WU RIVER VARIATIONS

PANG BEI

Translated by
JAMES TRAPP

SINOIST

Published by Sinoist Books (an imprint of ACA Publishing Ltd)
London - Beijing
info@alaincharlesasia.com ☎ +44 20 3289 3885
www.sinoistbooks.com

Published by Sinoist Books (an imprint of ACA Publishing Ltd) in arrangement with People's Literature Publishing House and Hua Cheng Publishing House

Author: Pang Bei **Translator:** James Trapp **Editor:** David Lammie
Cover Art: A. Bodrenkova **Proofreader:** Hui Cooper

Original Chinese Text © 乌江引 *(wujiang yin)*, 2022, People's Literature House and Hua Cheng Publishing House, China

ALL RIGHTS RESERVED. NO PART OF THIS PUBLICATION MAY BE REPRODUCED IN MATERIAL FORM, BY ANY MEANS, WHETHER GRAPHIC, ELECTRONIC, MECHANICAL OR OTHER, INCLUDING PHOTOCOPYING OR INFORMATION STORAGE, IN WHOLE OR IN PART, AND MAY NOT BE USED TO PREPARE OTHER PUBLICATIONS WITHOUT WRITTEN PERMISSION FROM THE PUBLISHER.

English Translation text © 2023 ACA Publishing Ltd, London, UK. A catalogue record for *Wu River Variations* is available from the National Bibliographic Service of the British Library.

This novel is entirely a work of fiction. The names, characters and incidents portrayed in it are the work of the author's imagination. Any resemblance to actual persons, living or dead, events or localities is entirely coincidental.

Paperback ISBN: 978-1-83890-569-9
eBook ISBN: 978-1-83890-570-5

Sinoist Books is honoured to be supported using public funding by Arts Council England.

WU RIVER VARIATIONS

PANG BEI

Translated by
JAMES TRAPP

Sinoist Books

PRINCIPAL CHARACTERS

Directory of the 2nd Bureau of the General Staff of the Central Revolutionary Military Council of the Chinese Soviet

Director General: Zeng Xisheng
Deputy Directors: Qian Zhuangfei, Song Yuhe
Decoding Section: Cao Xiangren and Zou Bizhao
Translation and Telecommunication Section: Li Zuopeng, Ye Chuping, Duan Lianshao, Dai Jinyuan and others
Investigation and Collation Section: Hu Lijiao, Qian Jiang, He Junzhen, Li Xinglü, Hu Beiwen and others

Part 1

Sketches

第一部 速寫

TONGDAO

The enemy were nowhere to be seen after we entered the Xiyan mountain range. The Gui Army from Guangxi did not follow us into the mountains and neither did the Xiang Army from Hunan, nor the "Central Army". The suspicion was that radio silence had been imposed since no signals were coming from any enemy station. This was highly unusual and had to be an indication of a major operation, which did not augur well for the safety of our troops.

Eight days after entering the mountains, we did indeed detect enemy information on the advance of the Kuomintang's "Pursuit and Suppression Army" to the front line at Xinning, Wugang, Suining, Jingxian and Hongjiang. On the tenth day, the 63rd Division of the 1st Corps had already arrived in Suining, and the 62nd Division was advancing on the same location. We reported the situation to the Field Army headquarters.

Following the blood-soaked route taken by the 6th Red Army Corps, the Central Red Army has now advanced to Tongdao in Hunan in three divisions, left, right and centre. From the time of our breakout at the Xiang River to the present, we have been moving by night towards the Xiyan mountain region on the Guangxi-Hunan border. Although the Gui Army has not actually followed us, day after day they have sent out spies to observe activities in every one of our Corps' encampments. They are setting fire to the houses of the local Miao people and attempting to shift the blame for their actions onto our Red Army to undermine public confidence in us. Commander-in-Chief Zhu has ordered every Corps to conduct rigorous patrols with orders for each soldier to respond to any fire alarm they encounter in order to extinguish the conflagration and provide emergency support for the people to mitigate any harm. Any of the arsonists who are captured are immediately to be put on public trial and then executed. On the tenth day, the 2nd Division of the 1st Red Army Corps occupies the county town of Tongdao, and the enemy defenders assess the situation and flee. We march in with one of the Military Commission's columns and establish our position there.

In the middle of the night on the eleventh day, we decipher the following deployment order issued by Liu Jianxu, commander-in-chief of the 1st Corps of the Kuomintang Army:

> **Orders to:** Commander Li Yunjie, Commander Li Yunheng, Commander Tao Guang, Divisional Commander Wang, Divisional Commander Zhang, Divisional Commander Chen, Director He, Acting Brigadier Liu Dai.
>
> The main bandit force seems to be on the border between Longsheng and Tongdao counties.
>
> The so-called 1st Corps has already fled westwards from Chang'anying, Yanzhai and Mulukou. Its vanguard has reached the line formed by Linkou, Xiaxiang and Jingwuzhou. The vanguard of my own Xue Corps has already arrived at Huitong. Half of the Gui Army is in pursuit towards Longsheng and Guyi.
>
> To cooperate with other friendly forces in the ongoing pursuit and annihilation of the main bandit force on the Hunan-Guizhou border, it has been determined that this Corps will deploy as follows:
>
> The 1st Route troops under Commander Tao, in addition to sending one force to blockade the Guiyang-Suining Highway in order to cut off the bandits' main escape route to the north, is to accelerate sending its main force to locate the bandits in the

direction of Linkou and Tongdao and to intercept and destroy them.

4th Route troops under Commander Li are to hasten into Suining to provide coordinated support for the 1st Route troops in the destruction of the bandits.

5th Route troops under Commander Li are to hasten to station themselves in Changpuzi to await further orders.

Troops under the command of Acting Brigadier Liu Dai, other than those left behind to garrison Chengbu, are to hasten to Yanzhai and Mulukou to pursue and eliminate any bandit stragglers. On reaching Yanzhai, they are to send a detachment to stand guard over Chang'anying.

Troops under Director He are to proceed from Changpuzi via Huangsangping to intercept the bandits on the cliff path to the west of Mulukou.

On the 12th, Liu Jianxu will proceed to Suining to take overall command.

Three pages in total
Liu Jianxu 2030 hours on the 11th

This was the telegraphed order from Liu Jianxu to the 100,000 Xiang Army troops under his command. We had a fierce battle with him when the Red Army crossed the Xiang River. We crossed the river in its upper reaches in Guangxi where first, Bai Chongxi's Gui Army had a vicious encounter with our 3rd Red Army Corps, then Liu Jianxu's Xiang Army intercepted our 1st Corps at Quanzhou. Our forces lost position after position with commanders and soldiers suffering disastrous casualties and the Corps commanders sent "most urgent" and "exceptionally urgent" telegrams requesting the central column to march at double time, night and day, to cross the river. But the massive transport team with its mountain guns, machine tools and huge quantities of provisions could only progress at forty *li* a day, or about twelve miles. The 1st Red Army Corps gave its all in bloody hand-to-hand combat with the enemy in the dense pine forests, but the Xiang Army made a sudden and unexpected outflanking move to attack the Corps' command post. It is said that Chief of Staff Zuo Quan was sitting down to eat when he saw the enemy rushing in with fixed bayonets, and he immediately directed his guard unit to counterattack. Regimental Commander Lin Biao and Political Commissar Nie Rongzhen also drew their pistols.

Liu Jianxu was the top general under He Jian, commander-in-chief of the Pursuit and Suppression Army, who was a fellow countryman from Liling in Hunan and a fellow student from the third intake at the Baoding Officers' School. In early 1929, he had travelled a great distance to chase down Zhu De and Mao Zedong's Red Army, which had broken out of the Jinggang Mountains. At the end of 1934, Liu's deployment again became very aggressive, giving every indication that he wanted to re-engage with us and trap us in another desperate situation. How should our army respond? The tragedy of the Xiang River was still fresh in our minds. The coded telegram also meant we could not stay long in our current position.

Deputy Section Head Zou Sheng opened the little black leather-bound notebook to ensure the Decoding Section had the most up-to-date record. This little black book is the crowning glory of the section. The date of this latest notation was recorded as: Midnight, 11 December 1934. When he had finished making the note, his head lolled to one side, and he immediately fell asleep. He had been hard at it for three days and nights on less than three hours sleep, his innards were numb with hunger and his mind had been beginning to wander.

Deep into the night at 0200 hours, our field army headquarters issued a notification to the whole Army:

> 1st, 3rd, 5th and 9th Corps: (most urgent decoding). First, according to the orders of our enemy Liu on the eleventh: (i) he estimates that the main body of our forces is on the Tongdao-Longsheng border; (ii) our enemy Xue's vanguard is already at Hongjiang; (iii) the enemy Liu has deployed thus...

Zou Sheng remained asleep throughout. Another urgent telegram from the Xiang Army was waiting to be decoded, but the section chief could not bring himself to wake him up. He could see that Zou's hair was still wet from the cold water he had poured over his head earlier to stay awake. Section Chief Cao Daye had also toiled for three days and nights and slept less than three hours in total. All of us are "people made of special materials", and those of us in the 2nd Bureau are the most special of the special. He was suffering an attack of malaria at the time. In the courtyard of the rustic mansion in a small town in southern Hunan, he was wrapped in a tattered blanket, but his forehead was sweating. Chief Qian was going to be back soon, wasn't he? Section Chief Cao needed a shot of quinine.

Section Chief Cao was clutching the latest coded telegram sent to him by the Decoding Section. There were still a few characters that had not been deciphered, and the message was not fully coherent. The workload of the 2nd Bureau was very heavy, and he was renowned for the speed and rate of his decoding. Every codebreaker has their own style, and he excelled in his bold arrangement of characters and his multi-directional attack. At this moment, he was sitting facing a wall, one hand scribbling on the paper of the telegram as his teeth chattered. In the Investigation and Collation Section next door, the radio sets were emitting a non-stop storm of beeps.

This storm of beeps reminded us of our time in the Central Soviet Area when we had our own station. In Meikeng in the Soviet capital, Ruijin, there was a bamboo grove outside the window of the radio room, and one day, one of our team came out of a dazed sleep to the sound of a barrage of beeps outside the window. Crisp, rapid, continuous beeping, like the sound of a telegram. Who could be sending a telegram in the bamboo grove? I went outside with a lantern to search, and it turned out to be an autumn cicada! It is a common insect in the south.

Through the crude glass of the window, you could look out at the old Gongcheng Academy. It was not cold but a little damp, and the raggedly dressed passers-by walked with their shoulders hunched. The sky was gloomy, but the morning sun coloured it with a splash of blood red. A bugler could be heard practising in the distance. It seemed he was not very familiar with his instrument, and the sound was rather shaky.

When Zou Sheng woke up in the early hours of the morning, Chief Zeng Mian was deciphering a coded telegram being held by Deputy Chief Cao. Chief Zeng's eyes were red-rimmed, but his gaze remained sharp and resolute. Chief Cao had already cracked one code and Chief Zeng had insisted he got some sleep, only to have him wake up suddenly just a little while later! There was an anomalous signal in the Detection Section next door, and he had rushed over to remind the detector that it was a very important communication, and he must take care not to omit any part of the code when copying it out. He fell back onto the bamboo bed and immediately fell into a deep sleep again. Chief Zeng glanced at the bed. He had already broken the last code and hurried to the Decoding Section next door. He gave Decoding Section Chief Li a brief explanation, and the codebreaker translated the proof text according to the key that had been provided. Chief Zeng hurried into the next-door Investigation and Collation Section. The section was filled with the smell of burning gasoline – the Hamlet brand generator was broken, but the work of the section could not be affected. He tried pulling on the starter handle several times, but the charger just beeped and gave off black smoke. The Decoding Section quickly finished decoding and checking the communication down to the last word, and he took the telegram to the commander of the field army.

* * *

The 2nd and 6th Corps under He Long and Xiao Ke respectively were in Xiangxi, and the Red 1st Front Army was heading north to join them. However, our decipherment of the coded telegram clearly showed that He Jian had already rapidly constructed four lines of fortifications in Xiangxi with more than two hundred blockhouses. The enemy had spread their net wide and were waiting. Chiang Kai-shek, on the other hand, wanted to drive the main force of our Red Army into the Guangdong-Guangxi region and annihilate it, forcibly preventing it from joining He and Xiao. The 6th Corps under Xiao Ke was the vanguard of the Central Red Army and, as early as the beginning of August 1935, had evacuated its Hunan-Jiangxi base to move on to central Hunan, not just to reconnoitre the route but also to harass the enemy. At the end of October, the 2nd and 6th Corps joined forces in Xiangxi to the east of Guizhou. Our 2nd Bureau's intelligence had already identified this danger. After we entered the Xiyan mountain range, the enemy were no longer in close pursuit, but they had certainly not given up the chase. They had determined that we wanted to join up with He and Xiao, so they used shortcuts to overtake the Red Army and spread their net across the road that we had to take to the north. In these circumstances, could the Central Red Army still follow the route reconnoitred by the 6th Corps? Heading west for more than two months, we had lost all contact with the Comintern and had no way of receiving timely instructions from Moscow.

Cao Daye woke up at noon, still with a high fever. He had been sick for several days. As chief of the decoding section, he said that he could not get sick, by which he actually meant he would not stop working if he fell ill. At this moment, he opened his eyes and stared at the map of Hunan. Cao Daye modelled himself on Bureau Chief Zeng, in that he was increasingly thinking about the bigger picture. Both Chief Zeng and Deputy Chief Qian wore glasses. They were intellectuals, and now they were both revolutionaries. Chief Zeng was a product of the era of the Great Revolutionary War, even though he was still only in his thirties. He cleaved to the bigger picture, saying that our 2nd Bureau should make intelligence-gathering on the enemy's military dispositions its priority. These two section chiefs were both from the great metropolis of Shanghai and had seen something of the world. Chief Cao woke up with another chill, shivering all over and his teeth chattering. We gave him half a bowl of ginger water to warm him up, which helped for a while. When he saw Deputy Chief Qian Chao approaching, he asked again about "long-distance" contacts. Our radio transmitter had limited power and any communication with Moscow had to be relayed via Shanghai, where the secret transmitters had been destroyed by the Kuomintang quite some time ago. Deputy Chief Qian replied that the White Terror in Shanghai was getting worse by the day, and he was afraid it would be a long time before the transmitters were up and running again. Moreover, our 3rd Bureau's 100-Watt transmitter had been lost during the crossing of the Xiang River. Luckily, we still had our 50-Watt transmitter and there might still be some hope of re-establishing contact with Shanghai, but he was afraid it wasn't powerful enough.

Deputy Section Chief Qian gave him a quinine injection and told him to get some rest and not to talk any more. Deputy Chief Qian was a doctor, and when he first arrived at the 2nd Bureau, he was bureau chief of the Military Commission's Political Security Bureau, but as far as the rank and file knew, his public post was director of the Red Army Theatre Company. Our 2nd Bureau was a top-secret outfit, working only with the Central Committee and the Military Commission; even the Corps commanders didn't know about us. The commander of the 1st Corps, Lin Biao, was a general, but even he was in the dark about us. When the 2nd Bureau was first established, it was not deemed appropriate to divulge the source of our codebreaking intelligence, even to Ye Jianying, who was the former chief of the general staff of the Military Commission. The bureau was still small in scale, and the intelligence it obtained could only be used in the main theatre of conflict. During our fourth "anti-encirclement and annihilation" campaign, Ye Jianying was principal of the Red Army School and commander-in-chief of the Southeast Front fighting against the enemy's Left Route Army, but this was only a subsidiary action. Zhou Enlai and Zhu De also sometimes sent him bulletins on the enemy's dispositions, and these messages often contained the words "The Military Commission Organisation confirms...", but Zhou and Zhu did not specify the source of the intelligence. "Counsellor" Ye Jianying was nobody's fool! Based on this, he inferred that the 2nd Bureau of the Military Commission already had codebreaking capabilities. He naturally wanted us to provide more secret information for the Southeast Front, so he circumspectly asked Zhou and Zhu, "Can you ask the Military Commission to 'organise' another..."

Initially, knowledge of the work of the 2nd Bureau was limited to Bo Gu, chief of the Central Committee, Li De, military adviser of the Comintern, Zhou Enlai, general political commissar of the Red Army, Zhu De, commander-in-chief of the Red Army, and Mao Zedong, chairman of the Provisional Central Government of the Soviet Republic. Peng Dehuai, commander of the 3rd Red Army Corps, knew about it too; he was also vice chairman of the Central Revolutionary Military Commission.

Bureau Chief Zeng, Section Chief Cao and Deputy Section Chief Zou are the best codebreakers in the 2nd Bureau. After Zeng and Cao gloriously cracked the Kuomintang army's Zhan Code, the 2nd Bureau has gone on to crack, one after the other, the Meng Code, the Qian Code, the Qing Code, the 7893 Code, the 3819 Code, the 3237 Code, the ◯ Code...

These achievements were all recorded in the black leather-bound book of Deputy Section Chief Zou.

Deputy Bureau Chief Qian was gesturing at the map and Section Chief Cao had still not gone back to sleep. He didn't speak, but just picked up a newspaper and began reading it. Deputy Chief Qian had brought along several of last month's issues of *Shanghai News* with headlines such as "Ji Hongchang shot dead by Tianjin Party headquarters of the Kuomintang" and "Shi Liangcai, editor-in-chief of *Shanghai News*, assassinated in Shanghai by agents of the KMT"... We asked again about what was happening with the 34th Division of the 5th Corps. The rearguard 34th Division was stuck on the east bank of the Xiang River and was unable to move west to join the main force. Deputy Chief Qian said that he had heard the head of the radio team of the 5th Corps, Li Bai, say that the 5th Corps, which was still under the command of Divisional Commander Chen Shuxiang and Political Commissar Lai Yuhong, was continuing to fight in southwest Hunan. We were delighted to hear this and wished them victory in their isolated action. Deputy Chief Qian suddenly took out his watch, looked at it, then hurried out of the room.

We couldn't ask any more. It was a question of discipline. What shouldn't be talked about, wasn't talked about. What shouldn't be asked, wasn't asked. We watched him through the window as he jogged along the road to the nearby Academy. The poised and elegant Deputy Chief Qian even looked good as he ran.

A local family was celebrating a wedding near the Academy. The women wore brightly coloured head scarves, silver collars round their necks and silver bracelets on their arms. Their pleated skirts were edged with lace.

On this early winter day, the streets of the mountain town present a different aspect from usual with the slogans painted on the walls by Red Army soldiers. The soldiers are asleep in the streets and alleys and under the eaves of the houses. They haven't forced their way into those houses but instead have helped the locals draw water, chop firewood and go about their other daily chores.

Yesterday, when we had set up camp, one of our soldiers, Ah Gen, had gone to the well to draw water. A young country girl was about to run away at the sight of a soldier, but Ah Gen hurriedly gestured to her, saying, "Don't be afraid, little cousin! Us soldiers and you poor folk are all one family."

The girl asked, "Whose battle cry do you shout?"

"The Red Army's!" Ah Gen replied.

"How come a Red Army soldier has to draw his own water?"

Ah Gen said, "We suffer hardships, just like you." So saying, he rolled up his sleeve to reveal a deep scar. "A bastard moneybags gave me this!"

Ah Gen wasn't much older than the rest of us, but he was like an older brother, looking out for us wherever we went. He was a man of few words normally, but he had the liveliest eyes and was always on the go. And there was this usually taciturn man, talking away like a regular guy beside the well. We teased him about it, and his sunburnt face blushed slightly as he turned his head away, apparently in annoyance, and lit up his tobacco pipe. He took a few solitary puffs, then he noticed a strip of cloth in a corner of two walls. His eyes lit up, and he hurried over to pick it up. He pulled it through his hands a few times, and when he felt its strength, he flashed a grin at us. He was going to use it to make straw sandals. We all knew how to make straw sandals, but sometimes we were short of the raw materials, or the straw wasn't strong enough so then we would add some strips of cloth or some hemp rope to make the shoes both light and hard-wearing. The little imps in the Red Army particularly liked to collect bits of coloured wool to make into red and green pom-poms to prettify the tops of their shoes.

Our Ah Gen was a canny fellow. Normally very quiet, he never lost his temper but just smiled and smoked away at the tobacco from his little pouch. As part of the transport squad, he was often in the advance guard and, as the advance guard was often in a hurry, he had to run fast carrying heavy machinery. I remember one occasion when he came off the advance guard. Everyone had pitched their tents but had no way of cooking because he had lost the matches he was carrying when he was running. The advance guard received a sudden order to move out and no one had eaten all day. Ah Gen got out his tinderbox and flint but found he had no tinder. Even so, he found a way. He took a cartridge and pulled off the tip, then he put a wad of cotton into the barrel of his rifle. When he fired the cartridge, it caused a spark which ignited the cotton in the barrel. We were overjoyed and called it "revolutionary tinder"!

When we saw him pick up the strip of cloth that time, we all thought maybe he had something else in mind and wasn't just going to use it to make straw sandals. Just like when he produced that tinder, who would have thought that he had a wad of cotton about him! Especially as it was summer and we were all wearing thin, unpadded clothes. On this occasion, when he had finished his pipe, he looked as though he was going to drop off to sleep. We didn't feel comfortable reminding him that now wasn't the time for a proper sleep, but a short nap would be all right. He and the troop commanders all thought that we could rest and regroup where we were for a few days, but, in truth, the situation was not favourable. Most of the big, rich households had made themselves scarce, and we were hard put to buy sufficient provisions. The troops were busy investigating the local petty tyrants and gangsters, targeting people who used their wealth corruptly. The doors of the county jails had been thrown open, and the Red Army had set free anyone who had been falsely imprisoned. A lot of these were people who had refused to pay taxes and levies, and the Red Army had asked local blacksmiths to pry open their leg irons. There were hundreds of these tax prisoners locked up in small towns all over the area. The Red Army had done the same thing as they crossed Guangxi. The life of the common people was extremely hard, but the warlords were still sucking the marrow from their bones, and all manner of exorbitant taxes were as numerous as the hairs on an ox.

People were putting themselves in hock to the following year's harvest, to the extent that the next five years' land tax was being levied in advance, so how could the people on the lowest rung of society ever break free of their chains? The soldiers sang lustily, extolling revolutionary principles to the public and expressing their intention to establish a Soviet there. Nonetheless, we were on tenterhooks there and it was no place for us to linger. But when the Red Army departed, it looked like we were going to have difficulty making our way north. Our intelligence indicated the dangers to us, but we were not comfortable with the thought of staying put.

We had to be patient, and patience was one of our strong points. We experienced front-line soldiers had it in abundance.

When Bureau Chief Zeng returned, the guards at the courtyard gate saluted him, which he just acknowledged with a quick wave of the hand. He was carrying a small lantern. It consisted of a stub of candle inserted into a large tea mug, which he carried by the handle with the base of the mug facing backwards and the opening facing forwards, so it was like a hand lamp, the flame protected from the wind and illuminating the people in front of him. He usually walked in a slow and dignified manner, but he was moving a little more quickly on this occasion. We watched the light. The bureau chief's return was observed by men from every section peering out of their windows. We noted the unusual briskness of his pace and the somewhat relieved look on his face. That look was also one that we hadn't seen for some time. After several months of gloom, the expression on Bureau Chief Zeng's bearded face seemed to have lightened. Although he wasn't all sunshine and cloudless skies, and there were just a few signs of pleasure crinkling the corners of his eyes, that was good enough. No more sullen frowns, no longer a single message of tension and stress, no more intimidating bristling of his beard. It was clear he wasn't going to lose his temper that day.

"Well, comrades, what's the mood like in here?" Bureau Chief Zeng asks upon entering the room. The hearts of the comrade code-breakers already feel lighter.

"The mood is pretty good, except we're rather hungry. If we could just have a square meal, we would have all the energy we need." Zou Sheng's voice is a little hoarse and he does indeed look really hungry.

"So, what's good to eat here?" It seems that Bureau Chief Zeng is quite hungry too.

"Not much, the best we've got is some thin congee." Zou Sheng shakes his head with a bitter laugh.

"We in the Second Bureau have special privileges. The Red Army gets two meals a day, but we get three!" Section Chief Cao struggles to get up, but Bureau Chief Zeng hurriedly makes him lie back down.

"I think a chicken would go down particularly well at this moment," says Bureau Chief Zeng, his tone making it sound as though he is making fun of himself, but he does have a pleased expression on his face. "After the revolution is won, won't it be good to have an egg every day!"

"How about a chicken every day?" Zou Sheng's mouth seems to be watering copiously.

"All right, all right, a chicken a day it is! Clear stewed chicken soup is really delicious too! If you think about it that way, at least your stomach won't be in revolt! And while we're on the subject of the victorious revolution, that's why we're heading west tomorrow."

Everyone is stunned by this sudden change in direction of the conversation. Bureau Chief Zeng takes three wild oranges out of his pocket and gives one each to Cao and Zou.

"The route north to Xiangxi to meet up with He Jian and Xiao Ke used to be all right, but there are problems with it now. Our own Second Bureau intelligence and what we have received from Liu Jianxu and others make it clear that Chiang Kai-shek knows we want to head north, so they've deployed a huge force and are waiting for us to fall into their nets. That route is a death trap. Central Command called an emergency meeting today to resolve operational issues and they decided we should first divert our advance westward."

Bureau Chief Zeng hesitates briefly. The men under him know better than to interrupt at this point, as the chief will pick up again when he is ready. "On this occasion, Comrade Enlai has shown great resolution. He has made preparations. There are two aspects to those preparations. One is that he invited Comrades Zedong, Luo Fu [Zhang Wentian] and Jiaxiang to participate, and, of course, Old Boss Zhu was there too, so they could not just be dismissed as the 'Team of Three' any more. The other is that, because of the intelligence obtained by us at the Second Bureau, he arranged for myself and Bureau Chief Qian to attend the meeting. Comrade Zedong has been 'sidelined' for a long time now – he's no longer in command of the army, but isn't he still a member of the Politburo and still the president of the Soviet Republic? He has not made his voice heard for a long time, but now he had the chance to speak out in public. It was the first time he had attended a major military conference since the meeting at Ningdu. He said that Chiang Kai-shek had laid a big trap for us and was just waiting for us to walk into it.

"He wants to give us a taste of our own medicine, so how stupid would we have to be to just take it! In truth, it was Comrade Zedong's proposal to abandon the plan to go north to Xiangxi that forced Comrade Bo Gu to hold the meeting. When Comrade Zedong looked at our enemy's position and saw that the plan for tomorrow's advance was still to go north, he lost his temper and went to Enlai and Bo Gu and said, 'If our army continues to go north out of western Hunan, we are playing right into the enemy's hands and signing our own death warrants. If you insist on sending the Red Army into the enemy's trap, ensuring its destruction, if that's what you really want to do, then you will be destroying both the army and the Party. How can you even consider it!' That's what was behind this extraordinary meeting. Comrade Enlai showed great determination and spoke with considerable emotion, which is unusual for him. As for Comrade Li De, he was pinning all his hopes on a rendezvous with the Second and Sixth Corps, and at first still insisted on going north as planned, accusing Comrade Zedong of being too subjective. Comrade Bo Gu also still supported Li De–"

"But the enemy is at our gates! Did Comrade Bo Gu not read the All Army Report that came out at two o'clock in the morning?" Section Chief Cao was a very impatient man, and this was clear in the way he spat out the question. It was also clear in the way he had already finished his orange.

"He believes Li De. Li De says we can dodge our pursuers who are on a parallel course to us. Because the enemy are using the main highway, after we suddenly turn north, we can bypass their line of fortifications, swiftly join up with He and Xiao and establish a new Soviet. You all know that Comrade Zedong wants to head west, and a few days ago he told everyone to get hold of a copy of Zuo Zongtang's *Account of the Pacification of the Miao*. He was examining the possibility of advancing towards Guizhou where the enemy forces were comparatively weak. He kept pushing this idea at the meeting, but Li De was stubborn in his opposition. Comrade Zedong wouldn't give an inch, and Enlai, Old Boss Zhu, Luo Fu and Jiaxiang all supported him but couldn't get a word in. At that point, Comrade Enlai told me to produce the secret telegram we had just intercepted, showing that Chiang Kai-shek had ordered every unit in western Hunan to spread their nets for us with forces six times the size of our own. Bureau Chief Qian also produced a map, annotated in Russian, showing the deployment of the Hunan Army, and Li De finally seemed to get the point... Ha! That was central democratic decision-making in action, and it all stemmed from the actual changes made in the enemy's deployment. In truth, this was the first time Comrade Zedong's opinion had gained any support since we first set out westward, and, in fact, it had the support of the majority of the Central Committee. It really was a question of 'seeking truth from facts'! When Comrade Zedong was young, he attended Number One Normal School, where the motto on the wall was 'Seek truth from facts'. I was only at Number Three Normal School, but even I understand that. Listen to the person who is in the right, that's not a hard principle to grasp, is it!"

Bureau Chief Zeng offers the orange he was holding to Cao Daye, but Daye gives him a tight smile and refuses it. Seeing that Zou Sheng had almost finished his, Chief Zeng breaks the orange into two halves and hands one to each of them.

"That's real Communism for you!" Bureau Chief Zeng says with a laugh.

"Huh! Is that all Communism is? A few oranges?" Cao Daye replies, very seriously. "If that's the case, who's going to follow it? We need heads to be broken and blood to be spilled too!"

"To be accurate, all you can say is that it is Communist thinking, isn't that right?" Zou Sheng says thoughtfully.

"Yes, Communist thinking, that's right. It's all about having good awareness. You're just nineteen, aren't you, Xiao Zou? You may not have any eggs to eat at the moment, but at least you've got these oranges! They're a speciality of Tongdao. And they're good for you. And you, Daye, you're just twenty, aren't you? Is that your nominal age or your real age?"[1]

"Well, what about our information on the enemy positions?"

says Section Chief Cao as he takes the orange, looking a little embarrassed as he returns to the main topic. "Have we still not had a signal from the Fourth Front Army?"

Bureau Chief Zeng shakes his head, then turns to look out of the window, staring silently at the smudge of distant mountains.

"It's strange. Just when we need support, there's no signal." Section Chief Cao purses his lips doubtfully. "The Third Bureau is sending several reports a day. You don't think they're deliberately abandoning us, do you?"

"Nonsense!" Bureau Chief Zeng shouts back fiercely.

(Supplementary note: on 4 January 1935, the Military Commission received a secret communication from the Red 4th Front Army giving information on the deployment of the Sichuan Army. It was signed: Tao)

Bureau Chief Zeng's older brother is, in fact, the commander of the Red 4th Front Army. Section Chief Cao smiles bitterly and stubbornly returns to his questioning: "So... have we given up on the idea of joining up with the Second and Sixth Corps?"

"As for that... I've said a bit too much today. Perhaps I've been in too good a mood. But just because I'm in a good mood doesn't mean I can't lose my temper! Of course, top-level meetings should be kept confidential, but we in the Second Bureau are a special case, so it's right that we get more information. It still needs to be kept confidential, though! The best thing is to keep your mouth shut... The Comrade Counsellor was really embarrassed at losing face and that's why he insisted on skirting round the enemy lines and going north as originally planned. Comrade Bo Gu didn't say anything in opposition, but he did try to fudge the issue a little. He has now agreed instead to head for the southeastern part of Guizhou where the enemy forces are comparatively weak, but that was really just a detour as he still wants us overall to stick to the original plan and head for Xiangxi to join up with the Red Army under He Long and Ren Bishi. After all, there is no need to go north immediately, and certainly not tomorrow. This is just adapting to the circumstances, and it shows a rare degree of flexibility! From a Marxist philosophical point of view, losing contact with the Comintern is both a good thing and a bad thing. Forgetting the bad side, the good side is that it means we can act on our own. I had a presentiment yesterday when we were stationed at Pingdeng and I was looking at the octagonal drum tower on the Pingdeng River. Today, in this little county town of Tongdao, things really are changing. Just think! Pingdeng! Tongdao![2] Maybe these names are good omens – a way through and a new way of life! Even so, if we go north, our future may still be annihilation– "

"It's a more dangerous situation than the battle at the Xiang River..." Deputy Chief Zou turns around and brings the map over. "When we left Ruijin, we had more than eighty thousand men, but after crossing the Xiang River and breaking through this blockade, we are left with just these thirty thousand."

At 1930 hours, Zhu De, chairman of the Central Revolutionary Military Commission, and Vice Chairmen Zhou Enlai and Wang Jiaxiang issued an urgent telegram to the entire army: "Turn! Go west in the direction of Liping in southeastern Guizhou!"

Go west! The Xiang River almost caused the destruction of the main body of the Red Army.

Even heading for Guizhou, another big river was bound to block our way. The bugles were blaring and the wind was moaning mournfully. It was time to strike camp and march out. The soldiers hurried to board up the doors, bale the hay, and clean and sweep the places where they had been sleeping. Looking out of the window, we could see the personnel of the Disciplinary Inspection Committee rushing around carrying out inspections, ensuring that even a needle borrowed from the locals was returned, and expressing our warmest gratitude. We were already packed and ready. The comrades on duty that night had been the first to pack their bags at midnight and the others had been resting, already in battle order. The baggage was very simple, as many of the few personal items that were owned had already been given to the poor. Out of class sympathy, some comrades gave away the last piece of dry food in their ration sack and their last piece of silver.

When the order was received to move out, Ah Gen loaded several document bags from the Decoding Section onto the back of a horse, and, as Bureau Chief Zeng had still not emerged from the building, he gave the beast a handful of hay. It was a handsome back horse with a glossy mane, and we all loved it. Bureau Chief Zeng was very fond of it too, and sometimes he would brush it or feed it the freshest, tenderest hay as he considered some difficult problem.

Bureau Chief Zeng had still not come out but remained gazing pensively at the map on his desk. It was a 1:100,000 map of the whole of Hunan Province.

"Does Guizhou have a major river?" Zou Sheng asked softly as he walked past.

Chief Zeng slowly drew a diagonal line on the left side of the map.

"The Wu River."

MOVING WEST

The road west was smooth going to begin with, as it was an area where the enemy had no bases. We had made the turn so suddenly they had not yet had time to deploy. After crossing the Xiang River, we were entering the deep rear of the enemy's territory, and their troops no longer had the benefit of railways, roads and river transport. Xue Yue's pursuing forces had to go by foot, just like us, and we were faster than them. Previously, we had been travelling on mountain roads while the enemy were on highways, and we had found it hard to shake them off. Then, they had been able to carry out flank attacks from their parallel course, but now we both only had mountain roads to travel along. Once we were in Guizhou, we no longer had to move at night by torchlight. There, where you never get three clear days in a row, the sky is mostly overcast and the clouds and mist in the mountains protected us, so the enemy aircraft were no longer a threat. They didn't dare fly too low, so found it difficult to locate us and impossible to bomb us. There was a lot of singing on this march and it was those perpetually cheerful youngsters of the "Little Red Army" who sang:

Brothers of the White Army,
We are the Red Army,
We are all poor labouring folk together.
You should not be fighting us,

And we should not be fighting you,
Brothers, please make up your minds

Our 2nd Bureau was incorporated into the 1st Field Column (the Red Star Column) under the commanders of the Field Army, Zhu De and Zhou Enlai. There were more than thirty technicians, six radio teams as well as a guard squad, a transport team, a catering team and stockmen, totalling several dozen altogether. The forty-*jin* transceiver could be carried on the shoulder, but the sixty-*jin* battery and the ninety-*jin* Hamlet generator needed carrying poles. The main army employed porters, but we could not let any outsiders have contact with us, so we could only use our own loyal and reliable soldiers. The hardest worker of all was Ah Gen, who rushed to be first to do all the hardest jobs. The men of the transport team worked to the limit of their energy, people fell over, and, with machinery involved, Ah Gen suffered frequent injuries.

At the beginning of the month, we crossed the Laoshanjie Mountains, the highest peaks in the Xiyan range. The further we went, the narrower the mountain roads became, and when we crossed Leigongyan, we had to use a perilous "sky ladder". This consisted of more than a hundred steep, narrow steps carved out of the cliff face. A towering precipice loomed above and a deep valley below. As the men watched so many horses and mules slip and fall, several of them felt their energy drain, their legs buckle and their bodies twist, and they tumbled down the cliff too. Looking at the sky ladder from a distance, we could not help sweating and trembling for the fate of the big black horse, but to everyone's surprise, it remained remarkably calm. We could see that Ah Gen was very calm too, as he stood at the bottom of the stone steps, stroking the horse's neck and whispering into its ear. A short period of silence followed as man and horse looked at each other, then Ah Gen took hold of the horse's reins, drawing man and beast even closer together. Ah Gen walked quietly in front, with the horse's head tight behind him, and in this fashion, they made their way upwards, testing every step. Neither man nor horse looked down, and they both kept their bodies stuck close to the cliff wall. We held our breath as we watched the two of them climb the sky ladder. Ah Gen placed his feet very softly at every step and the big black horse did the same as they made their way quietly up towards the top. Even when Ah Gen took the last step, he didn't stop immediately but slowly kept on going. Only when the horse reached the top of the stone staircase did he turn round, stretch out his arms and gently embrace the horse's head... Ah Gen had protected that big black horse, and from then on he took on two responsibilities, both as part of the transport squad and as groom to the horse. He became the horse's official protector. This horse was Bureau Chief Zeng's mount, but he was quite happy not to ride it and go on foot with everyone else. He said it was good exercise for him, and if he didn't have strong legs, how was he going to manage when he didn't have a horse? He wanted to let the horse carry the heavy generator, but Ah Gen wasn't happy about it, saying, "This is a fine horse, not a draught animal." He was a man of few words, and when he had finished, he looked at the other men of the transport team. They just picked up the generator and set off. There was nothing else for Bureau Chief Zeng to say, so he ordered a sick member of the Decoding Section to ride the horse instead.

We marched in relay as before, detection and equipment personnel forming two teams. The forward division would advance a stretch then stop and start up its detection equipment. At the end of the shift, the rear division would hurry along the road to overtake the forward division, so the two divisions were engaged in a continuous game of leapfrog. In this way, they could not only maintain radio surveillance of the enemy under all conditions but could also keep in close contact with the senior officers in our general headquarters and not fall behind.

After the Field Army's great breakout, the situation was very different from that in the base area. In the base area, you could still rely on the locals to obtain information about the enemy's deployments, but now the army was constantly on the move, there could be no information coming in about covert work, and our 2nd Bureau became the only source of combat intelligence. We worked ceaselessly, without a moment's rest. After the Field Army entered Guizhou from Hunan, the Qian Army became the focus of our intelligence gathering. Being few in number, we focused on what was key. We didn't have the capability to pay attention to too many different aspects, but occasionally we would turn our detectors back to listen out for enemy stations we had left behind us. It was a month since the Red Army had left Guangdong. On 4 December, we cracked Chen Jitang's Silver Code. We didn't intercept any further messages from the Guangdong Army, but while we were on this journey into Guizhou, we did still pick up information relating to it. The last coded telegram we had obtained in connection with it was Chiang Kai-shek's reprimand to Chen Jitang:

> In normal times when you requested pay for your soldiers and weapons, you obliged in every respect, but once a real emergency presented itself, you acted only in your own interest... this time, your troops were not mobilised, and the Communist bandits were allowed to flee westward, which has caused a great stain on our National Revolutionary Army that will remain for the rest of our lives.

At this juncture, we became aware of Chen Jitang again. On 11 December, Chen Jitang from Guangdong and Li Zongren and Bai Chongxi from Guangxi sent a coded joint telegram to the Nanjing Central Party Office, the Fifth Plenary Session of the Central Committee, the Guangzhou Southwest Executive Department, the Southwest Government Affairs Council, Chairman Lin of the National Government, President Wang and Chairman Chiang of the Military Commission:

> ...these provinces of Sichuan and Guizhou and the entire southwest of the country are full of deep mountains and remote forests, far removed from the safety of Jiangxi and Fujian. If we do not take advantage of this time when the bandits are exhausted and afraid to attack, and overwhelm them with even greater vigour, then, once they have recuperated and reorganised, they will be able to advance northward to turn the northwest Red and open up international lines of communication. To the south, they will be able to disrupt Guizhou and Guangxi and influence Fujian and Guangdong. They will undermine the peace of East Asia and endanger that of other friendly countries, and there will be no way to save the Party, the nation and the people from destruction. Jitang,

Zongren, Chongxi and others have repeatedly received praise and encouragement from their comrades, and they must continue fully to exert themselves. We humbly believe that until the Communists bandits are removed, and China's difficulties are resolved, all plans to save the country are just empty talk. The military forces of Guangdong and Guangxi always put patriotism before anything else, and they plan to deploy strong detachments immediately. They will first form a pursuit and suppression force, led by Zongren and, together with all the friendly armies, continue to harass and persecute the enemy in order to achieve complete success. If our recommendation is accepted, we would humbly request you to issue an express order to this effect, and we would humbly ask Chairman Chiang to give instructions to facilitate compliance at all times.

"Chen Jitang, Li Zongren and Bai Chongxi are asking Lao Chiang to fight! What a magnificent and impassioned piece of writing! What a 'petition for battle orders' it is!" Chief Zeng was shouting at Cao Daye. In fact, what he was really doing was testing Cao Daye's opinion.

"According to the secret intelligence we have obtained, Xue Yue's eight divisions are already close to the border of Guizhou. Xue Yue's Central Army and Wang Jialie's Qian Army are joining forces against the Red Army, but the tensions between them..." Cao Daye was thinking it through as he talked. "The Qian Army is particularly afraid that the Central Army will enter its territory, while the Central Army is taking advantage of–"

"So why do Guangzhou and Guangxi want to get involved? Guangxi is afraid of the Red Army entering its territory but even more afraid of the Central Army invading... yes, that's right, do you still have that report from after the river crossing, the one Bai Chongxi sent Chiang Kai-shek? Xiao Zou!"

Zou Sheng was lost in thought, staring at an old-fashioned "horseshoe" alarm clock, and despite the strength of the bureau chief's voice, he simply didn't hear it. He opened the clock's cover and moved the hands on with one finger. Seeing his absorption, Cao Daye didn't disturb him and hurriedly hunted out the telegram for himself.

The 2nd Bureau crossed the Xiang River inside the Guangxi border, which marked the fourth blockade line of the Kuomintang Army. The Red Army suffered heavy casualties, but its main force still effected the crossing. Chiang Kai-shek loaded the blame on Bai Chongxi, but Bai Chongxi was disrespectfully unconcerned about it.

"The Red Bandits have been encamped in Jiangxi and Fujian for seven years," Bai Chongxi stated, "and they have been besieged from east to west, north to south, with a force of over a million men. It's a shame the bandits escaped from the siege so easily, and now they have entered Hunan and taken up residence in Yizhang. I have pursued and suppressed each of their forces but the order to stop and rest up, discontinuing further attacks, was particularly misconceived. When the bandits came fleeing west along the Xiyan mountain range, Guangxi took the brunt of it...

"....our National Army had more than a million men but could not prevent the bandits from breaking out of strict containment and crossing three rivers, the Gan, the Lei and the Xiao. So how were we supposed to be able to stop them from crossing the Xiang with a smaller army?

"It appears that our current problems lie not just in the planning but in the actual offensive actions themselves, particularly in the way we believe our own lies with flowery reports of false victories, and in the dishonest behaviour towards neighbouring countries."

When the main force of the Red Army crossed the Xiang River, Bai Chongxi was suspected of letting it through. But Bai Chongxi refused to admit this and just sneered at Chiang. If that was the case, why, within a few days did he, Bai Chongxi, take the initiative to petition for war? Besides, wasn't he teaming up with Chen Jitang from Guangzhou?

The 2nd Bureau deciphered a large quantity of enemy intelligence, and the secret information submitted to the chief of the Military Commission first had to be analysed and evaluated for accuracy. At this moment, Chief Zeng and the others were making that evaluation.

"'Betrayal of neighbouring countries'... which neighbouring countries? Is Bai Chongxi saying here that his Guangxi is an independent country? That must have made Chiang Kai-shek furious! But things are different now from the time when Bai teamed up with He Yingqin and Li Zongren to force Chiang out of office. The current situation is that, as far as the Guangdong-Guizhou warlords are concerned, defending Chiang is more important than resisting the Communists. Now the Red Army has left Guangdong and Guangxi, Chen Jitang has no reason to petition Chiang for battle orders again, and nor do Li Zongren and Bai Chongxi." Bureau Chief Zeng was talking to himself, his eyebrows raised. "Good God! Could they all be putting on an act?"

"Is it just playacting? Playacting for Chiang's benefit! Doesn't it sound just like a movie? In the Battle of Jieshou, Lao Chiang airdropped funds, battle plans and secret messages for him, and he certainly fought for real then. But once the Red Army left Guangxi, he went back to playacting. He rounded up our wounded soldiers and civilians and hired some other civilians to pretend to be prisoners, and got his General Political Training Office to make a film called *Seven Thousand Prisoners* which he sent to Chiang Kai-shek to watch. He also sent it all over the place for screening, boasting about the achievements of the Guangxi Army and calling it the greatest military exploit since the five 'encirclement and annihilation' campaigns! The Fifth Plenary Session of the Kuomintang Central Committee is about to open, which is also a great opportunity for him. What a great director this 'Little Zhuge Liang'[1] is! He thinks he can easily pull the wool over Chiang Kai-shek's eyes!"

Deputy Bureau Chief Qian was waving the telegram in his hand. He was the best man at situational analysis and very good with words too. "You can be as slick and clever an operator as you like, but you have to be ruthless too! Before the 12 April Shanghai Massacre, he proposed to Chiang Kai-shek that he remove Xue Yue from his position as divisional commander in case he was sympathetic to the Communist Party. What Bai Chongxi did not know was that Xue Yue rushed in person to the Central Committee of the Communist Party in Shanghai and suggested that the counter-revolutionary Chiang Kai-shek should be arrested! Xue Yue was dismissed from office, and Bai Chongxi gave the direct order for the machine guns to be turned on the massed ranks of the workers. Do you remember? The whole Moscow circus protested about what they called the Shanghai White Terror. Under the word 'White' it was specifically noted that it referred to Bai Chongxi [the surname Bai means 'white']–"

"See how a great wave washes away the sand! You have made everything clear. You're not just an actor, you're a director too! I trust your judgement on this."

"That's why I say that, on this occasion, they are both acting and watching the action play out–"

"They know that Chiang Kai-shek won't let them compete with the Central Army for the territory, and all they can do is sit back and watch. And watching the Central Army fighting hand-to-hand with the Qian Army is even more fun because it is Xue Yue's Central Army–"

"Chiang must have seen more than his share of this kind of petition for battle orders and all these other old tricks."

"Why don't you find something new for him, Lao Qian?"

"I'll give him a new play to watch if he comes to Guiyang... the Red Army Drama Company's latest production. I've already got a title for it–"

"Excellent, excellent! What's it called?"

"*Wang Jialie*[2] *Taken Alive!*"

Now we could no longer follow the same road as the 6th Red Army Corps. Previously, we had scrambled across the Xiang River at the same crossing point as them. Once across, we were still heading into the Xiyan Mountains following in the bloody footsteps of the 6th Corps. From time to time, we saw notices and slogans posted by them on the mountain roads. They had been the vanguard of the breakout and had already joined up with the 2nd Corps in Xiangxi. They had orders to give coordinated help to the Red 1st Front Army in their own breakout.

Turning for Tongdao was our only viable plan to avoid running into the net spread by the enemy. Chiang Kai-shek had wanted to drive the Red Army towards Guangdong and Guangxi, but now we were in fact heading for Guizhou. We kept alert as we marched into Liping. The conference at Tongdao had required the detour via Liping, but our destination remained Xiangxi. The head of the Military Commission was expecting the 2nd Bureau's report on the situation in the north.

In the afternoon of 16 December, the 2nd Bureau sent its report on the enemy's latest dispositions to the Field Army Command: The enemy is still severely impeding our army's progress to the north.

It was no longer possible to take a detour from Liping into Hunan. The situation was such that the Central Politburo had to meet to consider it. On 18 December, the Politburo meeting discussed the future direction of the Central Red Army's movements. Mao Zedong did all he could to explain the reasons why we should abandon the original plan to join He and Ren in western Hunan, and strongly urged that the Red Army should be redirected to the Sichuan-Guizhou border. The first step was to gain a foothold in northern Guizhou and build a new Soviet centred on Zunyi. They needed to consider whether we could first establish ourselves in northern Guizhou, where we would have opportunities in both directions. Heading northwest we could, when occasion allowed, join up with the powerful Red 4th Front Army, and to the northeast we could coordinate with the 2nd and 6th Corps. If that was no good, we would have to head for Sichuan, which was in accordance with Stalin's thinking – years before he had urged the Red Army to move to Sichuan. Because this was what Stalin had once said, Bo Gu did not insist on entering Hunan to join up with the 2nd and 6th Corps.

At 1800 hours on 19 December, Commander Zhu and Chief Political Commissar Zhou Enlai issued the order: Advance into northern Guizhou with Zunyi as the focal point.

Build a new Soviet! Everyone was overwhelmed with emotion and excitement. Even though it was only the faint light of a star flickering in the distance ahead of us, it represented a longed-for new hope. Only recently, we had a multitude of bases! In the Central Soviet Area, we had the Soviet Republic. As the whole Red Army headed west, our feelings for that Republic that we had left behind naturally became more remote, gradually turning into a dream of the past. Nonetheless, its brightness truly still remained! Not so long ago, Ruijin changed its name to Ruijing [*jing* means "capital"] as the capital of the Chinese Soviet Republic. There you could find the Great Hall of the Central Government of the Chinese Soviet Republic, the Central People's Commissariat for Land, the Central People's Commissariat for Food, the Central People's

Commissariat for Labour, the Central People's Commissariat for Finance, the Central People's Commissariat for Education, the Central People's Commissariat for Justice, the Central Discipline Inspection Commission, the Central Taxation Office, the Central Treasury, the National Bank, the Supreme Court...

As far as we knew, these institutions that we could no longer see might well have disappeared in a sea of fire. We were following the Party's Central Army, but now, the Central Party Committee had no fixed building in which to hold meetings and all its most important documents were contained in some tin attaché cases. The Committee leadership normally had two mules each, one to ride and one as a pack animal. Those tin attaché cases were on the mule that followed Bo Gu on the march. In accordance with Red Army security regulations, the cases had to be fitted with internal incendiary devices.

I still remember Luo Fu's editorial: "Everything for the protection of the Soviet". That was the initial slogan of this breakout, and the article said that the move was necessary preparation for a major counterattack to fight our way to the far rear of Chiang's rebellion in order to open up a new Soviet area and then better defend the old one. The article went on to say that we should be victorious, could be victorious and, no matter how, must be victorious! But now, it was clearly a major retreat and where was that distant rear of our enemy? And there were countless beloved comrades left behind, including those many million workers, farmers, brothers and sisters in the Soviet area...

Marching across the mountain ranges, we saw no news or newspapers of any kind. Before we crossed the Xiang River, the enemy dropped a storm of handbills saying they had occupied Ruijin. The forces that seized Ruijin were the Kuomintang's 10th and 36th Divisions. Li Mo'an, commander of the 10th Division and Song Xilian, commander of the 36th Division were both part of the first cohort to graduate from the Huangpu Military Academy and had, at one stage, joined the Communist Party. They resigned from it after the Zhongshan Incident in 1926 in which Communist elements of the Nationalist army in Guangzhou were purged by Chiang Kai-shek. The Red Army soldiers hurrying through the wild mountains were completely unaware of the current situation in the

Soviet Area. Only we knew the terrible truth from the scattered reports we picked up from the enemy: following the Red Army's breakout, the occupied Soviet Area was a sea of blood...

...intelligence showed that the bandits numbered 100,000, and if they were currently allowed to spread further, not only would the province of Guizhou turn red, it was feared that Sichuan, Hunan and other provinces would also be endangered. In addition to concentrating troops to attack and intercept them, the central government was urged to send orders to all the armies in Hunan to move westward to the border of Guizhou, and all troops in Guangxi Province should cross the border to attack in order to round up and destroy the bandits to resolve the troubles in Guizhou. This action would be very gratefully received... Wang Jialie had no option but to request troops from Lao Chiang, and Chiang's Central Army could then enter Guizhou with impunity. It was said that the Qian Army was composed of "two-barrel soldiers", those barrels being their infantry rifles and their opium pipes. Their weaponry consisted only of guns such as barrel shroud Hanyang rifles,[3] nine-round Mausers and Winchester M1866s, and each battalion only had two or three machine guns. It was said that when they went into battle, each soldier had a bamboo basket on their back which held a thin quilt, an opium pipe and an opium lamp. "A bean curd army that would collapse at the first blow!"

The composition of the Qian Army was as follows: Wang Jialie was simultaneously the warlord provincial governor and commander of the Guizhou Province 25th Army, and he controlled the 99th and 100th Divisions, which included six brigades and eighteen regiments. The overall second-in-command was You Guocai, the commander of the 99th Division was Bai Huizhang, and the commander of the 100th Division was Hou Zhidan.

Latest intelligence report from the 2nd Bureau: three regiments of Lin Xiusheng's brigade under the overall command of Hou Zhidan are entrenched along the Wu River from Yuqing in the east to Weng'an in the west.

Our current principal opposition: two columns and eight divisions of Xue Yue's corps (four divisions of Wu Qiwei's 7th Column and four divisions of Zhou Hunyuan's 8th Column); two divisions of the 25th Army; and Liu Jianxu's Xiang Army in conjunction with the Central Army.

"Tiger Boy" Xue Yue had been following us all the way from Jiangxi to Guizhou. The Red Army ran faster than the White Army. We were the "muddy legs" who knew how to run and how to endure hardship. Some soldiers had been running barefoot since Jiangxi! When it came to a foot race, the enemy would always lose.

Know yourself and know the enemy. Chief Zeng of the fourth intake at the Huangpu Academy told us about Xue Yue's origins. It turned out that this Tiger Boy was also a veteran. Xue Yue, courtesy name Boling, was a native of Lechang, Guangdong. In 1921, when Sun Yat-sen was inaugurated as president in Guangzhou, a guard regiment was set up at the Presidential Palace, with Xue Yue, Ye Ting and Zhang Fakui as the 1st, 2nd and 3rd Battalion commanders, and in 1922, when President Sun fled disaster on the battleship Yongfeng, there were two men with him: one was Chiang Kai-shek and the other was Xue Yue. In 1927, Xue Yue, in collaboration with Chen Jitang, blocked the southward movement of our Nanchang Uprising in the area of Chao Mei, and the opponent he was then facing was Ye Ting. In the same year, he also suppressed the Guangzhou Uprising led by Zhang Tailei and Ye Ting. This time, Chiang Kai-shek wanted to send Chen Cheng to lead the Central Army in chasing and putting down the uprising, but Chen Cheng recommended Xue Yue instead.

22 December, the Winter Solstice. The extreme end of *yin* and the birth of *yang*. We advanced into the north of Guizhou with Zunyi as our focus. We will create a new Soviet Area.

The next day, the 2nd Bureau reported to the Central Military Commission on the enemy's situation: our enemy Xue decided to take Wu's column towards Zhenyuan and Zhou's column minus the 99th Division set out to pursue and destroy from Tianzhu towards Shibing. They have decided to launch an offensive against us after 26 December. Liu Jianxu's Xiang army will attack Jianhe with one division from Jinping.

In light of this, the Military Commission decided that the whole army should quickly move north to Weng'an and make haste to cross the Wu River before the enemy could catch up with them.

THE WU RIVER

The Lord of Heaven made the last day of 1934 a beautiful one and gave us a truly festive celebration with a heavy fall of snow. The 3rd Red Army Corps occupied Weng'an, and the enemy defending Yuqing fled without a fight. The local militia and despots had run away at the mere sight of us, so the Red Army confiscated all the possessions they had been unable to carry away with them and divided them among the "dry people". These dry people called us "Mr Red Army"; they were in need of food, salt and bolts of cloth. The dry people who were dressed only in rags, had certainly already been squeezed dry, squeezed very dry indeed. Needless to say, they were stick thin and, even though it was winter, teenage girls were not wearing trousers! Of course, it wasn't because they didn't mind the cold, nor because they wanted to smash feudal traditions; it was simply because they didn't have any to wear.

Houchang is one of the four great market towns of northern Guizhou. Now, it presented a scene of a different kind of bustle and liveliness. Freshly painted slogans for the "Expand the Red" campaign and other propaganda filled the streets, adding to the festival atmosphere. Our own slogans swamped the enemy announcements about collecting grain levies and press-ganging the able-bodied. Our two most frequent slogans were "Down with Warlord Wang Jialie" and "Long Live the Soviet of Workers and

Farmers". The members of the Red Army Women's Propaganda Team loudly and enthusiastically proclaimed, "The Red Army is the army of the poor and destitute! It is the army of the dry people! We have come to rescue you! There are never three sunny days in a row, or three square feet of level land and no one has even half a cent of silver. The landlords and moneybags make sure their lives are good but don't let anyone else live at all! But you dry people don't have to accept this fate, so you must rise up and support the Revolution!"

1934, a year of continuous artillery fire, ended on the march. We were overjoyed to receive our holiday allowance. It was a little more than the amount given to officers and men of the regular army because we in the 2nd Bureau always received preferential treatment. Some of the shopkeepers were setting off firecrackers to welcome the New Year and to entice us into their shops.

Our New Year banquet was necessarily very simple, unlike our time in the central revolutionary base area, when it was customary to hold a grand occasion where the banquet and entertainment were particularly lively and enthusiastic. Even the senior officials were sometimes forced to appear in the show. As we were on the march, however, the banquets and entertainments were conducted in quite small work units. Everybody's attention was focused on the upcoming fighting, so there was an unusually tense atmosphere to the occasion. In such fraught times, our 2nd Bureau didn't dare hold even the simplest of entertainments. A straightforward banquet was good enough for us! Everyone had plenty of sweet and fragrant delicacies, and their fill of the best cuts of meat. It had been a long time since we had last seen fat floating on top of a bowl of stew. There were great bowls of wine too! It was the local rice wine of Guizhou. The truth was, a lot of us had no head for wine. The revolution was a time of suffering and before it, many had been woodcutters and cattle herders, so where were they going to get wine from!

No one dared get drunk! Our comrades from the army corps were still strolling around the streets but we had no option but to start up our equipment. There were already two receivers running in the Investigation and Collation Section, but we needed to get some more going. The enemy signals had suddenly begun to come in thick and fast, but we still had to let the rest of our comrades enjoy their meat. This was the wonderful year 1935 and they should be able to welcome it in properly and not to celebrate the Red Army's victory with thin maize gruel!

Four enemy divisions of Wu's Army arrived in Shibing yesterday and continued their advance towards Xinhuangping, with some of them chasing us in the direction of Laohuangping. Our enemy Zhou's Army is still advancing towards Xinhuangping via Shibing Dongkou, with its leading division arriving at Shibing Dongkou on the 29th and still there the next day; the 4th Division of the Qian Army is in Zunyi...

2nd Bureau's "Report on enemy deployment" on 31 January:

The enemy does not seem to be in hot pursuit. On the basis of the current enemy deployment, the Central Political Bureau decided at the Houchang Conference on 1 January to resolutely implement the decision of the Liping Conference to create a new Soviet area along the Sichuan-Guizhou border and immediately cross the Wu River with the whole army. "The creation of new base areas can only be achieved in harsh, brutal and victorious battle. Resist all temptation to run away and all inclination to stop and rest."

The corps commanders did not attend either the Tongdao Conference or the Liping Conference. They received a telegram from the Military Commission during the march. They immediately conveyed it to the army cadres, who received it with delight. This sudden change in direction disrupted Chiang Kai-shek's original deployment, and the Red Army returned to a position of agile and adaptable command and action. Chief Zeng told us that Corps Commander Peng Dehuai sent a telegram to the Military Commission to express his firm support for the new strategic policy. Corps Commander Peng has been depressed for a long time; he is an open and honest person and always the most daring in speaking the truth. At the battles of Guangchang and the Xiang River, he was so angry that he was often reduced to cursing and swearing. In this shift of strategy, the combat troops provided mobile flanking cover for the huge central column as it "moved house", and this kind of channelled advance turned every combat corps into "sedan chair bearers" carrying the heavy "wedding sedan" of the central column. Peng Dehuai said they weren't carrying a wedding sedan but a coffin instead. After the turning point for the troops at Tongdao, as the war shifted in our favour and the Red Army was revitalised, Peng's mood was greatly improved, and he was sometimes heard cracking jokes with his men. He took the initiative to send a telegram to the Military Commission, suggesting that we should seize the favourable opportunity to cross the Wu River. When Chief Zeng told us this, the meaning was clear: the 2nd Bureau's intelligence had had a major effect. Things like this, from decisions at the very top level to the responses of our commanders and warriors, were what motivated us to work harder.

Previously, a decision was taken at the Liping Conference that Liu Bocheng would return as chief of the general staff. Comrade Li De, our international adviser, was said to be indignant. Liu Bocheng was a veteran revolutionary who had taken part in the Xinhai Revolution. In his time at the Frunze Military Academy in Moscow, he was admired by Li De but during the fifth anti-encirclement and annihilation campaign, Liu opposed Li De's dogma and was relegated to the position of chief of staff of the 5th Red Army Corps. It was said that when Li De was absent from the Liping Conference because of malaria, General Political Commissar Zhou showed him the Russian text of the meeting's decision, and the two of them had a stand-up argument. General Political Commissar Zhou was essentially a gentle and refined person, but he also had a sharp eye, and it was this sharpness that revealed his revolutionary fervour. Li De's interpreter, Wu Xiuquan, was not present, so they argued in English. The guards witnessed Chief Political Commissar Zhou slamming the table so hard it made the oil lamp jump!

At the Houchang Conference, it was also decided that the Military Commission would have to report to a meeting of the Politburo on the direction of operations and on the choice of time and place of those operations.

Previously, all military operations had been decided by the Team of Three, with Li De as the supreme military commander.

Bo Gu officially announced Liu Bocheng's appointment and Liu immediately reported to General HQ.

The heavy responsibility for the forced crossing of the Wu River fell to none other than Liu Bocheng. The Wu River is known as "Heaven's Moat". This first major river in Guizhou, it divides the province into two halves, north and south. It is a little wider than the Xiang River, with black cliffs on both banks and a swift current, like a green-black dragon rushing towards the northeast. The local people said the river was so fierce that even a goose feather could not float on it and would sink to the bottom. There were Qian Army fortifications and artillery at the crossing, and the same locals said it would be difficult to build a pontoon bridge. Some years ago, Wang Jialie and the warlords fought a war against each other and failed to build a bridge despite trying for many days.

"See how you get on, Red Army lads!" the people said. "Mind you, crossing the Wu River and taking Zunyi is a prize beyond price."

"Cross at all costs! We must cross no matter how!" This became the new slogan of the commanders and fighting troops. Our "big move" had got this far and, as the enemy said, we had well and truly flown the nest. There was no way back, and if anyone tried to intercept us, we would have to fight tooth and nail, no matter what the cost.

…Intercepted coded telegram from the commander of the Zhuchang River defence:

> "The river defences are heavily fortified, the officers and soldiers are tireless and diligent. They can see off the danger and hold the position without any problem."

Li De was still warning, "Do not cross the Wu River. Do not try to establish a new base near Zunyi. The Wu River may well be another Xiang River!"

2nd Bureau's latest report on enemy deployment: the Central Army is advancing at full speed towards the Wu River…

There is a saying that goes, "You may have travelled the whole world, but the Wu River is still hard to cross." Our reinstated chief of staff, Liu Bocheng, had great hopes of victory. He had once been a general in the Chuan Army and had led his troops into battle here back then. This was also his first battle since his reinstatement.

Zunyi was an important town in northern Guizhou, but Tongzi was the lair of Wang Jialie, the opium-addicted chairman of Guizhou. It was said that although the county town was not particularly big, it had a very foreign atmosphere and was known as "Little Nanjing". This was because Tongzi had produced a powerful figure who had total military and political control of the province and whose friends and family had also enjoyed a meteoric rise to power and influence. Between them, they occupied all the key posts and they had used the riches they looted from the ordinary people to return to their hometown to buy land and build themselves various Western-style houses. The so-called "natural stronghold of the Wu River" is indeed a natural defence for Zunyi and Tongzi, so the capture of those two areas was part of the military strategy to create a new revolutionary base. The 2nd Division of the 1st Corps was ordered to form the vanguard of the operation. Receiving the responsibility for such an important task ensured that every commander and every soldier embraced belief in their victory and it gave them the determination to sacrifice everything to break through, no matter how much of a "natural stronghold" confronted them.

The commanders stood on the snowy ground synchronising their watches, taking the lead from Old Boss Zhu's timepiece. In such a largescale operation, coordinated timing was essential, and watches could not be a second slow or a second fast. The enemy would be hot on our tail, so we had no line of retreat, and even less was there any time for hesitation. Crossing the river meant victory, and the hope of that victory was a fleeting one, like a snowflake in your hand – if you studied it for too long, it would melt away through your fingers. But the snow in Guizhou did not come in large flakes, it felt more like pinpricks of ice, and when it fell on the ground, the ground became slippery as an oil slick...

At midnight on New Year's Eve, the 1st and 3rd Red Army Corps were ordered to march up to the Wu River across slippery, slushy snow. Comrade Liu Bocheng, chief of the general staff, personally accompanied an engineering unit, and the latest enemy information we had intercepted was that the pursuing enemy, four divisions of Wu Qiwei's men and four divisions of Zhou Hunyuan's men, were less than two hundred *li* from the Wu River. If we did not manage to cross the river, we would have a fight to the death with the troops pursuing us.

Order from Lin Biao to the 1st Red Army Corps: Make haste to take the ferry crossings before the enemy!

The force that left for the riverbank to make a sudden assault on the opposite bank from three crossing points comprised the valiant soldiers of the 4th Regiment of the 2nd Division, the 1st Regiment of the 1st Division of the 1st Red Army Corps and the 13th, 14th and 15th Regiments of the 5th Division of the 3rd Red Army Corps. "Swim across the river!" The river was too bitingly cold to be crossed bare-chested, while bamboo rafts were swept back by the currents and a pontoon bridge was washed away. The officers and men of the engineering company were possessed of exalted class consciousness and comprehensive operational skills, so there was no difficulty they could not overcome, no matter how great. In the face of concentrated fire from the Qian Army, the 4th Regiment of the 2nd Division constructed more than sixty bamboo rafts, made three tiers of rafts into pontoons, then, anchoring them firmly at either end to the riverbanks with ropes made from bamboo strips, used more than a hundred of those pontoons to construct a floating bridge. They fought all through three days and nights before a huge pontoon bridge appeared on the surface of the river. This bridge to victory bisected the Wu River like a razor-sharp steel knife. The valiant 4th Corps implemented a large-scale forced crossing. Success! We saw white signal flares streaking into the night sky.

On 3 January, the Qian Army's Wu River defensive line collapsed entirely. We followed the senior officials of the Military Commission across the river, but Wang Jialie sent Chiang a coded telegram saying that the Qian Army was in the middle of a fight to the death with the Red Army and that the enemy had twice unsuccessfully attempted to force a crossing. "Dug into a stalemate on either side of the river."

Lao Chiang did not think Wang Jialie's whitewash of his efforts merited any attention and decided that this was the great opportunity he had been waiting for to root out the enemy and clear them from the area. Xue Yue understood Lao Chiang's intentions very well. On the day our army marched towards the Wu River, the first day of the New Year, we cracked the secret order given by Xue Yue to Wu's and Zhou's columns. He ordered them to pursue the Red Army with only a part of their forces and directed their main force to Wang Jialie's base camp: Guiyang.

> This Route Army's purpose is swiftly to pursue westward and suppress the Communist Army's invasion of Guiyang, and then to urge our central city command to take advantage of the situation and advance on and attack Sichuan...
>
> This Route Army is fully deployed with the Ou Division in the villages of the northern suburbs, the Han Division in the villages of the western suburbs, the Tang Division in the villages of the southern suburbs and the Liang Division in the villages of the eastern suburbs... it must not divulge its positions even to friendly forces.

"It must not divulge its positions even to friendly forces." The happy days of sole domination of one side for Wang Jialie, the leader of those "friendly forces", had clearly come to an end.

As far back as September 1927, Wang Jialie led his troops to Yuanling in Hunan. He wanted to attack the peasant army of the Autumn Harvest Uprising led by Mao Zedong, but before he came in contact with the insurgent army, he fought the Hunan-based warlords for territory and was forced to return to Guizhou. Relying on Lao Chiang, he finally made his stand in the warlord in-fighting in Guizhou, but now that the Central Army was chasing the Red Army, he was counting on both the Red Army and the White Army just passing through. However, instead of chasing the Red Army with his main force, Xue Yue was more interested in the provincial capital, Guiyang.

Analysis of Xue Yue's coded telegram: clearly, Xue Yue wants to take possession of territory of his own.

On the north bank of the Wu River, the Red Army's spoils of war were scattered everywhere. As it fell apart, the Guizhou Army dropped their rifles, their smoking guns and a lot of scarce mortar shells! The commander-in-chief of the southern Sichuan frontier,

Hou Zhidan, hurriedly ordered the troops to retreat to Zunyi. But his officers and soldiers were already in a panic, and they skirted Zunyi and fled even further north than Tongzi.

We ran through the fog, more than twenty miles of muddy mountain road hardly drawing breath, straight to Zhuchang where the River Defence headquarters were located. We heard that the leading troops had already beaten the local tyrant landlords and caught their households' fat pigs. They didn't have time to kill them, so they let the locals beat them to death with hoes. They were also too late to shave off the bristles, so they divided them up and gave everyone a piece. We didn't notice our hunger as we were keener to get our hands on the enemy's coded communications. We went straight to the River Defence headquarters, but we were disappointed. Lin Xiusheng, commander of the River Defence, had fled. Although the headquarters staff had left many confidential documents, the one thing we were most eager to find, their codebook, was not there. We did find one quite interesting draft telegram among the documents left behind: "The Red Army is crossing the river. Their firepower is very fierce."

While in Zhuchang, we decided to cross the Wu River. So far, we had gained victory within three days of reaching Zhuchang, and Zhuchang had turned out to be very entertaining indeed! When the Qian troops guarding the river fled there, one of our forward units chased their four army corps with great ferocity. One of the key company commanders, Hou Zhidan, was gravely wounded. The Red Army bound him hand and foot and carried him with them when they left, but unfortunately he died before they reached Zhuchang!

THE BIG CITY

On 1 September, we braved the rain to enter the city with the column of the Military Commission. The Red Army soldiers were covered in mud and dirt, and the first thing everyone did was wash their faces in a nearby river. We entered the city from the south gate of the new city, and when we saw the welcoming crowd as we crossed Fengle Bridge, the chiefs dismounted, and the crowd lit firecrackers. Zunyi is not very big, but it was the first major city we had captured on our westward expedition. It is the second largest city in Guizhou, and it was where Wang Jialie started out. The largest city is Guiyang, which was occupied by Xue Yue and his Central Army on 7 September. In a telegram to Xue Yue, Chiang Kai-shek once denounced the Guizhou warlords as "making fish and flesh out of the people". The warlords and tyrant landowners of Guizhou were so arrogant that, although there were so many dry people who could not make ends meet, they spent their days living in luxury in Western-style buildings! I heard that Guizhou's economy was monopolised by several warlords, and they controlled all the main commodities such as salt, sugar, cloth and grain. This was their idea of "virtuous government"! The evil stench of wine and roasting meat assailed us at the gates of the red-walled mansions, while outside, the streets were littered with frozen bones. This contrast stirred up old hatreds and gave birth to new desires for vengeance in the Red

Army soldiers, and also provoked in them a higher class consciousness.

Where is the enemy? This was the constant task of our 2nd Bureau, every moment of every day, and it was the prime concern of the head of the Central Committee.

Sunzi said, "Foreknowledge cannot be obtained from gods and ghosts."

We knew where the enemy was. Wang Jialie begged Chiang Kai-shek to send troops to blockade and encircle us, but Chiang was currently stretched thin. We analysed the coded telegrams frequently exchanged by various enemy troops and discovered that the enemy forces around Zunyi were very sparse.

On the day we entered the city, we decoded an order from Chiang. He Jian, commander-in-chief of the Pursuit and Suppression Army, passed on Chiang's demand that the Pursuit and Suppression Army destroy He Long and Ren Bishi's Red Army in Xiangxi, and also the Central Red Army. He Jian also asked Xue Yue's troops to "pursue and press home the pursuit", but as far as an attack on the Central Red Army went, Chiang Kai-shek's order was just a kind of posturing, and He Jian's deployment was merely a show of following orders. Twenty regiments of He Jian's Xiang Army went to Changde to engage the 2nd and 6th Red Army Corps. Liu Xiang's Chuan Army was positioned on a front on the southern sector of the Yangtze River and were reluctant to advance southwards because they did not know the true state of our army. Xue Yue, the frontline commander-in-chief of the enemy's Pursuit and Suppression Army, was intent on controlling not just the Guiyang area but the whole of Guizhou Province. They were all located on the southern bank of the Wu River and showed no sign of pursuing us. To the north of the Wu River, Hou Zhidan lost both the river defences and Zunyi; the Qian Army was really not up to their task.

However, the divisional commander of the Guizhou Army sent telegrams to a series of his superiors to ask for help. First, he said that he was stubbornly resisting alone and was outnumbered. Then he expressed his determination to kill the enemy: "Even if only the rivers and mountains remain, my lofty ambition can never be ground down." Finally he begged that "the central authorities issue an early order for encirclement and annihilation". The man was a joke! He sent humble petitions to such a long list of his superiors: the Central Party headquarters in Nanjing; Chairman Lin of the Nationalist government; President Wang of the Executive Council; and Chairman Chiang of the Military Commission. Also a variety of ministers: Minister He in Beiping; Deputy Commander Zhang in Hankou Director He; Chairman He in Baoqing; Commander-in-Chief Li in Nanning; Deputy Commander Bai in Liuzhou; Commander-in-Chief Chen in Guangzhou; Governor Liu in Baxian; Chairman Long in Yunnan; Chairman Wang in Guiyang; and Army Commander-in Chief You.

With the enemy in this position, the Red Army finally had time to rest and expand the Communist Revolution. Every corps had reached its designated defensive position: the 1st Red Army Corps was in the north of the city, the 3rd Red Army Corps was in the south of the city, and the 5th and 9th Red Army Corps formed the southeastern defence line. With Zunyi at its heart, the territory under control by our Army was about 400 miles long from north to south and 200 miles wide from east to west. This was the transportation hub of Sichuan and Guizhou, the economic and political centre of northern Guizhou, and it was ideally suited for our army to develop in all directions. Would this, then, become our new base?

There was something of a feeling of returning home to the old Soviet area. People waving colourful flags came swarming around to see us, shouting all the time. Some of them insisted on seeing the "water horses" because, to cover their shame at their defeat, the enemy had put it about that the Red Army had used water horses to cross the river and the army was composed of heavenly generals and heavenly soldiers! The Red Army seized Wang Jialie's salt business, which was worth several hundred thousand silver dollars, and his Platinum Dragon cigarettes worth tens of thousands of yuan and which were ordered from the Shanghai Nanyang Company and prepared as a New Year's gift to Xue Yue's Central Army. They distributed some of the confiscated salt and cigarettes among the poor, and the rest they sold at less than cost price. We changed the cash we received from the sales into Soviet banknotes because we used both cash and this paper money printed with the head of

Lenin to make purchases. The Soviet bank was able to open on a daily basis and, one by one, shops that had closed down were able to re-open their doors for business. Worthy of special mention at this point are the boys and girls of the Friends of the Red Army Society who enthusiastically handed out leaflets on the streets.

The girls presented an exhilarating new spectacle by dressing in colourful *qipao* with white socks and black cloth shoes. The boys spread the word that anyone following the Red Army would have food to eat, clothes to wear and an escape from their oppression. The girls called out to their country sisters that the aim of the revolution was liberation. They said that when the day of world unity came, our children would be educated for free. We heard that the girls exclaimed in admiration at the foreign dancing of one Red Army soldier, and we think they must have been talking about Captain Xiao Jinguang of the Red Cadre Corps. He had studied in the Soviet Union and was particularly skilled in Caucasian dance. When we were in the Central Soviet Area, Li Bozhao also danced the Soviet tap dance for us. Under the tall, densely grown camphor trees, the principal of the Gorky Drama School taught the soldiers to sing. Now the city was full of people celebrating, and freshly painted slogans adorned every street: "The Red Army is fighting for the Agrarian Revolution!"; "The Red Army never takes anything from the masses!"; "Smash the rich, save the poor. Poor people rise up!"; "Down with Chiang Kai-shek. Workers and peasants rule the country!"

Fighting local tyrants and redistributing wealth requires a degree of education, but fortunately these are not difficult subjects to master. We heard it said that some people didn't know how to fight at first. They went to the Yang family mansion at the south gate to fight the local tyrants, but they didn't know how to. They only knew that the word for "fight" meant "to hit", so they picked up benches and smashed the Yang mansion's lattice windows! Some Red Army soldiers explained to them that smashing things was not the same as fighting the landlords; what it actually meant, to quote a previous report by Mao Zedong, was "slaughtering the pigs and making a fresh start". The locals immediately took them at their word and slaughtered all the landlords' pigs to help celebrate the New Year. As the New Year arrived, the festive atmosphere grew more and more pronounced, and the kids began to let off firecrackers. The Red Army soldiers taught them songs, and the Red Army Drama Group put on a new play called *Down with the Warlord Wang Jialie*. Of course, the play was a form of propaganda, and only after the performance was over was the food distributed. We heard that the 9th Red Army Corps held a commemorative meeting for Carl Liebknecht and Rosa Luxembourg and also opened a Soviet bank in Meitan County.

In this festive atmosphere, the wives of the Red Army chiefs were also able to join their husbands. Deng Yingchao and He Zizhen, who were married to the two commanders, were normally part of the General Health Ministry's Cadre Recuperation Company, accompanying seniors like Dong Biwu and Xu Teli on the march. As far back as the Jinggangshan period, there was a rule that couples could only meet on Saturday evenings. The only exception was the wife of the commander-in-chief, Kang Keqing, who was not part of the Cadre Recuperation Company; she was the political instructor of the Central Column Command and a front-line woman soldier. There were more than a dozen more female cadres in the Cadre Recuperation Company. They did propaganda and political agitation work, and more importantly, they helped carry stretchers, fetch medicine chests and cared for the wounded (the "recuperating personnel" of the Cadre Recuperation Company were limited to cadres above the regimental level and confidential secretaries). They were referred to as "political soldiers". Comrade Xiao Yuehua and the commanders' wives were all integrated into the Cadre Recuperation Company, and because of her special status as Li De's wife, Xiao inevitably became the subject of humorous observations. We too took the opportunity to have a bit of a laugh. This time we heard that they had quarrelled again. However, the German political adviser sent by the Comintern, whose name was Otto Burn but was known as Li De, did not speak Chinese and Xiao Yuehua did not speak any foreign languages, so how could they argue with each other? Wu Xiuquan could not act as their interpreter all the time. Bo Gu was also known to comfort Xiao Yuehua, saying she should make some allowance for Li De because his German lover had died for the revolution and he no longer had any family in his homeland; his suffering was dedicated to the world revolution. To be honest, it had been a long time since we had a quarrelsome couple around, and it seemed to bring us a little taste of normal life. There was always something interesting to be reported when the commanders and their wives got together. Some of us liked to imagine that the first thing that happened when husband and wife were reunited was that she took off his underwear to search for lice. Everyone was happy to see these women busy about the place as it brought an atmosphere of peace and contentment. In addition, as it was approaching New Year, the sound of firecrackers became even more common. Of course, firecrackers and gunshots can sound very similar, and firecrackers give off gunpowder smoke just like guns. So the smell of gunpowder was real, but the sounds this time came from a benign source.

The work of establishing base areas really began. The Red Army went deep into the surrounding villages and towns, mobilising the poor and establishing Party organisations and revolutionary order. A meeting of 10,000 people was held in the large playground of the Old Town Middle School, which was full of red flags and slogans. Bo Gu presided over the meeting, Mao Zedong and Zhu De spoke, and the masses were able to see their real faces that day. They discovered that Zhu Mao was not one person but an amalgam of Zhu and Mao. Nor, of course, were they the red-browed, green-eyed, blue-faced, dripping-fanged, violent monsters described in the stories. Those were all rumours spread by the Kuomintang and the reactionary militia. In the flesh, Zhu De's face was honest and simple, and his tone of voice quite gentle. As for Mao Zedong, he was more like a scholar than anything else. After their enthusiastic speeches, the representatives of the Red Army and of the masses spoke, and Bo Gu then announced, "The Provisional Workers', Farmers' and Soldiers' Government of Zunyi is officially established!" Everything seemed to be just as it had been in the past, back to the scene when the Soviet State was established in Ruijin. This made everyone reminisce about the good times of the Ruijin Soviet Republic. Some people said that the Soviet Republic would now take Zunyi as its capital, Zunyi being considerably larger than Ruijin.

What a pleasant time it was! At the end of the conference, the Red Army held a friendly basketball match with the local middle school. At a shrill note from a silver flute, the game officially started. Commander-in-Chief Zhu took part, happily grabbing the ball and running with it. Although he probably hadn't touched a basketball ball for a long time, Zhu De, who had lived and studied abroad, got so excited he occasionally shouted a few words in English, and the local students whispered to each other, "He's a university student!" It was a real eye-opener for them.

The chairman of the Military Commission took up residence in the Bai Mansion at the top of the hill. It was the private home of Bai Huizhang, commander of the 99th Division of the 25th Army of the Kuomintang. It was the most stylish building in Zunyi City, being a two-storey brick and wood structure, part Chinese part Western in style with black brick columns, carved doors and windows, spacious corridors and balconies, and a locust tree in the yard. We had our quarters in another small Western-style building nearby, the sizeable property of another important local tyrant-landlord. A lot of stuff had already been taken away, but a few things were still left behind. There was half a bottle of brandy in the drinks cabinet, and cans, cigarettes and illustrated magazines scattered about the study. Burning hard, white charcoal to keep warm, sitting in a rocking chair with a cigarette in hand, and flipping through *Good Friends* from Shanghai, certainly gave us a taste of the bourgeois lifestyle.

All that was missing were bright electric lights. This local tyrant had also left behind a large opium pipe, and the smell of the drug had not yet dissipated, but that was something we couldn't touch. We preferred to go window shopping. Both the old city and the new city were adjoined by shops: commercial banks, pawnshops, silk houses, foreign goods stores, bookshops, restaurants, everything you could want, all part of the urban landscape. We had been crossing deep mountains and wilderness recently and, for a long time, all we had seen were deserted villages and thatched huts. Now that we had entered the big city, it seemed that the streets really did have everything. The first thing we wanted to do was eat chicken. Chief Zeng was a generous host and invited us to eat at the best Sichuan-Guizhou restaurant in Zunyi. There we had something better than just chicken: *lazi jiding*, popcorn chicken with dried chilis!

Our 2nd Bureau was a particular concern of the chairman of the

Military Commission and on this occasion, he gave us lots of leather goods and several pairs of waterproof overshoes, all of which came from the tyrant-landlords. Deputy Bureau Chief Qian said we should all make ourselves leather coats! After we had had a big dish of *lazi jiding*, Li Jianhua from the Investigation and Collation Section, our only female comrade in the 2nd Bureau, led us off to look for a tailor's shop. Strolling the streets that afternoon in the lazy winter sunshine was a heart-warming experience. At this time, we didn't dare think too much about it. The sun seemed to be tinged with blood. I thought of the blood in the Xiang River from the casualties of air attack and artillery shells. I thought of those young soldiers who left their hometowns and sacrificed their lives, those who studied and fought with us, and looked forward to the victory of the Revolution. All close comrades in arms, along with those lovable army horses that were terrified and killed by bombing, the thought of them brought tears to my eyes...

There were even more newspapers to read now we were in the big city. There was news of the bounty ordered by Chiang Kai-shek for the heads of Communist leaders, and of the murder of comrades in the Central Soviet Area. The *Dagong Bao* gave details of the tragic sacrifice of Chen Shuxiang, commander of the 34th Division of the Red Fifth Army. The 34th Division was defeated, and Chen Shuxiang led his troops to cover the main force of the Red Army as it crossed the Xiang River, but they themselves failed to make the crossing. Master Chen was wounded and captured. He refused medical attention and went on hunger strike. He also refused to divulge secrets about the Red Army's operations. He disembowelled himself while under escort by the Kuomintang security forces. The enemy had hung the head of our Commander Chen, an esteemed cadre of the Soviet Revolution, from the city gate tower of Changsha, not far from his family home.

Everything added to the continuous memories and tangled thoughts. Our relatives in the Soviet Area, holding newly made cloth-bound straw sandals, were standing by the river, eagerly saying their farewells. How could they anticipate the distance we would travel! Those voices, those tender remembrances still seemed to be ringing in our ears:

"When you come back, bring us some useful goodies!"

"Buy a torch and also some cloth for your sister!"

"Brother, capture more divisional commanders!"

All those who have died, all those who have sacrificed their lives for victory, and even more nameless martyrs! Their image has already faded and in the future, there will not even be the faintest shadow of them to be seen.

We passed a photographer's studio and everyone wanted a group photo. But a sign on the studio door read: "Looted by Qian soldiers. Temporarily closed for business." The wooden planks of the door were smashed in, and that was obviously the work of Wang Jialie's Qian Army soldiers. Chief Zeng said that Geng Biao, commander of the 4th Regiment of Heroes, had a camera, which he had taken when he attacked Zhangzhou. But he had no film, and sometimes, for fun, he would get people to pose and then say, "Oops, I forgot! No film!"

Colonel Geng's men led the way and were the first to arrive at the south bank of the Wu River. I wondered if there was any film in his camera that time. Many people died in that icy river.

There was a second-hand bookstore next to the photo studio, and its door was open. As we were about to go in to buy some pencils and pads, we heard Section Chief Cao greeting someone inside. It turned out to be Huang Zhen from the political bureau of a unit directly under the Military Commission. Zunyi is a big city, and the shop owner was carrying a Western-style walking stick and seemed to be very much of the new school. Huang Zhen told us to come in and then went on to tell the owner of the store, "You don't have to close your business and hide. We in the Red Army buy and sell out in the open. You businessmen have been suffering, but we are now here to protect you. We give those corrupt officials, landlords and bullies short shrift."

Huang Zhen was a graduate of Xinhua University of the Arts and joined the Red Army during the Ningdu Uprising. He had also performed on stage in the Central Soviet Area. He was a famous painter in the army, and his enormous painting "Crushing the Enemy's Encirclement and Annihilation Campaign" was a huge success when the Second Congress of the Soviets was held. He had come out to buy brushes and paper. Since we couldn't take photographs, and it was rare to catch an artist at leisure like this, we called out to him to paint our portrait. He showed us a painting called "An Old Hero on the Night March", the subject of which was Comrade Lin Zuhan, finance minister of the Soviet Republic. He was holding a stick in his right hand and a lantern in his left as he strode confidently through the darkness. His thick spectacles were also very expressive of his spirit and seemed even brighter than the lantern he was carrying.

From the time we left the Soviet Area until we crossed the Xiang River, we were marching almost exclusively at night, and I never imagined that an artist could represent such a scene. The vast line of torches wading through the mountains under the night sky was a magnificent sight. We ourselves had seen Master Lin holding up his lantern to light the way for people at the crossing, and clearly the artist Huang Zhen had seen him too. During this westward expedition, Master Lin was also director of the General Confiscation and Expropriation Committee and head of the General Supply Department. Huang Zhen said it was just a "quick sketch". He explained there are many things whose loss would be regretted in the future if they were not recorded at the time. Our political commissar said that our revolution would surely come to fruition, but we ourselves might not live to see that day. The new world would not forget us in the future, but even so we would do well to leave some record of our deeds.

It was no surprise that the head of the propaganda section of the Political Bureau would also be an effective political councillor, but this sketch of his was also very accomplished. He had just finished it, which was why he still had it with him. Section Chief Cao asked why he referred to it as a "quick sketch", and was there such a thing as a "slow sketch"? Huang Zhen laughed and said, "There are also 'slow paintings', things like formal style paintings which are rather like silk embroidery. Surely you don't have time for embroidery when you're on the march!" Everyone laughed. Huang Zhen went on, "A sketch uses broad lines and strokes, but the most important thing is to catch the spirit of the subject. There are lots of different types of sketch from brushstrokes to words, recording both people and events."

We also went with Chief Zeng to look at the huge oil painting. First, he nodded his head in appreciation of the quality of the painting, then he turned to us and said, with great seriousness, "Good! He hasn't left out the quotation marks!"

Chief Zeng was referring to the quotation marks around the phrase "encirclement and annihilation" in the title of the painting. While we were talking like this, Chief Zeng was leafing through an old book from the shelves. He was a very studious person, and whenever he marched into a place, he would search for a bookstore. He always lent us the books he bought so we could read them. Even though they were supposedly on loan, he never wanted them back and, in fact, we seldom returned them. Inevitably, one would get lost, but he didn't mind buying the same book four or five times. He said it was always a pleasure. This time he wanted to buy the book he was looking at, and we thought nothing of it. He asked the store owner for the price, and the store owner said he could have it as a gift. Chief Zeng offered three silver dollars, but the store owner said it was too much. We were rather surprised, but Chief Zeng said it was just the right amount and the sale proceeded smoothly. The store owner couldn't help but exclaim that his customer was "a master of culture and civilisation". The book was Xue Fucheng's *Supplement to Yongan's Text* written in the late Qing dynasty. The store owner took out a packet of Hatamen cigarettes, respectfully offered them to Chief Zeng and then gave one to each of us men. The smokers lit up and the non-smokers tucked the cigarettes behind their ears. Chief Zeng was engrossed in the book, but he still took notice of what we were saying to each other. He took a luxurious drag on his cigarette, then said to Section Chief Cao in a serious tone, "Recording people and events can be done in 'sketches', and always remember that in our struggle with the Kuomintang, we are also fighting a war of words. You young people have only studied for a few years, and although you know a bit, it is far from enough. We are all human beings. As such, we need always to be seeking new knowledge. Even better is the ability to write well. Would you all be able to write an essay?"

The question came out of the blue. It was like suddenly receiving a new coded report; there's nothing you can say straight off. However, Chief Zeng shook the old book he was holding at us and fixed us with a stare, as much as to say that there was no escape from answering his question. It was just like a coded report that had to be deciphered accurately. We talked all round it, but Chief Zeng just shook his head slightly, his expression still very serious.

After we left the bookstore, Chief Zeng told us that Comrade Mao Zedong was reading that very book, and as soon as he, Zeng, entered Guizhou, he had asked the troops in the vanguard to look for it. We were intrigued. Chief Zeng also said that there was a sentence in Chiang Kai-shek's recent secret telegram, which he was pretty certain also came from that book. This meant that Chiang Kai-shek too was reading the same book! Seeing that understanding was dawning on us, Chief Zeng explained that the book described the historical event of Shi Dakai's passing through Guizhou and his final defeat on the Dadu River.

"But this essay is about something that happened thousands of years ago. Let's not talk about things so far in the past. For the sake of our work, for the sake of writing our revolutionary essay, you must read more and put more work in on your brushmanship when you have the time. Why not learn from that great artist Huang Zhen and start by practising your sketching? That is my suggestion."

BUREAU CHIEF

So, I could do worse than take advantage of the absence of the sound of gunfire on our tails and, amid the sound of firecrackers celebrating the New Year, cherishing the hope of establishing a permanent base here, see whether I can find the time to write a few chapters. Records of people and events can all be done as sketches, but aren't what I have written so far factual memoirs, so can they really be called sketches? However, as for sketches of people, surely, I must start with the bureau chief since that was what he wanted us to do. He said it was his opinion, but really it amounted to an order. Of course, these are just my scribblings and not well written so I don't dare show them to him. I'm working on it. Bureau Chief Zeng is a pretty learned man himself, but his constant eagerness to learn more means we don't dare try to get out of it. Besides, being able to write a good essay in neat handwriting certainly is an enviable talent. I still remember how, when we took the county town, the Military Commission built barracks so that we could stay in the county yamen. The county mayor was new in office and everyone had already left, but there was still a pair of black ink calligraphy couplets on the gates. "May honour and good fortune be bestowed by Heaven; let everything thrive." When Chief Zeng saw this, and before even entering the courtyard, he exploded with anger. He seized a bucket of whitewash out of the hand of a passing member of the propaganda team and obliterated the old couplet with a few strokes of a hemp brush and replaced it with a new one: "Grasping officials and corrupt mandarins; dog farts every one of them."

This event triggered the memory of an earlier couplet of his, which he had written when he was still only a schoolboy. Bureau Chief Zeng was both a scholar and a soldier but he himself said he was really not even half a scholar. He once told us to study one of Mao Zedong's essays – it was during the time we were in the Jinggang Mountains, the revolution was at a low ebb and Mao Zedong wrote a letter to Lin Biao. "A single spark can start a prairie fire." Chief Zeng wanted us to appreciate what Mao wrote by saying, "When I say that the great surge of the Chinese revolution will soon be with us, that is in no way the same as the empty, unattainable things other people say may possibly come. It is the tip of a ship's mast that we can just see out to sea as we stand on the shore. It is the bright orb of the rising sun that we can see looking east from a mountain top. It is a baby on the verge of maturity stirring restlessly in its mother's womb."

Revolutionaries seldom talk about their past. Back during the period in the Jinggang Mountains, both Zhu's and Mao's wives were killed by the reactionaries, but no one else broached the subject, nor did they themselves say very much either. It is the same for everybody, there are so many emotions buried deep inside. Bureau Chief Zeng really is a very straightforward person. Sometimes he is so caught up in the decoding work that he doesn't speak for three days. Sometimes he jokes with us, and sometimes he talks about the history of past revolutions to improve our technical and combat capabilities. As an example, when he broke the very first secret Kuomintang telegram, he didn't just talk about it to us, he naturally told all manner of new recruits about it too.

When Bureau Chief Zeng was instructing the comrades new to the 2nd Bureau, he quoted a matching couplet[1] from his youth. The two vertical lines read, "A director who has no ability never achieves anything; in his favour, he gets on with everyone despite his self-regard", and the crosspiece read "All raw opium welcome".

He was explaining how to seek out the repeat codes. Codebreaking is like climbing a cliff, you have to find a crack to gain purchase. Even the smoothest rock face has cracks, and the repeat codes are those cracks. We all have experience of climbing a cliff. Faced with an incomprehensible text, these repeat codes are the breakthrough point. As our comrades searched out these chinks in the great mass of the enemy army's coded telegrams, they clattered away counting their frequency on ox-bone abacuses and then relying on challenging guesswork. The first character decoded was 所 but there are many other characters that can combine with 所. Supposing your next guess is 长, if it makes sense when you put it into the communication, then you have decoded the character 长 as well...

The couplet was co-written with his brother when he was eleven years old at the County High School, and his brother Zeng Zhongsheng was fifteen. When war in Europe broke out and Japan forcibly occupied Qingdao, Yuan Shikai agreed to the "Twenty-One Demands", the country's troubles were all coming to a head, and even the Opium Suppression Office was a billowing mass of black smoke! All you could see was people bustling in and out trying to look busy, and in the office new orders were being decided by playing rock-paper-scissors. It certainly did not present a scene of noise and excitement! The director of the Opium Suppression Office himself usually relied on force to get things done, using blackmail and extortion all over the place and always demanding "favours" for the slightest task. So much so, in fact, that he was generally nicknamed Favour. The two brothers were taking a stroll in the area of the office and when they saw how much Favour's business was still thriving, they almost exploded with anger. They ran back to their dormitory, one ground the ink, the other plied the brush, and the couplet was soon written. In the middle of the night when no one was around, they quietly posted the couplet on the door of the Opium Suppression Office. There was quite a show the next morning. The two brothers took their classmates to watch, and they saw a great crowd of people gathered in front of the office. Some were reading out the couplet at the tops of their voices and others were clapping their hands and laughing. Sometime mid-morning, the superintendent came out of the office yawning, and when he saw what was going on, steam seemed to come out of his every orifice. "What snivelling cowards did this? They're done for! Kill the lot of them!" Even talking about it so many years later,

Chief Zeng was still amused by the memory of the superintendent's outraged appearance.

He also talked about the language of the couplet and how one character could have different pronunciations, and one word could have many meanings. The enemy's messages were just as complex. As well as the standard commanders' positions and names, unit numbers, battle plans, troop deployments, tactical manoeuvres, times, places and directions, often there were also the commanders' courtesy titles or names. For example, Chen Cheng was also referred to by his courtesy name Cixiu. The rhetorical language was also very carefully chosen and sometimes quite eccentric in style. These telegrams were generally long and contained uncommon Chinese characters and simplified phrases, with which we translators and decoders had to be familiar. Chief Zeng had an old-school educational background and came from a well-known local family with an ancestral history of martial arts training. This had given rise to a tradition of martial arts training among the Zeng children. Many of the early revolutionaries were people who respected both literature and martial arts. In their youth, the two brothers studied at the Huang Yang Academy run by their grandfather, who also had someone come in to teach them martial arts. People who practise martial arts are mostly very competitive, and this is what we saw in his character. There was a stone roller weighing more than eighty *jin* at the Huang Yang Academy, and he could lift it with his feet and catch it with his hands, repeating the exercise seven or eight times without showing any change in his expression. He was already a kung fu master by then, and his brother, Zeng Zhongsheng, was also very skilled. He could put both hands behind his back and use a rope in his teeth to pull a basket packed full of rice and weighed down with a thirty-*jin* millstone, three times around the central courtyard!

The Zeng brothers were both scholars and martial artists. The elder brother was also one of the first three members of the Standing Committee of the Central Military Commission. The other two members were Zhou Enlai and Guan Xiangying. He was also the leader of the Hubei-Henan-Anhui Soviet. Although Chief Zeng too wore glasses, he was very different from Deputy Chief Qian. The bearded bureau chief had a fiery temper. Heavy responsibilities brought pressure, and pressure made him restless. We were naturally afraid of him losing his temper, but we knew it was all in the cause of the revolution.

Chief Zeng has the build and appearance of a fierce warrior, very similar to Corps Commander Peng. They are both from Hunan so love spicy food. Commander Peng came from a poor background, and it was said that he started out on the revolutionary road to fight injustice. He burned the barns of the local tyrants to feed the poor and needy. Chief Zeng also came from a farming family, but although the household was in straitened circumstances, it still owned a certain amount of land and was moderately well-off. When the commander's father was appointed to public office in the township, the family grew more prosperous by the day. His father sent him out to collect the rents, and when he saw how bad the harvest had been and what a pitiful state the farmers were in, he decided to reduce their rents and did not take even a single grain of rice from those who were in the direst straits. To avoid any arguments with his father, he simply issued them with false receipts for their taxes. In his father's eyes, he was a prodigal and a wastrel, but he himself had his own goals and ideals. He did not want to carry on his father's business but hoped to continue his education like his older brother and find his own way in the world.

Hunan Province's No. 3 Normal University is located in Hengyang. It is the highest-level educational establishment in southern Hunan. It is as famous as the No. 1 Normal School in Changsha and No. 2 Normal School in Changde. On the archway in front of the school, there are four big characters 南学津梁, which mean "Southern Learning Spans All Obstacles", and the couplets on either side of the school gates read, "My road comes from the south, originally from the Lianxi line; East of the great river is nothing but the backwash of the Xiang River."

What an impressive atmosphere that creates! "Lianxi" is one of the names of Zhou Dunyi, a philosopher of the Northern Song dynasty and a native of Dao County in southern Hunan. There is also a line in the school song of No. 3 Normal University: "Lianxi in front and Chuanshan behind". "Chuanshan" is the philosopher Wang Fuzhi of the late Ming and early Qing dynasties, who came from Hengyang in Hunan Province. Bureau Chief Zeng uses this school song to teach his comrades rhetoric. He had read all the ancient texts from his grandfather's place before going to high school. His calligraphy is also very handsome but, as we didn't have his childhood training, we cannot master that particular skill. Chief Zeng doesn't expect us to write calligraphy, but our characters have to be correct. Of course, he can't possibly demand fine penmanship in the face of the enemy; sometimes we can't even find a red or blue pencil! Everything is on hold until the day of victory in the revolution!

Today's revolution is no longer the revolution of the "Three Principles of the People". We are implementing a programme of agrarian revolution. We are fighting for victory in this revolution for the millions of poor people in the world. In the old days of the Great Revolution, the Kuomintang were our friends. Dr Sun Yat-sen founded the Huangpu Military Academy, Chiang Kai-shek was the principal and Comrade Enlai was the director of the Political Department. "Rage is surging, the Party flag is flying, this is the Academy of the Revolution. Principles must be implemented. Discipline must not be relaxed. We must be prepared to be in the vanguard of the struggle. Fight a bloody path, guide the oppressed people, join hands, and move forward..." The academy's motto "Comradeship, Spirit, Integrity" was in Chiang Kai-shek's own calligraphy. The students loved each other like brothers, and they had a resounding slogan: "No regard for money, no regard for our lives, love the country, love the people!"

In the autumn of 1925, the Zeng brothers became part of the fourth intake at the Huangpu Academy. At that time, Guangzhou was the birthplace of the Revolution, and cohort after cohort of enthusiastic youngsters decided to go south, just as they went to Wuhan during the Revolution of 1911. They travelled to Guangzhou because they were attracted by the Huangpu Military Academy, where they could find the new spirit of the age. Almost all of these young people who were seeking a way forward were genuinely full of passion. They came to the "True South", threw themselves into the torrent of the Great Revolution to overthrow the great powers and the warlords! The students sang the school song every day: "Water the flowers with blood; make the Academy our home..." In line with the Kuomintang's slogan, "Unite with

Russia, unite with the Communists, support the peasants and workers", the Kuomintang and the Communist Party cooperated in good faith and the revolution was in an excellent situation. Zeng Mian asked to join the Communist Party of China as soon as he enlisted in the army, but some of the Party branch members thought he was just doing it to be fashionable and considered him too young to stand up to the opprobrium and mockery he would face. He withdrew his application in a fit of anger. He could not stand people thinking his request was just an attempt to show how trendy he was. But the revolution ended in failure, with Chiang Kai-shek wielding a butcher's knife at his allies of the day before, with comrades being turned into enemies, with the Communist Party driven underground and with some of the less committed defecting from the Party. It was during the White Terror, when faced with the severest of tests, that he finally joined the Communist Party.

Speaking of that day, Chief Zeng told us, "I didn't just act in a fit of pique. My thinking at the time was that, just like the ebb and flow of the ocean, the revolution also had its ebb and flow. It was at low tide when you could see who the real Communists were." Even back when he was studying at Hengyang Normal School, he had read many progressive magazines, such as *Guide*, *Pioneer*, *New Trend* and *New Youth*, and the progressive teachers had shouted the slogan, "We must follow the Russian road". At No.3 Hunan Provincial Normal School, he joined the revolutionary group known as The Heart Society and formed a student movement with Huang Kecheng and other students. He also heard Mao Zedong speak many times.

In the eyes of us youngsters, Chief Zeng seems like a mature and sophisticated Communist. Of course, Communists can lose their temper too, but it is always for the success of the revolution. Equally, it is preferable not to lose one's temper, and that day was at last the one when he recovered some of his long-absent good humour. It was the day he brought back some oranges to share with his comrades, and the good humour was because our intelligence had offered the Red Army a new direction. It is because of this new direction that we are here now and the Red Army commanders and soldiers are no longer in a state of confusion. We have captured the city and it will become our new Red base.

At this moment, it does indeed almost feel as if we are back in the Central Soviet Area. The view from this small Western-style house, looking out over the mountain town at night, is of a new play being presented on a distant stage, with torches blazing and people milling about. The audience are both Red Army soldiers and locals; they are strolling the streets, one eye on the play, and their excited singing drifts up on the night breeze along with the faint sound of a bugle. That young trumpeter is working hard too. The Red Army has more than three hundred different bugle calls which are more complex than semaphore signals. Previously, those calls had been heard in the mountains and forests, but now they are ringing out over the city streets. The bugle calls are the secret language of the communication of the Red Army.

It's not easy to be a qualified bugler. It requires an ability to read music, the lung power to play the instrument and both a good musical ear and good hearing. Very early on, an excellent trumpeter was transferred to our reconnaissance department as we needed people with good hearing to detect enemy radio transmissions. The head of the Military Commission long ago gave a clear order that we can select people for the 2nd Bureau from anywhere in the entire army, and any suitable candidates are to be transferred to us as a priority. To begin with, we intercepted a wealth of material, but we couldn't read any of it. The dense code of those documents from the ether was just irritating blocks of numbers. Where was the enemy? What were its deployments? With the life and death of the entire Red Army at stake, that was what most interested the head of the Military Commission.

The pressure was on Bureau Chief Zeng and Cao Daye. In a corner of the wall were two big baskets filled with documents that we couldn't read. Chief Zeng said that no matter what they were, we had to understand what they said. He told us that there is nothing truly difficult in this world; as long as you put the effort in, there is nothing you can't achieve. He mulled it over for a long time, then suddenly remembered that when he was working on subversive measures to incite the enemy to defect or rebel, he had heard an operator say that a password could always be cracked. During the Northern Expedition, he was involved with propaganda and was the head of the propaganda team of the National Revolutionary Army's Frontline Political Department. Once the propaganda team arrived in Changsha, their unit was reorganised by Tang Shengzhi of the Xiang Army. Tang Shengzhi was a Buddhist, and he educated the troops in the "Buddhist spirit" and required them to burn incense and worship the Buddha before going into battle. Faced with such great obstacles, Zeng Mian and his comrades carried out an arduous programme of ideological agitation and reinforcement to make the troops understand that it was the National People's Revolution that they were fighting for. The Northern Expeditionary Army advanced into Hunan and Hubei like a hot knife through butter.

The masses of workers and peasants supported the Northern Expedition, and for its part the Northern Expedition promoted the workers' and peasants' movement. The revolutionary storm was so swift that Zeng Mian's family was affected. As a minor landlord, his father actually became a target of the peasant movement. The local peasant association arrested him. He thought he was going to be beheaded, so he cried out in complaint about the Communist Party, saying that both his sons worked for the Party, but now he had ended up like this! In fact, Zeng Mian had not yet joined the Party at that time. Fortunately, the peasant association went on to conduct an investigation. The father was released on the grounds that, first, he was only a small-time landlord and had no blood debts, nor had he committed any evil deeds; and second, that his two sons were fighting for the revolutionary cause. Zeng senior felt two emotions on returning to the village. One was that he was grateful to the peasant association for being reasonable. The other was that he no longer resented the fact that his sons had run away from home because their participation in the revolution had proved beneficial to him. At that time, he raised more than 800 yuan to send the brothers to study in Japan so that they could have a rewarding future after their return. However, the brothers were adamantly opposed to the idea and grew angry at the mere mention of Japan!

Japan was an imperialist country, and they had no desire to become old-school officials. They wanted to do something to save the country and the people. Their father jumped up and down in fury and cursed them when he heard this. His behaviour persuaded the brothers to leave home as soon as possible. Zeng Mian borrowed twenty silver dollars from his mother-in-law's family and slipped away quietly with his brother. More recently, however, the two brothers' success had changed their father's mind, and he became more understanding of the Revolutionary cause his sons espoused. However, that revolution unexpectedly hit a reef, and the situation took a sharp turn for the worse with the monstrous counter-revolutionary current of the Kuomintang. Communists were hunted down and killed, and the first shot of armed resistance was fired in Nanchang. It turned into open warfare, but a covert underground struggle was also essential. Zeng Mian secretly joined the Communist Party while on the surface he was still a mid-level officer of the Kuomintang, as this provided excellent cover for covert military operations. He organised the masses in the areas ruled by the Kuomintang reactionaries and set up revolutionary factions within the Kuomintang Army. He then sought out the Party organisation in Shanghai, and the Central Military Department sent him north to Yantai to infiltrate Liu Zhennian's section of the Kuomintang Army.

When Zeng Mian returned to Wuhan at the beginning of 1930, the Communist Party already had more than twenty regions within its Soviet movement. The Central Party Committee changed the Military Department, which directed military work in the provinces, into the Central Military Commission, whose job was to unify the Red Army throughout the country. In August, the Central Military Commission appointed Liu Bocheng as secretary of the Military Commission of the Yangtze River Bureau. Zeng Mian became secretary general of the Military Commission, but only a month later, a person from the Hankou District Committee of the Communist Party of China was arrested and defected, followed by someone from the Wuhan Municipal Committee. Zhou Enlai and other leaders of the Central Committee decided to evacuate Liu Bocheng and Zeng Mian to Shanghai. In Shanghai, Zeng Mian became head of the Intelligence Section of the Central Military Commission's General Staff.

To meet the needs of the struggle, he formed a mock family with He Shuheng and Huang Jie, a Party communications officer. As the older, He Shuheng played the part of the father and Huang Jie was the daughter. He Shusheng looked like a schoolteacher, but Zeng

Mian looked so different it was not realistic for him to pretend to be his son, so he took the part of Huang Jie's brother-in-law who was living as a guest in his sister-in-law's marital home. In fact, Huang Jie was Zeng Mian's sister-in-law in real life. She was married to Zeng Mian's brother Zeng Zhongsheng and was also a graduate of the Huangpu Academy. However, even as his sister-in-law, Huang Jie didn't know what Zeng Mian did. He lived alone in the rear wing of the house, often locking himself away in there to get on with his top-secret, classified work... Our beloved He Shuheng stayed behind in the Central Soviet Area. He said he would shed the last drop of his blood for the Soviet...

At that time, the Central Military Commission did not really have many sources of intelligence. Zhou Enlai had direct access to the upper echelons of the Kuomintang, but radio communications were limited to contacts with the Comintern and the Southern Bureau in Hong Kong. There were some insiders in the Shanghai Concession, but these channels remained very limited, and the main military intelligence still came from the press. At that time, the Kuomintang did not exert strict control of military news, and newspapers often disclosed military developments. Zeng Mian locked himself in the back room, capturing the detail of the enemy's military situation from the newspapers and sometimes sorting through secret reports provided by insiders. It was in this way that he uncovered the Kuomintang's three encirclement and annihilation campaigns.

His time in Shanghai turned out to be short-lived, and the situation was to deteriorate rapidly and fatally. In April of the following year, Gu Shunzhang defected. As an alternate committee member of the Central Political Bureau, he violated the discipline of the struggle in the White Zone by showing his face in places of entertainment! He was recognised by traitors, arrested and he subsequently defected. Not long afterwards, General Secretary Xiang Zhongfa was arrested when he stayed out overnight without permission, and he also defected. Of the three members of the Central Special Committee – Xiang Zhongfa, Zhou Enlai and Gu Shunzhang – two out of three defected, and the Party's central office in Shanghai had to be hurriedly dispersed. Bo Gu, Zhou Enlai, Qu Qiubai, Xiang Ying, He Shuheng, Deng Fa, Chen Yun... most of them took a direct boat from Shanghai to Hong Kong, then proceeded through Shantou, Chaozhou and Da Pu, bypassing the Nationalist blockade, into western Fujian, and then through Tingzhou to Ruijin in the Central Soviet. Zeng Mian arrived in the Soviet area at the end of the year. Before that, the Central Committee sent Ren Bishi, Wang Jiaxiang and others to the Soviet area, and Ren Bishi brought the "Haomi" or "Hao's Secret", which was the Communists' first radio code. It was created by Zhou Enlai and others in Shanghai and given its name after Zhou Enlai's pseudonym, "Wu Hao". Ren Bishi went to Ruijin disguised as a priest, and the Bible he carried was actually the codebook. The Haomi was itself encrypted in the book numbers, page numbers, line numbers and word order of the Bible.

From then on, Shanghai and Ruijin were connected by the Haomi. The encryption level was so high that the Red Army's enemies feared it would be very difficult to break it. Even so, we still had to decipher the enemy's secret telegrams. This was the mountain that blocked the Red Army's path to victory, and it proved a most stubborn stronghold.

At last, the day came when the stubborn stronghold was breached by Chief Zeng and Cao Daye. We had crossed the mountain!

It was August 1932. The Red 1st Front Army was looking to engage the enemy in the area of Le'an and Yihuang, which is on the northern edge of the Central Soviet. The bulk of the 2nd Bureau formed the 2nd Bureau of the Front, following the headquarters of the Red 1st Front Army. To make a breakthrough in our decoding, we needed to obtain the codebook of the enemy army in Jiangxi, as all its divisions were equipped with radio transmitters. Chief Zeng suggested to Zhu De and Mao Zedong that an immediate onslaught be launched to annihilate the divisional positions. This led to the Great Victory of Yihuang, in which the Red Army annihilated the bulk of the 27th Division of the Kuomintang Army and the 9th Route Army under the command of Sun Lianzhong, capturing two radio transmitters in the process. Chief Zeng hoped this battle would result in the seizure of codebooks, and he personally led the 2nd Bureau to advance with the main attacking force. The troops burst into Yihuang City and went straight to the enemy's divisional headquarters. They rushed into the radio room and searched for the confidential messages left behind by the enemy. The radio room was already a mess, with Mei Lanfang brand cans, cigarettes and papers with portraits of Chiang on them. Chief Zeng and his men recovered two large boxes of paperwork, but they were mostly back copies of incoming and outgoing telegrams, not the codebooks he most wanted.

Chief Zeng did make one great discovery. Among the many telegrams was a secret communication sent by Sun Lianzhong, commander of the 9th Route Army, to his subordinate Ji Hongchang. It had been sent in Spread Code. There were more than twenty code groups which incorporated more than thirty Chinese characters. To have more than thirty characters already deciphered was an extraordinary clue to the code. Chief Zeng set up an investigation post to focus on intercepting the secret messages between Sun Lianzhong and his men, and, together with Cao Daye, "followed the thread", starting with the thirty or so known decodings. Using them, they made every effort to work out and translate the rest of the message. The enemy did not know that this message had been captured and they were still transmitting in Spread Code. Chief Zeng was very good with words, and Cao Daye was familiar with the code used in enemy reports, so the two of them took the individual characters already deciphered and compared them with the reports on enemy positions in Spread Code that were being continuously intercepted. On this basis, they went to and fro guessing characters and making connections. The Kuomintang telegrams were complex in content and unusual in style. Whenever Zeng and Cao encountered difficult military language, Commander-in-Chief Zhu and General Political Commissar Zhou would often come together to compare guesses and to study the format and grammar of the enemy reports. Titles, designations, strengths, deployments, times, routes... using this process of constant supposition and deduction, more and more words were decoded, and the content of the enemy's secret report gradually revealed itself.

It was an order of battle from the Kuomintang Army. The military situation was urgent, and this was the first time the 2nd Bureau had deciphered an enemy telegram, so no one dared to speak with certainty. For the sake of thoroughness, Chief Zeng asked the head of the Military Commission for advice, then sent it to the base areas of Hubei, Henan, Anhui, Hunan and Jiangxi, with the caution, "I do not know if this is accurate. For reference only".

All those bases reported success! After receiving the secret information, the leaders of the base area urgently deployed troops to attack, and they fought a wonderfully successful battle. This good news meant that the Red Army's intelligence was accurate and extremely effective. It was as though Zhuge Liang was conducting operations. The predictions had an almost God-like accuracy, without the slightest discrepancy.

Deciphering the Spread Code was a huge and pioneering victory. It was October 1932, at the Red 1st Front Army headquarters and Zhou Enlai and Zhu De, the chiefs of the Military Commission, were also very excited. They immediately issued merit awards to the 2nd Bureau. The Red Army had broken the White Army code for the first time. From then on, we could start a code war with the enemy! We comrades of the 2nd Bureau were encouraged by this great victory, which also demonstrated the bureau's abilities in both radio detection and the deciphering of secret reports. To strengthen the deciphering power of the bureau, Zou Sheng was transferred from the Red 1st Front Army. He was an outstanding operative of the 1st Red Army Corps.

The Kuomintang Central Army used a Universal Code, which was based on plain text, and words not found in the codebook were replaced by plain text in brackets. Shortly after the decipherment of the Spread Code, the 2nd Bureau intercepted another coded telegram sent by the Kuomintang Army using the new codebook with the group "(2407)" in it. In the plain text crib, next to (2407) was the character 敖 (áo). Chief Zeng deduced that the phrase was a place name, so he searched for the word "Ao" on the map of the enemy's area of activity, and there it was, Aocheng! This meant that the encrypted word "2407" should be the word 城 (cheng, meaning "city"). Aocheng is in the southwest of Ji'an, Jiangxi, and this coded message must have related to a hostile Red Army operation in the Hunan-Jiangxi Soviet. Based on this, Chief Zeng made a breakthrough. Through the General Staff Department, he asked the Red Army of the Hunan-Jiangxi Soviet Area to verify the situation during the period covered by the enemy's report, and then, through inspired interpretation, deciphered the enemy's secret telegram based on the relevant information about the enemy. On this basis, he cracked the enemy's new codebook within a very short time.

January 1933, the Battle of Fengshanbu. The 2nd Bureau deciphered the operational orders of Wu Qiwei, commander of the 2nd Column of the Encirclement and Annihilation Army, and the Red Army engaged with the enemy and destroyed part of them. The enemy retreated to the Fuzhou area. In early 1933, almost all of the Jiangxi Nationalist Army switched to a new code known as the Meng Code.

The Meng Code was a special codebook with enhanced security, which made it far more difficult to decipher. Chief Zeng promptly adjusted the organisation of the 2nd Bureau, separating detection and deciphering functions. Cao Daye and Zou Sheng were to specialise in deciphering, and another adjustment and division of labour was made with regard to the listening stations, so that each station had a relatively fixed target for detection, ensuring that there were people listening out for every radio station of the enemy's main divisions, night and day. In this way, the enemy's Meng Code was not in use for long before it was successfully broken by the 2nd Bureau. This was the first time the Red Army had broken one of the Kuomintang's special codes.

The fourth encirclement and annihilation campaign was even more savage, involving 400,000 troops. Chiang Kai-shek flew to the headquarters in Nanchang and personally took command of the Encirclement and Annihilation Army. But the Provisional Central Committee had also moved from Shanghai to the Central Soviet, with Bo Gu in overall charge. The direct leadership of the Red 1st Front Army and the Central Soviet was the Central Bureau of the Soviet Area, and, under Xiang Ying's command, it implemented Bo Gu's risky offensive strategy. With the arrival of Comrade Bogunov,[2] Zhou and Zhu's autonomous command was subsequently restricted. In 1933, Bo Gu was only twenty-six years old. This slim young man, with his thick glasses, knew nothing about the military and, being nervous and fearful, worshipped his foreign adviser as if he were a god. The foreign adviser, Li De (Otto Braun), whom Bo Gu described as a "brilliant Bolshevik militarist", was always referred to by his Chinese name so as not to give away his identity or his real name. Li De always wore a leather jacket and lived in his own "detached house". He directed the army according to the Soviet Union's manual of regular warfare. He said he was only an advisor, but when Bo Gu gave him this supreme military authority, he always considered his tactics to be the most correct... The enemy's situation was critical, and Chief Zeng led the 2nd Bureau in staying close to Zhou and Zhu in order to provide a sound and up-to-date foundation for their front-line command. The troops under Chiang's direct command were equipped with radio communications to the regimental level, and our 2nd Bureau did not miss any key secret information. Every telegram sent by Zhou Enlai was marked "Fully Confirmed"!

The Kuomintang Army withdrew from the Central Soviet, and the Red Army's resistance to the fourth encirclement and annihilation campaign ended in victory. This was the sixth year of the Red Army's existence, and the Military Committee of the Central Revolutionary Army requested the Government of the Central Soviet stipulate that the anniversary of the Nanchang Uprising on 1 August 1927 would be the anniversary of the founding of the Red Army; also that the Red Star Medal should be awarded on this anniversary to Red Army officers of particular merit. There were three grades of medals: gold, silver and bronze. The ceremony was held in the early hours of the morning in Ruijin to avoid attacks by enemy aircraft. Additionally, to confuse the enemy, a fake venue was set up in Lenin Park in Changting, dozens of miles from Ruijin, as had also been done for the First Soviet Congress. This was the first time that the Red Army of the Workers and Peasants celebrated its own Army Day and the first time that medals of merit were awarded. Thousands of torches lit up the venue, parades marched past, oaths were sworn and medals were awarded. Xiang Ying, acting chairman of the Military Commission of the Chinese Revolutionary Army, read out the list of awards. First-class medals were awarded to: Zhou Enlai, Kuomintang general political commissar of the Red Army; Zhu De, commander-in-chief of the Red Army; Peng Dehuai, chief of the 3rd Red Army Corps; Lin Biao, chief of the 1st Red Army Corps, and others; second-class medals were awarded to more than twenty people, including: Wang Jiaxiang, director of the General Political Department of the Red Army; Liu Bocheng, chief of the general staff of the Red Army; and Nie Rongzhen, political commissar of the 1st Red Army Corps. Bureau Chief Zeng was also awarded a second-class medal, and dozens of others, including Section Chiefs Cao and Zou Sheng, were awarded third-class medals. The awarding of prizes to the personnel of the 2nd Bureau had to be done in secret, however. The bureau's secret celebration was also held in the evening, with General Political Commissar Zhou and Commander-in-Chief Zhu personally attending. With their own hands, they hung the Red Star medals around the necks of Zeng, Cao, Zou and the others. The award for Chief Zeng had actually been proposed by Zhu and Zhou, as he was the "founder" of the Red Army's intelligence work and had made an outstanding contribution to "snatching a critical victory from the jaws of defeat".

The Red Star Medal is our army's highest award for merit. It has been said in jest that this award should be called "Gold Medal for Avoiding Death". This is of course a very old-fashioned and feudal statement, but Article 16 of the Interim Regulations on Discipline of the Workers' and Peasants' Red Army does contain relevant provisions: "Anyone who has received the Soviet Order of Merit and violated the spirit of that order shall be subject to having it downgraded accordingly."

Sacrifices are inevitable in a revolution and they may be demanded at any time. But what we understood by "sacrifice" was death by the enemy's bullets, shells or butcher's knives. In the bloody Battle of the Xiang River, the troops of Zhou Zikun, commander of the 22nd Division, were scattered and he himself was wounded as he broke out of the enemy's encirclement. Li De ordered him to be tied up and executed according to military law, but it was said that Mao Zedong prevented this. The divisional commander was carrying out the wrong orders, and if the divisional commander was responsible, then those higher up in command were even more responsible. The crossing of the Xiang River was very slow. Although it was part of the breakout, the central column was still carrying all those pots and pans, and the huge transport team had to carry those cumbersome lithographic machines, bomb-making machines, money presses, X-ray machines and filing cabinets! The waters of the Xiang River were stained with Red Army blood! Who would take responsibility for that?

Mao Zedong and Peng Dehuai opposed the crossing of the Xiang River. While the Red Army was marching through southern Hunan, our 2nd Bureau had intelligence that the enemy had mobilised twenty defensive divisions along the Xiang River. Mao and Peng advocated advancing into central Hunan to seize the opportunity to destroy the remaining troops of the Kuomintang Army and then create new base areas. Mao and Peng were not in the majority, and Bo Gu and Li De insisted on crossing the river to join the 2nd and 6th Red Army Corps in western Hunan. This alerted Chiang Kai-shek to the intentions of the Central Red Army, so he appointed He Jian, a Hunan warlord, as commander-in-chief of the "pursuit and annihilation army", and his troops were divided into five columns to intercept, pursue and annihilate.

The intelligence coming out of our 2nd Bureau was quite clear, but everything depended on how the military commanders used it. Our Military Commission crossed the Xiang River on 29 November, and there was no sound of fighting then. The fighting broke out the next day, and the sky was full of enemy planes. Commander-in-Chief Zhu urged the central column to speed up, but the "heavy-mover" transport team, which was dozens of miles long, found it difficult to move at speed, and progress was very slow. The Central Red Army suffered heavy losses when it crossed the Xiang River. Had it not been for the intelligence of our 2nd Bureau, which enabled the Red Army to seize the undefended crossing two days before the enemy arrived, the consequences would have been even worse.

Thus, the role of the 2nd Bureau was valued by Mao Zedong, although he had no military authority at this time. How our intelligence is used is a matter for the military commanders. We have no right to interfere, but we must provide the most timely and accurate secret information for the very top commanders to make their decisions. Bureau Chief Zeng has a resilient spirit. He identifies the goal and charges forward, not looking back if his head is broken, not accepting defeat and not fearing any hardship or danger. He has the strength to win the ultimate victory. He was the first to break the Spread Code, and in the year that followed, the 2nd

Bureau has broken more than a hundred kinds of enemy code, each of which Zou Sheng has recorded in that little black leather-bound book.

We could only celebrate in secret, and we could only speak in secret. Chief Zeng naturally knew exactly what to say and what not to say, and every time he ended up reminding us in his particular way: Secrecy! Confidentiality! One day in the Investigation and Collation Section, after talking about a specific decipherment case, he asked the question, "Do you remember how we got started?"

"During the first anti-encirclement and annihilation campaign, we captured half an enemy radio set."

"What do you mean by half a radio set?"

"The soldiers had never seen anything like it before, so they smashed it... It could only receive, not send–"

"Ah! So, it could only receive, not send... The same is true of what we were talking about today!"

Revolutionaries are made of special materials, and we are indeed even more special than the special. Our names cannot be made public, our achievements cannot be publicised, and our grievances cannot be aired. There are a lot of things we can't say more about. That is the iron discipline of secrecy. Revolutionaries can die at any time, but careless leaks are as serious as intentional betrayals and both must be severely punished. We never tell anything to our parents, our wives or our children. In fact, many of us have already lost our parents to famine, disease or reprisals by the reactionary forces. None of us has wives or children either. Maybe there was a lover once, but our hometowns are far away now. Maybe there is the memory of a plant or flower like the amaranth flowers in autumn..."

Deputy Chief Qian is a married man, and it is said that he has two wives. Out of respect for their mother-in-law, the two ladies treat each other with courtesy and live in harmony. He was engaged to his first wife before going to university, and the second was a college classmate who was two years older than him. The old lady didn't like the new "big foot daughter-in-law" in Beijing, although she was, in fact, from a well-known family in Tongcheng, Anhui Province; there were prime ministers among her ancestors, and the family was very well off. Now, however, no one knows where they are. We consider Deputy Chief Qian to be our elder. He is several years older than Bureau Chief Zeng. It was he who designed the Red Star Medal in 1933, and far away in Yeping Village, Ruijin, the cannonball-shaped Red Army Martyrs' Memorial Tower and the octagonal hat-shaped Great Hall of the Soviet in Shazhouba were also his designs. He is chief designer of the six major commemorative projects in the Central Soviet Area, deputy director of the 2nd Bureau of our Military Commission and the map interpreter for Li De, the political consultant from the Comintern. In the Central Soviet Area, his public identity was as editor and director of the Red Army Drama Club. This club is entrusted with the task of spreading revolutionary literature and art. In 1933, the play *Attack on Lushan* was the grand finale of the cultural performance celebrating 1 August. What an exhilarating spectacle that was! A stage was set up in the ancient temple, and bonfires were lit all around it. Deputy Chief Qian Chao was one of the scriptwriters, along with Li Kenong and Hu Di. Deputy Chief Qian played Chiang Kai-shek, Tong Xiaopeng played Song Meiling, Nie Rongzhen played Song Ziwen and Li Zhuoran played Hans von Seeckt, a German advisor. Von Seeckt was formerly commander-in-chief of the German Wehrmacht and is said to have devised the "Iron Barrel" plan for Chiang Kai-shek when he launched the fifth encirclement and annihilation campaign.

When Chiang Kai-shek betrayed the revolution in 1927 and stopped cooperating with Soviet Russia, he sought out this German again; of course, our military adviser, Li De, was also a German. So there they were, two Germans, in two opposing camps, both orchestrating a contest between two Chinese armies! Li De correctly analysed von Seeckt's strategy and tactics, so Bo Gu relied on him even more than before.

The Iron Barrel Encirclement and Annihilation plan: targeting the Central Soviet area of Ruijin, Yudu, Huichang and Xingguo, 1.5 million Kuomintang troops were mobilised and suddenly surrounded their targets from all sides at a specifically appointed time. It was a very elaborate plan, with many numbered squares drawn on the map, based on which, each unit had to arrive at its designated position at the designated time. They were then ordered to lay barbed wire fences, with gaps for the installation of "deer fences"[3] and "horse barriers"[4] and at the same time set up fields of fire, build blockhouses, forage stations and ammunition warehouses, as well as hospitals, dressing stations, wired telephone networks, relay stations and so on. Once the encirclement was formed, the troops would follow their orders to advance several *li* towards the centre of Ruijin every day. A barbed wire barrier was built every *li* of advance, equivalent to about 500 metres. Every five kilometres, a bunker line was built with the bunkers equipped with the firepower to form an extremely tight network of interlocking blockades. The plan was to advance twenty-five kilometres deeper into our territory each month, so that the Red Capital of Ruijin would be reached in six months, and 300 layers of barbed wire, thirty lines of bunkers and innumerable obstacles would have been erected around the Central Soviet. To prevent the Red Army from breaking out, minefields were laid between the barbed wire fences; in the event of an emergency, a large number of American military trucks were immediately available for deployment. As a prelude to the Iron Barrel plan, twelve divisions were sent to engage with the Red Army before the encirclement was formed in order to confuse the enemy and buy time. As soon as the encirclement was formed, the twelve divisions would be evacuated and at the same time all transportation to them other than military supplies would be suspended in order to seal off the Soviet area and cut off all sources of supplies for the Red Army.

Deputy Chief Qian played the part of Chiang Kai-shek, and everyone said he was an excellent actor. For the Red Army officers and soldiers outside the 2nd Bureau, his cover identity was that of a doctor. He was a native of Huzhou, Zhejiang Province. The Zhe River is also known as the Qiantang River, which has the Qiantang tidal bore (*chao*), hence his name "Qian Chao". Qian Chao went to Beijing Medical College before Beijing was renamed "Beiping". After graduating from the college, he was first listed as a doctor in Beiping, before transferring to the Beiping-Suiyang Railway Hospital as a doctor. He also worked part-time as a teacher at the art school and as an editor for the newspaper. His number two wife worked as a doctor at the Beijing Tiantan Infectious Disease Hospital. Her brother was an early Communist Party member, and his sister was influenced by his ideals to reform society. They used their profession as doctors as a cover for their secret work for the Communist Party. They carried medical bags painted with a red cross to indicate "Doctor on Visit", but the bags actually contained secret Party documents, propaganda, leaflets and the like. Back then, the signboard of the Infectious Diseases Ward also made an excellent contact point because the enemy did not dare approach. Sometimes the secret Party admission ceremony was held in the Infectious Diseases Ward. When there was no Party flag, they would dip their fingers in tea and draw one on the table. The oath ceremony remained very solemn. Qian Chao and his wife also founded the Guanghua Film Company as a cover for their underground work, for which he was both a scriptwriter and an actor. 1926 saw the filming of *The Hidden Swordsman of Yanshan* by Guanghua, with Qian Chao in the lead role and his name on the poster as Qian Xixi.

Deputy Chief Qian has a chivalrous spirit, and he is certainly far from being a reckless man; he is the great intellectual of our ranks. The rest of us cannot really compete with his erudition and versatility as we can only be considered minor intellectuals at best, or semi-intellectuals. The Democratic Government of the Central Soviet had long ago decided that intellectuals were also workers, workers who used their brains, and in the ranks of this revolution, the intellectuals are themselves revolutionaries. Deputy Chief Qian is a great revolutionary intellectual. One day when he was lecturing us on the materialistic interpretation of history, he lent us a copy of *The Essentials of Western History* compiled by Wang Chunyi. He said that the author's real name was Yang Pao'an, a famous Marxist proselytiser in the south who was both a member of the Central Standing Committee of the Kuomintang and of the Supervisory Committee of the Communist Party of China. It seems that even in revolutionary times there are such things as coincidences, and it happened that when Bureau Chief Zeng was at the Huangpu Military Academy, he had visited Yang's residence at the Yang Family Ancestral Hall in Guangzhou, and Zhou Enlai, head of the Political Department of the Military Academy, had also gone there for meetings. Moreover, Chief Qian said that when Yang Pao'an was executed by Chiang Kai-shek in Shanghai he refused all bribes and inducements and never betrayed his principles. However, his family was going to be left behind after his death, so he asked someone to take them a letter from prison saying that if it was impossible for them to live in Shanghai, they should go home to Guangdong but not to sell their sewing machine, as that represented the family's future livelihood. On hearing this, we couldn't help but remember that Deputy Chief Qian had also left his family behind in a faraway place... When he has free time, he gives cultural lessons to the young people in our bureau. One day he was talking about Percy Bysshe Shelley, who had written, "If Winter comes, can Spring be far behind?", and he called this romanticism. Some of his audience nodded and said they understood; adding that romanticism meant not being afraid of the cold! Keeping a straight face, Deputy Chief Qian replied, "It is also what is called revolutionary optimism!"

He also told us about "Mr De" and "Mr Sai" (democracy and science), and imparted some basic scientific knowledge and the principles of medicine. He can always explain in simple terms things which many of us have never heard of before, which is of great benefit to us. One day we heard thunder outside the house, and he told us about thunder and lightning. He said that lightning travels in straight lines, always takes the shortest route, and that we should try to stay away from trees and tall buildings when it strikes. He himself always follows this principle, and no matter how rudimentary the conditions are, his bed is always placed in the middle of the room, as far away from the walls as possible. He said it was best to lie flat on the bed during a thunderstorm, as even if lightning passed through your body, the electrical charge was lower when you were lying in bed rather than standing up.

I will never forget the time we ate a jar of lard we got from Chief Qian! Chief Qian's beautiful military art was a hit with Li De. Li De particularly valued it because he was a master draughtsman himself. He wanted to send Chief Qian to the front so that he could give a demonstration to the frontline staff officers. So Chief Qian gave away some things he didn't need, and we targeted a jar of lard that he had bought with the money he had been paid for his cartoons. Thinking that life at the front was going to be better than at the rear, he gave us the lard to eat. After a few days, Li De said that he didn't need to go to the front after all, but by that time Chief Qian's lard was gone!

The Central Soviet Area had been blockaded by the Kuomintang for a long time, and they burned and killed repeatedly, creating a huge area of uninhabited territory. Life in the Red Army was very difficult. The same was true for the Military Commission and the General Headquarters, where officers and soldiers were equal. Meals were strictly rationed, and each person had no more than half a catty of red rice a day, which was divided into two meals and cooked in little packages made of rushes. The personnel of the 2nd Bureau had to work the night shift and were allowed a vegetarian evening meal, which was already a special privilege, but they also craved oil and meat. Most of the 2nd Bureau transport personnel were big men, some of them very big, so they really didn't have enough to eat. Whenever they saw us, they would say they couldn't get enough to eat, and that sometimes they were so hungry their stomachs felt like they were on fire. They couldn't help but fantasise about having a full meal. Vegetables were also scarce, and salt was mostly obtained from the troops up ahead, but it was always bitter and unpalatable nitrate salt. In the worst times, bamboo shoots were boiled in water every day, without any salt, but they were long and fibrous and hard to digest. Chief Zeng developed a stomach ailment, and Zou Sheng once suffered a haemorrhage after eating bamboo shoots that had not been cooked thoroughly. It was only after Deputy Chief Qian gave him morphine that he was saved. To encourage frugality, the Central Committee of the Communist Youth League called for a "Three Quit" campaign: quit smoking, quit drinking and quit eating chillies. The campaign was overseen by Comrade Kang Keqing, an executive instructor at the General Headquarters. There was nothing to eat anyway and no chillies were allowed, so you can imagine what we thought of this! Once we had fried up half a basin of red chillies and were eating them, when Instructor Kang came to inspect us. We hastily covered over the chillies, but she still found us out. Instructor Kang criticised us for violating the Three Quits campaign, but Chief Qian had his own opinion on whether to eat chilies or not, and he had a fierce argument with her. To improve our life in Wushilong, Chief Zeng led us in planting pumpkins next to the house, but later on we had to move to Meikeng in Yunshishan County to avoid the bombing, so we never got to eat those pumpkins.

Chief Qian was a great revolutionary intellectual. He was certainly not born into the lowest rung of society, and even during the time he was undercover in Shanghai, the Party organisation asked him to pretend to be a man of refined tastes. In 1927, when the Nationalist reactionaries wielded their butcher's knife, Comrade Li Dazhao was killed by the warlords of the Fengtian Clique, the Northern Party leadership organisation was severely damaged and Qian Chao fled Beijing when his identity was revealed. In early 1928 he moved to Shanghai, made contact with the Party organisation and was incorporated into the French Concession branch. Later that year he worked in the Shanghai International Radio Administration, responsible for advertising and investment. This was a government-run foreign business agency of the Kuomintang government, specialising in sending and receiving international telegrams to and from foreigners in Shanghai. To counter the massacre policy of the Kuomintang, the Central Committee of the Communist Party of China set up a special operations section, whose main tasks were to protect the security of the leading members of the Central Committee, punish traitors, rescue arrested comrades, analyse enemy movements and keep the revolutionary base generally informed about the enemy. With Qian Chao working undercover in the enemy's camp, where he could master their methods of secret communication and gather useful information, the Party organisation decided to order him to remain there for an extended period, not to participate in other activities of the Central Special Branch, to pretend to have no particular political allegiance, to eat and dress well, not to talk about politics and to live in a small Western-style villa.

And now that we have captured this big city, our 2nd Bureau is itself living in a small villa. There is a gramophone in Chief Qian's villa. It has a burgundy-coloured wooden case and a turntable with a green felt mat, but it is broken. The soldiers of the security team wanted to listen to this "talk box" so much that Chief Qian started to fix it as soon as he moved in. He cranked the handle to wind up the machine, and a swooshing noise came out of the brass horn, but it wasn't music. The records on the turntable were traditional songs, one of which was *Plum Blossoms Yin* (梅花引). Talking about words and understanding characters comes as second nature to us

Comrades, and we are often asking about a word as the occasion arises. Agent Xiao He asked what the character 引 meant, and Chief Qian laughed and said, "Haven't you memorised the Kangxi Dictionary yet?" Xiao He said that a dictionary was not as good as a living person, and since a great master was standing right there in front of him, it would be a shame not to ask him for advice! Chief Qian replied, "Then I have a condition. Bring the dictionary along next time, and I will open it at a random page and see how much you have off by heart!" Xiao He agreed cheerfully. Chief Qian then explained that 引 referred to one type of theme for a *guqin* tune. Music composed for this ancient stringed instrument has both orthodox tones and overtones, and the overtones are what give the music colour. He went on to cite examples such as *Thunderclap Yin*, *Ultimate Bliss Yin* and *Returning Home Yin*.

What kind of sketch would the artist Huang Zhen have made of him if he had been present and seen him in such high spirits? It probably wouldn't have been in the same style as *Old Heroes on the Night March*! In fact, Chief Qian is a painter himself! Maybe he could do a picture called "Intellectuals on the Road West". He and General Political Commissar Zhou are both first-class, handsome and confident figures. General Political Commissar Zhou is more refined, calmer and more easy-going, with sharp, alert eyes; Chief Qian is freer and easier, more like a poet, with passion in his eyes and something of the uninhibited dreamer about him. He is also quite similar in temperament to Comrade Qu Qiubai, but the scholar-turned-author Ah Qiu has a more scholarly and diffident side. These intellectuals all wore their hair parted: Chief Qian had a side parting, Comrade Mao Zedong had a centre parting, as did the chief of the 3rd Bureau, Comrade Wang Zheng. Comrade Wang Zheng was liberated by us, but I don't know what hairstyle he had before then.

Chief Qian really should draw his own portrait. He designed the masthead and drew cartoons for *Red China*, and once he asked someone to be his model while he drew him. He had him lying on a wall, and also lying on the floor as if he was about to be beaten on the buttocks! He was also a very good calligrapher with a brush and called himself "Number One in the Soviet Area".

He can talk like this about himself, and no one minds. This man of legendary experience is reticent about talking about those legends. But we have still heard about everything from various sources, even though he himself tends to be evasive when asked about it. Every time, he acts very humbly, but we have a pretty good idea of the whole story. Once we forced him to talk about his romantic history and the women of Shanghai. Somehow, the topic turned to the word "Daybreak" and he began to talk about the traitor who used that codename. Xiao He managed to winkle more secrets out of him. Xiao He was a great admirer of Chief Qian. He himself had been born into a wealthy family in 1911, the year of the Xinhai Revolution. His father operated a small mine. He had taken the revolutionary road to avoid an arranged marriage. His father had made the match for him, but the youngster wanted to be free and live a romantic life. Among new wave students, almost everyone is at odds with their family. Xiao He is a musician and one day he talked about the Russian concert work *Rite of Spring*. He talked about the return of spring to the Earth and about offering sacrifices and making dedications. He explained his dream that, after the victory of the Revolution, he could go to the "far off place", Moscow. He had studied music and had excellent sound-recognition skills. When guns were fired at the front, he could identify the type and number of them just by listening carefully. He also had good writing skills, and although he was in the detection unit, he sometimes helped to decode telegrams and even occasionally took part in the "code guessing". Everyone could see that what he really wanted was to be transferred to the decoding section. He considered himself to be the right material for it. On more than one occasion, he half-jokingly said that at least the decoding section was still "good for something". In his free time, he went to Chief Qian ostensibly to learn a few words of Russian, but his real reason was something else entirely. Chief Qian was an enigma and he wanted to find out more about him. That was how we too got to hear more of the story behind the legend of Chief Qian.

A codebook of huge significance! On 25 April 1931, at around 10 pm, Qian Chao, who was on duty at the Zhengyuan Industrial Club in Nanjing, received some telegrams from the Kuomintang secret service in Wuhan. They were coded telegrams to Xu Enzeng, director of the Investigation Section of the Central Organisation

Department. Each of the six most urgent and top-secret telegrams had the words "Personally encoded by Xu Enzeng" written on them. They were being forwarded by Xu Enzeng to Chen Lifu, secretary general of the Central Party headquarters. As far as the general public was concerned, the Zheng Yuan Industrial Club was a front for the Investigation Section, but in reality, it was the highest secret command centre of the Kuomintang secret service. Director Xu Enzeng used his shrewd and capable fellow Huzhou resident Qian Chao as his assistant. As his confidential secretary, all information sent to Xu Enzeng had to be read by Qian Chao first. The "personally encoded" secret telegrams were supposed to be transcribed by Xu Enzeng himself. He had a codebook for communicating with senior Kuomintang officials, which he always kept in his pocket, but Qian Chao had already got his hands on it.

Xu Enzeng was addicted to sex. When Chen Lifu installed him as director of the Shanghai International Radio Administration, he asked Qian Chao to help his mistress settle in too. So Qian gave her the second-floor front rooms of his residence in the French Concession, thus earning himself more trust and favour. Xu Enzeng, who was in charge of the Kuomintang Investigation Division, also took Qian Chao with him to Nanjing.

One day, Xu Enzeng was going to a newly opened bordello on Nanjing Road in Shanghai, and Qian Chao reminded him that it would not be safe to take the codebook to a place like that, and that it would be a big problem if it got lost. Xu gave the book to his most trusted aide, Qian Chao, who said he would lock it in a secure cabinet. This was a specially designed locker, equipped with multiple alarms, for which there were only two keys, one for Xu and one for Qian. That night, Qian used a German micro-camera to take pictures of the codebook. On Saturday night, after the confidential messenger had left, Qian Chao took the opportunity to go into the secure room where he opened Xu Enzeng's telegrams and deciphered them, word by word from the codebook he had photographed. The first telegram read, "Daybreak has been arrested and has given himself up. If he can be quickly transported to Nanking, all the organs of the Central Committee of the Communist Party can be purged within three days."

Daybreak was the codename within the organisation of Gu

Shunzhang, a member of the Central Committee Special Committee and an alternate member of the Political Bureau of the Central Committee of the Communist Party of China. He had been arrested the day before in Wuhan. He had gone with Zhang Guotao to work in the Jiangxi-Hunan-Hubei Soviet. After completing his mission, to earn some extra money, he had broken his cover by performing magic tricks on stage at the Hankou amusement park without permission and was recognised by traitors. Among Gu Shunzhang's skills were contortionism, magic tricks, disguises and marksmanship, all of which he had learnt in the Soviet Union, where he had been sent by the Party organisation to study political security along with Chen Geng.

Gu Shunzhang assisted Zhou Enlai in leading the Central Special Branch, using the public identity of the famous magician, Hua Guangqi. He was alert and clever, capable and brave, and ruthless in the way he dealt with traitors. He once led an ambush to shoot Bai Xin on Xiafei Road. Bai Xin was the traitor who betrayed Peng Pai. At that time, Gu Shunzhang's "red team" assassination squad only had four pistols. Bai Xin had four bullet holes in his head, and the forensic examiner judged he had been shot three times simultaneously, with each bullet entering at a different point but sharing one exit wound. This time in Hankou, he not only performed magic tricks as Hua Guangqi, he also fooled around with dancers and prostitutes, and was arrested by the Kuomintang Wuhan Detective Office. He was not only chief of the Central Special Branch Operation, he also presided over the specific work of the Central Special Branch and was in charge of the lines of communication between Shanghai and the Soviet areas. He knew almost all the secrets of the Central Committee of the Communist Party of China. He also knew about Qian Chao and how close he was to Xu Enzeng.

Qian Chao copied down the contents of the Wuhan telegram, sealed it back in its original form, then sent an urgent telegram to the underground Party in Shanghai: "Dawn is over, Mother is critically ill, transfer to hospital immediately." In this message, "Dawn" represented "Daybreak". He also sent his son-in-law to Shanghai on a night train, instructing him to tell the Central

Committee that Daybreak had betrayed them and that big problems were heading their way.

His son-in-law left under cover of darkness and Qian Chao quickly tidied up the documents and telegrams, so he was ready for whatever might come next. It was around midnight when Qian Chao received another coded message from Wuhan: "Daybreak is already being transferred by boat under escort to Nanjing and will arrive in a couple of days." It was fortunate he was not being taken by plane as it meant they had a few days to respond. As soon as daylight arrived in Nanjing, all of Qian Chao's covert activities would be exposed, and the liaison station on the fourth floor of the Central Hotel and news agencies in various other places would also be broken up. Overnight, Qian Chao sent urgent telegrams to Shanghai, Nanjing, Tianjin and other places: "Chao's illness is coming back fast." This was the signal to the underground Party organisations to evacuate as soon as possible.

"I wonder if that first urgent telegram got through to the Central Committee?" said Qian Qiao. "I wonder if my son-in-law, Liu Qifu, arrived in Shanghai without any problems? Will he be able to find his 'uncle' Li Kenong, as tomorrow was not the day of the meeting? Will Li Kenong be able to alert the Central Committee in time?... A bloody storm is about to hit the Central Committee and the Communist Party is facing destruction!" Time was running out and Qian Chao was so anxious that he determined to go to Shanghai himself.

The next morning, Qian Chao acted as if nothing had happened and handed the secret messages to Xu Enzeng as usual. Then he pretended to go home to rest and calmly left the Kuomintang secret service compound. In fact, he had no time to go home and change clothes, nor to say goodbye to his wife and children. He jumped into a horse-drawn carriage and rushed to Xiaguan, where he boarded a train bound for Shanghai. In case Xu Enzeng sent agents to intercept him at the Shanghai railway station, he cautiously got off at the small station of Zhenru on the outskirts of Shanghai and took another detour by bus into the city proper. At noon, Qian Chao met Li Kenong, who had already sent the urgent telegram to the Party Central Committee with Chen Geng, the head of the

Intelligence Section of the Central Special Branch. What a thrilling day it was!

Zhou Enlai, secretary of the Central Military Commission, was not afraid of the danger and commanded the Central Special Branch to respond urgently before Chen Lifu and Xu Enzeng acted. By the evening of the same day, all the leading members of the Central Committee of the Communist Party of China were transferred to safety.

Qian Chao rushed to Shanghai on his own, while his family was still in Nanjing. He decided to ask his son-in-law, Liu Qifu, to return to Nanjing to look after them, as he had left a letter for Xu Enzeng on his way out. In the letter, he stated, "I take personal responsibility for everything, and you should not harm my family." He also warned Xu Enzeng sternly that if he did do anything to his family, he would inform the press about his, Xu Enzeng's, scandalous private life.

The incident happened so suddenly that he couldn't get his family out without arousing Xu Enzeng's suspicion. Instead, his family became his cover defence.

The three people who had infiltrated the Kuomintang Central Organisation Department – Qian Chao, Li Kenong and Hu Di – could no longer remain inconspicuous in Shanghai. In the spring of 1932, the Party Central Committee decided to evacuate them. They took a circuitous route via Hong Kong and Guangdong to reach Ruijin.

Gu Shunzhang defected, Xiang Zhongfa, general secretary of the Central Committee, was arrested, Yun Daiying, a member of the Central Committee, and Cai Hesen, a member of the Politburo Standing Committee, were killed, and Chen Geng, head of the Intelligence Section of the Central Special Branch, was left at severe risk. Zhou Enlai also had to leave Shanghai. All the main members of the Central Committee were evacuated from Shanghai, and thus the General Headquarters of the Chinese Revolution moved out of the big city.

In December, the following appeared on posters:

"Wanted by the People's Committee of the Provisional Government of the Central Soviet Area – concerning the apprehension of the revolutionary traitor Gu Shunzhang... The Provisional Government of the Central Soviet hereby issues a general announcement to the Soviet governments at all levels, the Red Army and the Red Guards everywhere, and informs the workers, peasants and toiling masses throughout the country that they should be strictly on their guard against the counter-revolutionary machinations of the Kuomintang and that they should apprehend the traitor Gu Shunzhang at any cost. If this traitor is encountered in the Soviet Area, he should be arrested and brought to trial by the Revolutionary Court. If this traitor is encountered in the White Terror zone, it is the duty of every revolutionary fighter and every poor worker and peasant to exterminate him. It is the conscious and glorious duty of every revolutionary fighter and member of the worker-peasant faction to apprehend and exterminate the traitor Gu Shunzhang."

Xiao He from the Detection and Collation Section asked Chief Qian, "That night after your son-in-law left, you had to prepare for whatever came next. What kind of preparations did you make?"

"I couldn't decide that until early the next morning when I saw Xu Enzeng. Daybreak was going to reach Nanjing in a day or two, and he wouldn't say anything until he had met with Chiang Kai-shek. Those one or two days were all the time we had for the urgent transfer of the central personnel... It wasn't just the Party Central Committee involved, he also held the secrets of Party organisations everywhere."

"Daylight knew you were working with Xu Enzeng, but he didn't say anything until he got to Nanjing. Did he want to give you some time?"

"You do try to see the best in people, don't you! My reading is that he was even more concerned for his own safety and wasn't going to say a word until he had seen Chiang."

"Supposing he let something slip on the journey... there was always that danger, wasn't there? The river route from Wuhan to Nanjing would have taken at least eight or nine hours, right? You'd got the information out, your mission had been completed, and you should have been safely evacuated that night–!"

"Daylight was in the Green Gang in Shanghai and was a

hundred times more resourceful when things went wrong, but he also had a tendency to keep his mouth shut. I had to take a gamble. After all, with a bit of luck, it would mess up the timing of their operations."

"If you saw Xu Enzeng again, there was a big risk he'd kill you–"

"I was prepared for that. There were only three options – evacuation, arrest or sacrifice."

"Sacrifice is not the best policy. But if I had been there at that time, and someone really did have to make a sacrifice–!"

"The revolution is what it's meant to be, and that's what it has to be."

"I would be willing to die for you."

"Don't talk about dying! You are all young, you haven't begun to taste life yet…"

SECTION CHIEF

Section Chief Qian has an eye for aesthetics, as though his glasses have the power to reveal beauty. He can even find beauty in these boring codes. In the year or so after deciphering the Spread Code, the 2nd Bureau cracked more than a hundred enemy codes, and every one of them was recorded in that little black leather-bound book, which Deputy Chief Qian even called the "Record of a Hundred Beauties", as if it were a scroll painting! This is of course a great credit to the decoding section, on which the soldiers on the front line rely to win battles. The 2nd Bureau has three masters of decoding: Bureau Chief Zeng Mian; the head of the decoding section, Cao Daye; and Deputy Chief Zou Sheng.

"I wouldn't dare take your head, but I will send you a good brain!" said Army Chief Peng as he laughed loudly down the phone to Chief Zeng. "Take your head" referred to what Peng said when he was raging on the front line about inaccurate intelligence. "Send a good brain" referred to him wanting to send Cao Daye, the outstanding intelligencer of the Red Army Corps, up to headquarters. Headquarters needed a "good brain", and Peng was not one to mince his words.

The personnel of the 2nd Bureau were the "most special of the special", and this was undoubtedly true of Cao Daye. He quickly showed his "God-given genius" in deciphering and soon became head of the decoding section. Chief Cao had an excellent memory and was a master of deciphering, working both fast and prodigiously. He was a hard-working, selfless and quite extraordinary operative. Code-breaking takes talent and aptitude, but in addition to these attributes, he had an almost manic enthusiasm. Often working around the clock, even when eating and walking around he was immersed in cryptographic guesswork. He often said, "If we shed one more drop of sweat, the men at the front will shed one less drop of blood."

To break the enemy's five-digit code, he did not go to bed for seven days and nights, and his nerves were stretched to breaking point until the code was broken. Then he collapsed in bed with pneumonia and a fever. Once in the winter, he was so engrossed in his work that he was oblivious to the fact that his shoes and trousers had caught alight from the charcoal brazier. No one dared to go over to him and put out the fire because he was staring fixedly at a tree outside the window, as if he was close to a flash of inspiration; the slightest disturbance would mean that all his previous work would be lost and the light would be put out. Luckily, only his shoes and trousers were burning, not his actual flesh. The people standing near him caught a strange smell, the smell of burning wool. They looked at each other and smiled knowingly: the money in his trouser pocket was on fire! The pulp used to make Soviet banknotes is mixed with fine wool to prevent counterfeiting. The smell of burning wool meant that the banknotes in his pocket were undoubtedly genuine. The fire was growing, the flames were jumping up and spreading, and he was in danger of having his eyebrows singed off, when finally, he cried out joyfully, "Got it!" Everyone rushed over to push him to the ground and roll him over a few times to put out the flames. Our intelligence gathering concerns the life and death of soldiers on the front line and the safety of the whole army.

Cao Daye took part in the attack on Changsha. In August 1930, the 1st and 3rd Red Army Corps joined forces in Yonghe City, Liuyang, to form the Red 1st Front Army. The commander-in-chief was Zhu De, the deputy commander-in-chief was Peng Dehuai, the chief political commissar was Mao Zedong and the deputy chief political commissar was Teng Daiyuan. The General Forward

Committee of the Red 1st Front Army decided to retake Changsha. However, the enemy proved too strong to risk it, and the Red Army retreated to Jiangxi. Mao Zedong reported to the Central Committee that the technical conditions were not in place, and we did not have any means of communication, such as radios, which resulted in poor contact between the two regiments. This was why the opportunity was lost.

In late October 1930, 100,000 Kuomintang troops attacked the Jiangxi Soviet on three different fronts. Lu Diping, chairman of the Jiangxi Provincial Government of the Kuomintang, and director of the Nanchang Battalion, commander-in-chief of land, sea and air, served as the "annihilation commander". Zhu De and Mao Zedong issued an order: lure the enemy deep into the Red area and wipe them out when they are exhausted. They also signed a special order: do not destroy any radios during the battle!

"Ten thousand maple trees glowed bright red from the frost," said Mao, "and the Red Army soldiers' anger shot up to the clouds. Fog enveloped the dark, rolling peaks of Longgang as our troops chanted in unison, killing the enemy at the front and capturing Zhang Huizan alive."

In the fog-filled Longgang Valley, the commander of the 18th Division of the Kuomintang Army, Zhang Huizan, was captured alive. The fat, red-faced man tried to disguise himself and escape, but the Red Army soldiers spotted his fox-fur coat and pulled him out of the cave where he was hiding. Zhang embezzled the soldiers' salaries, and he would beat, curse and insult his troops at will. On the day of his capture, the other soldiers of the 18th Division who had been taken prisoner ignored the Red Army's attempts to stop them and ran over to vent their rage at him by beating him up and cursing him. "Annihilation Commander" Lu Diping sat peacefully doing nothing in Nanchang for, although Zhang Huizan was apparently only the commander of the 18th Division, and overall commander of the right wing of the middle column, he was actually commander-in-chief of the whole encirclement and annihilation campaign.

Do not destroy any radios in battle. In this battle, the Red Army captured one enemy radio station and ten radio personnel. The radio had been damaged in the fighting and could only receive but not transmit. This was the radio used by the prisoner-of-war lieutenant and radio operator Wu Renjian. The Red Army treated prisoners favourably, especially technical personnel. Zhu and Mao also found time in their busy schedules to meet with the prisoners, and this contributed to their change of allegiance. Wu Renjian, Liu Yin and others joined the Red Army. Wu Renjian changed his name to Wang Zheng, acknowledged his mistakes and professed his new faith. Building on their victory, the Red Army pursued and defeated one more enemy brigade and captured another radio set.

Within a few days, a radio team was established at the headquarters of the Red 1st Front Army, with Wang Zheng as its captain. With only one and a half radio sets, it was impossible to establish complete communications, so the first thing Wang Zheng and his team did was carry out a search. They found rechargers, rechargeable batteries and dry batteries, but they could not find a transmitter or an antenna. There was plenty of bamboo in Jiangxi, and a single wire run up a stem of bamboo served as an antenna. They put everything together and set up a transceiver for themselves. Their reconnaissance work began, first by copying news from Chinese and foreign news agencies, and second, by copying enemy radio signals. At the First Chinese Soviet Congress, the radio team collated and mimeographed news items from the Central News Agency, Reuters and the United Press into their so-called *Reference News* for the delegates to consult. Intercepting radio signals from enemy stations was principally based on the QRC location code. As soon as the enemy established a camp, they had to establish contact, for which the QRC was required. That is to say, the new radio station reported its location, and the other party answered with the QRC. The QRC did not use "open code", but instead a "pass code", that is, the station code, which was the contact code between the stations. The replies comprised two characters, with another three characters for the location, but Wang Zheng and the others who had come over "from the other side" had no trouble deciphering them. The Red Army chiefs were pleased to know the enemy's movements but this just represented the simplest translation of contact information, and the enemy general staff did not use these station codes. So, we took the next step and transcribed the reports in order to decipher the enemy's deployment orders.

In the second encirclement and annihilation campaign, He Yingqin replaced Lu Diping as the "annihilation commander" and personally led the 200,000-strong Kuomintang Army. The Red 1st Front Army lured the enemy into their territory, and first concentrated its forces on attacking the two divisions of Wang Jinyu and Gong Bingfan. Our radio personnel followed our headquarters and moved to Donggukou. For more than twenty days and nights, they monitored every signal from the enemy radio stations, both QRC and QRG (subordinate self-reporting radio stations) and provided accurate reports on the enemy's movements and encampments. One evening, we finally received an open-code conversation from the enemy's radios, and the Red Army headquarters deployed accordingly. The first battle was launched the next day.

The fighting was fierce, and the radio team installed their receiver halfway up Mount Baiyun. In the afternoon, we received an SOS signal from Gong Bingfan's division, and not long after, Wang Jinyu's division also issued the same. The first battle was won, and the Red Army swept 700 miles from west to east. In the second victory against encirclement and annihilation, the Red Army seized three radio sets, one of which was the 100-Watt set belonging to Gong Bingfan's division. These radio sets were then distributed to the 3rd Red Army Corps, the 3rd Red Army and the 4th Red Army, and the large, 100-Watt set was given to the Central Bureau of the Soviet Area, which enabled the Soviet Area formally to establish radio contact with the Central Committee of the Communist Party of China in Shanghai. There was also wireless communication between the Red 1st Front Army headquarters and the Forward 3rd Red Army Corps. The Red Army had its own radio station. Before that, communications between the Soviet Area and the central government had to be transmitted by undercover messengers. The documents were written on bamboo paper and white shirts using invisible ink. The messages took anywhere from a month to several months to get through. Just imagine how much effort it took back then for Mao and Zhu to find each other before their meeting in the Jinggang Mountains!

Now that more captured radio stations were available, Commander-in-Chief Zhu and Chief Political Commissar Mao announced the establishment of a radio training course, asking all corps and armies to "select young people who can be sent to come and study with the radio team at headquarters". At the same time, Peng Dehuai's 3rd Army Corps also started a radio training class. In the summer of 1931, Cao Daye became part of the first cohort on this course.

June 1931. The third encirclement and annihilation campaign, with 300,000 enemy troops and Chiang Kai-shek leading his own army. The Red 1st Front Army "avoided the enemy's main force, attacked their weaknesses, and took advantage of their victory to pursue and destroy them". They won the first three battles and then two out of the next three, once again smashing the encirclement and annihilation of the Kuomintang army. Cao Danhui, a trainee radio operator of the 12th Red Army, was with the 3rd Red Army Corps when he intercepted a secret telegram from He Yingqin to the Kuomintang Army. It was encoded in Strong Code and deciphered using a captured codebook. It proved to be a message of great value that enabled the leaders of our army to understand the enemy's deployment, thus guaranteeing victory in the ensuing battle. Political Commissar General Mao asked the Adjutant General's office to give Cao Danhui some money to buy eggs. They gave Cao Danhui three dollars, so he bought chicken and meat and invited everyone to a blow-out meal.

In December, the 26th Kuomintang Army launched the Ningdu Uprising, with 17,000 officers and soldiers switching allegiance to the Red Army. These included more than forty radio communications personnel with eight radio sets. From then on, the Kuomintang Army became more vigilant and radio communications were fully encrypted by every department.

The Red Army's radio detection section was now in a difficult position with all enemy reports being fully encrypted. At the end of the year, Comrade Zeng Mian arrived in the Central Soviet. He had been head of the espionage section of the Central Military Commission when he was in Shanghai, and on arriving in the Central Soviet, he became head of the detection section of the General Staff. Soon afterwards, the Military Commission of the

Chinese Revolution changed the sections under the General Staff into bureaus, and the Detection Section was changed to the Detection Bureau, which was soon renamed the Intelligence Bureau. The Operations Bureau was the first bureau under the General Staff Department, so the Intelligence Bureau was called the 2nd Bureau. The Military Commission of the Chinese Revolution also assigned the radio detection section to the 2nd Bureau.

In February 1932, the Military Commission of the Chinese Revolution followed the Central Committee's decision to mount a strong attack on Ganzhou. Radio detection was largely ineffective as it was impossible to translate the encrypted telegrams of the Kuomintang Army, while the spies sent out had difficulty in feeding back information in time. The enemy suddenly mobilised several more regiments. The besieging Red Army was attacked from both inside and outside the city, and although they used their machetes to cut a bloody road of retreat from the battle, the Red Army suffered more than 3,000 casualties and more than ten cadres at division and regiment level died.

"Who gave us false information about there only being two regiments?" Army Chief Peng Dehuai asked angrily from the front line. Commander-in-Chief Zhu De telephoned him to ask, "How did the enemy maintain communications? Are you telling me they used signal fires?"

The battle was a fiasco due to the adventurist mistakes of the central leaders, but the lack of knowledge of enemy deployments was also a factor. The first problem faced by the 2nd Bureau was breaking the enemy's radio codes. In Jiangxi, they were using the Spread Code.

Faced with this enormous pressure, Chief Zeng rose to the challenge. The code must be decipherable. It had to be deciphered. He arranged for the detection section to make more copies of the coded enemy telegrams, separate them by section and give them serial numbers by time and date, analyse them according to the state of the battle, then compare the captured codebooks and telegram transcripts to try to determine the approximate content of the messages and consequently find a way to decipher them. At the same time, he questioned Wang Zhen and the other former enemy radio personnel in order better to understand the enemy's codes and telegram encryption system. He also asked Zhou Enlai for the benefit of his coding knowledge.

He asked the various Corps for men. The right people were really hard to find, as enthusiasm alone was not nearly enough. Chief Zeng asked the 3rd Red Army Corps for men, and Corps Commander Peng sent Cao Daye. This was in May 1932.

Cao Daye was transferred to the headquarters as a detection operative, whereas Comrade Zeng Mian was actually trying to find someone with deciphering potential. Cao Daye had attended private school for four years. He was a gifted and intelligent man who studied diligently and excelled in the radio training course of the 3rd Red Army Corps. As the enemy continued to encircle and blockade the Soviet Area, a severe shortage of all kinds of materials ensued. Conditions of study on the training course were very tough, with supplies of dry batteries and stationery often very difficult to replenish. There was no salt to eat, so they used alkali instead; no proper rations, so they ate pumpkins; no bed planks, so they laid down straw; no shoes, so they went barefoot. The teaching was even more difficult, as the instructors used the wall as a whiteboard and charcoal as a pen if they did not have a blackboard and chalk. There was only one buzzer to emit tiny signals to train the students' ears as they listened and copied down. Instead of a buzzer, the trainees use their voices to sound out the Morse code, with one person beeping while the others wrote on the floor with sticks. They also had fun practising transmitting messages, pressing the first three fingers of their right hands anywhere they could, either on the edge of a wooden table or on their own legs, and then oscillating their wrists up and down to get a smooth sequence of dots and dashes. The greater the difficulties, the more one is forced to find ways to overcome them. Cao Daye graduated with honours and became the best telegraph operator in the 3rd Red Army Corps. On arrival at the headquarters, he was confronted with several baskets of undecipherable coded telegrams, and Cao Daye began to study them together with Chief Zeng, in addition to his detection duties.

In August, at the Battle of Yihuang, they found Sun Lianzhong's coded telegram with more than thirty characters decoded. More than a month later, at the Red 1st Front Army headquarters at

SECTION CHIEF   95

Jianning in Fujian, they successfully cracked the Spread Code! Over the following years, they have cracked more than a hundred different enemy codes. In May 1933, Cao Daye became chief of the decoding section when he was not yet nineteen years old. In August, he won the Red Star Medal, Third Class.

The Spread Code was broken, and our fortunes in the Battle of Fengshanbu were transformed. This was in January 1933.

On 4 and 5 January, the Red 1st Front Army concentrated its forces on destroying a brigade of the enemy's 5th Division at Huangshidu and then occupied Jinxi. At 9 pm on the evening of the 6 January, the 2nd Bureau detected that Chiang Kai-shek had ordered the Kuomintang Army to attack Zuofangxu and Huangshidu near Jinxi in retaliation. On the left, Wu Qiwei led the 90th and 27th Divisions in the main attack with the 11th Division as back-up, and on the right, Zhou Zhirou directed the 14th and 5th Divisions to contain the enemy in the Langju area. The Kuomintang Army was commanded by Luo Zhuoying on behalf of Chen Cheng. The five divisions were all formed of Chiang Kai-shek's elite troops, of which the 90th Division was Zhang Fakui's division, known as the "Iron Army", and the 11th and 14th Divisions were also trump cards in the hands of Chen and Luo. In response to this enemy deployment, the Red 1st Front Army used Lin Biao's 1st Corps, Peng Dehuai's 3rd Corps, Zhao Bosheng's 5th Corps and Luo Binghui's 22nd Army to set up ambushes and wait for an opportunity to destroy the enemy. The enemy had 100,000 soldiers compared with the 40,000 of the Red Army.

Once the enemy issued an attack order, there were usually no changes in the situation to report. They maintained radio silence before the offensive, and our troops were already appropriately deployed to meet the attack. Only one detection set was operative in the 2nd Bureau and all the others were offline. At midnight, Cao Daye took over duty alone but suddenly found that the Kuomintang Army radio transmissions had sprung into vigorous life. All five enemy radio stations simultaneously issued a "most urgent" signal! Such unusual transmissions from the enemy had to indicate unusual actions. There must be a major military situation! But which enemy radio station should he listen in on first? The first message was too long, probably a camp report, so he switched to the 5th Division radio station, which was transmitting to Nanchang and had little relevance to the current battle. Cao Daye was listening and transcribing simultaneously. Signal into code, code into code frame, code into text, and all to be done instantaneously and all to be done in his head! The signal was unstable, and he was dealing with five stations at the same time. Finally, he tuned back into Wu Qiwei's radio and heard the crucial message. The signal was immediately translated into text in his head: "As follows: (1)". Wu Qiwei was issuing new orders!

"Take advantage of the Communist bandits' easing off after slight gains and wait for the opportunity to mount a sneak attack..."

It turned out that our army's offensive deployment had been discovered by the enemy, and the enemy army changed the direction of their main attack overnight. The left column moved the 27th and 90th Divisions towards Fengshanbu to mount a flank attack on Zuofangxu, and sent the 40th Division by a roundabout route to join up with part of the 5th Division to mount an attack on Huangshidu. Their plan was to cut off our retreat and implement a large-scale encirclement. Our army urgently adjusted its deployment accordingly. At 0400 hours on 7 January, the command of the Red 1st Front Army issued a combat order. The 1st Red Army Corps and the 22nd Army moved by night to the vicinity of Fengshanbu to confront the enemy, and the 5th Red Army Corps went to the southwest of Huangshibu to block the enemy's 14th and 5th Divisions. The 3rd Red Army Corps continued their offensive in the direction of Langju. We also gave the enemy the illusion of "easing off after small gains" to lure them forward. At 0800, the enemy entered our deadly baited trap, and our 1st Red Army Corps launched a frontal attack near Fengshanbu, like a tiger chasing a flock of sheep. By Bajiaoting, they had eliminated most of the enemy forces and the 22nd Army even captured Huwan and pursued the enemy to the other side of the Fu River.

The Battle of Fengshanbu ended in our complete victory. Without the information from the 2nd Bureau, if we had not been aware of this new enemy deployment in time, the main force of our Red Army and the headquarters of the Military Commission would have been surrounded and perhaps even destroyed. The

Kuomintang Army was defeated once again. A new round of encirclement and annihilation was bound to come.

The fourth encirclement and annihilation campaign was a fierce one, with 400,000 troops on the left, right and centre. It was February 1933.

On the night of 2 February, the 2nd Bureau broke the secret information about Chiang Kai-shek's decision to transfer three more divisions to Jiangxi. It then detected the battle formations, assembly times and locations of the three columns of Chen Cheng's Central Route Army. The Kuomintang Central Army had by now activated the Meng Code, which had been broken by Cao Daye and Zou Sheng.

As the enemy was strong and we were weak, the headquarters of the Red 1st Front Army suggested we should avoid pitched battles and destroy the enemy with a campaign east of the Fu River, but the Central Committee ordered a direct assault on Nanfeng. The Red 1st Front Army was thwarted in its attack on the city, and the main force retreated secretly to the Dongshao and Luokou areas, while the 11th Red Army disguised its main force by making a feint at Lichuan. The 2nd Bureau detected that the Kuomintang Army mistakenly thought that the main force of the Red Army was retreating to Lichuan. Chen Cheng led three columns of the Central Army to Lichuan and mounted an attack on different fronts. The commander of the first column, Luo Zhuoying, led the 11th Division south from Yihuang, and ordered the 52nd and 59th Divisions to advance eastward to Huangpi to join the 11th Division. They were then to advance to Guangchang and Ningdu to cut off the Red Army's line of retreat.

Acting on this information, the Red Army's main force was divided into two flanking columns on the left and right to covertly meet the enemy and set up an ambush of the 52nd and 59th Divisions, which were advancing eastward either side of Luozhang Mountain. Between them, the mountain was densely wooded and shrouded with clouds and fog. In the drizzle, the left wing of the 1st Red Army Corps launched a sudden attack on the 52nd Division, which had advanced to Dengxian Bridge, and fragmented it. Then the 3rd Red Army Corps joined the battle, wiping out the 52nd Division and capturing the division commander, Li Ming. Meanwhile, the 5th Red Army Corps assaulted and destroyed the 59th Division, capturing its commander Chen Shiji alive.

Li Ming and Chen Shiji were put on public trial and the personnel of the 2nd Second Bureau attended the event. Li Ming was a graduate of the Military Academy of the National Protection Army, while Chen Shiji graduated from the Baoding Army Military Academy. As divisional commanders of the "National Army", although they were both wounded, they were not persuaded away from their cause at the hands of the Red Army. And there was Cao Daye rushing to the stage, approaching them and muttering a few words to them. They immediately lowered their heads sheepishly and Cao Daye slapped them both in the face.

What exactly did Cao Daye say to them? He recited to them the contents of their top-secret telegram.

It was no bad thing to give them a few slaps to knock the arrogance out of them. Cao Daye was certainly delighted, but afterwards, when an organisational meeting was held, someone from the Party group criticised him. We had a strict disciplinary code. As far back as Jinggang Mountain, the Red Army already had a prisoner policy: killing prisoners was strictly forbidden, and no cursing of them was allowed. Those who surrendered their guns on the battlefield were not to be killed, while the wounded should receive medical treatment; those who wished either to leave or stay were to be treated according to their wishes, and those who wished to leave were to be given travelling money.

When Zhang Huizan was captured earlier, Zhu and Mao originally wanted to let him go. This man was an old acquaintance of theirs. He was also a young firebrand revolutionary during the Constitutional Protection Movement, when he expelled the pro-Japanese feudal butcher Zhang Jingyao from Hunan, and Mao went to Beijing as a student representative to petition for his rights. They had also had dealings with each other when the Nationalists and Communists were working together in Guangzhou. Zhu became acquainted with Zhang when he was in the National Revolutionary Army. So Zhu and Mao had wanted to let him off the hook. Secret negotiations were underway, the Kuomintang was eager to ransom him, offering temptingly generous terms of money, guns and medicine, just when the Red Army was in desperate need of such things! Mao Zedong also wanted to keep him in the Soviet Area, as he had undertaken formal military studies in Germany and Japan and would be very suitable as an instructor at the Red Army School which was in the course of being established. Chiang Kai-shek publicly promised to release a large number of Communist "prisoners" held in the White Areas if the Red Army would release Zhang Huizan. He was commander of the Nanchang garrison, and thousands of Communists died at his hands. Now this "Butcher Zhang" was begging for mercy from Zhu and Mao, although before he was defeated and captured at Longgang, he had been supremely arrogant!

During the "invasion and suppression" of Donggu, he carried out the "Three Every" policy: burn everything, loot everything, kill everyone. "Stones must be smashed with swords, and wooden benches must be burned with fire. All men, all women and children over the age of ten are to be killed! All houses, public and private, thatched and mud-walled, are to be burned before the troops retreat! Take all the food and supplies you can carry!" His 18th Division also daubed slogans on the walls of the houses in Longgang, saying that they would shave Zhu's and Mao's heads!

Zhu and Mao wanted to save Zhang Huizan's life, but there was no way the people in the Soviet Area were going to let him go so easily. The Donggu District Soviet convened a public trial at the insistence of the masses. Mao Zedong urgently sent He Changgong, commander of the 8th Red Army, to try to swing the balance in Zhang's favour, but before the decision of the Central Committee could be passed down, Zhang Huizan's head had already been separated from his body. The scene at the trial had been out of control. Zhang Huizan had been taken back to Donggu from Longgang, wearing a dunce's hat and tightly bound "five-flower" style. As soon as Butcher Zhang, who had left countless families in ruins and wives widowed, arrived at Longgang, the crowd's anger flared up on the instant, with cries of "Skin him!" and "Stretch his tendons!" The Red Army soldiers in charge of keeping order at the venue were from the 3rd Red Army, which had also suffered heavy casualties during the battle of Longgang, and they too hated Zhang

Huizan. Blood debts and the fury of the crowd inevitably led to the public trial deciding to execute him on the spot. Zhang Huizan died under a hail of sticks and rocks, and his head, placed on a wooden plaque, drifted down the Gan River to Ji'an before being retrieved by Chiang's troops.

As a result of Zhang Huizan's execution, Chiang Kai-shek cancelled all promises of negotiation and replaced them with even more frantic reprisals, first by massacring the Communists in prison and then by intensifying his tactic of encirclement and annihilation.

How could Chiang Kai-shek not be shocked by our victory in our fourth resistance to his encirclement and annihilation efforts, when we captured two enemy division commanders alive thanks to the accurate intelligence of the 2nd Bureau? They were escorted to the stage during their public trial, but they still refused to concede defeat, since how could they know that the victory was thanks to our secret intelligence work!

There was another divisional commander who was also completely in the dark.

That was Li Mo'an, commander of the 10th Division. Li Mo'an was ordered to follow up after the main attacking force. He had a feeling that the 52nd and 59th Divisions had been annihilated, and although he was lucky not to reach Dengxianqiao and be captured alive, he was very much weary of the war. He sent a few lines of poetry to his wife in Shanghai in a coded private message. How could he have known that we would decipher that "private" message?

The last line of the poem read, "How many bright red tears will begin to dry as we cross the Heavenly Bridge to ascend to immortality?"

Cao Daye had been sent to us by the 3rd Red Army Corps, and Zou Sheng by the 1st Red Army Corps. Two months previously, Chief Zeng and Cao Daye broke the first enemy code, and the information obtained led to a glorious victory for the Red Army. The 2nd Bureau was greatly valued by the head of the Military Commission who wanted to strengthen its decoding power.

Zou Sheng is definitely made of the "special material" needed for decoding.

SECTION CHIEF

Zou Sheng joined the Red Army at the age of fifteen. He first served as a logistics officer in the 1st Red Army Corps. At seventeen, he was chosen to participate in the radio training class at headquarters. He was privately educated, had an excellent memory and could recite Morse code fluently. Like Chief Zeng and Section Chief Cao, he too has the strength of will never to admit defeat, the momentum to overwhelm all enemies and the ability to put in maximum effort. But they are very different in character. Bureau Chief Zeng and Cao Daye are straightforward and quick-tempered, but not quite in the same way. Bureau Chief Zeng is the overall leader, and although he has a fierce temper, which sometimes turns into a blazing fire, he is generally calmer and more sophisticated. Section Chief Cao is sometimes a bit wild and impulsive, but he has a cheerful disposition. Zou Sheng is introverted and quiet and speaks in a soft voice; you rarely see him get angry.

What they have in common is also obvious. They are diligent and eager to learn, straightforward and persevering, and both have a "good head". They were calm when they needed to be calm as, when the cannon were roaring outside and the sound of slaughter was overwhelming, they still had to keep control of their voices, breathe calmly and immerse themselves in the codes.

When Zou Sheng was transferred to the 2nd Bureau of the Military Commission, his original post was that of telegraph operator. Like Cao Daye, he was able to operate several radio sets simultaneously and recognise the subtleties of the enemy's fingering. By the end of 1932, the troops under Chiang's direct command had been equipped with radio communications up to regimental level, and there were hundreds of enemy divisional, brigade and regimental radio posts on the northern front of the Soviet Area alone. Because the 2nd Bureau had so few operators, they had to work very hard to ensure that critical information was not missed!

The 2nd Bureau did it! No key intelligence was missed. In early 1933, when General Commissar Zhou reported the enemy's battle deployments, every time they were marked "definitely confirmed".

On 21 January, Chief Zeng gave a comprehensive report on the enemy situation as recently detected to General Political Commissar Zhou and Commander-in-Chief Zhu. The same day, Commissar

Zhou called the central authorities and secretly reported to the Central Committee, "It is confirmed that, on Chiang's orders, Chen Cheng instructed the 11th Division to return to the area between Yongfeng and Le'an; the 23rd Division to move to Le'an; the 43rd Division to move to Yongfeng, Jishui, Xiajiang and the Futian area; the 52nd Division to assemble east of Ji'anshui; the 59th Division to move to the vicinity of Ji'an once Tan Daoyuan had sent a team to relieve the garrison at Anfu..."

Two days later, the 2nd Bureau again confirmed that the enemy had identified the 5th, 6th, 10th, 11th, 14th, 52nd, 59th, 80th and 90th Divisions as the "advance and annihilate army" and the remaining divisions as the "clear and annihilate army". This latter group would then take on the defence of all the county towns. It also confirmed movements reported on 21 January that Chiang Kai-shek would come to Nanchang in the near future and had ordered all ministries to prepare for the transport of medical supplies and the construction of roads, and that his major attack was scheduled for February. On the same day, Zhou Enlai sent a telegram to the Central Office with the "definitely confirmed" information to be forwarded urgently to the Central Committee.

On 24 January, despite the imminent large-scale attack by the "encirclement and annihilation" army, the Central Office of the Soviet Area ordered Zhou Enlai, Zhu De and Wang Jiaxiang to "concentrate all our main forces on taking Nancheng and then consolidating and maintaining it", and to "give special attention to arrangements for the occupation of Nancheng and Nanfeng".

The 2nd Bureau confirmed, "Chiang Kai-shek has arrived in Nanchang and has convened a meeting of generals from all sides… the encirclement and annihilation offensive is about to begin."

Zhou Enlai had no choice but to send another telegram to the Central Office of the Soviet Area, to propose an alternative plan focused on eliminating enemy reinforcements. On 4 February, the Central Office of the Soviet Area sent another telegram to Zhou, Zhu and Wang: "Following instructions received from Shanghai, we have discussed that in line with the general political task, Fuzhou should be made the principal strategic zone and that, at the moment, it would be appropriate to attack Nanfeng first."

"Instructions received from Shanghai" always means they are the instructions of the Comintern. The highest-level instructions.

At dusk on 12 February, the Red Army launched an attack on the enemy's 8th Division, which was guarding Nanfeng City. The enemy stubbornly resisted with heavy fire from the bunkers and artillery towers outside the city walls. The following day, after the attack failed, Zhou Enlai sent a telegram to the Central Office of the Soviet Area to be forwarded to the Provisional Central Committee, requesting that the attack be changed to a feint and that every effort be made to target the enemy's reinforcements.

The 2nd Bureau obtained information that the enemy had concentrated their forces in advance in response to the threat of our attack on Nanfeng. On 15 February, Zhou re-reported this development to the Central Office of the Soviet Area and suggested that the Red 1st Front Army should meet Luo Zhuoying's first column. A week later, the 2nd Bureau detected that the enemy commander-in-chief, Chen Cheng, had ordered Wu Qiwei's 2nd Column, Zhao Guantao's 3rd Column and Luo Zhuoying's 1st Column to work together to surround and destroy our troops in Nanfeng.

Bureau Chief Zeng reported this news of the enemy to Zhou and Zhu, who came to a firm decision: abandon the original offensive strategy and immediately return to the hinterland of the Soviet Area in a strategic retreat to carry out a counter-offensive against the enemy's first column which had penetrated deep into the Soviet Area. At the same time, the 11th Red Army was sent to make a feint in the direction of Lichuan, creating the illusion that this was the destination of our main force's retreat.

Chiang Kai-shek and Chen Cheng were taken in by this ruse and ordered the three divisions of the 1st Column to advance towards Guangchang and Ningdu in an attempt to cut off our retreat. On the afternoon of the 27 February, the 59th Division of the enemy's 1st Column advanced from Xiyuan to Huangpi, and the 52nd Division advanced to the front line of Qiaotou in the vicinity of Huangpi, Jiaohu, Dalongchang and Dengxianqiao.

The 1st and 3rd Red Army Corps, who were waiting in ambush, suddenly attacked like a tiger descending the mountain, annihilating most of the enemy's 52nd Division, and wounding and capturing Division Commander Li Ming. Meanwhile, the 5th Red Army Corps launched an attack on the 59th Division, annihilating most of the enemy and capturing the commander, Chen Shiji.

It was only then that Chen Cheng realised he had been duped. During those few days of March, Chen Cheng was mobilising his troops to find out where the Red Army's main force was heading, while the Red Army was seeking opportunities to destroy the enemy's main force, and the 2nd Bureau was keeping an eye on changes in the enemy's operational policy. On the night of 19 March, Commander-in-Chief Zhu De, Chief of General Staff Liu Bocheng and Director of Operations Zhang Yunyi were analysing the enemy's situation in the courtyard of a landlord's residence in Wucun when Bureau Chief Zeng delivered a report on the enemy's deployment. Zhang Yunyi read it out loud: "The enemy's vanguard, the 14th, 10th and 90th Divisions, and the rearguard, the 5th Division, are advancing towards Ganzhu via Dongpi and Xinfeng. Its 9th Division is occupying positions in the Dongpi Mountains, and its 11th Division has moved into Huangpi."

The commander-in-chief said that our strategy was to destroy every one of them. Chief-of-Staff Liu proposed to prepare for battle at Caotaigang. The commander-in-chief asked Director of Operations Zhang to draft the orders. It was not long before another report on the enemy came in from the 2nd Bureau, saying that the enemy's 11th Division's rearguard had stopped advancing towards Caotaigang and that its leading troops could be withdrawn in three hours. So the order that had just been drafted was scrapped and the battle plan was re-examined. The rooster crowed for the first time and the second battle plan had just been drawn up, when a third report from Bureau Chief Zeng arrived, saying that the enemy's 11th Division had been constructing fortifications all night, that the advance guard had not retreated northwards and that the whole rearguard would arrive before dark the next day. Chief of Staff Liu laughed out loud. "Heaven help me!" he said. "Let's give the order, Commander!" The commander-in-chief asked Chief Commissar Zhou to join them, and Liu reported on the changes in the enemy situation and the deployment of our troops overnight. Chief Commissar Zhou read the order for himself and expressed his full agreement. The order was immediately signed and issued by Zhu and Zhou, and the attack was launched at dawn on 21 March.

At dawn, the 3rd Red Army Corps launched the first attack and was followed in by the 1st Red Army Corps. By dusk, the majority of the enemy's 11th Division was wiped out, except for the division commander Xiao Qian who was wounded but escaped. More than 3,000 prisoners were taken.

The 11th Division was the trump card of Chen Cheng, commander-in-chief of the encirclement and annihilation army. On receiving this news, he was so distressed that he vomited blood. Chiang Kai-shek was also very disturbed, saying, "This setback is so tragic. It is the great secret pain of my life."

The 2nd Bureau investigated the situation and learned that Chiang Kai-shek was still putting on a show of bravado after the fiasco. He was on an inspection visit to Chen Cheng's headquarters in Chongren, and the Red Army headquarters had just moved to the southeast of the city. The 2nd Bureau also confirmed that Chiang was scheduled to return to Nanchang during the day, travelling by river so he could admire the scenery, "showing he may have been defeated but was not discouraged".[1] Zhou and Zhu urgently sent troops to set up an ambush. The Chongren River is not big, so it is easy to intercept someone travelling on it. Regrettably, a coded enemy telegram indicated that Chiang Kai-shek had changed his mind on the spur of the moment and taken his car back to Nanchang instead, So his luck held and he got away...

Raging revolutionary enthusiasm and fighting spirit are all hidden under his calm, quiet character, but every time he talks about this, Zou Sheng shows a rare excitement, and he heaves a long sigh when he finishes. If Chiang Kai-shek had been captured alive that time, we would definitely have stayed in the Central Soviet Area, a bigger and stronger Central Soviet Area, and perhaps the revolution would have been victorious sooner. Then, of course, there would have been no need to travel all this way westwards. In any case, this was the great victory that Zou Sheng witnessed on his arrival at the 2nd Bureau. Our victory against the enemy's fourth encirclement and suppression campaign was achieved under the wise command of Chief Political Commissar Zhou and Commander-in-Chief Zhu. In the course of it, the Red Army soldiers fought bloody battles, and of course there were also the "definitely confirmed" reports on the enemy's deployments from the 2nd Bureau. Zou Sheng was both a telegraph operator and a decoder. At first, he learned his codebreaking skills from Zeng and Cao when he was on duty, but he picked up those skills with extraordinary speed, and he was soon able to work independently. On this occasion, in countering the encirclement and annihilation campaign, his and Cao Daye's top priority was decoding.

Codebreaking is first of all guessing the translation, guessing the password, guessing the report, guessing the individual characters. Then, analysis, assumption, inference, confirming or disproving, stripping out of all the various types of encryption, synthesis, induction and restoration of plain text information.

Chiang Kai-shek's ciphers were originally based on plain-code telegraphic reports, and the only code changes were made on the corner codes, horizontal codes and straight codes. This coding method has a limited number of possible changes, and the key is to find the repeat codes. Later, the enemy discovered how to introduce random numbers into the code, so that the repeat codes were hidden by those random numbers. Now, the random numbers had to be stripped out first to restore the original repeat codes.

Our analysis from the traces we uncovered suggested that Chiang had hired a foreign expert, probably a Dutchman, to improve the enciphering. Around the time of the fourth encirclement and annihilation campaign, Chiang's direct line of communications abandoned the use of plain code as a base, and made up their own codebook, which we call the "special book". It is a "self-edited" book with many variations, the most complex of which is a mixture of single characters and single words not grouped according to initials, which we call "come-and-go". Based on the same code, the enemy operator must compile his own codebook for each outgoing and incoming message, and this immediately increases the difficulty and workload of deciphering. In the case of a code based on a plain code telegraph codebook, there must be some connection between the top and bottom, left and right of every character, but this is not the case with the "come-and-go" book. As a result, when a character is decoded, it is only decoded for that particular character, and the same is true for words. Some self-edited codebooks have multiple codes for each character of commonly used words. For example, decoding the character 军 (army) once, does not mean you have the coding for every time it is used. Moreover, these self-edited books are seldom reused. They also have a kind of self-edited password, and the passwords are changed frequently; some passwords are even changed to five-digit numbers.

The 2nd Bureau only had three decoders: Bureau Chief Zeng, Cao Daye and Zou Sheng. But these indomitable geniuses met with success after success! First, the special Meng Code was broken, and then all the enemy's passwords were broken like stems of bamboo. Every time a secret was broken, Zou Sheng made a note in his little black leather-bound notebook.

"Broken!" In Nanfeng in Jiangxi, when Cao Daye and Zou Sheng unravelled the last set of digits of the Meng Code, Chief Zeng slammed his fist on the table. Ever since then, they have followed this custom. Whenever they break a code, they no longer say "Guessed it!" or just nod silently, but they shout the word "Broken!" instead, with great gusto and even more confidence, and always with a sharp blow on the table. Their great brains have been working away in close confinement for days, seeing nothing, hearing nothing, so when they break through, there has to be action, there has to be noise!

In April 1933, the Red Army flag was changed from a black axe and sickle to a hammer and sickle inside a white star on a red background. In May, the General Headquarters of the Chinese Workers' and Peasants' Red Army was established. At the same time, the 2nd Bureau of the General Staff of the Central Revolutionary Military Commission of the Chinese Soviet was established at Wushilong in Ruijin. The 2nd Bureau of the Front was set up in Jianning, Fujian, under the charge of Bureau Chief Zeng Mian, who remained at the front with Cao Daye. The 2nd Bureau of the Rear was still in Ruijin, under the charge of Deputy Chief Qian Chao, with Zou Sheng transferred to the 2nd Bureau of the Rear to be responsible for the decoding work. The 2nd Bureau of the Front separated the detection and deciphering work, and expanded the decoding section, with Cao Daye as its section head. Zou Sheng joined the Rear 2nd Bureau, which was relatively small in terms of manpower and only had him as the one decipherer. But he quickly got the section up and running and worked continuously deciphering the enemy-coded telegrams, averaging one every two days. The enemy information was forwarded to all Soviet zones across the country, and the results proved successful in actual combat. The Hunan-Jiangxi Soviet, in particular, won two battles in a row in May, destroying two enemy regiments, using information from the decoded telegrams.

There are more than a hundred broken codes recorded in that little black leather-bound notebook which Deputy Bureau Chief Qian calls the Record of a Hundred Beauties. In August 1933, the glorious sixth anniversary of the founding of the Red Army, the Provisional Government of the Central Committee of the Chinese Soviets and the Military Commission of the Chinese Revolutionary Army decided to award the Red Star Medal to the "most meritorious" members of the Red Army. The 2nd Bureau of the Military Commission, which fought on the "underground front", received the highest awards. Bureau Chief Zeng received the Red Star Medal second-class, while Section Chief Cao and Deputy Section Chief Zou received the Red Star Medal third-class. Zeng was twenty-nine years old, Cao was nineteen and Zou was eighteen.

That evening, Chief Political Commissar Zhou and Commander-in-Chief Zhu were personally present at a secret meeting of the 2nd Bureau, which was also an award ceremony and a congratulatory celebration. "The Comrades have worked hard. The Comrades have triumphed!" "The Chief has worked hard. Victory to the Revolution!" Zhou and Zhu hung the shining medals on their recipients, and together with the comrades of the 2nd Bureau, they admired the Record of a Hundred Beauties, and everyone told stories and sang songs, staying up celebrating until late into the night.

The 2nd Bureau had three main targets: the Fujian 19th Route Army, the Guangdong warlord Chen Jitang and the Hunan warlord He Jian. Theirs was a vital task in the field of communications, and Zou Sheng was responsible for establishing contact with the 19th Route Army and the Guangdong warlords. Their coded telegrams were deciphered by Zou Sheng of the 2nd Bureau without going through the central government's Special Branch, so this came under the classification "extremely secret".

Back in 1927, when the forces of the Nanchang Uprising entered Guangdong, Chen Jitang led his division to Chaoshan to stop them, but he was not under the personal command of Chiang Kai-shek. He really just wanted to be a "Southern Heavenly King". He supported the building of the Sun Yat-sen Memorial Hall and was said to be more qualified than Chiang to carry on the spirit of Dr Sun. Basically, he was not willing to act as Chiang's pawn...

At the end of 1933, the 2nd Bureau of the Front returned to Ruijin along with the General Headquarters of the Front, and soon afterwards the two Bureaus of the Front and the Rear were formally merged, still bearing the title of the 2nd Bureau of the Military Commission of the Chinese Revolution. After the merger, the three men still engaged in deciphering work were Zeng, Cao and Zou, with Cao and Zou doubling up in detection as well. They continued to withstand the pressure of the urgency of their work, not only breaking one four-digit cipher book after another in rapid time but also getting the better of the five-digit cipher of the Kuomintang army.

The fifth encirclement and annihilation campaign began in September, with the Kuomintang amassing a million troops and 200 aircraft. The ciphers of Chiang Kai-shek's direct line of communication were now completely self-coded, and many of them had been upgraded to five-digit ciphers. The frequency with which they were changed was also significantly accelerated. Even so, they were soon cracked by Zeng, Cao and Zou. For more than a year at the beginning of this campaign, they stuck to their task and deciphered 352 enemy codes, almost one a day. What the enemy transmitted, we received; what the enemy communicated, we passed on. The copy rate of the main command stream was almost at maximum, the rate of decipherment and transmission was also "one in, one out", and at many crucial moments, there were frequent miraculous examples of "simultaneous transmission and decipherment". However, the command of the Red Army was in the hands of Bo Gu and Li De, one of whom did not understand the military and the other was arbitrary in his decision-making. As a result, our top-secret information was reduced to the status of wastepaper. Li De was indeed aware of the importance of intelligence, but his strategy was one of territorial warfare, "fighting for every inch of land", "short, sharp raids" and "keeping the enemy at bay". The powerful enemy forces built up a broad defensive base and moved steadily, advancing and entrenching step by step while maintaining a total economic blockade on the Central Soviet Area. The enemy was strong and we were weak, but Li De still insisted on defending across the whole front. April saw the fall of Guangchang, the northern gateway to the Soviet, and in August, all positions south of Guangchang were lost. The enemy had German-made Bofors guns with a maximum range of almost twenty *li*! In mid-September, the only areas left in the Central Soviet were Ruijin, Huichang, Yudu, Ningdu, Changting and some other narrow strips, and manpower and material resources were almost exhausted. The situation was such that the only option was an urgent breakout.

A breakout was imminent. The only possible route was to the west. The Red Army had recently been in extensive secret contact with the Guangdong warlord Chen Jitang, and Zou Sheng was responsible for this highly confidential encoding. The breakout had been scheduled for late October or early November, but the situation was becoming increasingly dangerous and the opportunity for Chen Jitang to let them through could not be missed. In addition, the 2nd Bureau had detected that a major attack by the Kuomintang was being brought forward, so Li De decided to go ahead. That evening, a bridge was thrown across the Yudu River and the river was swiftly crossed.

On 10 October, the Central Red Army began its great transfer. A telegram from Zhou Enlai was received by the Guangdong Army radio station and they relayed it to the Red Army representatives who were negotiating at Junmenling. "The pigeon you were feeding has flown," it read.

The Red Army set off from Yudu. The wind rustled in the autumn air, and a lingering autumn rain persisted as the columns of the rank and file crossed the pontoon bridge in the hazy moonlight. They were dressed in neat, new, monochrome uniforms, with conical bamboo hats hanging down their backs beside straw sandals and bags of dry rations. They were loaded down with guns and ammunition slung across their shoulders. Walking with heavy steps, we kept looking back, waving a tearful farewell to the mountains, hills and rivers of the Central Soviet Area, to this happy land created by the Party six years ago and to the friendly people who lived there. We are just saying goodbye not farewell. We will fight our way back, we will definitely fight our way back...

Riding our luck, we passed through the first blockade line of Chiang's forces by making use of a road in the territory controlled by the Cantonese Army. After this, Chen Jitang stopped communicating with the Red Army. Once having crossed the Xiangjiang River, we no longer had any kind of military relationship with him, and Deputy Chief Zou no longer detected and collated coded telegrams from the Cantonese Army.

TUCHENG

A beautiful dream shattered in a matter of days. Zunyi is not somewhere we can stay for long, and it is not a suitable place for a new base. The "pursuit and annihilation" army is coming, and it is not just the "pursuit and annihilation" army of the Central Army, it is a six-pronged offensive: the Xiang Army in the east, the Qian Army in the west, Xue Yue's Central Army in the south, the Chuan Army in the north, the Qian Army and Central Army in the northwest and the Dian Army in the southwest. They have 400,000 troops, German ordnance, an air force and plenty of ammunition and supplies, while we have only 30,000 men, half of whom are non-combatants, and most of whom have no guns in their hands. There are still enemy planes bombing us from above and reactionary militia groups on the ground. The fun times are about to end, and the spicy chicken will definitely run out in a few days. The girls of Zunyi City will not be able to see our Captain Xiao Jinguang dancing the Caucasian dance again.

From 11 to 15 January, the 2nd Bureau's decoding section broke three enemy codebooks and learned that Chiang Kai-shek had deployed Xue Yue's troops to join forces with the Chuan, Qian, Gui, Yue and Dian Armies to close in on the Red Army in order to encircle and harass it in the area northwest of the Wujiang River. The eventual purpose is to round up and destroy us. On 15 January,

He Jian, commander-in-chief of the "pursuit and annihilation" army, ordered an all-out attack. Enemy forces were about to pounce on Zunyi from all sides. It is the day the Politburo is due to meet.

"He Jian is going to attack in full force, but he has to transfer his officers and men first, so I don't think he'll get in position that quickly. We still have time for a meeting and a few days of rest." Bureau Chief Zeng has brought in this newly deciphered operational order and is analysing it. "This Commander He, it's just Hunan he wants to protect, isn't it? Aren't we already in Guizhou?"

Deputy Chief Qian is also giving the matter serious thought: "He Jian is the commander in chief, and Xue Yue is the chief operational commander. Will Xue Yue be convinced? He Jian leads a powerful local faction, and Xue Yue is commander of the Central Army. Chiang's instructions are quite explicit. The only explanation is that Chiang wants him to leave his province to fight."

"At this time and in that place, he is sitting pretty in Hunan territory," Deputy Chief Qian continued. "I don't think he is going to be easy to transfer out of there, is he? He was asked to besiege the Red Army but the Red Army's frontline assault troops are all from Hunan too, and are old adversaries of his! Oh, and I have a story about He Jian that might help you understand all this. During the National Revolutionary Army's Northern Expedition, he was commander of the First Division of Tang Shengzhi's Eighth Army, and I was the political instructor at the Third Division's barracks. This man led a surprise attack on Hanyang and took Wuchang by trickery. He was the first commander to distinguish himself on the Northern Expedition, and Chiang Kai-shek twice sent him congratulatory telegrams. Oh, and He Jian's division was the first to break open the West Gate of Wuchang, and who was the first to storm into the city? Liu Jianxu's brigade! After the battle, He Jian was promoted to commander of the Thirty-Fifth Army and became one of the most famous generals of the Northern Expedition in one fell swoop. Tang Shengzhi was promoting Buddhist teachings among his troops, and this He Jian was also a believer in the power of the Buddha. When he was afraid that his officers would not listen to him, he summoned a monk and made all the officers from warrant officers upwards get ordained as Buddhist monks. There was only one battalion commander out of the whole First Division who didn't accept this. Guess who it was?"

No one could guess. It is a very interesting story!

"As for the rest of the story, I've already given you all the clues you need!"

"It's Peng Dehuai!" Zou Sheng shouted. "He's from Hunan! It's our own Peng Dehuai!"

It suddenly dawned on everybody.

"They're all from Hunan," said Bureau Chief Zeng, suddenly sounding rather depressed.

"So, what happened next?"

"What happened next? Do you think I'm some kind of storyteller? All right then. Next, the first of the Kuomintang armies to attack Jinggangshan was led by none other than He Jian, and it was Peng Dehuai who was defending it. That was in 1929. Then, the only one from our Red Army to attack the provincial capital was Peng Dehuai, and it was He Jian who was defending Changsha at the time. What year was that?"

"1930!" Cao Daye snapped out excitedly. "In July I fought in that battle! The Third Red Army!"

"How old were you then? Fifteen, eh? Later, he executed Mao Zedong's wife and dug up the Mao family's ancestral grave..."

We look out of the window and see the figures approaching. The weather is overcast, and their steps seem a little heavy. It is dusk and the chiefs enter the Bai Mansion one after another. Vice Chairman Wang Jiaxiang is still lying on a stretcher, and so is Nie Rongzhen. Chief Zeng sounds very solemn, weighing his words as he says, "If you are poor, you must make changes, and if you change, you will make it through. In holding this meeting... we have problems to solve and it is essential we do so."

The next few days were even more tense and hectic than usual, as we toiled away day and night in the radio room, wanting to pin down Xue Yue's Central Army and keeping an eye on the radio stations of the provincial warlords. In this dense hail of radio beeps, the swarms of lice were providing their own crazy interference, but we had no time to boil them up to eat!

It was late at night when Li De walked out of the Bai Mansion in a dejected mood. Li De, a foreign adviser, was only an attendee at the enlarged meeting of the Politburo of the Central Committee of the Communist Party of China. By the acacia tree in the courtyard, Chief Zeng met Li De's interpreter Wu Xiuquan. Wu Xiuquan said quietly to Chief Zeng that he was exhausted from all the translating, that the meeting was very ill-tempered, and the arguments were heated. Everyone was talking so fast that he was finding it difficult to keep up. Li De was complaining that he wasn't getting to hear everything, but there was no doubt that he got the general idea and knew that he was the man in everyone's sights. He sat in a chair by the doorway, chain-smoking moodily. This attendee at the meeting was about to find out what it felt like to be left out in the cold. We had lost all contact with the Comintern, and Li De no longer held the "imperial sword". On the road on this Western Expedition, there was no private communication between Li De and Mao Zedong, except for the few times they shared leaves from wild mountain trees, which they used as tobacco. Mao also suffered from malaria more often than not, and he spent most of the time lying on a stretcher and travelling with Luo Fu and Wang Jiaxiang. Chief Zeng had an unusually happy expression on his face as he told us that the meeting was not yet finished and would continue after dinner the next day.

Back at the 2nd Bureau, Chief Zeng talked to Deputy Chief Qian about Li De's and Bo Gu's arguments at the meeting, saying that they believed the main reason for the failure of the anti-encirclement and annihilation campaign was that the enemy was too strong and that it was essential to fight a territorial war. They also said that the Central Column could have crossed the Xiang River faster if they hadn't "dragged their families with them". Combat troops had become palanquin bearers, and the people in the palanquins complained about the people carrying them.

"Li De argued that he was only an advisor… and perhaps there was some truth in that."

"His real power lay in the fact that he had been appointed to the highest level of military command. He hadn't earned it in combat but was given it by our Central Committee, by Comrade Bo Gu. That was how he could play the role of 'emperor'. Telegrams that came from the front were first sent to him, having been translated by us and turned into simple sketch maps for his evaluation. After he had looked at them and given his opinion, we turned it all back into Chinese and sent it to Vice Chairman Zhou. Vice Chairman Zhou generally dealt with them at his discretion, with anything major being referred to the Military Commission or the Politburo for discussion."

"I mean to say... we haven't seen any actual documents, any authority from the Third International. There doesn't seem to be anything like that, not even a telegram!"

"There was a long-distance phone call that came via Shanghai before Bo Gu arrived in Ruijin, but the instructions in it were couched in very vague language. It only said that Li De had the authority to make suggestions." At this point, they all fell silent.

* * *

The third day was still overcast, and the meeting continued into the evening, still in that room on the second floor of the Bai Mansion. I heard that the commanders of the 1st Red Army Corps were staying in a local tyrant's house at the south gate of the old city, and that the commanders of the 3rd Red Army Corps arrived half a day late for the meeting. They came on horseback and stayed on the ground floor of the Bai Mansion. However, they only attended the meeting for one day before hurrying back to their troops, because fighting had kicked off between the 3rd Corps and the Qian Army on the southern defensive line. On this occasion, it was Bai Huizhang, commander of the enemy's 25th Army's 99th Division, who was leading the Qian Army into battle! It was in his mansion in Zunyi that the Red Army was holding its meeting!

The day after the Politburo meeting ended, we intercepted another telegram from the chairman of the Nationalist Government's Military Commission:

> "Investigation has exposed Hou Zhidan's repeated loss of key positions and his secret flight to Chongqing. He has already been arrested and is awaiting further investigation."

So, the commander-in-chief of the southern Sichuan border defences, who lost the battle over the Wu River, had fled all the way to Chongqing! What a way to get yourself killed! After the Red Army occupied Tucheng, Chiang contacted Xue Yue and Wang Jialie to follow up on the crime, and Xue Yue sent a telegram to Chiang to demand severe punishment for ineffective combat leaders in order to enforce military discipline. When Hou Zhidan failed to fight with sufficient commitment and fled the scene without permission, Chiang ordered him to be apprehended, and Hou was taken into custody by the Kuomintang Military Commission Staff Corps.

Another change of destination. Zunyi was abandoned. The idea of building a base area with Zunyi at the centre was rejected at the Liping Conference. This expanded meeting of the Politburo in Zunyi was first and foremost to discuss the destination of the strategic transfer. The information our 2nd Bureau intercepted clearly showed that the enemy's 400,000-strong army was converging on Zunyi and that Zunyi was not somewhere to linger for any length of time. Liu Bocheng and Nie Rongzhen suggested crossing the Yangtze River to establish a base in northwest Sichuan. The first reason was that the 4th Red Front Army had its base in Sichuan-Shaanxi to support it; the second was that Sichuan was the richest province in the southwest, densely populated and ripe for development; third, Sichuan was inaccessible to the outside world and the Chuan Army was hostile to outsiders, so it would not be easy for Chiang to move the Central Army into Sichuan. Liu and Nie's suggestions were accepted. Both men are from Sichuan.

Our direct opposition was going to be the Chuan Army. When we arrived in Zunyi, we at the 2nd Bureau had made deciphering the Chuan Army's codes our top priority, but we had no idea how quickly it would become urgent. The Kuomingtang Central Army's code offered no difficulty, nor did the Xiang Army's, as they had previously been our principal military opponents, and we were already familiar with them. The Chuan, Dian and Qian Armies have now been added to the list of opponents, with the Chuan Army being the most important. The Central Army used "general codebooks" to communicate with the local armies, while "special codebooks" were used within the Central Army and the local armies. The special codebooks were much more difficult to break.

On 19 January, we detected Chiang Kai-shek's plan to encircle and annihilate the Central Red Army on the south bank of the Yangtze River:

> Our army will chase the bandits with a "pursuit and annihilation" army, press them hard in the area on the south bank of the Chuan River, and join with the operational forces and the defensive forces at various points south of the Chuan River to attack and annihilate them.

This was an order from Chiang to the Central Army's Xue Yue, commanding Xue's corps to join the Qian Army in crossing the Wu River on 15 February, and to join up with the Chuan Army to sweep away the Red Army in the Zunyi area. One piece of information in Chiang's telegram about the deployment of the Chuan Army revealed that the enemy was weak in the area of Chishui County in northern Guizhou and that Xue Yue's "pursuit" was to take place twenty-five days later. Chief Zeng reported all this to Zhou Enlai and Mao Zedong. The Politburo meeting had co-opted Mao Zedong as a member of the Standing Committee, which previously consisted of four members: Bo Gu, Luo Fu, Zhou Enlai and Xiang Ying, the last of whom had remained in the Central Soviet. The meeting stripped foreign adviser Li De of his authority to make military decisions, which was something that everyone had been hoping for. Someone had to be held accountable for the tragic defeat of the fifth anti-encirclement and annihilation campaign, the loss of the Central Soviet Area and the sacrifice of so many lives in the crossing of the Xiang River. The blood of the Red Army soldiers must not have been shed in vain! Blood stained the water of the Xiang River, but when Bo Gu held a pistol to his head, it was Nie Rongzhen who took the gun away from him. Bo Gu had good reason to despair, and he had a hard time accounting for himself to the Comintern. The fate of the Red Army was a far more important issue than personal responsibility, and the future of the revolution could not be sidelined. The problem was resolved when the Politburo meeting abolished the previously established Team of Three and thenceforth Zhu and Zhou remained the military commanders, with Zhou being the one responsible for making the final decisions on military command entrusted to him by the Party.

As far as the next move was concerned, the decision of the meeting was to cross the Yangtze River in the north and enter western Sichuan to seek possibilities for further development. The latest information from our 2nd Bureau showed that Xue Yue's corps was still on the south bank of the Wu River, and Pan Wenhua's corps of the Chuan Army had not yet arrived. Mao and Zhou therefore decided to take this opportunity to implement the plan to cross the Yangtze in the north.

On 19 February, Zhu De issued an order to rename the column of the Military Commission as the Central Column, and the Central Red Army evacuated Zunyi along three routes: left, middle and right. When the Military Commission left the Bai Mansion, the same Bai Huizhang followed the Central Column with his troops, not daring to pursue them but equally not willing to let them go; he settled on following them very closely. The Red Army rearguard stopped by a small bridge in the north of the city and confronted the pursuing Qian Army, separated by only 200 metres or so. A Qian Army battalion commander was about to drive his men forward, but as soon as he moved, he was shot down by a Red Army rifle.

The next day, the Military Commission of the Central Revolutionary Army officially issued a plan for crossing the river: "The basic policy of our Field Army is to cross the river from the north of Guizhou to the south of Sichuan and then move to a new area to carry out a general counter-attack from the northwest of Sichuan in coordination with the Red 4th Front Army. Then we will use the combined activities of the 2nd and 6th Red Army Corps in Sichuan, Guizhou, Hunan and Hubei to clamp down on a potential encirclement by the enemy in southeast Sichuan, and, as a result of this counterattack, crush the enemy's new attempts at encirclement and fight for the return of Sichuan to the Communist fold."

Addendum: It was here in mid-January that Liu Xiang, chairman of the Nationalist Sichuan Provincial Government, convened a meeting in Chongqing of officers above regimental rank. Liu Xiang judged that the Red Army would move north along the Chishui River out of Hejiang and across the Yangtze River to the north; or they might leave Luzhou via Gulin and Xuyong. He had anticipated our movements! He also moved the new provincial capital to Chongqing to stop the Red Army from crossing the river. We had no idea he had such foresight! It is a pity that his ideas did not appear in any coded telegram; otherwise, if we had deciphered it in time, we would not have spent the next two months on that particular route. We had intended a surprise crossing, but he had already worked out that we would go via the Chishui River.

It was a rainy morning, and the north wind was strong enough to fill our battle flag. The bugle calls seemed extra loud and clear as we moved out towards Chishui. After their ten-day rest in Zunyi, the Red Army soldiers were well fed and rested, their weapons and ammunition were replenished, and they had more Mausers and more new straw shoes, some with leather soles. Now with a clear direction of movement, new woven rush raincoats and new hats, the Red Army was no longer a spent force, it was a team with its morale at its peak again.

After a few miles, we heard gunshots in the mountains in the distance. The "dry people" stood at the side of the road with bamboo baskets on their backs. Some watched with tears in their eyes as the army marched away. "Mr Red Army" had helped them to stake out ownership of the fields, but now the troops were moving out, they were afraid that those allocations might not materialise. Some of them simply went with the army. It is said that the young women of the "Friends of the Red Army" were brought into the army by Li Bozhao,[1] and many young men also wore dark green uniforms. We followed the arrow markers left by the troops ahead of us. During the march, the "little Red soldiers" were also excitedly learning to read. This was an invention of Comrade Luo Fu called the "Looking at the Back" literacy class. The soldiers in front had strips of white cloth tied to their backs with Chinese characters written on them, and the soldiers behind learned them by rote. Ah Gen was part of the heavy transport team of the vanguard, and he kept stealing glances at the character sheets on our backs as we hurried past. He did not know how to read himself, but he was too embarrassed to be seen openly learning the characters in the same way as the "little Red soldiers". Since leaving the Central Soviet Area, the Red Army had been travelling on proper roads, and Mao Zedong rode his tall white horse.

The Central Red Army marched in multiple parallel columns along the highway, the whole mighty team advancing in orderly fashion. The forward team of our 2nd Bureau had to make haste to the front and get far ahead of the main force. We needed to set up tents, erect antennae and then start listening. Chief Zeng's big black horse was laden with equipment, and we all trotted along together. We had to go right through the main force and take the lead. Whenever a soldier shouted out, complaining about our lack of discipline, a cadre would reply quietly, "Ah, it's the Second Bureau! Make way for them and be quick about it!"

The ordinary cadres did not know the exact nature of our 2nd Bureau's work, but they all knew it was important and that they had to make way for our forward team. They always saw us following the leaders of the Military Commission, saw our tents and antennae, and sometimes heard the buzzing of motors and the ticking of the telegraph. The 2nd Bureau had radio sets, and radio sets were important. At times of the greatest urgency, the troops simply circulated the order to turn back temporarily so that a passage would suddenly open up, allowing us to get through at speed. At this point, the soldiers whispered about which section we were from and also loudly complimented our big black horse.

Addendum: Passing through Tongzi. The city is not large, but it is more beautiful than Zunyi. The big city of Zunyi has no electric lights, but the smaller Tongzi does. It is said that some soldiers, seeing electric lights for the first time, unscrewed the bulbs as they left, wanting to take them back for illumination or for lighting their cigarettes. When the enemy started a rumour that the Red Army was the "Long Hairs" (referring to Shi Dakai's troops in the Taiping Heavenly Kingdom), Tongzi was left in a state of panic and all the powerful officials fled with their families and belongings to Chongqing and Guiyang, while the ordinary rich folk took refuge in the large caves on the outskirts of the city. When the Red Army broke into the Panglong Cave, the people inside came streaming out. The Red Army seized all the belongings of the landed gentry who had been sheltering in the cave and distributed these ill-gotten riches among the poor as the fruits of our victory. Our 2nd Bureau made an unexpected discovery: among their number was the director of the Tongzi County telegraph! We replenished our stores of batteries and petrol and added a few vacuum tubes. Tongzi merits its nickname of "Little

Nanjing", and the names of its residents are quite elaborate and worthy of note. That telegraph chief's name was Linghu Dafang, and the wife of the man who owned the house we stayed in was Leng Bingru, his widowed sister-in-law was Linghu Shouzhen and his sister-in-law's younger brother, who lived with them, was Linghu Bage. The owner of the house himself had run away to hide. On this day of heavy frost and bright sunshine, that same owner returned and saw that the Red Army had not committed any crimes and his wife was sitting sifting rice for the Red Army while a Red Army soldier was carrying a big jar of water across the yard. The man carrying the water was our Ah Gen, whose wounded leg was still oozing blood through his puttees.

"I've never heard of such a virtuous army, let alone seen it with my own eyes. How well-behaved the Red Army is!" the landlord exclaimed. "There seem to be a lot of people called Linghu here," we said. "Is it one big family clan?" Younger Brother Linghu responded, "The rich die rich, the poor die poor. It's class that matters, not family clans." The landlord opened a lunch tin and said, "Red Army friends, have a taste of a poor man's snack..."

Tucheng: a small town in the middle reaches of the Chishui River, surrounded by mountains to the north, south and east, with the preferred crossing point of the Chishui River in the west. Tucheng is the main point of entry into Sichuan from the north of Guizhou. The road from Tongzi to Tucheng is a major one, with several sections of metalled surface suitable for cars and a gradual uphill gradient.

On 24 January, the Red Army's advance guard reached the vicinity of Tucheng, and Hou Zhidan's division, which had retreated to this area after the defeat at the Wu River, did not dare engage with them. Hou handed over command of his division to his cousin, the deputy divisional commander Hou Hanyou, and fled in great haste with only his guards and his family (it was said that this local Tucheng tyrant was fleeing towards Sichuan). Hou Hanyou led out the remnants of the 100th Division to resist the Red Army but was soon routed.

On the 25th, the 1st, 3rd and 5th Red Army Corps and the Central Column had all reached Tucheng, and the 9th Corps was advancing towards it.

On the 26th, Pan Wenhua, the commander-in-chief of the Nan'an "bandit annihilation force", ordered Guo Xunqi's brigade and other Chuan Army troops to pursue the Red Army. Guo Xunqi's brigade advanced from Xishui with murderous intent, and our intelligence team reported the enemy's strength at four regiments. If we did not beat the enemy forces that were pursuing us, we could not cross the Yangtze River northwards as planned.

On the 27th, the Central Revolutionary Military Commission adopted Mao Zedong's suggestion and decided to continue to block the Chuan Army troops advancing on Tucheng with the 1st and 9th Red Army Corps, and to destroy Guo Xunqi's Chuan Brigade in Tucheng with the 3rd and 5th Corps. Qinggangpo to the east of Tucheng is a gourd-shaped mountainous area, with peaks fringing the low valley. With our pursuers isolated there, we could ambush them on this highly advantageous terrain. This would be a decisive battle for the northern crossing of the Yangtze. In the afternoon, the 2nd Bureau arrived at Tucheng with the Military Commission and immediately made strenuous efforts to locate the radio station of Guo Xunqi's brigade. At 1500 hours, the advance regiment of Guo Xunqi's brigade advanced to Qinggangpo and engaged in heavy fighting with the Red Army on the opposite side of Nanmu Mountain. The enemy swooped in like a wolf pack and quickly seized a number of the high points, including Qinggangpo. The battle lasted until dusk, but the two sides were locked in a stalemate, and it was difficult for our troops to expand the field of engagement. Guo's brigade began to build fortifications in preparation for the next day's battle. We suffered heavy losses in this battle, and our troops carried the wounded from their positions under the dismal light of the waning moon.

At 0500 hours on the 28th, the 3rd and 5th Red Army Corps launched a fierce attack on the Chuan Army positions at Qinggangpo, with the 3rd Corps taking the main attacking role, fighting for four hours. However, the enemy still proved difficult to drive back. The two sides repeatedly fought for position, but the enemy was getting the upper hand. The Chuan Army brought fierce firepower to bear and advanced on Tucheng, which is only a few miles from Qinggangpo. The situation was so desperate that Mao and Zhou ordered the 1st Red Army Corps, which was already attacking Chishui City, to return to the rescue, and they also ordered Chen Geng and Song Renqiong to lead their cadre corps into battle. Charges and counter-charges, more and more Chuan Army troops, more and more firepower, until they reached the front line of the Military Commission headquarters!

The smoke of battle was not far away, and the sound of gunfire was so intense that we had to struggle to block out the distractions and maintain our intense concentration. The doors and windows of the ramshackle temple we occupied were very solid, and when they were closed, the sound of gunfire disappeared. Then, the silence was unbearable, and we felt suffocated. Our heads were clamped tightly by our earphones and began to go numb from the pressure, but when we opened a window, we heard the roaring, whistling sound of the wind. It was so loud we had to shut the window again. Before we shut all the windows the first time, there had been no roaring and whistling, in fact there hadn't even been a breath of sound from the wind, only from the gunfire. The trees of the woods on the mountainside opposite were also still. In fact, when we tried opening the same window again, there was indeed no sound of wind, but when we shut it, there must have been a slight gap because there was the roaring and whistling again. The mountain wind was carrying the sound of the gunfire, and that sound was now even crisper than before. It was that slight gap or crack in the latticed window that was causing the sound of the wind. The wind in itself was silent, only making a noise when it encountered an obstruction. Deputy Chief Qian had told us about the principle of resistance, so this must be "wind resistance". The sound of the wind was amplified by the gap in the window, allowing us to hear it. We had to find that gap as soon as possible, then locate the sound we actually wanted, the signal from the Guo Xunqi's brigade's radio, and amplify that.

With the battle raging along the front, we didn't know what was really going on over there, nor did we know that Commander-in-Chief Zhu had also established a position! All our radios were on at once, doing their best to capture the signal from Guo Xunqi's brigade. We were expecting news of victory. On the way to Tucheng, the head of the Military Commission also told us that we might take a large number of prisoners in this battle and that the 2nd Bureau would get some of them to replenish our transport team. It would be even better if there were radio personnel who could be liberated for our use. The commander told us to cook more food and get ready to receive the prisoners. He also said that after this battle, we would cross the Yangtze near the Hejiang River and join the 4th Red Army Corps in Luzhou... Fighting broke out at Qinggangpo yesterday afternoon, but no prisoners were sent to us. Yesterday's fighting did not end in victory for our troops, and we were fighting again today. We worked hard to locate the signal from Guo Xunqi's brigade radio station, and, after finding it, we had to copy down the code and decipher it, so we didn't even have time to eat. Good news is often delayed, and the door was suddenly thrown open. Two people rushed in: Zhou Enlai and Wang Jiaxiang. The two vice chairmen of the Military Commission were here!

They were out of breath and covered in dust, and must have run all the way. We could immediately tell that all was not well. Vice Chairman Zhou anxiously asked Chief Zeng, "Guo's Brigade has a radio station, right?"

Zeng: "We found it and are copying down its transmissions."

Wang: "Has the code been broken? It must be broken in a hurry!"

"We're working as fast as we can. As soon as we arrived yesterday, we got straight onto it... we've been at it ever since... we're making every effort to crack it."

"Well, hurry up and work out the enemy's deployment while we help make you some food!"

It had to be cracked in a hurry. Guo Xunqi's code was the Upright Code, self-coded and a complex "come-and-go" cipher. It had to be broken, no matter how complex it was, and it had to be broken quickly. Revolutionaries are not afraid of failure, but this was not the time for failure. They may be hungry, but they don't feel their hunger!

The phone rings with news from the front: the captured Sichuan men have been interrogated and we learn that yesterday's battle was fought by Guo Xunqi's brigade and today's is being fought by Pan Zuo's brigade. Both of these are "model brigades", have not two but three regiments and are very well equipped.

How many enemy troops are there? We are deciphering as we receive the reports; the military situation is critical. It is abnormally quiet, and everyone can hear their own breathing, even though it makes no noise. The immense pressure on us in the 2nd Bureau, at a time when the soldiers on the front are fighting for their lives, is so intense. A suffocating pressure, but we have to breathe normally, and our brains have to work at high speed. There is no danger of being wounded, our lives are not at risk, but, make no mistake, this is a battlefield without the noise of battle. But these three valiant warriors, these three commandos, are all forcing themselves to work through illness: one with a stomach ailment and abdominal pain, one with pneumonia and fever, and one with insomnia and dizziness. Chief Zeng paces slowly along the wall and squats down to wash his face with cold water again, scooping up the water in cupped hands and thinking hard as he does so, wiping his hands only once and then grabbing a copy of the Kangxi Dictionary and excitedly turning to a particular page. Cao Daye turns to the fire pit and uses a poker to stir up some heat. He stares blankly at the blue flames, then scribbles something down on his sheet of paper. Zou Sheng ducks his head to compare several coded messages, and takes another sip from the tea jar, which has long since reached the bottom... This broken-down old temple is not far from the front and the enemy radio station is quite close. This broken-down old temple is also in a corner of the battlefield. Our soldiers are fighting on the same hillside, and the sound of gunfire rattles our eardrums and shakes our antennae.

We have never done this before: listening out for the messages and deciphering them on the spot.

> ...the 3rd Independent Brigade is making haste to reinforce, and the 2nd Instructors Brigade is also detouring to Tucheng...

"Broken!" Chief Zeng slams his fist on the table. At 0300 hours, Guo's brigade's coded telegram is finally deciphered. Such a complex "come-and-go" cipher! A single character is cracked, and the entire text follows. Only now do we fully understand the enemy's deployment: there are nine brigades surrounding us!

Update on the enemy's deployment: there are three brigades in the east Guo Xunqi, Panzuo and Liao Ze, with the 3rd Independent Brigade on its way to reinforce them; in the west there is the 2nd

Instructors Brigade detouring towards Tucheng; there are two brigades in the northwest, one regiment moving towards the Red Army's flank and rear; in the southeast are Xue Yue's massive forces.

The Chuan Army's coded telegram also contains the latest report on the current situation. In this engagement, "machine guns have been deployed and there has been much hand-to-hand combat" with "2,000-3,000 Red Army officers and men killed and 3,000-4,000 wounded or captured". In addition, "the captured Red Army soldiers gave up with scarcely a struggle, being equipped with no guns and only a handful of bullets".

Pan Wenhua, commander-in-chief of the Nan'an Chuan Army, telegraphs,

> "There is still fierce fighting at the eastern end of Tucheng. My two brigades, Da and Liao, are attacking hard towards Tucheng and are expected to work together with Guo's and Pan's divisions to destroy the enemy. The bandits' main force is all gathering at Tucheng, and the encirclement has been established, so please send small detachments from each friendly army to intercept them. Liu Xiang, commander of the Chuan Army, orders the 'hungry and exhausted' Red Army to be wiped out!"

The 2nd Bureau's own coded message states that the enemy forces are rushing to assemble and that an encirclement is rapidly forming. Currently, the encirclement has not yet been fully closed and there is still a gap. By now it is five o'clock in the afternoon and the battle is still raging. An emergency meeting of the Politburo is held in the command post on the mountain behind Tucheng. The plan to cross the Yangtze to the north is no longer possible. We will have difficulty proceeding north from Chishui to Sichuan, and to preserve the strength of the Central Red Army, we must withdraw from the battle immediately.

The night is misty, the enemy's searchlights light up the sky and flares continue to streak across the darkness, signalling that even greater danger is on the horizon.

The latest coded message from the enemy states,

Troops west of the Chishui River are depleted, and we are extremely worried about the Red bandits taking advantage of the opportunity to move in.

Before the enemy army finally close up and while the enemy's strength is depleted to the west of the river, the Military Commission has decided to cross the Chishui River immediately.

Our engineers built the bridge overnight, with Zhou Enlai taking personal command on the spot. In the early hours of the morning, the army crossed the pontoon bridge three abreast. We were still working when Chief Zeng took an urgent telephone call and shouted at us, "Radio sets off! The Military Commission wants the Second Bureau to take the lead."

On the critical afternoon of the Battle of Tucheng, Chief Zeng was working with Cao and Zou to decipher the Upright Code while also dealing with other urgent matters. He dashed over to the Investigation and Collation Section where the telegraph operator Qian Jiang was on duty. Chief Zeng took out a sheet of squared paper covered in scrawl; this was a handwritten order from Mao Zedong. Mao was instructing the 2nd Bureau to establish a dedicated radio station to locate and master Long Yun's radio station and all its subordinate stations within three days.

Long Yun was the "King of Yunnan", chairman of the Kuomintang Yunnan Provincial Government. We were fighting here in Tucheng, in Guizhou, to go north, and the battle was still raging, but before it was over, Mao suddenly had the weird notion to get us to turn our attention to the south. Perhaps this was a kind of foresight, as there is always something different about those who are wise beyond their years. We gradually came to see Mao in a new light. He was not a disciplined soldier; although our uniforms were ragged and dirty, there were also times when we changed into new ones. Mao always preferred to leave his coat unbuttoned.

During those years of his "enforced idleness", we would see him smoking, reading and thinking. As chairman of the Central Executive Committee of the Soviet Republic, he was not completely "idle", as he had meetings to chair, speeches to give and research to undertake. He was ill when the Red Army broke out of the encirclements, but he still helped to build a bridge across the Yudu

River. However, the military struggle was his priority and the loss of command of the army was, to him, the "enforced idleness" of dismissal from office. He loved to read ancient books, grew his hair long and had something of the romantic poet about him. He was very humorous, not to say witty, in his speech. Sometimes he would crack jokes or moan about something, sometimes he would argue a point or just chat about everyday life. Everybody understood what he had to say, and the Red Army soldiers and the local people of the Soviet all wanted to listen to him.

He was transferred away from the front line at the Ningdu Conference and was removed from his position as general political commissar. Later on, he was not seen openly clashing with Bo Gu and Li De, indeed he did not have the position or seniority to participate much in the discussions. Now, we don't even know how to address him. In the Central Soviet, the locals naturally called him "Chairman Mao", as he was chairman of the Soviet Government. However, that is a position with little practical significance now that we have lost the Soviet Republic. In this strategic breakout, real power within the army is of course the most important thing, and everything is secondary to the fighting.

If we continue to refer to him as "Chairman Mao", it would seem alienating and a little out of place. It might also be seen to touch on a kind of secret pain, and not just because we lost our base in the Soviet Area. When on the march and in battle, we have the commander-in-chief, the general political commissar, the chairman and vice chairman of the Military Commission, but Mao holds no such position. He is a member of the Standing Committee of the Politburo of the Central Committee, but this is not a unique post. There are many members of the Standing Committee, and he is just a new addition. Fortunately, there is still the title of "comrade", and so that is what we call him: Comrade Zedong.

Sometimes we would see him smoking cigarettes and staring into the distance through narrowed eyes, like a poet. But his expression would be markedly depressed, thoughtful, a little disconnected, a little inscrutable and his gaze a little restless. Now that he is no longer depressed, we still see him smoking a leisurely cigarette, but he is even more mysterious.

When he wrote this note for Chief Zeng at Tucheng, were his

wandering eyes straying to look south to the territory of Yunnan? If this was some kind of foresight, it is exactly what we need to march into battle. Chief Zeng has also stressed many times that we have to be prescient in our work because we are the eyes and ears of the Central Red Army. After the westward crossing of the Chishui River, because so much is demanded of us, he also asked us to question ourselves over the loss of Tucheng.

"There are two very dangerous situations. One is when you see a guest off, and the other is when you greet one." Chief Zeng held a meeting of the whole bureau in Gulin after the crossing of the Chishui River. This choice of words seemed rather whimsical at first, but when we saw the chief's expression, it was clear there was much more to it and we became very solemn. With everyone silent, he continued, "On the nineteenth, we set off with the column of the Central Commission – ah, the centre column that is to say – and we had only just left the city when the scene unfolded–"

"That was when the Qian Army intercepted us! A company suddenly appeared on the hillside, firing at us from above, with our entire column in range."

Section Chief Cao Quickly took over: "I heard that the guard company did not have enough firepower, and it was fortunate that Ye Jianying led his men quickly to... We were marching at the rear of the troops, and we could not really see everything that was going on up ahead. All I heard was that Political Commissar Zhou hurriedly greeted everyone, and then, they all scrambled into a ditch to hide. Fortunately, it was a false alarm and there was no real danger. Comrade Zedong was clearly in a jovial mood as he stood up, patted the dirt from his body and said, "Our host is being so polite, accompanying his guests such a long way as we take our leave!"

Everyone laughed heartily.

"On the twenty-eighth, the battle for Qinggangpo was fought with over three thousand casualties. The Third and Fifth Red Army Corps ran out of bullets and fought a long hand-to-hand battle with the Chuan Army. The political commissar of the Tenth Regiment of the Fourth Division, Yang Yong, led the charge and was shot through the cheek, losing six teeth. As he could no longer issue verbal battle orders, he wrote them down with a pen and paper. His face and hands were so covered in blood that his written orders were drenched in it too. The Chuan Army broke through the Red Army's blockade and charged up to the Military Commission headquarters. Commander Zhu unholstered his Mauser C96 military pistol and took up position himself. The other commanders could not dissuade him. It was like a scene from a tragedy...

"Section Chief Cao and the others were there too, and the cadre corps stepped up as well! Sending the cadre corps to the frontline shows what dire straits we were in. We had underestimated the strength of the Chuan Army. On arriving in Sichuan, we were entering their territory. They had already seen off the Red Fourth Front Army, and they were going to do their best to stop us too. They were a much tougher prospect than the Qian Army. They also excelled at mountain guerrilla warfare. We had lost that advantage too. Commander-in-Chief Zhu and Commander-in-Chief Liu are both Sichuanese, and Commander Liu and Guo Xunqi are old acquaintances. The first time we come up against the Chuan Army, and this is the greeting we get!"

Everyone nodded in understanding, but Chief Zeng adopted a harsher tone.

"We are not clear about the enemy's deployment, and the intelligence is not being followed up."

"This..." Section Chief Cao shook his head in confusion. "How can that be? Have the chiefs of the Military Commission criticised us?"

"We only arrived at Tucheng on the twenty-seventh, and we had already broken Guo Xunqi's Upright Code within a day and a night." Deputy Section Chief Zou hadn't slept for yet another three days and nights, and his voice was thin and weak, as if he might fall asleep at any moment.

"No one is blaming us," Section Chief Cao continued, "but the top brass did reflect on their own performance. They feel that they were too easily blinded and should not have been so gullible and engaged in a decisive battle so readily. Zhu and Liu were familiar with the Chuan Army, and both believed it was faction-ridden with little combat power or will to fight. But it is no longer the same as it was in the past, and it is also much closer to Chiang Kai-shek. They might not show much commitment or effort in battles over external affairs, but they will fight to the death if you invade their own territory! They also had new equipment. Czech mortars!

"If our commanders are reflecting on their own performance, we should reflect on ours too. Although it is not our responsibility if tactical mistakes are made, based on our intelligence, it has to be said that if we had paid more attention to Guo Xunqi's Upright Code sooner, we would have been less blind going into combat. Since we are at a disadvantage in terms of strength in any battle against the Kuomintang, we should always be at an advantage in terms of intelligence, and it should be a decisive advantage. Our numerous victories against the encirclement and annihilation campaigns demonstrate this!"

Bureau Chief Zeng could see how exhausted everyone was, so he lightened his tone a little: "Of course, we did break Guo Xunqi's code in time, and that was a miraculous effort. Just think of the consequences if we hadn't had that information and if we hadn't evacuated in time. Liu Xiang reckons he would have wiped us out in one fell swoop! So many of our central command, so many Red Army generals, are here in one place... No matter what the circumstances, we can see the crucial role of our own intelligence, and more important, we can see the harsh lesson we have been taught. Being casual won't cut it and being careless even less so.

"We have to be in full command of the enemy's deployment at all times. We have to decipher one hundred per cent of their reports, so if things change with the enemy, we change too. We have to be self-aware and self-critical, and I have to take the lead."

"Can I make an observation?" Xiao He from the Investigation and Collation Section asked cautiously and diffidently. "The three of you sometimes drive yourselves to your absolute limit, physically and mentally. Surely there'd be no harm in it if you lent on the rest of us for some strength, and maybe we could take on just a little of the work–"

"OK there, you little imp! It's not surprising you've been memorising the dictionary from cover to cover and burning the midnight oil! Next time you can take on a little bit of it!" Bureau Chief Zeng immediately seemed energised by the suggestion.

The praise made Xiao He feel a little shy, but he continued to speak his mind: "I just realised what Chief Zeng meant when he said there are two very dangerous situations. It is indeed unwarranted that the heads of the Military Commission should be in such danger. We are all willing to be sacrificed for our leaders because they are irreplaceable and hold the fate of our Red Army in their hands. We in the Second Bureau, especially you three, are also irreplaceable. The task of decoding is so daunting and formidable, you simply can't be allowed to collapse–"

"Let's hope you are soon up to it yourself, then!" Chief Zeng said with a great laugh.

The Battle of Tucheng ended in defeat, and Chiang had already sent massed troops to guard the northern bank of the Yangtze. Liu Xiang's Chuan Army presented an even sturdier defence, making it next to impossible for our troops to cross the river there. The battle saw Guo Xunqi defeat the Red Army, and Chiang immediately promoted him and issued a telegram, commending him for his loyalty and courage, and promoting him to lieutenant general of the Twenty-First Model Army Division as an example and an encouragement.

Report on the enemy situation by the 2nd Bureau on 2 February:

> Chiang has adjusted his strategic deployment. He Jian is made commander-in-chief of the 1st Route Army and Liu Jianxu becomes general commander of the enemy front charged with opposing He Long's and Xiao Ke's 2nd and 6th Red Army Corps. Long Yun is made commander-in-chief of the 2nd Route Army and Xue Yue becomes general commander of the enemy front charged with opposing our Central Red Army. Zhu Shaoliang is made commander-in-chief of the 3rd Route Army and Yang Hucheng becomes his deputy commander and general commander of the enemy front charged with opposing Xu Xiangqian's Red 4th Front Army and Xu Haidong's 25th Red Army.
>
> *The 2nd Route Army has adjusted its operational order:*

Wu Qiwei's division now forms the first column, Zhou Hunyuan's division forms the second column, Sun Du's division of the Dian Army forms the third column, Wang Jialie's division of the Qian Army forms the fourth column, Li Yunjie's division of the Xiang Army forms the fifth column, Guo Xunqi's division of the Chuan Army forms the sixth column and Li Yunheng's division of the Xiang Army forms the seventh column.

So Guo Xunqi made another move, up to column commander! The 2nd Route Army was formed from Xue Yue's division of the Central Army, along with the Dian, Qian, Chuan and Xiang Armies, and the "King of Yunnan" Long Yun became commander-in-chief. Xue Yue was still only commander-in-chief of the enemy front, and nominally he had to accept orders from Long Yun. On the afternoon of the fierce battle at Tucheng, Mao Zedong ordered the 2nd Bureau to locate Long Yun's radio station within three days. Now, only a few days later, here was Chiang Kai-shek making a big show of that same Long Yun. It was as if they were secretly betting on a game of chess, with Long Yun being the key piece. Except it was possible that the two players were not using the same opening gambit.

Chiang clearly wanted to motivate Long Yun so that he would make every effort to link up with the Chuan Army to circumvent any blockades. The Dian Army was well armed and well fed, and Long Yun's internal control was stronger than Wang Jialie's. Wang Jialie was nominally commander of the 25th Army and provincial chairman, but in reality, You Guocai controlled Panjiang Bashu, Hou Zhidan controlled Chishui, Renhuai and Xishui, and Jiang Zaizhen controlled all the counties along the river in Zheng'an, so the only two divisional commanders he could personally mobilise were He Zhizhong and Bai Huizhang.

This set of reassignments meant that He Jian was moved from the command of the "pursuit and annihilation army" to take charge of the 1st Route Army, primarily targeting He's and Xiao's armies in Hunan. It was also clear that Chiang was making the southwestern provinces his principal target as that was where the Red Army forces were concentrated.

"Each one of them has ulterior motives, and each province is trying to protect their borders and secure their people," said Deputy

Chief Qian. "What they are all really doing is trying to avoid the reality of the situation and preserve their own strength." Deputy Chief Qian looked at the map and suddenly things fell into place. "They are trying to defend themselves against both the Communists and Chiang by making sure neither one wins nor loses, while Chiang is trying to kill two birds with one stone by wiping out the Red Army and unifying the southwest at the same time. His Central Army can enter Guiyang, but it may not be able to enter Kunming. Long Yun is not as easy to deal with as Wang Jialie."

"He's trying to get others to do the dirty work and then keep the profits for himself," said Deputy Chief Qian. "Wow! What a situation! They are playing soldiers and playing politics at the same time!" Then, turning to Deputy Chief Cao, he continued, "Do you remember that coded telegram he sent to Xue Yue. It wasn't long after we set out and it was about the method of pursuit–"

"He said 'Move when the bandits move, stop when the bandits stop.' That bandit Chiang deserves to die himself!"[2]

FOUR CROSSINGS

On the New Year's Eve of the Jiaxu year according to the lunar calendar, 3 February 1935, Zeng, Cao and Zou overcame all difficulties in cracking the Chuan Army's code while faced with high mountains and treacherous roads and enduring cold, hunger and fatigue in the middle of nowhere on the ancient salt road to Zhaxi.

At 1600 hours on 2 February, Pan Wenhua, the Kuomintang's "encirclement commander" in southern Sichuan, sent an order to Fan Ziying, Chen Wanren and Guo Xunqi, the commanders of the 1st and 2nd Armies under his jurisdiction, and the commander of the General Reserve:

> 1. Based on the current situation of all parties, excepting that there are 3,000 bandits fighting fiercely with our Zhou regiment outside Xuyong City, the greater part of the enemy's incursion into the mountains seems to have been broken up.
>
> 2. On this basis, tasks are urgently reassigned as follows: apart from dispatching a regiment from the Liao Brigade to Chishui to stand guard over the transport road, the Guo command, comprising the Guo, Pan and Liao Brigades, are to proceed to Gulin.
>
> 1800 hours, 4 February, Field Command's Circular on Enemy Deployment:

To all divisions:

> On 2 February, the enemy Pan Wenhua said:
> 1. General situation: Except for my 3,000 people who are fighting fiercely with the Zhou regiment outside the city of Xuyong, most of my forces appear to have been broken up.
> 2. With the exception of one regiment from the Liao Brigade to be dispatched to Chishui to stand guard over the transport road, Guo Xunqi's command, comprising the Guo, Pan, Liao (minus one regiment) brigades are to proceed urgently to Gulin....

Our intelligence report on the enemy on 4 February was the result of deciphering their telegram of two days earlier. It was exactly one week from 28 January, when we were thwarted in the battle for Tucheng by lack of information on the enemy, to 3 February, when we deciphered the coded telegram from the Chuan Army.

The battlefield meeting at Tucheng on the evening of 28 January was an emergency meeting of the Politburo held while the battle was still raging. It was decided there that Mao Zedong, Zhu De and Liu Bocheng would stay on the mountain slope behind the city to command the battle. Zhou Enlai was to be responsible for throwing a pontoon bridge across the Chishui River before dawn, and Chen Yun was to be responsible for seeing to the wounded and disposing of any materials that hindered the ease of march. At 0300 on the next day, Commander-in-Chief Zhu issued an order to cross the Chishui westwards and continue in that direction to the south of Gulin.

The Red Army evacuated its position at Tucheng, with the enemy in hot pursuit. The commander-in-chief's wife, Kang Keqing, one of the few active combatants among the women of the Central Committee and the Military Commission, is an expert with a gun, and at that time she was bravely blocking the enemy at the end of the column, with guns in both hands. The bullets were whistling round her ears, the enemy was charging into plain sight, but she was still firing calmly. When a Chuan Army soldier grabbed her backpack, she turned round and flung it at him before disappearing into the night.

A night of chaos and tension! Gunfire was still fierce in the direction of Tucheng, and Red Army assault troops on the Chishui River were again exchanging fire with Qian Army troops on the opposite bank. The Central Committee's plan for the river crossing was for the central column to cross downstream from Tucheng, while Peng Dehuai commanded the left column in crossing upstream from Tucheng, and Lin Biao commanded the right column in crossing at Yuanhouchang. The engineers used wooden boats they had managed to gather together to build the bridge while Zhou Enlai ran around directing operations.

At dawn, the three pontoon bridges were ready as ordered. To be able to advance relatively unburdened, at noon, the columns discarded another batch of provisions, gritted their teeth and threw the lithographic printer and the money printer they had struggled to carry all this way into the waters of the Chishui River. They also buried the X-ray machine that had needed so many people to carry; any spare guns and cannons were also discarded. While these actions were a source of regret, Mao Zedong said there was no need to mourn their loss. We had arrived at the front to fight the enemy a day early and the enemy would have replacements for all these things ready and waiting for us.

The Red Army crossed the Chishui at speed from three different crossing points. The sappers paid off the boat owners and then blew up all the pontoon bridges.

Although this was a desperate retreat in a desperate situation, the purpose of crossing the Chishui was to find an opportunity to cross the Yangtze to the north. However, the enemy had already noticed our movements and taken action accordingly. We had deciphered Pan Wenhua's code. He was the "encirclement commander" in southern Sichuan but was completely unaware his security had been breached. At 1500 hours on 4 February, he went ahead and secretly ordered Chen Wanren, Guo Xunqi and Fan Ziying, together with the 3rd Route Army, to withdraw to the front lines of Gaoxian, Changning and Xuyong in southern Sichuan to mount an aggressive defence to prevent the Red Army from approaching the southern bank of the Yangtze River.

The way into the Xuyong and Gulin areas of southern Sichuan was to bypass the Sichuan defences and cross the Yangtze to the north, which is almost exactly the route taken by Shi Dakai of the Taiping Heavenly Kingdom back in the 19th century. We had all read about it in that book, the *Supplement to Yongan's Text*. When Shi Dakai led an expedition to Sichuan via Guizhou, he also passed through Zunyi, Renhuai and Xuyong.

We originally wanted to cross the Yangtze northwards from Xuyong, but it would be a long time before we could attack Xuyong. The two secret telegrams from Pan Wenhua on 2 and 4 February showed us that the area around Xuyong was heavily defended by the Chuan Army in order to intercept our Red Army.

With Xuyong off the table, the Military Commission decided that the Field Army would move to the areas of Gulin and Changning, and advance northwest again to cross the Yangtze River in the Yibin area. However, the 2nd Bureau detected that Pan Wenhua had ordered a pursuit and blockade of the area around Changning by eight brigades of the Chuan Army.

It was impossible to cross the Yangtze from southern Sichuan, and the Military Commission prepared to implement the plan to cross the Jinsha River via the Sichuan-Yunnan border. Accordingly, it ordered all divisions to change "advance to the northwest" to "continue to the west", and to gather in the Zhaxi area in Yunnan.

The 1st Red Army Corps was in the vanguard of the northern crossing of the Yangtze River when the military commission ordered it to assemble at Zhaxi. Its commander, Lin Biao, was unaware of the change in the enemy's deployment and sent a telegram to the military headquarters questioning the order: "Our position is a long way from you, and now we are ordered to turn around and move south. What exactly is the intention? Why do we keep going round and round?"

It was no longer possible to make a north-south crossing of the Jinsha, so we tried to cross on the Sichuan-Yunnan border instead. However, this road was also blocked. On 5 February, the 2nd Bureau detected that the main force of the Dian Army, Sun Du's column, was coming from Bijie and Zhaotong to block and outflank the Red Army from the west.

Chiang Kai-shek and Long Yun had obviously fully deployed their troops.

At 1 am on the 6th, the Central Revolutionary Military Commission contacted Lin Biao and Peng Dehuai, the commanders of the main force of the Field Army, saying, "In the light of current intelligence on the difficulties the enemy presents to our crossing the Jinsha River and the Dadu River, the Military Commission is reconsidering the feasibility of making any kind of crossing. If it is not possible, our Field Army will make a determined stand to fight the enemy on the Sichuan-Yunnan border and create a new Soviet Area."

This is how we came to arrive in Zhaxi, a sparsely populated place in northeast Yunnan. Here the snow is like heavy goose down as opposed to the great chunks of ice that fall in Guizhou. As we marched blindly through the snow, the local militia and bandit troops hid in village blockhouses. The local landlords and petty gentry also built bunkers to defend themselves. They hid their provisions and we couldn't find any anywhere. There were lots of blockhouses and bunkers like this in the region and, to facilitate our passage, we took no action against anyone who seemed supportive of us and opened their doors voluntarily. There are few rice fields in this mountainous area, and the locals eat maize as their staple food. It was the fourth day of the Lunar New Year, and the cadres charged with grain collection were running around doing their best to find enough to give the officers and soldiers a decent meal. They tried their hardest to persuade the locals that the Red Army was dedicated to working for the good of the people, in the hope that they would sell some of their food. Ha! Even on New Year's Day, we didn't get to eat our beloved *lazijiding*. All we each got was half a bowl of thin congee to drink, as we huddled round braziers eating roast sweet potatoes.

The Military Commission said in a briefing that "the current situation will unfold into victory in battle", and we really needed a victory. We lost the Battle of Tucheng, which was the first engagement with Mao in command after he regained military power. We lost and, as a consequence, we had had to come all the way west to arrive here. Where should the Red Army go next? The officers and men were all confused and at a loss.

The Red Army headquarters was located in the main hall of the Jiangxi Temple, which was an old-style, old-world temple building. Apparently, it did have some connection with Jiangxi! I heard Commander-in-Chief Zhu say to a soldier from Jiangxi, "After months of fighting, we may not have ended up in Sichuan, but we have ended up in your home province of Jiangxi!"

How could we not feel homesick, so far away from the Central Soviet Area in Jiangxi? How far were we going? Bureau Chief Zeng returned from Jiming Sansheng on horseback. The name means "the cock crow is heard in three provinces" and it is a small mountain village on the border of Yunnan, Sichuan and Guizhou, where a rooster crowing can indeed be heard in all three provinces. There were not many families in the village, which was where Mao Zedong was staying. Chief Zeng said that the Politburo had held a few more meetings and adopted the resolutions of the Zunyi Conference, and the Standing Committee had a new division of labour, with Luo Fu replacing Bo Gu and taking overall responsibility for the Central Committee.

This was of course a major change in personnel and, on this far-flung frontier, we didn't have to use our imagination to picture what form this transfer of power would take; it was all down to Bo Gu's big tin box file. From now on, it would be following behind Luo Fu, and inside it was the great seal of the Party Central Committee.

According to the new division of labour among the Politburo Standing Committee members, Mao became Zhou's assistant in matters relating to military command. We were now in Long Yun's territory, and we had followed Mao's orders to locate and intercept Long Yun's radio station. We also cracked the secret telegram sent by the commander of the Dian Army to Long Yun, to the effect that because the Red Army had entered Yunnan, but Xue Yue's troops still showed no signs of leaving Guizhou, Wang Jialie was complaining that the Central Army treated the people of Guizhou even worse than the imperialists had. He said that Guizhou folk were suffering the "profound grief of losing their province".

We were excited to decipher the coded messages of the Dian Army, and we laughed at Wang Jialie's grievances. As a result, we also gained some understanding of the strength of the Dian Army.

To be honest, we were really surprised. The Dian Army had not yet fought against the Red Army, but they were equipped with new weapons, all purchased from France, the Czech Republic and Belgium. Not only could the Qian Army not compare to this, even the troops under Chiang Kai-shek's direct command were not that well equipped.

If we want to settle on the border of Yunnan, Sichuan and Guizhou, we first need a big victory. We must fight: fight pain, fight fear of the enemy, and fight until the "pursuit and encirclement" enemy forces are temporarily withdrawn. Only then can we divide up our troops to mobilise the masses and create a new Soviet Area. The nature of the march will also change. We must actively seek battle, not just retreat and move on. We need to mount a counter-offensive. This must be fought with care; the first battle must be won and victory must be secured. This can only be achieved by choosing the right target and the right timing to engage the enemy.

To achieve this, we at the 2nd Bureau have had to keep our ears to the ground, with each radio set tracking one or two enemy armies and listening in every hour to keep tabs on the enemy's every move. At the same time, we are also focusing on detecting Chiang Kai-shek's overall deployment to ensure that the leadership of the Military Commission can seize on the one-in-a-hundred mistake that will give them their opening.

Of course, the Dian Army did not want us to hang around for long and intended to drive the Red Army out of Yunnan as quickly as possible. Chiang Kai-shek ordered Long Yun to marshal the Dian Army at Bijie to link up with the Chuan Army's defences. Now that he had been appointed commander-in-chief of the 2nd Route Army, Long Yun had become even more energetic. He said in a telegram that "the bandits are in tatters and in the killing ground", and that "they have been on the move day and night, not even able to catch their breath. Even if they are made of iron, they can't keep this up", and "their total annihilation is only a matter of time".

Under Long Yun's general command, Sun Du's column was advancing towards Zhaxi, but more in the general direction of Dawanzhen to the south of Zhaxi.

Mao and Zhou therefore planned to make Sun Du's column their main target for the first battle. The 1st and 3rd Red Army Corps would advance southward to Zhenxiong, and when Sun Du's vanguard troops penetrated Dawanzhen, they would hit them hard. However, on 7 February, the 2nd Bureau intercepted the "Operation Strategy" which Long Yun had announced that day, and we submitted a comprehensive report on the enemy deployment to the Military Commission:

> "At present, the Chuan Army is attacking southwest from Changning and Gongxian with its main force and is holding the two banks of the Jinsha River. They have ordered three of its brigades to deploy towards the Yunnan side, on the line from Daba to Lianghekou, and that one section of them be used to pursue and attack. The three brigades of the Dian Army will concentrate on the line from Dawanzhen to Zhenxiong and press us hard. The main force of Xue's troops and the Qian Army remain in the southeastern section of the Chishui River."

In the light of this intelligence on the enemy, if the original plan to fight them when they had entered Dawanzhen were to be followed, we might be caught in a north-south pincer attack by the Chuan and Dian Armies. It would be a difficult victory to win and could end in stalemate. Accordingly, the field army headquarters summed up the situation: "The Chuan pursuit forces are almost all heading west; the Dian Army is blocking our entry into Yunnan; the Qian Army has not yet joined in the 'pursuit and encirclement'; and Xue's forces are not hastening in their pursuit of us."

Our target was the Qian Army and Xue Yue's forces. Mao and Zhou decided to cross the Chishui River to the east and then seek opportunities for further development in northern Guizhou. On 11 February, the Military Committee of the Central Revolutionary Army issued an order:

> "To prepare for the battle with Wang Jialie and Zhou Hunyuan's division of the Qian Army, and to develop our position towards the east bank of the Chishui River, our Field Army will now advance towards Gulin and the territory to its south and seize the first opportunity to cross the river."

Two days later, the 2nd Bureau intercepted a telegram from Chiang Kai-shek to Xue Yue, the former enemy commander-in-chief of the 2nd Route Army, ordering that "the 2nd Route Army must work with the Chuan Army to annihilate the bandits fleeing westward in the area south of the Yangtze River and east of the Heng River and Junlian".

All eight divisions of Xue Yue's Central Army were resting and reorganising in the area of Guiyang. This order revealed Chiang Kai-shek's general approach to the campaign and coincided with Long Yun's Operational Strategy. However, the coded telegram also gave up an important piece of information: Wang Jialie's forces in northern Guizhou comprised only a single division, and this was the weakest point in the Kuomintang's defences.

Chiang Kai-shek had finally revealed a weak point. Mao and Zhou seized the opportunity. They swung their troops eastward with murderous intent to attack Wang Jialie's lone army in northern Guizhou.

At 2000 on 15 February, the Military Committee of the Central Revolutionary Army ordered,

> "Our Field Army has the main operational objective of crossing the Chishui River to the east in order to destroy the Qian enemy's army of Wang Jialie. It is ordered to cross the Chishui River from Lintan through the sector from Taipingdu to Shunjiangchang, and then split up and advance towards the area of Tongzi. They should be ready to eliminate the Qian forces as they arrive from Tongzi, or to attack and destroy them by going directly to Tongzi."

Going back into northern Guizhou would be to adopt Sunzi's strategy in *Art of War* of "avoiding the enemy's strength and targeting their weakness". It would involve the Red Army having to turn around and retrace its tracks. The sky was gloomy, reflecting the depressed mood of the commanders. Some of the men complained that although it was no big deal walking eighty or a hundred *li* a day, going round in circles was unbearable! First east then west, we are like the shuttle on a loom! Where the hell are we going anyway? Even if my legs will keep moving, why should I listen to any more orders I don't understand? At least if we keep going north, we'll end up fighting the Japanese!

The troops needed a clearer idea of what they were doing as they marched on eastwards through the drizzle. However, specific tactical motives cannot be stated explicitly because they are military secrets. They cannot be voiced openly, let alone communicated or given as reasons for mobilisation. Ever since they first evacuated the Central Soviet Area, the cadres and soldiers kept asking where they were heading. The corps commanders could only say in general terms that it was a strategic transfer and that they would reach their destination after crossing a few mountains, but later they did have to say explicitly that it was a rendezvous with the 2nd and 6th Corps. When that rendezvous was abandoned, they were avoiding the enemy's encirclement, but when they turned west, they were still repeatedly besieged along the way, weren't they? The original orders said to go to the west of Hunan, then changed to go to northern Guizhou. Then they said abandon northern Guizhou and head for southern Sichuan. When the northern crossing failed, the orders changed again to go to the Sichuan-Yunnan border to create a new Soviet Area there. Then, out of the blue, the orders were to turn back to Guizhou...

For the time being, our 2nd Bureau personnel could only remain tight-lipped about the most recent enemy deployments. As for why we had been "going round in circles", all the Central Military Committee could say was that it was a matter of strategic aims. On 16 February, the Central Committee of the Communist Party of China and the Central Revolutionary Military Committee issued their "Report to All Red Commanders", stating: "We must seek favourable opportunities and regions to destroy the enemy, and under unfavourable conditions, we should avoid the kind of risky engagement where we are unsure of victory. The Red Army must therefore frequently shift its area of operations, sometimes to the east, sometimes to the west, sometimes by big roads, sometimes by small roads, sometimes by old roads, sometimes by new roads, with the sole aim of seeking victory in battle under favourable conditions."

On 18 and 19 February, the Central Red Army crossed the

Chishui River eastward from the crossing points of Taipingdu and Erlangtan.

On the 19th, Chiang Kai-shek telegraphed Xue Yue, stating, "Our army aims to round up and destroy the bandits south of Xuyong and Gulin, west of the Chishui River, and north of Renhuai and Bijie. We intend to bring together all our armies to encircle the bandits."

The Red Army had already crossed the river to the east, but Chiang Kai-shek was still intending to wipe it out west of the river. They were having great difficulty deciphering the Red Army's coded communications, but we could detect their movements at any time we pleased. The Red Army's movements were erratic, and Chiang Kai-shek sent frequent telegrams with orders to move first east then west. Both the forces under his direct command and the local armies were constantly changing their codes, and our 2nd Bureau's decoding section was at full stretch keeping up with them. In the first half of the month, over four days, we were able to break six new codes one after the other! It was entirely because of our accurate and timely reports on the enemy's movements that the decisions of the Military Committee changed almost daily over the ten days following the crossing of the Chishui River.

Mao Zedong's observation about all this was that, given our current strength, we could not seriously engage the enemy. To do so would be like a beggar competing for treasure with a dragon king. For the time being, we can only dodge when we see the need to dodge and hide when we need to hide. When the time is right, we will give the enemy a good battering.

When the enemy changes, we change. The Military Commission can only make decisions based on intelligence, but this is not something that can be explained to the troops, and all they are expected to do is to obey orders. Only we can see the real result, which is that we are keeping one step ahead of the enemy.

We could see where the enemy was whenever we wanted. From Chiang Kai-shek's operational plans down to the specific deployment and movements of the various "pursuit and annihilation armies", we were able to detect them all as promptly as necessary. The enemy, however, did not know where we were. The Kuomintang's reconnaissance relied mainly on aircraft, supplemented by field reports. Aerial reconnaissance relied on visual inspection, and the rain and fog of spring in Guizhou meant the opportunities for aircraft to take off were few and far between. Not to mention the fact that the region was heavily wooded, and the Red Army operated mostly in mountainous areas, so as soon as we heard the sound of aircraft, we took cover in the forests and underbrush. Furthermore, we usually marched at night, and even if we were on the move during the day, we would deliberately set out to confuse the enemy. When their planes were approaching, we pretended that we were too late to hide and purposely moved in the opposite direction to the one we were actually heading. We even deliberately exposed the pontoon bridges erected over rivers. The result was that the reconnaissance aircraft would either not find the Red Army at all or get a false picture of the situation. As for the so-called "on the spot" reports, even fewer of these were of any use, and by the time Chiang's troops arrived, the Red Army was long gone. These so-called surveys were neither timely nor comprehensive, were often just hearsay and almost always turned out to be misleading.

It would have been better for Chiang Kai-shek never to have sent that telegram on 19 February, as it not only revealed his ignorance of the Red Army's whereabouts, but, at the same time, revealed to us an important piece of information that confirmed our previous judgement that Wang Jialie's was the only enemy strength in northern Guizhou.

This telegram reinforced Mao and Zhou's determination to engage with Wang Jialie!

We quickly moved east and recrossed the Chishui River. On 16 February, Liu Xiang sent a telegram to Xue Yue:

> "The bandits fleeing southward are under pressure from our Dian troops and appear to be returning to Xuyong and Gulin. This telegram is to request Commander-in-Chief Xue to order the troops in Gulin to attack."

Xue Yue sent back:

"The positions near Gulin are fully equipped, and once the enemy arrive, our combined efforts will ensure victory."

Liu Xiang's telegram was already too late, and it was even more ridiculous for Xue Yue to sit back on his heels and wait because the Red Army had already sneaked past him to the south of Gulin. The Red Army knew how to be stealthy but also how to be quick, and its soldiers were very fast indeed.

It was only the Chuan Army, which was closest to the Red Army, that noticed the discrepancy in what was occurring. The Red Army left Zhaxi moving rapidly eastwards, while, on the other side of the mountain, the enemy was still advancing rapidly from all directions towards Zhaxi.

We were passing through the only gap in the enemy's encirclement.

2nd Bureau Confidential Information: Xue Yue has been appointed director of pacification in Guizhou.

"Let's see how Wang Jialie feels about that!"

Chiang Kai-shek must have been greatly surprised when the Red Army suddenly swung its advance eastwards. On 23 February, the 2nd Bureau reported that Chiang had ordered the troops in northern Guizhou to block the Reds' eastward advance, and that a part of the Qian Army had left Loushanguan with six regiments and advanced to Zunyi.

Xue Yue was more aware than Chiang Kai-shek that the troops in northern Guizhou were hardly a match for the Red Army. He ordered Zhou Hunyuan's column of three divisions to cross through Chishui towards Tucheng and the other regions to follow up on the pursuit and annihilation. Wu Qiwei's column of two divisions was ordered to cross the Wu River to reinforce Zunyi.

Only a few of Wang Jialie's troops were left in Zunyi to guard the city. The Central Revolutionary Committee, taking advantage of the fact that most of the pursuing troops had not yet arrived, decided to quickly take Loushanguan and then Zunyi.

That night, our Red Army launched an attack on Tongzi County.

The part of the Qian Army that had entered Tongzi was very aware of its own limitations. On hearing that the Red Army was coming to kill them, they were afraid of being annihilated and abandoned the city to retreat to Loushanguan. Tongzi, a major town in northern Guizhou, became deserted and the Red Army Corps made all haste south towards it.

At midnight, both sides issued battle orders almost simultaneously. Zhu De ordered the 1st and 3rd Red Army Corps to attack to the south, while Xue Yue ordered Zhou Hunyuan and Wu Qiwei's two columns to advance and annihilate to the north.

On the following day, the two armies marched to meet each other. Both sides were on the move as ordered, but the steep hills and winding roads of this part of Guizhou meant that even if they were across the river from each other, it would take more than a day's effort to detour across a bridge to pursue the enemy on the other side. Their encounter was going to take place at Loushanguan.

The Dalou mountain range, north of Zunyi, runs east to west for many dozens of *li* with towering peaks. The winding road up the mountain between Zunyi and Tongzi forms a line running through its highest peaks. The narrow pass it follows is Loushanguan, the Loushan Pass. It is a dangerous place, easy to defend and difficult to attack, and is a key stronghold that military strategists have fought over for many centuries.

The 3rd Red Army Corps took prisoners from the Qian Army on its march and thus learned that the enemy at Loushanguan only consisted of Bai Huizhang's three regiments. It was a tempting but unattainable target, as the encircling enemy forces were bound to arrive sooner rather than later. We also intercepted a telephone call which told us that Du Zhaohua's brigade was at the Black God Temple, five miles south of Loushanguan. We must fight, but how? The enemy's deployment around the area was key, as our success or failure depended on it. Our strength was limited, and we could not afford to squander our capital on this one battle. Just how trustworthy were prisoners' confessions and intercepted communications?

The leadership of the Military Commission were undecided when, at that moment, the 2nd Bureau sent them the latest deciphered intelligence on the enemy deployment: "Bai's and Du's two divisions which are guarding Loushanguan and the Black God Temple are probably the six regiments comprising the 1st, 4th, 8th, 15th and 16th Corps of the Qian Army or maybe only three corps in one division. They can block our passage south with the possibility of an opportunist sortie from Loushanguan and take shelter in Zunyi to wait for Xue's troops to reinforce them."

The Military Commission then issued an order: "Our Field Army will use one division to block the pursuit of enemy forces in Sichuan, while the main force will resolutely destroy the Qian Army forces at Loushanguan. They will then take advantage of their victory to seize Zunyi City in order to take the fighting to the enemy."

Commander-in-Chief Zhu ordered that the 1st and 3rd Red Army Corps and the Cadre Corps should be commanded by Peng and Yang.

Addendum: after this great victory, Mao Zedong wrote the emotional poem Remembering Qin E – Loushan Pass. Peng Dehuai joked that, without the information from the 2nd Bureau, he would have forgotten that legendary daughter of the Duke of Min, Qin E!

At dawn on 25 February, the 3rd Red Army Corps launched the battle to seize the pass. Commander Peng ordered the vanguard of the 13th Red Regiment to seize their main position at Loushan Pass and make sure it was taken before nightfall the following day. To ensure victory in the battle, the whole 3rd Red Army took the battlefield without leaving any troops in reserve. If we didn't take Loushanguan, our centre would be in danger of being surrounded. Bugles were blaring, guns were firing, war cries were being yelled, the hills were resounding with noise, and the valleys responded. The Red Army officers and men were fighting to the death! Bullets flew, bayonets bent, sabres carved out openings as the three corps took the high ground of Loushanguan in one fell swoop, defeating the six regiments of the Qian Army. By the afternoon of 26 February, before nightfall, the heroic 1st and 3rd Red Army Corps had successfully captured the pass. The Qian Army fled in the direction of Banqiao.

The 2nd Bureau reported the enemy situation: the nine defeated regiments of the Qian Army that had retreated in defeat from their stations at Loushanguan, Banqiao and Siduzhan had already reached Zunyi. Chiang Kai-shek and Xue Yue gave strict orders that both the old and new cities of Zunyi must be held at all costs, and Zhou Hunyuan and Wu Qiwei were further ordered to lead three divisions of the Central Army to reinforce Zunyi.

Based on the position of the two divisions of Wu Qiwei's advance provided by the 2nd Bureau, the Military Committee judged that the enemy would have difficulty in reaching Zunyi that day. At 0000 hours, they issued an order to pursue the routed enemy in the direction of Loushanguan.

It is second nature to the Red Army to mount a fierce pursuit of a defeated enemy. If you don't win the battle, nothing more can be done, but if you are victorious, you must be fierce in your pursuit. Attack fiercely, charge fiercely and chase fiercely: these are the Three Fierce Styles of the Red Army. On 27 February, the 1st and 3rd Corps attacked Zunyi with great force, and Wang Jialie abandoned the city with the remnants of his troops.

So, we occupied this great city again. Less than a month had passed, and there were mixed feelings about it. Naturally, celebration feasts were held, with meat and large bowls of wine, but when the toasts were being drunk, some people burst into tears, remembering their comrades who had sacrificed their lives, while they survived. In pursuit of this victory, Deng Ping, chief of staff of the 3rd Red Army Corps, had advanced with the vanguard. He was shot and killed by the Qian Army in the north of the city.

When Chief of Staff Deng was buried, Section Chief Cao, who had originally come to the 2nd Bureau from the 3rd Red Army Corps, went to pay his last respects. Chief Deng had been very upset when Peng gave Cao Daye to us. They had known each other since the days of the 5th Red Army, when Deng Ping and Peng Dehuai led the Pingjiang Uprising in 1928, and the uprising forces were reorganised into the 5th Red Army, with Peng as commander and Deng as chief of staff. They were comrades in arms through countless bloody battles. Section Chief Cao came back and told us that when Commander Peng saw Deng Ping's body, he wept hot tears of grief. Deng Ping was only twenty-seven years old. Peng washed his face and put him into a new uniform. That night, Commander Peng issued the order to attack: "Take Zunyi City and avenge the chief of staff!" We did indeed recapture the city. Peng bought a coffin and buried Chief of Staff Deng outside the city under a cherry apple tree.

This time, the sadness around the capture of Zunyi diluted the joy of victory. Our fond memories of the bustling markets, the enthusiastic crowds, the bright red oranges, the soft, sweet cakes, all seemed such a long time ago when we were trying to create a new Soviet Area. Now the people had been betrayed by the warlords, most of the citizens had fled and the markets were run down and depressed. When we evacuated the city last month, Bai Huizhang chased us out with his troops and then turned back for three days of slaughter outside the walls before entering the city. At Tuanxi, he killed more than seventy people in two days. Once back in the Bai Mansion, he ordered the killing of more than a hundred in one day. The local landed gentry regrouped and organised militia groups to support him. The sick and wounded of the Red Army we had left behind, the heads of the Party organisations who had stayed to fight and the poor people who had offered shelter to our soldiers, all died under their butchers' knives. A peasant family of six was killed, and even their two-year-old child was not spared. Some members of peasant associations were sliced open and disembowelled. Such was their crazed revenge! They blockaded roads and mountains, hunted our people down and slaughtered them with broadswords. The Kuomintang district chief personally hacked to death more than twenty wounded Red Army soldiers, and finally said to a young soldier, only fourteen or fifteen years old, that he could live if he was willing to commit to working for him for the rest of his life. The youth replied, "I'd rather die than work for you!" He was slaughtered and left lying in the gutter. Some of the Red Army wounded still threw themselves at the enemy even though their heads had been slashed open; they went into battle with the tyrant landlords, clutching their bleeding scalps. One wounded soldier of the 3rd Red Army Corps who was found in the search had his legs broken but proclaimed he would rather die than kneel to his captors. He was cut down on the spot and, as he fell into the mud, his eyes looked in the direction of the departing Red Army.

As Mao wrote in his poem *Remembering Qin E*, "The west wind is fierce, the arching sky is full of geese calling to the frosty morning moon. The sound of horses' hooves clattering, the sound of trumpets sobbing... The mountains are like a sea, the sun is like blood." We are here again, and we can still smell a faint scent on the mountain breeze. It is the smell of blood from that massacre.

Vengeance for the death of our comrades! A fury burned in everyone's heart. When the Battle of Loushanguan and Zunyi began, Chief Zeng ordered the 2nd Bureau to keep an eye on the enemy troops that might reinforce the Qian Army: Guo Xunqi's column of the Chuan Army, which was chasing us across the Chishui River towards the northern front; Zhou Hunyuan's column of the Central Army, which was set to enter Renhuai; and Wu Qiwei's column of the 59th and 93rd Divisions, which had crossed the Wujiang River into Zunyi on the southern front.

On 28 February, the 59th and 93rd divisions of Wu Qiwei's column advanced to the south of Zunyi and repeatedly fought with our Red Army Corps for Laoya Mountain south of the city. The 2nd Bureau detected that the command post of Wu Qiwei's column was located in Zhongzhuangpu, south of Zunyi. The leaders of the Military Commission judged that Guo Xunqi's column was currently engaged in retaking Tongzi and could not immediately go south to reinforce. It also believed that Zhou Hunyuan's column, even if it did move east to engage in the battle for Zunyi, would not arrive for several days; and our 5th and 9th Red Army Corps could monitor both of these two enemy fronts. Our 1st Red Army Corps had a full day's rest and the 3rd Red Army Corps had taken the old city of Zunyi. The remains of Wang Jialie's troops were now like birds startled by the mere twang of a bowstring, and Wu Qiwei's column was isolated deep in our territory. On this basis, the Military Commission decided to use the 3rd Corps to engage with the enemy's 59th Division in a counterattack on Zunyi Old Town, and the 1st Red Army Corps to attack the enemy's 93rd Division and Wu Qiwei's general headquarters in Zhongzhuangpu.

The battle was fought that very day. This was the end of the overall Battle of Loushanguan and Zunyi, and an engagement of supreme importance. Chief Zeng ordered the reconnaissance station to keep a close eye on the reactions of Wu Qiwei and Xue Yue. In the evening, Wu Qiwei did ask Xue Yue for help. At midnight, Xue Yue sent back a telegram advising that they could disengage from the battle and cross the river at Dadukou. Chief Zeng reported all this to Mao, Zhou and Zhu. Zhou ordered the 3rd Red Army Corps to pursue the remnants of Wang Jialie's forces westwards as they fled to Yaxi and the 1st Red Army Corps to make all haste to pursue Wu Qiwei's regiment. "Pay great attention to surrounding them from both sides," he said. "Force them to the Wu River and destroy them to achieve complete victory."

1 March. The 3rd Red Army Corps carried the chase to Yaxi, and Wang Jialie led his survivors in flight to Daguxinchang. The 1st Red Army Corps pushed their lightning pursuit to the Wu River ferry crossing, with the commander and political commissar of the 2nd Division leading the way, and nearly 2,000 Kuomintang officers and soldiers were captured. Before that, Wu Qiwei refused to cross the river and sat on the ground weeping loudly. His bodyguards dragged him across the river, and he immediately ordered the pontoon bridge to be cut loose. The officers and soldiers on the bridge tumbled into the river, and those who did not manage to cross were taken prisoner.

"If a squad retreats together, only the squad leader is to be executed; if a platoon retreats together, only the platoon leader is to be executed; if a company retreats together, only the company commander is to be executed; if a battalion retreats together, only the battalion commander is to be executed; if a regiment retreats together, only the regimental commander is to be executed; if a division retreats together, only the divisional commander is to be executed; if an army retreats together, only the commander-in-chief is to be executed; if the commander-in-chief does not retreat when the whole army retreats, but the commander-in-chief is killed in action, his divisional commander is to be executed."

Chiang Kai-shek personally formulated the "Revolutionary Law of Associative Punishment" when he was at the Huangpu Military Academy, and it is a tradition that the Kuomintang Army continues to this day. But the defeated commanders had their own protectors: Wu Qiwei had Xue Yue, Xue Yue had Chen Cheng and Chen Cheng had Old Chiang himself. There are no jokes in the military, but for its senior officers, the so-called "being dealt with according to military law" and the "taking responsibility with your life" are so often just empty and insincere sentiments...

Just imagine, at that moment the Generalissimo must have been incandescent with rage in his field headquarters in that mountain city. "Go to hell, the lot of you!" What a war room it must have been! A war room with a flag showing the white sun in the blue sky on the wall, maybe also a portrait of the late, former president of the Republic and maybe the four big characters 礼义廉耻, meaning "righteousness and integrity". It would be an orderly, well-regulated war room, not like ours with the generals and senior officers clustered round the commander. Instead, the Generalissimo would be standing at one end of a long table, with the senior officers seated along either side in order of rank. They would be dressed in neat military uniforms with their badges all polished and shiny. They would be wearing clean white gloves. Their "New Life Movement" was already well established and accordingly they had to dress quickly, stand up straight, keep quiet when eating, limit their meals to four dishes and one soup, and refrain from spitting wherever they pleased. "To revive the nation, we must start by washing our faces with cold water." At that moment, they would be looking straight at the map, at the wandering lines and arrows on it that represented how they were following us...

A great victory in the Battle of Loushanguan and Zunyi! The first great victory of our westward march! Our two main forces automatically worked together in this battle, with Peng Dehuai (Uprooting the Mountain)[1] capturing Loushanguan and Lin Biao[2] (Three Tigers Roaring in the Mountain Forest) raiding Zhongzhuangpu. In five days, they defeated and annihilated eight regiments of Wang Jialie's Qian Army and two divisions of Wu Qiwei's Central Army, killing more than two thousand enemies, taking more than three thousand prisoners, capturing a large number of guns and supplies, especially ammunition and salt, and replenishing the Red Army's strength as never before. The soldiers said it was more satisfying to fight the Central Army because Chiang Kai-shek supplied it with such good guns!

The results of the battle greatly exceeded expectations. The original aim was just the elimination of two brigades of the Qian Army, but in the end two divisions of the Central Army were pursued and annihilated as well. This victory was the first step in a response to Chiang Kai-shek's fifth encirclement and suppression campaign and pursuit plans. Now, we had to work harder and more circumspectly to build on this victory to create a new Soviet Area in Yunnan, Guizhou and Sichuan.

The 2nd Bureau intercepted Xue Yue's coded telegram to Chiang. To hide the truth of his defeat, Xue Yue deliberately understated the number of casualties in the Central Army, and to protect the position of his direct subordinate Wu Qiwei, he specifically put the blame on Wang Jialie. Xue asked Chiang to punish him.

The Red Army was capable of winning again. Since the failure of the fifth anti-encirclement and annihilation campaign, the Red Army had been beaten everywhere it went, but now the proper command of the Central Committee and the Military Commission was back in place. Morale was high and people were happy. On 4 March, the latest issue of *Red Star* published an editorial, stating, "Prepare to continue fighting to eliminate the Zhou Column and Sichuan warlords." The editorial pointed out, "This victory was achieved after the enlarged meeting of the Politburo of the Party Central Committee opposed Comrade Hua Fu's purely defensive line and adopted correct military leadership. Under the correct military leadership of the Party Central Committee and the Central Military Commission, we developed our strengths in mobile warfare and defeated more than twenty enemy regiments in six days. This shows that with the right military leadership, we can defeat and destroy any enemy as long as we are not afraid of fatigue and fight bravely."

After being relieved of his supreme military command, Li De stopped writing about war and the revolution under the pseudonym "Hua Fu". Since then, he has been sent down to the 1st Red Army Corps to "experience life" with an active army unit. It is said that his haughty demeanour has disappeared and that he still has a mischievous and innocent smile when his comrades occasionally joke with him. Wu Xiuquan continues to act as translator for him, and the Military Commission has sent a small team as bodyguards. Li De is tall and rides a big white horse, which makes him an easy target for air strikes, so he is particularly afraid of aircraft. On the other hand, those of our soldiers with experience in ground-to-air shooting get very excited when they see enemy planes approaching. While some of the troops drop to the ground and take cover at the sound of the sirens, they calmly fire into the air with whatever rifle or machine gun they have in their hands. They want to stop the planes "laying eggs" (dropping bombs) and are hoping to "have flying chicken for dinner" (shoot down an aircraft).

Mao and Zhou were also looking for an offensive opportunity, but the right one was hard to find. They were keen to win some more battles to force the enemy to suspend their "pursuit", thereby facilitating the creation of new Soviet Areas. On 1 March, Xue Yue sent a telegram to Chiang Kai-shek, saying, "I am waiting to be disciplined, and I ask for my punishment so that I may expiate my transgressions." Chiang Kai-shek denounced the incompetence of his subordinate, saying that the defeat at Zunyi was "the greatest disgrace since the start of the National Army's pursuit of the Red Army". The following day, he flew to Chongqing with his wife Song Mei-ling, Chen Cheng and a number of his aides and other staff to chair a meeting of the General Staff Committee of the National Government Military Commission. His aim was to plan a new round of encirclements and draw Zhu and Mao into a decisive battle.

Chiang Kai-shek's plan was detected by our 2nd Bureau. His initial judgement was that the Red Army had to head eastwards, cross the Wu River and enter Xiangxi to join up with He Long's and Xiao Ke's Red Armies. From 2-4 March, Chiang sent several coded telegrams: he ordered Zhou Hunyun's column of the Central Army to march along the south bank of the Wu River and cross to the north bank when the opportunity presented itself in order to "prevent Zhu and Mao from joining forces with He and Xiao". Liu Jianxu's Corps within He Jian's Xiang Army was ordered to march westwards and "take up positions along the east bank of the Wu River". Guo Xunqi's column of the Chuan Army was ordered to attack the Red Army in Zunyi, while Wu Qiwei's column was ordered to provide coordinated support on the south bank of the Wu River.

The Wu River was blockaded. At 2300 hours on the evening of 5

March, the forward headquarters of the Military Commission at Yaxi ordered the Red Army to ambush Zhou Hunyuan's men, while at the same time, Chiang Kai-shek sent a special secret message from Chongqing to Xue Yue and Zhou Hunyuan.

"Urgent message to Chief Xue and Commander-in-Chief Zhou to be sent using individual special codes:

> According to the afternoon aerial reconnaissance report, the bandits have more than 10,000 troops moving southwest towards Yaxi, and observation suggests only two possible reasons: a) they will abandon Zunyi and continue their flight westwards to achieve their original purpose; b) they will first seek a confrontation with our Zhou column and then press on southwest to Guizhou. At this time, our army should respond as follows:
>
> Wu's column will remain on the south bank of the Wu River tomorrow, concealing their activity for the time being, and once the bandits' movements become apparent.
>
> Zhou's column will assemble in the vicinity of Changganshan, throw up strong fortifications and, for the time being, enact an aggressive defence.
>
> It is reported that the codebook of Han's division has not been lost. Everyone take note."

Chiang specified that this telegram should be sent using individual special codebooks. These were his special instructions to Xue Yue and Zhou Hunyuan of the Central Army to adopt temporary defensive positions.

There was a suggestion of deliberate avoidance of engagement with the enemy in this, and it was essential that the local troops did not get wind of it. At the end of the report, it said that "Han's division codebook was not lost", referring to Han Hanying's 59th Division of Wu Qiwei's regiment. In the Battle of Zunyi, the ten regiments of our three army corps suffered heavy casualties. Honghua Ridge is the protective barrier for the old city of Zunyi, as it commands every direction. The main peak, Laoyashan, was captured by the enemy's 59th Division and it was fortunate that, at this critical moment, Lin Biao's 1st Corps mounted a surprise attack on the enemy's headquarters in Zhongzhuangpu, and Wu's Column fled in panic!

The story is that the 1st Corps was hiding in the hills to the east of the city, ready to attack. Lin Biao was secretly watching the battle through his binoculars in the woods on a small hill. When Wu Qiwei's forces were all getting close to Laoyashan, where the 3rd Corps was located, Lin waited until most of the enemy troops had entered the mountain valley at the foot of Honghua Ridge and then ordered his bugler to sound the charge. The 1st and 2nd Divisions charged down the mountain like tigers, and Wu Qiwei's army turned round and fled.

Lin Biao tore a piece of paper in half, marked the direction of the pursuit in red and blue pencil, and wrote the word "chase". The 1st and 2nd Divisions had received orders to give chase immediately and energetically! It was said that "three tigers" were involved: the 1st and 2nd Divisions were two of them and they gobbled up two divisions of Wu's column; the third tiger mounted a direct attack on Wu's command post. When Han's division saw from their position on the mountain that their commander was trying to slip away unnoticed, they realised what an unfavourable position they were in, abandoned any intention of holding the main peak and were immediately driven down from the mountain by our 3rd Corps and the Cadres Company. This was a battle that the enemy had already won, but then that victory was suddenly and unexpectedly turned into defeat. Chiang said that although Han's division had been routed by the Red Army, the radio codebook had not been lost. Needless to say, this was another of the "special codebooks".

"Broken! 'Special code', my arse! To Hell with Baldy Chiang!" Section Chief Cao and the others were very excited to break this code. Although Baldy Chiang was scrupulous about protecting his secret codes, what he didn't know was that we weren't entirely reliant on his "general" codebook. He sent this telegram using a "special" code, and we broke that too! To celebrate this victory, we asked the cooks for some better food. The head cook ran over to the 4th Bureau and asked Chief Song Yuhe for some century eggs, and we were just about to try them when we realised something was wrong.

What we realised was that this coded telegram of Chiang's countermanded the orders he sent in his telegram of 3 March. In that first coded telegram, he ordered the Zhou and Wu Columns of the Central Army to step up their attack, but this new telegram ordered them to stay on the south bank of the Wu River and "temporarily enact an aggressive defence". We immediately reported to the head of the Military Commission and highlighted this change.

On the morning of 6 March, when the main force of the Red Army arrived at the intended battlefield, Zhou Hunyuan's men were nowhere to be seen, and on the following day, our field army headquarters briefed the various corps on the recent enemy deployment, copying the same message as detailed above, but replacing the words "temporarily enact an aggressive defence" with "temporarily enact a fully defensive defence". The enemy was making a show of "attacking", but in reality, they were "defending". The change in wording was a definite recognition from our Central Military Commission of the current state of the enemy forces. They were all, in fact, passively avoiding engagement. On the basis of the coded telegrams intercepted by the 2nd Bureau, it was universally judged that although Wu Qiwei, a general under Chiang Kai-shek's direct command, had started his encirclement and suppression of the Red Army in Jiangxi, and had been in relentless pursuit all the way over mountains and rivers, once he had almost been captured at the Battle of Zunyi, he no longer dared engage with the Red Army.

Zhou Hunyuan also knew that the Red Army was looking for an opportunity to fight him, but the knowledge of Wu Qiwei's disastrous defeat made him wary of doing so. He ordered his troops to adopt a "leap-frog" tactic with units alternately digging in and advancing so they could always provide covering fire and not be broken up by Red Army attacks. Xue Yue particularly warned Zhou Hunyuan to learn the lesson from Wu Qiwei and not to go into combat with the Qian Army assigned to his command so as to prevent being dragged down with it when it was assaulted by the Red Army.

The task of the Chuan Army's Pan Wenhua Corps was to block the Red Army's crossing of the Yangtze in the south, and as long as the Red Army did not approach the river, he was not going to concern himself with it. The only reason he ordered Guo Xunqi's column to participate in the pursuit was to put on a show for Chiang. When the Dian Army's Sun Du Column set out, Long Yun specifically explained that its mission was to work with the Central Army to stop the Red Army at the Guizhou border, and, if the opportunity presented itself, it would be best of all if it could swallow up Wang Jialie's division. Wang Jialie's Qian Army had no real fighting ability and no one respected them, but that suited them nicely because it meant they never had to take on the main combat role.

Although Chiang Kai-shek had instructed all of these commanders to be proactive in seeking to engage the enemy, none of them obeyed and instead deliberately shrank from combat, leaving the Red Army unable to find any suitable opportunities to fight. The Red Army could only exploit the enemy's weaknesses if they were in motion, so they repeatedly tried to lure them out, but the enemy did not prove easy to provoke. However, Chiang Kai-shek persisted in issuing forceful orders, so the enemy commanders were obliged to start playing bureaucratic tricks by occasionally issuing orders and making offensive deployments but never carrying them through so the troops never actually moved.

It was difficult for us to determine which enemy orders would be carried out and which would be ignored. Every coded message had to be intercepted and deciphered, as this was far preferable to missing out on useful information. We had to put up with the hardship involved because, while the front-line troops were not fighting every day, we were on permanent battle duty.

Deputy Chief Zou's little black leather-bound notebook is running out of blank pages. Recently he has been writing in smaller print to save pages, and also because he has a belief that the day he uses the last page will be the day the revolution is victorious. He is convinced that this one notebook will suffice, and he does not want to start a new one. Even so, he still wrote in slightly larger characters when deciphering Chiang Kai-shek's "special codebook".

On the other side, it was clear that Chiang no longer dared take the Red Army lightly, and his tactics changed to "prolonged pursuit and steady fighting". He denounced the bad habits of the "National Army" by saying, "In peacetime, military discipline goes by the board and in times of trouble, they let golden opportunities slip through their hands." On 6 March, the 2nd Bureau intercepted a coded telegram from Chiang to Liu Xiang and Pan Wenhua of the Chuan Army:

"To Commander-in-Chief Liu and Chairman Liu in Chongqing and Commander-in-Chief Pan in Yibin, inner circle only:

> It is reported that when the former Zhu and Mao bandits fled through southern Sichuan, they did not harass or mistreat the people in any way. If they picked radishes from the fields because they were hungry, for every one they took, they would replace it in the soil with a copper coin. When they reached Xuyong, they captured four regimental commanders but executed only one for corruption and released the others to confound the expectations of the local people and gain their love. We hope that the troops and other teams under our command will strictly follow last month's orders about how to comport themselves in their participation in the war and will look after the people so that they are not exploited by the bandits.

Chiang Chung-cheng Sealed under battle orders, 0300 hours on 6 March"

Coming from him, "look after the people" sounded like a bad joke, given how strict he was with his subordinates. It might be genuine but, even so, it was not an easy thing that he was asking of his men. From ancient times, it has been those who win the hearts of the people who win the world.

Wu Qiwei's column was defeated at the Battle of Zunyi, and the Party Central Committee and the Military Committee decided to target Zhou Hunyuan's column again. To this end, Chairman Zhu De of the Central Revolutionary Military Committee and Vice Chairmen Zhou Enlai and Wang Jiaxiang signed an order on 4 March: To strengthen and unify operations, a command post for the area of enemy contact is hereby established for this campaign, to be commanded by Comrade Zhu De with Comrade Mao Zedong as its political commissar.

In his capacity as political commissar, Mao Zedong was de facto commander-in-chief of the campaign. On 8 March, the Central Column was stationed at Gouba in the Zunyi region. On the same day, the *Red Star* newspaper published a letter from the Party Central Committee to all Party comrades: "Dear comrades… the decisive battle to crush the enemy's new encirclement has begun. Our central slogan for this moment is to win a great victory to turn the whole province of Guizhou Red!"

Our army was eager to fight. The Central Red Army was resting, reorganising and waiting for an opportunity in the area of Zunyi, Yaxi and Bailakan, casting around for Zhou Hunyuan's column, while the enemy concentrated only on staying put. At 0100 on 10 March, Lin Biao and Nie Rongzhen of the 1st Red Army Corps sent a telegram to the Military Commission proposing an attack on Daguxinchang, where You Guocai's 3rd Division of the Qian Army was located.

After the establishment of the forward command, Zhu and Mao were again able to sign combat orders together, but the telegram from Lin and Nie sparked a disagreement. The forward command was set up to fight Zhou Hunyuan, but Lin and Nie wanted to fight the Qian Army. Zhu De thought this battle would open up the way to the west, while Mao disagreed, believing it to be a rash offensive.

"Daguxinchang" is a very conspicuous placename. Mao Zedong consulted the newly deciphered enemy report from the 2nd Bureau and learned that Chiang had judged that the Red Army might "flee along the line of Daguxinchang, Qianxi and Anshun" and had ordered "the Qian Army in the area of Daguxinchang to mount a tight defence, and blockade and intercept" and the Dian Army to "advance Sun's column to the line of Xinchang and Bailakan to provide coordinated support".

More coded messages from the enemy indicated that the Qian and Dian Armies had been massing at Daguxinchang, which Chiang Kai-shek valued as "a place the Communist Army must pass through to escape westwards". On 10 March, Mao suggested that Luo Fu call an extended Politburo meeting to discuss the matter, with more than twenty leaders of the Central Committee and Military Commission in attendance. All were in favour of Lin and Nie's proposal, except Mao, who opposed it. Mao's forceful objection was that the line between Daguxinchang and Qianxi was Chiang Kai-shek's chosen battlefield to realise his plan to round up the Red Army and wipe it out. Moreover, Daguxinchang was in imminent danger of being encircled by the enemy. Finally, after a democratic vote, the minority ceded to the majority and it was decided to attack Daguxinchang. Mao left the venue angrily. His position as political commissar of the forward command was revoked, and Peng Dehuai temporarily took up the post of commander-in-chief.

So, Mao Zedong lost his military command once again, and the results of the Zunyi Conference were likely to be undone. We only heard about the incident that night in Gouba Township. Chief Zeng emphasised the importance of every enemy action, and from then on, we gathered even more information. Mao Zedong returned to his residence that night, deeply worried about the future of the Red Army.

There were big risks involved in attacking Daguxinchang, and even if we squeaked a narrow victory, although we would have won a battle and gained some supplies, it would still just be a victory in one battle, whereas what we needed was victory in the whole campaign. This battle was all about escaping the enemy's encirclement.

Mao Zedong decided to seek out Zhou Enlai again to make a last stand, so he walked three or four miles up the mountain to Zhou's residence in the middle of the night, carrying a horse lantern. He asked Zhou to hold off on issuing any orders or, at least, take some time to reconsider. At that point, Zhou received an urgent report from the 2nd Bureau: the Qian Army's You Brigade had retreated to Panshui and was now advancing towards Daguxinchang; the Dian Army's Lu Brigade was reinforcing Daguxinchang from Qianxi; the Dian Army's An Brigade and Gong Brigade were also advancing on the same spot; the Chuan Army and Zhou Hunyuan's column of the Central Army were assembling. If we attacked Daguxinchang, the Dian and Chuan Armies would have the potential to outflank us.

Zhou also carefully studied the reports on recent enemy

deployments intercepted by the 2nd Bureau and, overnight, reconvened a meeting to further explain the enemy situation to everyone. It was decided to give up the attack on Daguxinchang. At 0130 hours on 11 March, Zhu De called Lin, Nie, Peng and Yang to give the order not to attack.

Twenty-four-and-a-half hours elapsed between the time of Lin and Nie's call and Zhu De's order not to fight, and Mao regaining his command. A major factor contributing to this change was the special importance Mao and Zhou attached to the 2nd Bureau's intelligence reports. After the establishment of the forward command, Mao personally headed the decoding section of the 2nd Bureau of the Military Commission, and Zhou strictly controlled the flow of the information that was deciphered.

Something to think about: the truth is often in the hands of a few. This is very true.

We were looking for the right opportunity to engage with the enemy, but their situation was always changing. Our troops were always in action, and decisions had to be made on the spot. The leaders of the Central Committee and the Military Commission were also concluding that military command cannot always be conducted on the basis of "the minority falling in with the majority", and that it cannot always be a discussion between twenty people. The Gouba fiasco was testimony to this. When conducting a battle, power has to be highly centralised. It was not unreasonable for the Team of Three of Bo Gu, Zhou Enlai and Li De to be in full command of the military initially, but, of course, they then had to take responsibility for any mistakes made while they were in charge. At the Houchang meeting, it was decided that the Military Commission must report to the Politburo, but the enlarged Politburo was not up to the task of dealing with the urgent military situation. Before crossing the Wu River, the Central Committee decided to set up a three-person military leadership group to facilitate effective decision-making. This was another Team of Three, comprising Zhou Enlai, Mao Zedong and Wang Jiaxiang.

The new Team of Three decided that the first target would still be Zhou Hunyuan's column of the Central Army. Instead of attacking Daguxinchang, the new tactic was to "surround the target and attack the reinforcements". This was because the 2nd Bureau had deciphered Xue Yue's latest order to destroy the Red Army east of the Chishui River. The Central Revolutionary Military Commission then issued an order to use the 9th Red Army Corps to block the Chuan Army and Wu Qiwei's column on the Zunyi-Tongzi line, while the Central Red Army was to use its main force to destroy the 3rd Division of the Qian Army, thereby threatening Zhou Hunyuan's column and drawing it in for a decisive battle.

Xue Yue's order was not carried out, and the victory planned by Mao and Zhou was not won. At 2000 hours on 14 March, Dong Zhentang, commander of the 5th Red Army Corps, and Political Commissar Li Zhuoran reported that Zhou Hunyuan had advanced one division south from Renhuai to Lubanchang and Sanyuandong, but they had not yet completed their fortifications. Mao and Zhou were determined to attack Lubanchang. At this moment, the 2nd Bureau detected a coded telegram from Zhou Hunyuan to Xue Yue, saying that his main force would assemble at Lubanchang the next day and would mount a joint attack on our troops when Wu Qiwei arrived.

At 2100 hours, the Central Revolutionary Military Commission issued a combat order.

Lubanchang has nothing to do with the ancient engineer Lu Ban; it is just a small market town. Surrounded by mountains on three sides, it is situated at altitude, high up in the mountains, easy to defend and difficult to attack. It is about forty miles from the town of Maotai on the upper reaches of the Chishui River. Before the battle began, Mao Zedong had sent engineers to set up two pontoon bridges at the Maotai crossing.

At 1000 hours on 15 March, the 1st and 3rd Red Army Corps attacked Lubanchang, where four of Zhou Hunyuan's regiments were stationed. The enemy's blockade line had been formed, with bunkers every fifty metres and they were holding it with strong fortifications. Their artillery fire was so heavy that it was difficult for our main attacking team to get close. The Red Army soldiers charged back and forth under a hail of bullets. After a day of bitter fighting, our troops had suffered more than 1,500 casualties and the Red Army was in a stand-off with the enemy. As the rain fell at dusk, the enemy still had the upper hand. That night, to avoid further losses and to protect our remaining forces, Peng Dehuai and

Lin Biao proposed to abandon the frontal assault. The 2nd Bureau intercepted messages indicating that enemy troops were rapidly closing in on Lubanchang with the intention of surrounding it.

The attack had been an extended affair and left the main force of the Red Army very exposed; it would only become more and more ineffective the longer the fight went on. On 16 March, the Central Committee issued the order: abandon Lubanchang and evacuate northwards immediately; all troops to be across the Chishui River by noon the following day.

The Battle of Lubanchang was lost and we were unable to fight a decisive battle with Zhou Hunyuan. If you can win a fight, then fight; if you can't win, then walk away. That was all we could do. If we don't defeat Zhou Hunyuan, our plan to turn all of Guizhou Red will be very difficult to achieve.

The secret information obtained by the 2nd Bureau showed that there was heavy encirclement in the east, north and south, and only in the west was it slightly weaker. The Military Commission then ordered another westward crossing of the Chishui River. It was difficult for the active corps commanders to question this, as a military order is as immutable as a mountain: you go where you are told to go, when you are told to go, and you follow the order in all respects. The motives behind the order could not really be explained. They were so secret they could not be laid before the commanders or used as fuel to fire up the troops. When we left Lubanchang for the westward crossing, Mao Zedong asked Liu Bocheng if the pontoon bridges he used when he crossed the Chishui River were still operational. This was the section between Erlangtan and Lintan. Liu subsequently ordered engineers to secretly repair and take charge of the two bridges.

This time, we crossed the river from the two ferry crossings in Renhuai and Maotai Township. We swaggered across the river in broad daylight. The 1st Red Army Corps training battalion took the lead, occupying Maotai on the evening of 16 March. The Military Commission ordered the troops to rest in the woods after crossing the river and stand by for orders.

After crossing the river with bugles sounding and flags waving, our troops waited under cover for their next orders, maintaining total radio silence. However, the 1st Red Army Corps dispatched a regiment with a radio set to Gulin and sent frequent signals. Chiang Kai-shek was bound to intercept those transmissions and would surely be convinced that the Red Army was going to cross the Yangtze northwards from Gulin.

Addendum: Maotai township. This small riverside town is not very large, with houses and muddy lanes crammed onto the steep banks of the river. It was the home of the warlord Hou Zhidan, who built several small Western-style villas there and also had a monopoly on salt, cloth and Maotai wine. There were many wine cellars in the town, and I even heard that the Retired Cadre Centre was quartered in a distillery that the owner and workers had left deserted. Maotai wine was confiscated from the homes of the corrupt local tyrants and landed gentry. These homes were full of vats and jars of wine, and most of the owners had fled. When the hatches of the wine cellars were opened, the smell of wine was overwhelming. The Red Army confiscated personal possessions, grain and wine from the families of the local tyrants and distributed them among the poor. The soldiers brought the Maotai wine out from the tyrants' houses and filled their own kettles. Those who liked to drink, drank to their heart's content, drinking to the victory of the great Soviet nation! Several people were unsteady on their feet after drinking half a jug of wine. Those who were not drinkers dipped their enamel mugs into the jars of wine, tasted a mouthful out of curiosity and then filled their own water bottles because the wine was also good for massaging into tired muscles and stimulating the circulation. In the field hospitals, the wine was used to clean the wounds of the casualties and to disinfect swollen feet. Another excellent use for the wine was to rub it into the hair a few times to get rid of lice. Passing by the tall, spacious villa of the old Chengyi Distillery, I heard that there were several hundred large wine vats inside, each with a capacity of twenty to thirty piculs[3] of fine wine, and the owner of this house had also fled...

The westward crossing was a feint, a probe for opportunities to engage the enemy and intended to redirect them from northwest Guizhou to southern Sichuan. The enemy troops were indeed deceived, and Chiang Kai-shek hastily ordered his divisions to launch an attack towards the south of Sichuan. First, five enemy planes arrived to harry us. One flew low near Maotai Township and was hit by an anti-aircraft company belonging to our 3rd Corps. The enemy aircraft burst into flames and crashed far to the west of the river, while the others fled. It was 18 March, the anniversary of the Paris Commune. Weather: overcast, clearing slightly.

In order to take the initiative in locating the enemy and finding suitable ground to engage them, our 2nd Bureau was doubly vigilant and made sure not to miss a single suspicious message. On 18 March, the Military Commission informed the whole army of the enemy situation: Zhou Hunyuan and Wu Qiwei's columns had all recently moved from the south bank of the Wu River to the north of Guizhou, concentrating on the narrow area west of the Sichuan-Guizhou Highway and north of the Wu River. They were constructing blockades in the areas of Tucheng, Gulin, Changganshan, Fengxiangba and Daguxinchang, and attempting to encircle and annihilate the Red Army in the area of Fengxiangba and Daguxinchang. The Chuan Army was still deployed along the line of Tongzi, Zunyi, Chishui and Hejiang. On 19 March, the 2nd Bureau broke three new enemy codes in Gulin. A number of coded telegrams bearing the signature "Zhongzheng" showed that Chiang Kai-shek was aware of the Red Army's position, but because of the Red Army's misdirection, he was unsure of their intentions. His plan was now to round up and destroy the Red Army in the region of Chishui, Xuyong, Gulin and Bijie. Chiang believed the Red Army was not strong enough to cross the river, so he telegraphed Xue Yue from Chongqing:

> "The Communist army has reached the limit of its strength and will be broken into pieces. They may wage a guerrilla campaign along the northern bank of the Wu River, the southern bank of the Yangtze River, and the eastern bank of the Heng River. There is no great risk involved in crossing the Yangtze..."

Although our army had won a great victory in Zunyi, it had also suffered heavy casualties, and only one regiment of the 3rd Red Army Corps could maintain its original formation. We were targeting the Zhou column of the Central Army but were afraid it would not be easy to destroy it any time soon. The Red Army could run, but so could the Qian Army; they could also climb mountains and were expert at mountain warfare. They were fighting on their home ground, and after Wang's main force was beaten, the Qian Army became increasingly desperate. The enemy had built a broad band of forts west of Chishui, just as they had done in Jiangxi. These forts, which we called "turtle shells", formed a new line of blockade. This made it difficult to carry out our tactics of seeking opportunities to destroy the enemy on the move, and the Red Army's main force would once again be in danger. At 1700 hours on 20 March, the Party Central Committee and the General Political Department sent a telegram to every corps commander:

> "This is a critical juncture in the development of the deployment of the Field Army, and all corps commanders must quickly and resolutely organise the river crossing. This must be accomplished within the established time limit...This time the crossing is to be made to the east. Orders must not be issued in advance to preserve secrecy."

This time we crossed the river by Erlangtan, Jiuxikou and Taipingdu. During the previous three crossings of the Chishui River, Liu Bocheng had given secret orders to defend the two bridges over the river. At the same time, Chiang Kai-shek ordered all the "pursuit armies" to speed up their operations in order to destroy the Red Army west of the Chishui River. Chiang's order stated: "With such a large army surrounding the bandits in a narrow area, this is a good opportunity to round them up and destroy them... Success in the war against the bandits is at stake, so gather your strength for a supreme effort!" If the Red Army was not destroyed, "how can we look the world in the eye again?"

The main force of the Red Army crossed the river to the east, as the Kuomintang Army hurried to the west of the river. The 1st Red Army Corps sent a regiment to cover the main force as it continued its march westward. They attacked the Chuan Army in Gulin with all guns blazing. Chiang Kai-shek was convinced that the Red Army wanted to cross the Yangtze northwards, so he ordered all his troops to march day and night to the south of Sichuan.

On the night of 21 March, Chiang Kai-shek finally came to his senses. What he most feared was the Red Army crossing over to the east again and returning to northern Guizhou. And that was indeed what was going on! He was particularly worried about the Red Army retaking Zunyi, as that would make him look very bad. Chiang sent a coded telegram to Xue Yue:

> "The Red Army has returned to the east to cross the Chishui River and seems to be following the Sichuan-Guizhou border to Youyang and Xiushan to rendezvous with He Long and Xiao Ke."

At 0000 hours, we intercepted another telegram from Chiang Kai-shek to Long Yun, which contained Chiang's deployment of troops in response to the Red Army's eastern crossing.

At 1300 hours the following day, Chief Zeng submitted the deciphered telegram to Mao Zedong. At 2200 hours, this enemy communication was included in the Red Army General Headquarters' "Bulletin of Enemy Information". It was sent as it was, with just some minor changes to make it sound like a Red Army communication:

> "A) Chiang has learnt that the field army crossed the Chishui River on the morning of 21 March in the area of Taipingdu and Erlangtan and then circled back east.
> B) Guo Xunqi's men are following in pursuit.
> C) All senior commanders are ordered to mount a resolute defence of their current positions in Zunyi, Tongzi and Songkan."

Astonishingly, the details of Chiang Kai-shek's troop deployment to encircle the Red Army entered the Red Army's chain of command on the same day it entered that of Chiang's own army. They were delivered on the same day to the various levels of commanders who were leading two armies that were currently at each other's throats. On 22 March, the whole of the Central Red Army crossed the Chishui River.

On the 24th, Chiang flew from Chongqing to Guiyang with his wife, his personal entourage, including the influential Australian journalist William Donald, and his aides and staff. He wore battledress and personally joined the front line. Believing this would be the final battle, Chiang high-handedly proclaimed: "The Communist bandits are at the end of their tether. They have been forced to flee into Guizhou and are now seeking to cross the river but don't know where to try. They are blocked ahead and pursued behind. The vast Yangtze River is like a rift valley and the mountains are ringed around with our blockhouses as numerous as the stars in the sky. All we need to do is tighten the noose of our encirclement, and the Red Army can be wiped out!"

The Yangtze River is like a rift valley, and their blockhouses are as numerous as the stars in the sky. Chiang Kai-shek is sitting in Guiyang preparing his celebration banquet. Our original plan to settle at the Yunnan-Guizhou-Sichuan border is now unlikely to be realised. The nature of our operations is about to change, as are the balances that need to be struck between strategic transfer and strategic attack and between walking and fighting – recently we have mainly been fighting but it seems that in the future we will mainly be walking.

Where are we to go next? We trekked from east to west with the aim of going north, and Chiang Kai-shek stopped us from crossing the Yangtze. The Wujiang River in the south, the Yangtze River in the north, the Heng River and Jinsha River in the west, are all heavily blockaded, and the enemy are five times stronger than us. The Central Committee and the Military Commission are studying new paths of action, and the relevant reorganisation of troops is being quietly carried out. A new plan is in the pipeline, and the ordinary soldiers can't really keep asking about the reasons behind every move. Military orders must simply be obeyed. During this reorganisation, Xiao He of the Reconnaissance Division has been assigned to the 9th Red Army Corps to strengthen its technical reconnaissance capabilities. Although he does not want to leave the 2nd Bureau, he knows that this is a necessary part of his revolutionary work and is also testimony to the organisation's esteem and respect for him, so he willingly complies. We are all sad to see him go. The young soldiers of the 9th Red Army Corps are the main rearguard of the Red Army, and they have the affectionate nickname the "Old Ninth". Able to fight on the run, the Old Ninth are a well-trained light infantry force that undertakes the most dangerous covering duties, often requiring deception and disguise. Remembering how Chen Shuxiang's troops had been almost wiped out when acting as the rearguard, we are all the more reluctant for

Xiao He to go, as we are afraid we might never see him again. But we do not say so out loud. Chief Qian mocks us for being so sentimental as he does not want the business to cast a pall over things. When Xiao He returns Chief Qian's copy of Bukharin's *Historical Materialism*, Chief Qian generously gives him a novel in exchange – it is the Russian author Maxim Gorky's *First Love*. Xiao He smiles sadly and looks a little melancholy, but he accepts the gift. Then we begin to tease him and everyone's mood lightens.

"Just suppose I actually manage to guess any words..." Xiao He looks at Chief Zeng, his expression more serious.

"Use the radio! Get straight in touch with us!" Chief Zeng laughs. "I expect you to make a real name for yourself!"

"Are you making a play to join the decoding section? Aren't you afraid I won't let you go?" says Hu Lijiao, head of the Detection and Collection Section.

"Well, we know the chief knows what he is talking about there," says Xiao He, acknowledging Chief Hu's remark with a mischievous grin.

"We will surely see each other again!" Chief Zeng exclaims. "The Old Ninth may be acting alone and fighting alone, but even if it is too difficult to meet up for a while, the day will always come when the revolution is won. We are sure to be victorious! We'll see you in Nanjing when the revolution is won!"

"See you in Nanjing! My treat at the Central Hotel!"

We all believed Deputy Chief Qian when he said those words. Back at the time when he was working with Xu Enzeng, the "Zheng Yuan Industrial Club" was located next to the Central Hotel. Deputy Chief Qian had actually moved away to become deputy secretary general of the General Political Department, but he was still willing to accompany the 2nd Bureau. After crossing the river, we just kept moving south, still looking for an opportunity to fight. After the Zunyi Conference, Li De no longer got to see Chief Qian's beautiful map markings, and Russian and English were no longer needed. Even though Chief Qian had already been transferred, as he was marching with the 2nd Bureau, he was still sometimes involved in our analysis of the enemy's situation. Any urgent report was, of course, immediately reported by Chief Zeng to the head of the Central Committee and the Military Commission. Based on the analysis of and predictions made from the large number of recent coded telegrams, it was essential for us to do so in order to provide the highest level of command with a basis on which to make their decisions.

Now, together, we are analysing where to go. Nearly six months after evacuating the Central Soviet Union, we still have no destination. We can't go to western Hunan, Guizhou is under siege, and it is difficult to establish a foothold anywhere. It is going to be very difficult for us to turn Guizhou Red and create a base here. So we return to the idea of going north.

Chief Qian is still writing on the map as usual, but in fact, we already know the names of these places by heart, including all those remote villages and townships, just as long as they have appeared once in the enemy's coded messages.

There are two ways to cross the river to the north: one involves going west and the other going south.

Westbound means travelling from the upper reaches of the Yangtze River to cross the Jinsha River into western Sichuan. This involves crossing the fringes of the territory held by the Zhou and Wu columns of the enemy's Central Army, the defensive zone of the main Dian Army column commanded by Sun Du, and the possibility of being pursued by Pan Wenhua's corps in southern Sichuan. Even if we fight all the way, we still may not be able to cross the river as we wish, and the risks are enormous.

If we go south, it means making a big circle from southwest Guizhou through northern Yunnan. It is several times longer, but it plays to our own army's superiority on the march and exploits the enemy's shortcomings in their slow and lazy way of marching. With the enemy's "pursuit and annihilation army" so far to our rear, this route would win us the time for an easy crossing of the river. Naturally, there are risks, as we would have to slip quietly past the edge of Guiyang, where Chiang Kai-shek was stationed.

It is like a bow: west is the bowstring, a shortcut; south is the stave of the bow, a detour. Of the two, going south is less risky.

The first hurdle to the south is the Wu River.

THE WU RIVER

The Wu River. Li De warned us to beware of the Wu River becoming another Xiang River, but we managed to break through, and the tragedy of the Xiang River was not repeated. But that was the first time, a surprise assault, and if we are to do it again, it will be much more difficult. The enemy has reinforced its blockade.

It is only we who are blockaded; the enemy themselves are coming and going quite freely. Some time ago, Wu Qiwei's troops were chased down by our 1st Red Army Corps. He had originally brought two divisions across the Wu River but was left with only one regiment. When he fled to the Wu River, Xue Yue forbade him to cross, and with the Red Army coming after him, he sat on the ground in despair and wept. He said he was going to die there, and his staff officers had to get some of his bodyguards to drag him across to the south bank. As soon as he reached the shore, he ordered the bridge ropes to be cut, stranding more than a thousand officers and men on the north bank as prisoners of the Red Army. We in the 2nd Bureau know very well that the two divisions under Wu Qiwei, who were destroyed by our 1st and 3rd Red Army Corps, are exactly the same two divisions we wiped out in Dongpi and Huangpi during the fourth anti-encirclement and annihilation campaign. They have retained their old unit numbers, and Chiang

Kai-shek has cobbled them back together. Unsurprisingly, they are particularly afraid of fighting the Red Army again.

Now that the two divisions had been defeated again, Wu Qiwei was unexpectedly restored to his former role. It was reported that Xue Yue had asked Wu Qiwei to redeem himself by giving him command of the 90th Division. He was to lead the newly defeated troops across the Wu River again to coordinate with Zhou's column in an attempt to mount a counter-attack on Zunyi.

Based on accurate information from the 2nd Bureau, at 2000 hours on 25 March, the Military Commission communicated the current positions of the enemy's columns, divisions, brigades and even regiments. They pointed out that Chiang Kai-shek was attempting to "cut us off to the east and block our southward advance" and said that the Red Army should move southwest. This was because Wu's columns were stationed in several different places, the Qian Army was even more scattered, the Dian Army was a long way away in Chishui and Bijie, and the Chuan Army was two days' journey away from us. At 2100 hours, Zhu De gave out the deployment details for each of our corps on 26 March, moving southwest from the position between Changganshan and Fengxiangba. An hour later, Peng Dehuai and Yang Shangkun of the 3rd Red Army Corps sent a telegram to Zhu De, arguing that "at present, it is very difficult to find an opportunity to proceed to the southwest. Before anything else, we have to break through the columns of Zhou, Wang and Sun, and this makes it very hard to complete the strategic task of reaching Qianxi and Dading". They suggested that "it is more advantageous to turn southeast to the Wu River basin". At 0100 hours on the 27th, the Military Commission accepted Peng's and Yang's suggestion and decided to "gather the main force to go south between Changganshan and Fengxiangba instead, and if Zhou's troops attack from Changganshan, they will be destroyed by our prowess in mobile warfare". Late that night, the 2nd Bureau discovered that the area between Changgangshan and Fengxiangba had been occupied by enemy troops, but the area of Yaxi and Bailakan was still open. At 0600 on 27 March, the Military Commission sent out an urgent telegram:

"The original plan for our field army to break out between Changganshan and Fengxiangba is no longer possible, so we have decided to move southwest from the area of Yaxi and Bailakan instead."

The space between Yaxi and Bailakan was the only gap in the heavily guarded enemy Zun-Ren blockade line. The Central Revolutionary Military Commission ordered the 9th Red Army Corps to disguise itself as the main force of the Red Army and become active in the area from Changganshan to Fengxiangba in order to attract the enemy troops. The gods smiled on us, and a torrential rainstorm provided us with cover. On 28 March, the main force of the Red Army moved swiftly south from the area between Yaxi and Bailakan, leaving most of the Nationalist forces on either side of the Chishui River, and immediately raced for the north bank of the Wu River in the area of Andi, Gouchang and Shatu.

The Field Army headquarters informed the whole army of the enemy's movements and dispositions: Chiang was not eager to seek an engagement between Yaxi and Tanchang, but rather deployed several defensive lines to the rear in an attempt to lure us deeper before engaging. Zhou Hunyuan ordered one of his divisions to take a shortcut from Zunyi and build blockhouses in the area of Shibanchang, Dadukou, Shatu and Andi. It was possible that this forward division of Zhou Hunyuan's might encounter us at Shatu and Andi.

On 28 March, Chiang's telegram to Zhou Hunyuan and Wu Qiwei read:

> "Judging from the bandits' current situation, they must be trying to break through between Tanchang, Fengxiangba and Bailakan and flee southward... You must not stick rigidly to the use of massed troops... but set up defences piecemeal to hinder the enemy's passage".

On 29 March, our 2nd Bureau arrived in Shatu with the field army headquarters. Xiao He, now of the 9th Red Army Corps, discovered that Zhou Hunyuan's division might reach the boundary between Zunyi and Jinsha that day. Chief Zeng passed this information on to Mao Zedong and Zhou Enlai. They immediately ordered the 5th Red Army Corps, who were charged with bringing up the rear, to monitor the enemy as closely as possible.

The Central Red Army reached Shatu on the north bank of the Wu River. The 9th Red Army Corps were still providing cover by making a feint towards the area of Changganshan and Fengxiangba. On 30 March, the 2nd Bureau detected that the two main enemy forces were now advancing towards Panshui and Xinchang.

The main force of the Red Army was waiting to cross the border in the area of Gouchang, Andi and Shatu. If Zhou's and Wu's enemy columns discovered this and changed direction to pursue them, the distance between the two sides would be only twenty to thirty *li*! At night, the lights of the Shatu field army headquarters were flickering and figures could be seen moving about. Mao Zedong, Zhou Enlai, Wang Jiaxiang, Zhu De and Luo Fu, as well as Liu Bo Cheng, chief of the general staff, Ye Jianying, director of the 1st Bureau of the Military Commission, Zeng Mian, director of the 2nd Bureau, and Wang Zheng, director of the 3rd Bureau, looked nervously at the large map on the wall, on which rectangular and triangular troop markers were inserted with large pins. From time to time, Guo Huaruo, the chief of staff, moved the markers around. Everyone was anxious, and at one point they fell silent as the red and blue markers on the map revealed a terrifyingly dangerous situation through the smoke. All the possibilities for breaking out had been analysed, and there was nothing else to be done. The situation was critical, and they were almost completely at a loss. The crossing of the Wu River was crucial for the success of the Chinese Revolution.

The 2nd Bureau obtained the latest information about the enemy: Guo Siyan's 99th Division of Zhou Hunyuan's column was near Guiyang, Tang Yunshan's 93rd Division of Wu Qiwei's column was in Yanglong Town, and Li Yunheng's 53rd Division of the Xiang Army was heading south from Zunyi via Yanglong. Yanglong is north of Xifeng, just half a day's journey from the south bank of the Wu River.

Current status of our Central Red Army: the 1st and 3rd Corps and the Military Commission are now assembling in the area of Shatu, Gouchang and Andi, and will finish crossing the river around noon tomorrow. The 9th Corps will first take cover north of the line of Changganshan and Fengxiangba, and then choose their opportunity to move south to cross the river. The 5th Corps will break off back to the area of Shatu, Gouchang and Andi, and prepare to hold off the enemy.

To the north the enemy were pursuing us and to the south they were blockading us. On the south bank were Tang's division and one each of Guo and Li's divisions, who were blocking our troops from crossing the river at Xifeng. On the north bank were the main forces of Zhou and Wu's columns. To the east, the Xiang Army was blocking us, and Chiang Kai-shek had ordered He Jian to strengthen the guard along the Wu River to prevent the Red Army from crossing it to the east. The greatest danger was to the north, where we were most worried that the main forces of Zhou and Wu would change direction and come after us.

The enemy are getting close to both the north and the south, and if they discover where the Red Army is crossing the river, they will mount a north-south pincer attack so that our men who have already crossed the river and those who are still preparing to do so, will both be forced to fight with their backs to the water. The result will be even worse than the bloody battle on the Xiang River! In that battle, we still had a few days to get across, but now the enemy on both sides of the Wu River are little more than half a day away. The space on the two sides of the Wu River is also much narrower and our forces are more concentrated.

They had no way out to the north, the west or the east that would not inevitably end with them being encircled by the enemy. Even if they went south, they would still be heading into tremendous danger.

That danger was immediate. If they met with the worst possible result, a battle even bloodier than the Xiang River, that would be catastrophic. The whole army would be wiped out...

A bright light sweeps through the night, the bright light of a waving torch. It is Chief Zeng who has returned, and he burst into our duty room in a blaze of glory. We can tell by the look on his face that a decision had been made at the highest level of command. His expression immediately changes to one of calmness, the kind of calmness that comes before a battle, and there is a very real tension just beneath that calmness.

He casually picks up a ragged copy of the Kangxi Dictionary that is lying on his desk. The Come and Go Code is the king of the codebooks. Ciphers are based on the Ming Code, which uses the Kangxi Dictionary as the source of characters. The Kangxi Dictionary has 47,035 characters and 214 radicals, of which 10,000 are coded in the Ming Code. After turning the dictionary over in his hands a few times, Chief Zeng charges over to Cao and Zou and says, "You pretty much know this dictionary off by heart, but I want to ask you this. There are plenty of characters which are homophones among the forty thousand-plus that are in here, but there is only one which has homophones but none of them in the same tone. Do you know which it is?"

This stops everyone in their tracks. It isn't that Chief Zeng is trying to embarrass them both; it is more like he is talking to himself, asking and answering questions as if he is alone with his musings.

"Ming," says Chief Zeng, referring to the word 命, meaning "order".

Realisation dawns on everyone, and they wait for Chief Zeng to continue.

"Send a message to Zhou Hunyuan and Wu Qiwei."

As soon as Chief Zeng says this, we understand. We are all materialists, but occasionally we cannot help but believe in fate. Lives are hanging in the balance, and those lives are in our hands. Never give up hope! We know the current situation like the back of our hand. Chief Zeng hardly needs to explain, we all understand his master plan: using Chiang Kai-shek's name, he can by-pass Xue Yue, the corps' commander-in-chief, and give orders directly to Zhou's and Wu's two columns.

What a brilliant move! Chief Zeng tells us that the leaders of the Central Committee and the Military Commission have given their enthusiastic approval, and we are immediately excited. We too feel at once that this plan could work.

From time to time, Chiang Kai-shek overstepped the normal boundaries of his command. At this moment he was in Guiyang to supervise the war and had actually taken direct command. He had sent telegrams directly to Zhou and Wu. Our 2nd Bureau was familiar with the procedures and rules of the Kuomintang Central Army's coded telegrams; Chief Zeng was familiar with the language and format of Chiang Kai-shek's messages; Section Chief Cao was familiar with both the common and special coded texts of the enemy army; and Deputy Section Chief Zou was able to imitate the rhythm and fingering used by the other side in sending telegrams. Pretending to be Chiang Kai-shek sending a telegram from Guiyang, he ordered Zhou's and Wu's columns to advance according to their original plan, thus hopefully avoiding an encounter between the enemy and our forces and ensuring that all our troops would cross the Wu River southward on the 31st.

The original orders for Zhou's and Wu's columns were to advance towards Panshui and Xinchang. This telegram simply ordered them to march according to the original plan and not to change their course of action without permission. It would be even better to find some reason to make them advance more quickly! The faster they went, the further away they would be from the Red Army.

A brilliant move, but of course a dangerous one.

"The leaders of the Military Commission were all banging the table and exclaiming in delight," says a grim-faced Chief Zeng, "but I told them this plan could only be used once. Comrade Zedong said that turning the enemy's intelligence back on them was a masterstroke, but if we used it again, we would be recognised and all our decoding work would be put at risk. Old Man Zhu said that this was top secret and should be kept strictly confidential forever. We should just keep it bottled up inside. They wanted to go through with it, but I could see they still had some doubts. What are they so worried about?"

"Suppose they spot the fake telegram," says a frowning Deputy Section Chief Zou. "What then?"

"There is no 'suppose' anything!" Section Chief Cao shouts. "It's foolproof!" Chief Zeng's fist slams down on the table.

A night bird is singing in the shadows, a strange, hoarse, elongated call. They listen to the call with bated breath, all unconsciously shaking their heads slightly. None of them knows the name of the strange bird, and they just look at each other, smiling.

Everyone relaxes a little and sets to work. Chief Zeng picks up a recently deciphered message from Chiang Kai-shek: "The actions of the Red bandits are erratic. When our army is fighting against them, speed is of the essence. Since I have been in control of military affairs, I have repeatedly enforced military law. However, all the divisions are still very lax. It is a disgrace that the government has failed to achieve anything even after four or five serious campaigns. The Guizhou border is a bad place for the bandits. It's what Sunzi calls the 'killing ground'."

Chief Zeng scanned the message, trying to get a feel for what the Generalissimo had written. Then he picks up the red and blue pencils on his desk. Abruptly, he puts the pencils down and grins as he pulls the Parker fountain pen out of his pocket. This is a trophy he was given by the 1st Red Army Corps. The ink is running low, and he would not use it in the normal course of events. He bends low over the pen and begins to draft a message.

"To my two brothers, Qianchu and Wusheng," Bureau Chief Zeng writes, and Section Chief Cao immediately translates his words into code. But then he looks up questioningly.

"Is it wrong?" Chief Zeng asks.

"On the last set of orders, he was more direct and wrote 'To the Zhou and Wu columns'," Section Chief Cao says. "But Lao Chiang likes playing around with courtesies and rhetorical flourishes! Last month he sent two telegrams to Wan Yaohuang, and even though Wan is only the commander of the Thirteenth Division of Zhou's column, in one he called him 'Comrade Brother Wu Qiao' and in the other, it was 'Wu Qiao, my brother'! He's always exceptionally cordial in exceptional circumstances. We need to think about this some more."

Chief Zeng writes a question mark on the paper and continues with the text of the message: "Top Secret. According to confirmation received from aerial reconnaissance, the bandits are moving south towards the Wujiang River with one force, while the main force is accelerating its march westward."

Bureau Chief Zeng and Section Chief Cao keep their heads down, writing the coded message, while Deputy Section Chief Zou sits in front of the transmitter, his fingers flying. For him, this is like a skirmish before a big battle. As Chief Zeng's right hand sweeps the pen across the paper, he ignores the cigarette in his left hand as it scorches his left index finger. "At this point, the westward march is to continue with all speed along the original route. Unauthorised diversions or delays are not permitted."

"Isn't that a bit too direct?" Section Chief Cao interrupts again.

"This is a direct order from him. It's got to sound stern."

Chief Zeng puts another question mark next to the words "are not permitted" and asks Section Chief Cao what Chiang had said to Xue Yue about the Wu River: "What was the phrase he used?"

"'The Wu River is the place where King Xiang died.'"

"Yes, that's it, that's it! You've got a good memory! We should get him to use that with Zhou and Wu too. Wu River! King Xiang! What a load of nonsense. He's just showing off."

"It's not right yet. This kind of telegram can't be too wordy, these are battle orders. I need to keep it short. This is of overall strategic importance, and it needs to be done immediately–'"

"Obey to the letter!" Deputy Chief Zou can't resist adding a final sentence. Chief Zeng grins at him. "Ha! Yes, it fits!" They worked together on getting the first draft finished, poring over every word.

They changed the wording many times and by the time they came up with the final version, the paper was a mess of red and blue pencil markings. "Zhongzheng. 1500 hours on 31st." Chief Zeng looked down at his watch as Chief Cao wrote the last piece of code. He put the red and blue pencils down to indicate he was finished.

Chief Zeng looked at it one last time and then handed the cipher to Deputy Chief Zou.

Deputy Section Chief Zou sat solemnly in front of the transmitter, coughed dryly and adjusted the hook-and-eye fastening of his collar once again, as if he was chairman of the Republican Army Committee and Commanders Zhou and Wu were awaiting his orders. "Separate telegrams to Zhou and Wu respectively. It's all down to you now," Chief Zeng said. Deputy Section Chief Zou smiled faintly, and his finger began deftly to operate the transmission button.

Chief Cao lit the lantern.

The coded message had been sent, but Chief Zeng showed no sign of leaving. We still couldn't stop worrying. We boiled a pot of water and grabbed a few eucommia leaves for tea. Chief Zeng sat at the reconnaissance desk and kept a close eye on the reactions of Zhou's and Wu's columns. The telegram had said that the 99th and 93rd Divisions could intercept the southward-bound Communist Army, and it was expected that Zhou and Wu would march their troops through the night to reach Panshui and Xinchang by tomorrow, so as to stop the Communists crossing through western Guizhou. They were told to spare no effort to advance rapidly and not to hesitate. Ha! It was vital that these orders were obeyed. Xinchang was more than a hundred *li* from Shatu so even if they discovered our troops were crossing the river, they would have to wait until the day after tomorrow before they could muster their own troops and turn around to pursue them. We could all cross the river tomorrow.

Chief Zeng had not slept for three days and nights, but once the telegram was sent, his demeanour relaxed, and he looked more than a little sleepy. He forced himself into some small talk to stop himself suddenly dropping off: "Just now in the headquarters war room, we were all worried about how to cross the Wu River. If we really do manage to cross it, it will look like we are leaving Guizhou. Southern Guizhou is not the same thing as northern Guizhou. Southern Guizhou is their defensive stronghold so even if we do get across, we have to get out of there in a hurry. And talking of getting out of Guizhou, Comrade Zedong is very emotional about the prospect. He said to me, 'Without the reports you gave us, Bo Gu would have kept on being Bo Gu and we would never have kept up with the times and changed the direction of our march. If we hadn't gone into Guizhou, we would never have reached Zunyi, let alone held the Zunyi Conference. You had a big hand in getting the army into Guizhou.'"

"When you talk about changing the direction of the march, do you mean Tongdao?" Deputy Section Chief Zou almost seemed to be talking to himself. "Who knows what would have happened if we had gone into western Hunan. That's really hard to imagine–"

"What he meant was that our reports were crucial in getting us into Guizhou, so let's see what kind of a masterstroke we can pull to get us out." Chief Zeng sounded rather solemn.

"Ha! Well, this is it, isn't it!" Section Chief Cao laughed contentedly.

"Let's hope. Let's hope they listen to us. Then we won't have to turn tail and go back. Into Guizhou, out of Guizhou... it's becoming a bit of a worry. Objectively speaking, this place has its advantages, there's coal, and the sources for waterpower are very rich too. I think, when the revolution is victorious, we can also come back to build a dam, really work on the water conservancy and get it right, then electricity won't be a problem and there'll be enough to create a 'miniature sun'. The sky's never clear for three days in a row here, is it? If we get that 'miniature sun' up and running, it will burn off the fog and we'll have clear skies, won't we!"

This talk of a "miniature sun" perked everyone up, and we wanted to hear more about his ideas, but he just smiled and stood up, swaying slightly as he took a sip of tea. Then he laughed and said, "I'm asleep on my feet! And my head's aching... looks like it's time for me to take a nap. But don't forget to wake me up in half an hour. If they don't take our advice, wake me up straight away. But the way I see it, they will listen! Anyone want to bet?"

None of us took him up on the bet. Us Red Army men couldn't afford to. All we could do was pray to the gods to grant our wish. We did at least have faith!

For the time being, no major force was pursuing our men along the northern road. The situation there was that the 5th Red Army Corps was closely guarding the areas of Kuchayuan and Gouchang to stop any enemy that might come after them from Panshui. Under the cover of the glorious vanguard of the 1st Corps, the 3rd Regiment of the 1st Division rushed through the storm to the river crossing. The enemy guarding the crossing at Daobashui was a battalion of Xue Yue's men. When we made the first breakthrough back at the Wu River at the beginning of the year, it was with a full-frontal assault, but this time we made a sneak attack. Using bamboo rafts and thick bamboo ropes, they crossed to the other side by night. On 31 March, the main force then crossed the river from the three crossings without incident.

We did not have to wake Chief Zeng and actually let him sleep for a quarter of an hour longer. Zhou's and Wu's columns were obedient and followed our instructions to the letter. We had convinced them!

Coded message from the 2ⁿᵈ Bureau:

> Wu Qiwei arrived at Panshui with the 90th Division on the 30th and advanced to Sanchongyan on the way to Xinchang on the 31st; the 96th Division under Zhou Hunyuan advanced between Sanchongyan and Xinchang on the 31st and the rest were within striking distance of Xinchang.

So, a fake telegram gave the Central Red Army a way to survive against all the odds and avoid being overwhelmed. Chiang Kai-shek did not realise that the Red Army had sent a coded telegram in his name, but planes sent from Guiyang spotted them crossing the river. On the day of the crossing, Chiang was informed of the situation, but it was too late, and he hastily deployed Sun Du's column of the Dian Army, which happened to be closest, to strengthen the defences around Guiyang. He also sent a severe reprimand to Huang Daonan, the head of the Wu River garrison, who was also under Wu Qiwei's command.

Naturally, we intercepted this coded telegram too. Chiang was so furious, you could almost hear him when you read the message:

> "...it seems that the bandits' main forces are now crossing major rivers at will. Moreover, our defensive forces cannot halt the bandits in time on the banks of the river or hit them when they are halfway across. Their main force has already passed us, but our army doesn't even seem to have noticed them. It is rare for the military to be so rotten and useless. The reason this has happened is that the officers in charge at all levels did not personally make a detailed inspection of the terrain along the river or investigate the crossing before deploying their defensive forces. When the troops were deployed, they did not always check that their men were doing their job and did not give their officers and men the rules they needed to follow. From top to bottom the army has been lazy, negligent and perfunctory in the performance of its duties. When the bandit gang forced their

way across the river, the same officers were at a loss what to do. I did not know such shame existed in the world and the same applies to ordinary soldiers too. The bandits took more than a day and a night to cross the river near the rear of the mountain, and the officer in charge of our troops in Xifeng did not even notice. How can our revolution succeed if we are so dull-witted? The officer in question, Huang Daonan, is to be dismissed from his post and severely punished as a warning to others who are lazy and negligent in their duties, and all divisions are to be informed. These are my orders!"

When the enemy failed in their pursuit, they turned to bomb us from the air. Sometimes they swooped in low to strafe us, sometimes they dropped bombs from high altitude. But, in the end, we had managed to cross the Wu River and had broken out of the enemy's tight encirclement.

In order to go north, we first went south. The Military Commission had decided to cross the river and go directly south between Zhenxiwei and Guiyang, but, on 1 April, our 2nd Bureau detected that Chiang Kai-shek had ordered Sun Du's and Wu Qiwei's columns to seize Zhenxiwei, and had sent Li Yunheng's division of the Xiang Army to intercept us at the Zi River. At the same time, Zhou Hunyuan's column was advancing on the Wu River crossing. To avoid a head-on collision with the enemy's main force, on the same day the Military Commission telegraphed all the army corps, informing them that the Red Army's path to the southwest was about to be blocked and that we would now change direction and go east from south of Xifeng in order to seek new room to manoeuvre. That same evening, the 2nd Bureau also detected that Guiyang was effectively deserted, with only four regiments of Guo Siyan's 99th Division of Zhou Hunyuan's column left to guard it. Those four regiments were spread out on the high ground around the provincial capital, amounting only to a few small detachments when put next to the huge area of Guiyang they had to guard. A section of the Red Army, pretending to be the main force, marched eastwards, making a feint of moving into Hunan to join the 2nd and 6th Red Army Corps, while the real main force marched through Xifeng and Zhazuo, pushing straight towards Chiang Kai-shek's temporary state residence in Guiyang. The Red Army marched east, out of eastern Guizhou and into western Hunan, which was just the situation Chiang was most worried about.

Attacking with the fierceness of a tiger and probing the enemy's strength to turn it into weakness. On 2 April, as the Red Army's vanguard approached Guiyang, Chiang Kai-shek ordered Wu Qiwei, Zhou Hunyuan and Sun Du, whose columns constituted the main force of the Dian Army, to "travel through the night" to come to the rescue. Sun Du's column had been stationed in the area of Bijie and Anshun, but by moving it to Guiyang, Chiang opened the way for the Red Army to advance into Yunnan. Chiang still believed that the Red Army "appeared to be heading eastwards", and to compound his mistake, Mao Zedong and Zhou Enlai then decided to seize the opportunity to make a feint to draw the enemy's mobile troops on the south bank of the Wu River off to the area of the Zi River.

Using outward appearance to hide the truth; there can never be too much deception in warfare. On 3 April, the Central Revolutionary Military Commission ordered the 1st Red Army Corps to execute the feint, to be followed by an advance by the 3rd and 5th Red Army Corps and the Central Column – it was a huge move! Chiang Kai-shek was completely taken in by it, and, willing to try anything in his desperation, he actually told the Gui Army to take part in the operation. Before this, in order to prevent any collusion between Li Zongren and Bai Chongxi of the Gui faction and Wang Jialie of the Qian faction, Chiang had never allowed the Gui Army to join in the pursuit and annihilation of the Red Army, so the two divisions of the Gui Army had only been able to wait around in Duyun and Dushan.

On 4 April, Chiang Kai-shek sent a telegram to Li Zongren and Bai Chongxi: "The main force of the bandits fled to the east from the southeast of Xifeng via the Zi River to the east of Weng'an", and the Gui Army at Duyun and Dushan "must advance to the area of Pingyue and Niuchang before the sixth to intercept the bandits fleeing east". He also telegraphed an order for Li Yunheng's division to "advance from the Zi River along the main Weng'an road, and to travel by night". On the same day, he also contacted Wu Qiwei, ordering his various troops to converge on the Red Army in the

Weng'an region and encircle it. Chiang Kai-shek was rushed off his feet organising all these different troop movements.

Chiang had taken the bait, so the Central Red Army returned south on 5 April. The 3rd Red Army Corps became the vanguard, the 5th Red Army Corps and the Central Column the main force and the 1st Red Army Corps the rearguard, thus turning the whole army around and heading straight back between Guiyang and Longli. Longli marks the eastern border of Guiyang district, and the two places are less than sixty *li* apart.

Chiang Kai-shek must have been furious beyond words and horrified at the same time. The fury would be at having been duped and horror at the weakness of Guiyang's city defences. At this time there were only four regiments on the outskirts of Guiyang; the city guard garrison and the military police amounted to less than two regiments, and the remaining troops were two or three days away. Chiang Kai-shek hastily called Sun Du into the city, gave him a sum of money and ordered him to take his troops to Longli immediately to stand guard there. At the same time, he urgently ordered a regiment of Tang Yunshan's 93rd Division that was left in Qianxi to rush to Guiyang with all speed. The situation was laid out for us in his frequent coded telegrams, and on learning of it, Mao and Zhou decided to continue the bluff even further.

On 6 April, the Central Revolutionary Military Commission ordered the Red Army Corps to be on the alert and reconnoitre Guiyang and Longli. The slogan "Take Guiyang City, Capture Chiang Kai-shek Alive" appeared outside the city at Guiyang. Chiang Kai-shek was at a loss as the Red Army pushed towards Guiyang. We were kept informed of the situation by his coded messages. Chiang had prepared two plans for his escape: one was a plane and the other a sedan chair with a fast horse and a guide. The coded messages also contained the word "Madam", so we knew that Chiang's wife was also there at this scene of panic. We heard that the couple referred to each other as "Darling", which was said to be the only word of English the chairman had learned, but it did not appear in the coded telegrams that we intercepted.

Addendum: Chiang secretly flew to Kunming on the afternoon of 7 April on the pretext of inspecting the Yunnan government, and only returned three days later after the "rescue" columns had arrived in Guiyang.

Our 5th Red Army Corps wanted to block the two divisions of Wu's column advancing from Baini to Yangchang, but as the bulk of Wu's troops had not moved, it only intercepted a commando unit driving from Machang to Yangchang. The 5th Army Corps then marched to the line of Maochang and Jichangba.

On 7 April, the vanguard of the 3rd Red Army Corps feinted to attack Longli. The 2nd Bureau detected that Sun Du of the Dian Army had finally reached the city of Guiyang and that a large force could well be following on behind him. Chiang Kai-shek seemed to have his mind made up and was again thinking of ways to destroy the Red Army. He still concluded that the Red Army was going east to join up with He Long, and that crossing the Wu River and forcing Guiyang was just an alternative route. Luckily for him, he had already ordered the two forces commanded by Liu Jianxu and Li Jue to set up a second line of defence in Xinhuang and Tongren, and Guiyang was already secured. He then ordered Wu Qiwei, Zhou Hunyuan and Li Yunheng not to come to Guiyang but to take a shortcut to hurry to Yuqing, Shiqian and Zhenyuan, aiming to arrive before the Red Army and block their eastward path. In light of these enemy manoeuvres, Mao Zedong let Chiang Kai-shek compound his mistake in simply letting the Red Army continue its eastward march and sent a part of it eastwards towards Weng'an deliberately to let itself be spotted by the enemy's planes, so that the enemy army would increase its pace eastwards. With the Red Army apparently heading for Weng'an, Chiang Kai-shek was naturally delighted that the Red Army really was "fleeing east" as it made for Weng'an! This reinforced his misjudgement that the Red Army could only move east, and east was where his heavy forces were concentrated. He thought the enemy had been trapped and that he was going to be able to set up a showdown, so, as he sent all his forces eastwards to "converge and annihilate", he also hurriedly ordered Sun Du's three brigades to follow them to Guiding and Weng'an. It was in this way that the Dian Army was mobilised out of its home ground and that mobilisation was a great victory for us. With Sun Du's Dian Army heading east and the troops under

Chiang's direct command doing the same and heading for Zhenyuan, the main road to Yunnan lay wide open.

At 2130 hours, Zhu De sent a telegram marked "Of Utmost Urgency" to the commanders of the 1st, 3rd and 5th Red Army Corps:

> "It is believed that Li Baobing's division of Wu's column and the Dian Army in Guiding will attack Yangchang. If they know that we are moving south, Wu's column will chase us to the Xima River via Songjiadu, and the follow-up troops of the Dian Army will open up Guiyang and Longli... our Field Army must encounter the enemy, make a feint towards Guiyang and Longli, then head south from between Guiyang and Longli to occupy Dingfan as quickly as possible".

On 8 April, the 3rd Red Army Corps made an energetic feint towards Guiyang city.

On the following day, some forty *li* east of Guiyang, the main Red Army force suddenly turned southwest and crossed the road between Guiyang and Longli! This was the only gap in the Kuomintang lines. There were enemy troops in both Longli and Guiyang, so to avoid being pinned down, our main force had to make the crossing quickly before the enemy realised what was happening. Liu Bocheng, commander of the Military Commission column, stood on a ridge and personally supervised the manoeuvre, urging over and over again: "Move! Move! Make sure you get over that hill in front of you before noon, or you'll be in trouble!"

Had Chiang Kai-shek been on his plane trip at that moment, he would have seen a very unusual battlefield: the two forces were running in opposite directions, the Kuomintang Army heading east and the main force of the Red Army speeding southwest. Moreover, the mountains in Guizhou are steep and the roads are winding and twisting. Even if two mountains actually face each other, and if the people from either side really want to catch up with each other, it can easily take two days or more.

The enemy troops chasing eastwards were left behind to the east of Longli. In this way we crossed the gap in the enemy's lines and then split into two columns, right and left, to put on a forced march. We marched 120 miles a day towards Yunnan, which was now empty of enemy troops! The enemy's main force was far to the northeast of Guiyang, and they were so exhausted by this point that they simply didn't have the strength to turn back and chase us.

The 2nd Brigade of the 3rd Column of the Dian Army sent a confidential telegram to Long Yun:

> "We have been ordered to follow and attack the enemy entering Yunnan, and the vanguard regiment has now seen a wide trail left by the Communist Army. They appear to be in dozens of columns, none of them of any great size and all moving fast. Given how confidently they are marching, we believe it is almost certainly their main force…"

The last hurdle to the south was negotiated without a hitch, and so brilliantly! So flexible and so inspired! Such amazing resourcefulness! The Central Revolutionary Military Commission's boldness in making this decision was largely based on the absolute accuracy and timeliness of the 2nd Bureau's intelligence. Ye Jianying, director of the 1st Bureau, was enormously impressed. As director of the Operations Bureau, he knew better than anyone that enemy troops were all around and this was the only gap, but the opportunity had to be taken quickly and with precision. One step too slow or one step too fast, and we would have been in an incredibly dangerous position.

The combat troops praised the inspired leadership of the Military Commission, and some said that in the past we had been beaten at every turn, as if we were marching in the dark, but now we had correct and reliable leadership, it was like a lantern on the road at night. They realised that this reliable guidance, this "lantern", was the correct leadership of the Military Commission. Hearing this, Mao Zedong smiled and said to Chief Zeng, "It is your Second Bureau that is that 'lantern on the road at night'."

Based on the timeliness, accuracy and reliability of our secret information, the wise commanders of the Central Committee and the Military Commission repeatedly foiled Chiang Kai-shek's actions. Compared with our analysis of the enemy situation, Chiang's own "enemy assessment" was completely off beam. Ever since the Red Army first entered Guizhou, Chiang and Xue misjudged the situation every time. Whereas the Red Army had the 2nd Bureau, and we knew where the enemy was at all times, they could not decipher our secret telegrams and could only rely on aerial reconnaissance. When Chiang was in Guiyang, he ordered all the armies to come under his direct command and told the troops to study the passage in Sunzi's *Art of War* about what he calls "entangling ground": "If it is easy to sally forth from but hard to reoccupy, it is called entangling ground. If you are besieged in entangling ground, you must use multiple means to mislead the enemy." Actually, that sounded more like the situation our Red Army found itself in. He seemed to be working to a strategy of knowing himself and knowing his enemy, but somehow or other he was allowing himself to become entangled in a maze of his enemy's making! If his judgement was at fault, all he could do was lead in the dark. The enemy army marched as ordered, but even though they tried their best, they often found themselves chasing their own tails for days on end, without seeing even the slightest sign of any Red Army. Sunzi also said that "a general who understands the use of the oblique has a source of tactics as inexhaustible as Heaven and Earth, which, like the Rivers and the Oceans, will never run dry". Although Li De was a brave man, he did not know how to use the "oblique" and was not good at deception. He only knew how to fight head-on. The Red Army was now "avoiding the enemy's strong points and exploiting their weaknesses, pretending to strike in one direction but actually attacking in the other" so "Commander-in-Chief" Chiang couldn't help but be led by the nose around in circles until he was dizzy. As far as he was concerned, we were appearing and disappearing like "wraiths and phantoms".

The phrase "entangling ground" comes from a chapter in the *Art of War* entitled "On Terrain", but the route we took as we headed southwards was more like a "recurve bow": first we turned to head through northern Yunnan, then we crossed the Jinsha River to the north.

Taking a "recurve bow route" south needed the corps commanders to fully understand what was going on. According to our comrades from the 1st Corps, when they crossed the Wu River on 31 March, as Mao Zedong passed by the 2nd Division's camp, the division's political commissar Liu Yalou asked suspiciously, "The Red Army is going all round the houses, but where are we actually heading?" Mao Zedong smiled and said nothing. He used a red pencil to draw an eye-catching line on a map. It led from Guizhou to Yunnan, into Yunnan and then turned back to point north to the Jinsha River.

It was quite a detour! "If we make a sharp turn, the enemy will break a leg as they chase after us!"

When we crossed the Beipan River into Yunnan, we did not head straight for the Jinsha River but turned towards Kunming in a feint to draw the defenders away. Just as in Guizhou, the Red Army's vanguard made directly towards Guiyang and were soon on the city's doorstep. But they did not attack, as this was just another feint to lure the Dian Army out of Yunnan and leave it undefended. This time, Chiang Kai-shek swallowed the bait completely, fell into a panic, and his first reaction was to give strict orders to all his armies to pursue and attack. However, ever since the Red Army crossed the Wu River and took over Zunyi in early January, the various "pursuit and annihilation armies" had been run ragged by Chiang for four months, and by now they had lost the will to go straight off chasing after the enemy again. Xue Yue said his troops needed to rest and reorganise, or at least change out of their padded cotton clothes into summer ones. Wu Qiwei simply claimed he was ill and took leave to recuperate in Guiyang. Liu Xiang's Chuan Army only sent Guo Xunqi to join in the "pursuit". He Jian's Xiang Army sent Li Yunheng's division to participate, but it was just a token gesture. Only Sun Du's column came from Yunnan, but now that the Red Army had entered Yunnan, it goes without saying that he really had no option. So this was the state of mind of the "pursuit and annihilation armies", while morale in the Red Army was buoyant. After crossing between Guiyang and Longli, the 1st and 5th Red Army Corps and the Central Column took the inside line, turning westward from the north of Anlong via Ziyun and Zhenfeng; the 3rd Red Army Corps took the outer line, pushing in westward from Jichang to Longchang to monitor the movements of the enemy's main force and advancing in parallel with the other corps. After a short rest, Xue Yue's "Central Army" followed us westward through Pingba, Guanling, Qinglong and Pu'an, while

Sun Du's column also followed our main westward route, but they were all a long way to our rear. In fact, they were about a week behind, a distance they could hardly make up, and the Red Army was always going to be faster on the march than them.

No clever words from a writer are as powerful as the real thing. Our troops said, "People say we have legs of iron, but even iron legs are quickly worn down", by which they meant, "Our legs are even stronger than any iron ones."

We are made of special stuff.

So, crossing the river to the south this time meant a farewell to all that zig-zag crisscrossing with the enemy, and we no longer had to weave to and fro to get past them. The enemy's encirclement and blockade strategy had failed completely! We were now able to travel unhindered. "You march along the highways and minor roads in order to destroy the enemy, but you follow a twisting path and take the long way round to be sure of victory in the revolution!" The cadres and soldiers were relieved of their doubts and had a better understanding of the Military Commission's strategy. They were happy to believe that there must be a "divine plan" behind their wise decisions, that they had some kind of magical power. Revolutionary optimism was back, and with it, a belief in victory.

We followed a long leg westward then detoured to the north via northern Yunnan in the hope that this would throw the "pursuit" army off our trail. The regiment from the 1st Red Army Corps, which had been sent out to make a feint towards Gulin, went straight on to the Wu River after the enemy withdrew from the Gulin area and crossed the river with the main force without incident. We all praised our intelligence operators for a job well done and reckoned they deserved a major commendation. Unfortunately, Luo Binghui's 9th Red Army Corps failed to cross the river and our Comrade He, who was with them, also remained on the other side of the river. After the main force of the Red Army and the Central Column crossed the river, the Red Cadre Corps stood guard over the pontoon bridge to wait for the rearguard 5th Red Army Corps to cross. When they heard that the 5th Army Corps had crossed the river from another crossing, they dismantled the pontoon bridge and chased after the main force of the Red Army. When Commander Zhu got the news, he ordered the Cadres Corps to rebuild the bridge and wait for the 9th Corps to cross the river. However, when the 9th Corps arrived on the banks of the Wu River, two hours later than the time specified by the Military Commission, the enemy had already taken control of the crossing and the main body of the pursuing troops was approaching, so the 9th Corps had to evacuate the area. They had distinguished themselves in covering the crossing of the main body of our troops but encountered difficulties in making it over themselves. The Military Commission ordered them to act on their own initiative and stay in Guizhou to fight as guerrillas and look for another opportunity to rejoin the main force. Our Old Ninth had to turn back in the rain and return to deep mountain forests. Later we received a coded telegram from Xiao He:

> "At Lao Mukong, on the upper reaches of the Wu River. Four regiments of the enemy's 100th Division and five regiments of the 99th Division. We are still fighting."

It was a fierce and grisly battle. The 9th Red Army Corps was the rearguard of the Central Red Army. They had fought numerous terrible battles and had suffered heavy casualties. We were told afterwards that the Old Ninth were outnumbered twelve to one, but they managed heroically to hold off the enemy and successfully covered our main force after it had crossed the river. While the battle was raging in Lao Mukong, we received an urgent telegram from the "9K" – the 9th Red Army Corps. At the time, we were at the side of the road receiving telegrams under enemy bombardment. That was the last coded telegram sent by Xiao He. Zou Sheng judged from the fingering of the transmission that he was already seriously wounded, but there was still just enough of a signal to get the message out. Section Chief Cao immediately read out the decoded words: "Another four combined regiments of the Chuan Army... Wu and Zhou columns are coming at us head-on."

Zou Sheng send the coded message to Xiao He: "Message received. You have fully discharged your responsibilities. Please switch off your radio. Retreat with all speed!"

Chief Zeng fishes out a cigarette, lights it and takes a fierce drag.

"Just worked one out, came to me suddenly just now... 16447...

梅..." Chief Zeng's eyes light up and he nods in understanding, but just at that moment, there is pain written all over his face.

"Dear comrades..."

Zou Sheng softly reads out the message.

"...farewell forever... you keep on going..." Zou Sheng's eyes are blurred with tears.

There is still an intermittent signal but getting fainter. Zou Sheng gets up, walks a few paces and, with his back turned, quietly wipes a tear from his face.

Section Chief Cao sits down next to the transmitter. He has left his headphones on and struggles to collect his emotions as he listens to the faint thread of a signal.

"Far away... mo--si--ke [Moscow]..."

The signal grows weaker and weaker, eventually falling silent. There is a sudden boom in the headphones.

Chief Zeng stands there, still and solemn, and Section Chief Cao sits numbly in a daze, his hands trembling. Chief Zeng slowly raises his right hand and takes off his military cap.

Chief Cao gently presses the transmission button and sorrowfully sends out his final farewell... and extends a Bolshevik salute!

Zou Sheng wipes away his tears and tries to make contact again, but he no longer hears anything from the other end. The display panel on the foreign-made transmitter reads: FAILED. Transmission unsuccessful.

We also lost our beloved Chief Qian at the crossing of the Wu River. Although he had been transferred to the General Political Department, he was reluctant to leave us and still travelled with the 2nd Bureau. We were attacked by enemy planes after crossing the river at Tiziyan, and Chief Qian disappeared as he took shelter from the bombing. The Military Commission had a clear standing order that no one from the 2nd Bureau was to be left behind, and that the protection of the 2nd Bureau was to be the responsibility of the 1st Bureau. The 2nd Bureau is top secret and very important. The 1st Bureau is a "combat bureau" and is charged with protecting secrets and keeping the 2nd Bureau safe. The personnel of the 1st Bureau always say, "We must keep the Second Bureau safe at all times. If we lose it, we lose our heads too!"

Shocked to hear that Chief Qian had disappeared, Chief Political Commissar Zhou scrambled a search party. Our comrades in the 1st Bureau leapt on their horses and the captain of the guard of the 2nd Bureau mounted up too, on the big black horse, anxious to help them. But they searched in vain until darkness fell, at which point the vicious reactionary militia groups also appeared. Even after dark, the units were still in contact by bugle call and messengers, gathering the scattered troops together. They found some of the wounded and others who had got left behind, but there was still no news of Chief Qian. I heard that Comrade Hu Di of the headquarters reconnaissance section also rode out to look for him, but there was no sign. We still had a glimmer of hope. The men of the reactionary militia were all poor local folk who had been pressed into service because they were fit and healthy. Even if he fell into their hands, with his great intelligence, he should be able to escape safely. Maybe he could even liberate the militias... of course, we didn't actually have any need of them and all we wanted was to get Chief Qian back.

We heard that someone had seen a horse by the riverside that looked very much like Chief Qian's white horse. By then the air raid had passed, and the figure of the horse appeared high up on the slopes above the river, shrouded in mist under the hazy light of the beautiful crescent moon.

AFTERTHOUGHTS

This prose poem, this collection of war notes, could be called a bundle of "sketches" if you use the artist Huang Zhen's terminology. It has to be completed because it is an assignment from Chief Zeng, but I wouldn't dare show it to him unless, by chance, he asks to see it one day. How could I dare take up his time with it when he is weighed down with military matters and the future of the Red Army is at stake! Even if I did show it to him, he would only criticise it for its lack of literary merit! The chances of any kind of praise are very slim indeed. I know I don't really have a way with words to begin with, but the hardest part is that what I have written is more a record of actual events, which can't be messed around with but has to be written just as they happened. Getting it right in every detail is incredibly challenging. Our Western Expedition was, after all, one of the most intense and remarkable events in Chinese history, and all I can do is put everything I have into creating this sketch of it.

My original intention was to show it to Chief Qian, to ask for his guidance, and perhaps one day he might suddenly have been inspired to make a few changes with a swipe of his pen, which, as I understand it, he could easily have done. But with his sudden departure, I felt I had lost the strength to continue writing, and I could not see any point in doing so. The only other time this subject was mentioned was in Zunyi. One day he showed me the latest issue of *Red Star*, which carried the headline story, "The Great Beginning – The First Battle of 1935". Comrade Deng Xiaoping was once editor-in-chief of this newspaper, and the words "Red Star" on the masthead were designed by Chief Qian. That day when he held that newspaper in his hands, I felt the weight of his words. He said that if you want to write well, remember that you have to see with your own eyes and write what you have seen; that is the one real necessity. As for style and rhetoric, those are not easily learnt and the process can't be forced, but that shouldn't prevent you from adding your own thoughts and feelings, especially your emotions, so that others can find truth in what they read. In this way, it becomes your own writing and not someone else's.

His words are still fresh in my ears, and I feel guilty whenever I think of them. I have tried my best to write with my eyes, but I have not added much of my own emotion. This is not a conscious omission, but more likely a matter of inertia. When I look back at these chapters, they are almost all written in the voice of "us" and "we". It is force of habit to omit personal emotions, although there are a few places where they are expressed, and they are indeed the feelings of all of us. We are a revolutionary team, a revolutionary collective, we have too many feelings in common! However, now this sketch is next to impossible to continue, I really don't feel the same way any more. It's not that I've put it aside entirely, but I've just stopped making it a priority to get it done. I should just write a few words. Even if they are fragmentary, that's good enough. Just a simple record is good enough.

That way, there is no great pressure on me. After all, we are marching to war, and, as deputy head of the decipherment and telecommunications section, my priority at the moment is to detect enemy intelligence, not to write fine prose. Now we are across the Wu River, we finally have a clear direction and a viable route. You could also say that we have seen the light.

Addendum: Meeting scene. The long, tall figure in the morning fog on that May morning in 1933 was our new Deputy Bureau Chief Qian. We shook hands warmly in the yellow morning mist, and Zeng and Qian seemed to be very much in tune with one another. It was the time when the 2nd Bureau of the Central Revolutionary Military Commission was established in Ruijin, with Zeng Mian as bureau chief and Qian Chao as deputy chief. The 2nd Bureau was temporarily divided into two: the 2nd Bureau at the front line was located in Jianning, Fujian, under the charge of Chief Zeng Mian; the 2nd Bureau at the rear was still in Ruijin, under the charge of Deputy Chief Qian Chao. Now I come to think about it, Qian Chao arrival at the 2nd Bureau was a momentous occurrence. Qian Chao, Li Kenong and Hu Di were the "Three Heroes of the Dragons' Pools": they fought together through situations as dangerous as dragons' pools and tigers' lairs and arrived in the Central Soviet one after another. There, Zeng Mian, Cao Daye and Zou Sheng were the "Three Great Codebreakers", the ones who deciphered the "documents from the ether".

In August of that year, Zeng, Cao and Zou were awarded the Red Star Medal, while Qian, Li and Hu compiled a new play called Death on Lushan. It was a great play, too, with its scenes of covert warriors! In the past, in Shanghai, Nanjing and Tianjin, Qian, Li and Hu were working in intelligence, both openly and undercover, but when they came to the Central Soviet Union, which was besieged by the enemy, and joined us on our westward expedition, we were mainly on the lookout for the enemy up in the skies and obtained our intelligence from the enemy's airwaves. In the past, when they were in Shanghai, Zeng and Qian were engaged in underground activities, but now they have had to turn to the heavens. Zhou Enlai said that Zeng's intelligence work made him "a rare immortal within the Party", and that without Qian's intelligence reports, "we would have been dead long ago". The meeting of these two chiefs was symbolic of our victory in the intelligence wars. Although Qian did not know how to decipher codes, he was very good at analysing the enemy's situation, and he had profound knowledge and revolutionary optimism and enthusiasm. Although we did not have an official political commissar in the 2nd Bureau, Qian certainly played the part in terms of propaganda, political agitation and boosting morale in the face of defeat. We were unlikely to see another play co-written by Qian, Li and Hu. Qian and Hu had both been film actors, and Comrade Li Kenong was a famous actor in the Red Army Drama Club, but now the whereabouts of both Qian and Hu were unknown...

2 May, a telegram from Long Yun to Chiang Kai-shek:

"Captured in Yangjie, a Communist staff officer called Chen Zhongshan, a native of Ruijin. He is now being transferred under guard to the government centre for interrogation. A bundle of reports was found on him, which includes coded telegrams from all parts of our army, all converted into Chinese characters. It is no wonder that the enemy is very clear about our armies' movements and knows how to avoid them. We are now studying these deciphered messages, in conjunction with our own codebook, and intend to work out his decipherment techniques and what methods of communication should be used in the future to avoid disclosure. I am pleased to report further details will be forthcoming."

3 May, Chiang Kai-shek's reply to Long Yun, sent in Liang Code:

"It is a serious problem that our messages have been stolen and deciphered by the bandits. The only way to deal with this matter is to have more ciphers prepared and changed daily. Each code should be used at most once in a week and changed on a daily basis. Each ministry shall issue ten different codes, one to be used per day, and ten more on each tenth day. As one measure, weather permitting, we will use aeroplane communication to address this problem. I request, Brother, that you compile and distribute the new codebooks and return here to handle this business."

When Chiang went on to say, "The danger is very great and the disgrace beyond words", Long Yun finally understood why hundreds of thousands of soldiers of the "pursuit and annihilation armies" could not intercept our mere 30,000-strong Red Army. Before Chiang replied to Long Yun, he must have consulted his code experts. One new code a day is, of course, a very serious countermeasure to code breaking, and it has certainly increased the workload of our 2nd Bureau, which only has three decoders, Zeng, Cao and Zou. Even so, these measures taken by the enemy remained futile in the face of our amazing 2nd Bureau experts. In fact, the Kuomintang Army had been changing its radio codebooks daily or every two or three days recently. From 14 January to 9 May, they had used at least fifteen different codebooks: Sui, Ke, Ting, Mou, Keng, Ji, Sheng, Zhi, Liang, Li, Zhou, Yi, Ye, Kai, Yan, plus several special codes. However, these different codes were not used in daily rotation. Looking at Chiang Kai-shek as an example, he knew that the Liang Code had been used on 24 February, and he was also well aware that the Red Army had broken it, but he still used it unchanged on 3, 8 and 9 May in telegrams to Long Yun. Seen in that light, it would seem that his cipher experts weren't up to the job.

Not only did the enemy change their codes frequently, they also began to use codenames: Chiang Kai-shek was "He", Long Yun was "Qian", Xue Yue was "Che", Sun Du was "Huo", Wu Qiwei was "Ai", Zhou Hunyuan was "Gui", and so on, but all to no avail. We broke them all.

Chen Zhongshan, staff officer of the decoding section, who was captured, was not a decoder himself but had the decoded messages with him. The good thing was that the task of deciphering had not been made more difficult for us, and Chiang Kai-shek's own code was not changed as a result. Rather, it was Chairman Long Yun, who already knew all about our decoding abilities and wanted to put them to the test. He deliberately stated in a coded Kuomintang Army communication that Commander-in-Chief Zhu had secretly sent someone to make contact with him, on condition that he would return Commander-in-Chief Zhu's property in Kunming. He was trying to play a diversionary trick on the Red Army leader, and as he hoped, we naturally intercepted and deciphered the telegram. But we just laughed it off.

For us in the 2nd Bureau, the Chen Zhongshan incident was a serious lesson as a result of which we had to make significant improvements. For this reason, Chief Zeng took more stringent measures to prevent such incidents from happening again. Objectively speaking, it was quite clear how that lesson came about. The only way to shake off the enemy was to run as fast as we could. Hundreds of miles of forced marches were commonplace, but often we were in a half-starved state and many soldiers had to run in bare, bleeding feet because their straw shoes were torn and useless. Most of them were poorly educated, many illiterate, and they did not understand much about theory and reasoning, but they were determined in their belief that only by following the Red Army would the poor have a way to survive and be liberated. And the only way to survive was to keep up with the Red Army and keep running. Once they fell behind, it was difficult to catch up, and then the enemy and the militia would come after them. The three main tasks of the combat troops were to march, fight and sleep, and there was always an element of surprise in the fighting. This routine did not hold entirely for us at the 2nd Bureau; we were on duty around the clock, whether marching or fighting, to detect and decipher enemy information at all times, every day. Although our personnel were divided into two shifts and we were able to fight and march, our sleeping time was greatly reduced. When the troops were on the move, we had to leave three or four hours before they did at one end and stay on duty three or four hours longer at the other. Even so, we still had to keep up with their progress, so we had to split into two shifts and take turns being on duty and sleeping. The forced marches were mostly at night, with uninterrupted bombing and strafing by enemy aircraft during the day. We were chronically sleep deprived, and it was not easy to keep our movements coordinated. Sometimes one of us might fall out of line when sheltering from an air raid, fall into a deep sleep and not be found when the troops moved on. It was during an air raid that Chief Qian fell out of line.

Those who fell out of line were in a bad spot. Suddenly I remembered our Xiao He and the telegram Deputy Chief Zou had sent: "Message received. You have fully discharged your responsibilities. Please switch off your radio. Retreat with all speed!"

He had passed on the information about the enemy to headquarters, his mission was complete, but he still wouldn't switch off his radio, he still wouldn't withdraw. He broke the code for the word 梅, and he wanted to tell us. If he had switched off his phone earlier, he might have had the strength to get away. His comrades were breaking out through the enemy lines, and at that moment, he must have been thinking that sending a message was more important than breaking out too. In a situation like that, the breakout is first and foremost a matter of individual escape, but if he failed while trying, he would never have a chance to send another message.

Our military discipline dictates that people die and machines are destroyed. There was a communications soldier in the 3rd Bureau of the Military Committee who jumped off a cliff in his final moments, still holding his radio. In the upper reaches of the Wu River at Lao Mukong, all we received was a signal from Xiao He. We couldn't hear the sound of the killing or see the flash of the bloody broadswords, and we couldn't see his expression at that last moment of his life.

As far as we could picture his position, he must have been on a cliffside as he sent us his last report and made his farewells.

29 April, decoding of Chiang's telegram: Wang Jialie has been allowed to resign from his temporary post and is transferred to be an adviser to the Military Council.

On the morning of 5 May, we crossed the Jinsha River at Jiaopingdu with the central column. This large river on the border between Sichuan and Yunnan is called the Jinsha but is in fact the upper reaches of the Yangtze. Our original strategic plan to cross the river between Yibin and Hejiang and enter Sichuan was now being realised here in Yunnan. What a mysterious and unpredictable detour!

Addendum: In the Three Kingdoms period, Liu Bei entered Sichuan with a map provided by Zhang Song, but this time the Red Army entered Sichuan with a map provided by Long Yun. Long Yun was sending military maps and medicine to Xue Yue by plane, but the pilot suddenly fell ill, so he used a car instead. The car was intercepted in the Qujing area and was found to be full of baiyao, ham and tea. The baiyao is a traditional Chinese remedy that was urgently needed by our army, and the dozens of military maps in the car were a lifesaver. It was on these maps that we found there were nine crossing points on the Jinsha River.

The valley is filled with the red flowers of the kapok tree, like a great conflagration. Bonfires are lit on both sides of the river, illuminating the tumbling waves. Six "leaf" boats go back and forth, with thirty-six boatmen taking turns to row. Passengers ride in the boats, horses wade through the water, people lead the horses and follow the boats. The mules and horses are pulled along by people in the boats and swim across the river with the boats. Our 2nd Bureau's tall, black horse also crosses the river in the same way, but its reins are not tied to the stern of the boat; Ah Gen is sitting in the boat holding them and guiding him along. Some of the more timid mules and horses have to be pulled and pushed by their grooms, and once in deep water, they have difficulty landing on their hooves and have to float along at the stern of the boat. Our big black horse, however, goes into the water on its own and swims with ease, seemingly without the need for the boat to drag it along, just following along at the side of the boat, looking so noble!

The river's banks are rocky and there are no houses to shelter in, only a few small cliff caves where we and the central commanders have taken up residence. The caves are hot and humid, with water dripping from the ceiling and moss on the floor, but we immediately set up our antennae and started work, using the rocks in the caves as our tables and stools. From the breakthrough at the Wu River in January to today's crossing of the Jinsha, in the challenging and unpredictable environment of enemy encirclements, in nearly four months of difficult and circuitous victories, our 2nd Bureau with Zeng, Cao and Zou, who are at the limit of their physical and mental endurance, have successively deciphered more than a hundred messages in different codes from the Chiang, Xiang, Gui, Qian, Chuan and Dian Armies. Every single one has been recorded in Deputy Chief Zou's black leather-bound notebook. He has switched to writing smaller characters to save paper, and the result looks much nicer. There are not many blank pages left in the black book, and the day of victory for the revolution can't be far off. Although we are materialists, we still carry this superstition, and we are all hoping that the remaining pages will be sufficient. If Chief Qian were still around, and if he were to look at the one hundred new records in the black book, he would say that it was an even more beautiful "Hundred Beauties". Thanks to the extraordinary brilliance of Mao and the Central Revolutionary Military Commission – that is Mao's inspiration and Zhou's meticulousness – the coded information we detect has been used to maximum effect. The situation is ever-changing, and the use of military force is unpredictable. Sun Tzu said, "Military strategy is like water that flows from high ground to low ground. So, in your tactics, avoid the enemy's strengths and attack his weaknesses. There are no constants in warfare, any more than water maintains a constant shape. Thus, a general who gains victory by shaping his tactics according to the enemy, ranks with the Immortals."

The ancients used water as a metaphor for the art of war, but now we were faced with a great river. This was no ordinary current; this river was like a giant python. The Politburo had resolved that the Red Army should try to cross the river quickly and go north to establish a Soviet base in western Sichuan.

The commanders of the Military Commission were in the cliff cave next to us, but unfavourable news was emerging from there: the 3rd Red Army Corps was unable to build a bridge at Hongmendu because of the swift flow of the river. Two days before, the 1st Red Army Corps had been blocked at Longjiedu, also because the river was too wide and fast, and the Corps commander, Lin Biao, had asked the Military Commission to advise them to stay put. Our two main forces were blocked from crossing the river, and Wan Yaohuang's division was close on their heels. If Wan's division made haste to the Jinsha crossing, with Xue Yue's other troops following behind to get involved, the 1st and 3rd Red Army Corps and the Central Column would be in danger of being cut off on the wrong side of the river. Wan's division was only a day and a half away. The leaders of the Military Commission were in a state of great agitation, but at a loss for a viable solution. At this point, Chief Cao deciphered a coded telegram from Wan Yaohuang to Chiang Kai-shek. It appeared that Wan was in no hurry to catch up with them! Wan falsely claimed that he had not found any sign of the Communists in the direction he was heading, so he had decided to rest for a day at Tuanjie and then retrace his route to join up with other friendly forces to encircle and annihilate the Red Army elsewhere.

The enemy's pursuit is slow, and their blockade is ineffective, as all the pursuit armies have their own agenda. Wan naturally wants to preserve his division's strength and is reluctant to chase the Red Army alone. When they see the telegram, the leaders of the Military Commission feel as though a light has been turned on. In the war room of another cliff cave, Mao Zedong points to the map on the rock wall with a pencil and says, "Look, we have managed to 'transfer' Long Yun's troops from Yunnan to Guizhou, and now

Wan Yaohuang's division is under our 'command' too! You all know the story of Zhuge Liang harnessing the east wind, right? We are now harnessing the conflict between Chiang Kai-shek and Wan Yaohuang to move our main force across the river. Future generations can write this tale too!"

The enemy had originally left us only a day and a half to cross the river, but now we had four or five days to do so. The Military Commission then ordered the 1st and 3rd Red Army Corps to come to Jiaopingdu and cross the river within the time previously agreed.

On the afternoon of 9 May, all the main forces of our Central Red Army crossed the river.

The next day, when Wan Yaohuang's division reached the river, there was no one to be seen (our rearguard was actually still at the top of the hill on the opposite bank to keep watch, but the enemy could not see them). They looked at the river and sighed since all they could see was river water, fish eagles skimming the waves and a few broken straw sandals on the strand. The planes flew over again and dropped the army pay for the Zhou column. The riverbanks were empty and silent, and there was no sign of the Dian Army troops. Xue Yue sent a telegram to Chiang to raise his doubts about the Dian Army, and we also intercepted one from Long Yun to Chiang:

> "The bandits have undoubtedly crossed the river. I am burning with anxiety at the news. The original plan was to drive the bandits to the riverside, and even if we couldn't dispose of them once and for all, we had to punish them severely, breaking them up beyond repair to save the nation from terrible harm and repay Your Honour's inestimable favour, even if only in the smallest way. Although no one could have anticipated this result, I am ashamed to the very depths of my martial spirit. No matter whether or not there was any effective blockade in place on the north side of the river, practical responsibilities were inadequately assigned, none of the "pursuit and annihilation" forces were strong enough and no one emerges with any distinction. I can only request that Your Honour is rigorous in deciding the appropriate punishment to express my contrition to the Party and the Nation."

Long Yun "humbly accepted the news" and requested that he be punished, but he was, in fact, secretly very satisfied. At first, he was taken aback when the Red Army tried to cross into Yunnan, but now we had crossed the river back into Sichuan, he could sit back and lord it as the "King of Yunnan" without a care. Yunnan is a fine place, with a pleasant climate and excellent produce such as Yunnan Baiyao (white medicine), Xuanwei ham and Pu'er tea. Moreover, most of the necessities for daily life in the cities were French goods imported from Annam. It was even said that Long Yun had a French-made aeroplane of his own.

Addendum: When Chiang repeatedly severely rebuked him, Zhou Hunyuan became depressed, and Wan Yaohuang tried, as a friend, to explain things to him. Over several coded telegrams, he explained: "The Generalissimo flew to Yunnan, and Yunnan has been returned to the control of the central government. The Communist bandits are like a medicinal catalyst to be introduced where the central government's power cannot reach. The entry of the Communists into Sichuan may seem to be a failure militarily speaking, but it is a success in political terms. The effect of their arrival will be that the warlords in Sichuan will not dare to unite to oppose me. Once we were across the river, we no longer intercepted any coded telegrams from the Guizhou or Yunnan factions.

Huili. Our siege of the city was frustrated for several days and eventually abandoned. Chiang Kai-shek flew over the city and dropped orders to the defending troops. He promoted Brigade Commander Liu Yuantang to lieutenant-general of the army and also dropped 10,000 yuan-worth of banknotes as a reward.

The Politburo held an expanded meeting on the outskirts of the city. We heard that a long letter to the Central Committee written by Lin Biao, the head of the army, was discussed. Lin Biao complained that the Red Army was taking a route "along the curves of the bow stave", which would wear the troops out, and that, instead, it should be taking the direct route "along the bowstring". He argued that Mao, Zhou and Zhu should simply accompany the army and preside over the general strategy, and that the command of the front should be handed over to Peng Dehuai so that they could quickly move north to join the Red 4th Front Army. Lin Biao was severely criticised at the meeting on the grounds that he had simply written the letter in a fit of pique.

"You are just a puppet," Mao said. "What do you understand about it?" The troops were indeed exhausted by all the running and never fighting. Lin's letter reflected the fact that the troops' grievances came about because they did not understand the Military Commission's overall strategy... "The Military Commission are not idiots. They will not abandon the 'bowstring' just for the sake of following the 'bow stave'. You can defend in order to attack later, and retreat in order to advance. You can turn to the side to face the front and follow a winding route to go straight ahead. Heaven's affairs do not move according to your will. If you adopt this approach, you won't achieve your aims all at once, but when you come back round again, everything will fall into place."

The Military Committee had to adapt to the rapidly changing enemy situation, even to the extent of changing orders overnight. The basis for the changes was the secret information on the enemy's deployment that our 2nd Bureau had expeditiously discovered, but the combat troops could not be told this explicitly.

We were following the same route that Shi Dakai had taken some eighty years before. His army was defeated at the Dadu River, and as that was precisely where we were heading too, we couldn't help but tell ourselves that great tale from history. When Shi Dakai's Taiping Army also marched all the way through Jiangxi, Hunan, Guizhou and Yunnan, only 40,000 men were left when they reached Anshunchang. They wanted to cross the Dadu into Sichuan, but they were foiled by the river because the melting snow in the mountains upstream swelled the waters and brought flash floods. As a result, they were surrounded by the Qing Army for several days, and eventually wiped out. That happened in the fourth lunar month of the second year of the Emperor Tongzhi. The fourth month of the lunar calendar equates to May in the solar calendar and now, as we hoped to cross the same river, it also happened to be May... Chiang Kai-shek too had long ago remembered what happened to Shi Dakai and he certainly wanted the Red Army to repeat the same mistakes. We intercepted a series of coded telegrams from Chiang to Xue Yue and Liu Wenhui. Chiang ordered Xue to make sure all his officers and men understood the story of

Shi Dakai's defeat at the Dadu River eighty years previously, and to exhort them to work with other friendly forces to attack the Red Army north and south of the Dadu River and destroy it. Chiang especially hoped that Liu Wenhui would follow the example of Luo Bingzhang, the Qing dynasty governor of Sichuan who captured Shi Dakai alive, so that Zhu and Mao's Red Army would become this generation's Shi Dakai.

The question was whether Liu Wenhui, commander-in-chief of the Chuankang Border Defence Army and also commander of the 24th Army, would follow Chiang's wishes. The latest story was that Liu Wenhui and his nephew Liu Xiang were fighting for supremacy in Sichuan, but Chiang Kai-shek was backing Liu Xiang, who became the "Governor of Sichuan", and Liu Wenhui retired to the barren and impoverished frontier, where his only option was to become the "King of Xikang" (Western Sichuan).

Our current task is still to "march" and "fight", but the Red Army is now down to 20,000 men. Many have died of starvation and exhaustion; dysentery is spreading and typhoid is beginning to appear. As for fighting, ammunition was already in short supply, and now it is not going to withstand any major demand. We have been forced into this western part of China, have had to trek across the sparsely populated eastern side of the Qinghai-Tibet Plateau, and all of us are covered in lice. With treacherous mountains, rivers, forests and snow, it is not only the enemy's pursuit we have to overcome, but also the ferocity of Nature itself.

The high mountains, dense forests, clouds and rain make radio signal reception very difficult and locating the enemy even more so. It is hard to get hold of fuel in these poor mountains, so oil for the radio has become a big problem. Always economising on consumption, we are searching for it everywhere.

We are still marching in relay combat formations, still moving between vanguard and rearguard, on duty, off duty twenty-four hours a day, constantly reconnoitring. To overcome interference from the terrain, the bodyguard squad and the transport team are helping us to raise our antennae, sometimes right at the very top of a mountain.

The enemy codes have changed again, and the two section chiefs, Cao and Zou, are solely focused on the challenge. Chief Zeng too is always engrossed in whatever sheet of code he is carrying, whether he is marching along the road or riding his horse. So much so, in fact, that he often trips as he walks or even falls off the horse.

After leaving Huili, the Red Army marched north through the Yi region of the Daliang Mountains. Fortunately, the local Yi guides and interpreters led the way, so we avoided any major attacks. On 25 May, we arrived at Anshunchang. Previously Chiang Kai-shek had flown to Kunming, where he had personally overseen the Dadu River campaign. This time it looked more as if he was sharing the hardships of his soldiers and officers, and we knew from the wording of the coded telegram that he had flown to the front himself and used his own message pouch to drop his "personal orders" to the unit commanders!

Chiang's relentless pursuit from Nanchang to Chongqing to Guiyang and Kunming, which he had personally followed all the way "regardless of suffering and hardship", was not going to let up. On 26 May he flew to Chengdu, where he had set up the Xingyuan battalion regiment to supervise the encirclement.

All that awaited him was failure. *The Red Star*, 30 May: "We have victoriously crossed the Dadu River." In the upper reaches of the Yangtze River, where Shi Dakai was defeated, our Red Army created a legend unprecedented in history.

On one side is Mount Gongga and on the other is Mount Erlang. Although the big river between the two mountains is not as wide as the Jinsha, it has strong waves and powerful currents, with a flow speed of four metres a second. There are towering peaks on both sides of the strait, monstrous rock formations in the river itself, raging waves battering the sides with a deafening roar, and everyone on the bank is shouting at the tops of their voices. The river is full of whirlpools and hidden reefs which make it incredibly difficult to build a pontoon bridge. In this season, the snow on the mountains in the upper reaches is melting.

We made the crossing a few days after Shi Dakai, and while the river is wider for the time of year, we are rushing across with the enemy in hot pursuit. When Shi Dakai began his crossing, there were no Qing soldiers behind him. We have only found three boats at Anshunchang, one usable, two waiting to be repaired, but the most any of them can carry is thirty people. Like this, it will take a full month for the Red Army to cross the river, and the information we have from the 2nd Bureau is that Xue Yue's Central Army is closing in fast, and Yang Sen's troops of the Chuan Army are only three or four days away. This valley may turn out to be the valley of death. If we cannot cross this treacherous river within five days, the Red Army really may follow in the footsteps of Shi Dakai.

Upstream of the Dadu River is the old Luding Bridge, and the Military Committee decide to take control of it immediately. Even though we don't actually know whether the bridge is still in place, we have no choice. The Luding Bridge is the main route from Sichuan to Kangding, where commodities such as tea, salt and sugar are distributed from Sichuan throughout the Kham region of Tibet. We split into two columns, left and right, and simultaneously head for the Luding Bridge along both sides of the river. The worst-case scenario is that if the left column fails to cross the river, the right army led by Liu and Nie can "head into Sichuan and create a situation".

Anshunchang is 320 *li* of mountain road from Luding Bridge, along a rugged path cut out of the rocky riverbank, with cliffs on one side and rapids on the other. With no knowledge of enemy dispositions along the way, our troops had to arrive in two and a half days, travelling a hundred *li* a day. Early on the morning of 27 May, the 4th Regiment of the 2nd Division of the 1st Red Army Corps made a rapid march towards Luding. They had made just thirty *li* of rapid progress upstream when they were engaged by Chuan forces. They fought as they marched, wiping out the enemy as they progressed. At midnight, they rested eighty *li* from Anshunchang.

The next morning, they continued their journey but did not get very far before encountering a corps messenger coming after them on a fast horse. It was a note from Lin and Nie to the regimental commander Wang Kaixiang and political commissar Yang Chengwu: "Wang and Yang: the Military Commission has sent a telegram firmly ordering the lefthand column to capture Luding Bridge tomorrow. You must proceed with utmost effort and resolute manoeuvring to accomplish this great and glorious task. This time you will have to break the records for the capture of Daozhou and the time when the 5th Regiment took Yaxi by running 160 miles in one day. You are heroes on the line of battle and model soldiers of the Red Army. We believe you will be able to accomplish this task, and we are ready to congratulate you on your victory!"

The Military Commission ordered the capture of Luding Bridge on 29 May. The distance on the map was 240 *li*, with only a day and one night to run there! This order was clear and unambiguous! The mountains were steep, the roads were wet and slippery, they were carrying guns and ammunition, and they had to fight the Chuan troops along the way.

They travelled along the west bank of the river towards Luding Bridge. The mist-shrouded road there winds and twists like sheep's intestines, rising and falling, sometimes with wooden walkways anchored into the rock, with steep cliffs on one side and dizzying turbulence on the other. Some people just couldn't run any more, others lost their footing and tumbled into the river, while those who could, just kept their heads down and ran.

At 6 am on the 29th, the 4th Regiment arrived at Luding Bridge on time.

At the bridgehead on the west bank, the bugle sounded, making the soldiers' blood surge! The regimental buglers blew their horns in unison, and the whole regiment opened fire with machine guns, mortars and grenades. Under this furious blaze of covering fire, twenty-two soldiers with sabres on their backs and grenades around their waists charged onto the swaying chains and planking of the bridge. They advanced in the teeth of enemy bullets onto the bridge over the mighty, tempestuous river! The enemy on the other side of the bridge were scared out of their wits, never having seen such courage. They set fire to the bridgehead on their side and turned and fled back into the forest. The courageous warriors charged forward, hurling grenades at the enemy with all their might. They had broken through!

On the east bank was the county town of Luding. The 4th Red Army Regiment swiftly overwhelmed Liu Wenhui's defending troops in one assault. One by one, the main force assembled at the bridgehead and waited to make their orderly way across. The crossing of this river marked a great victory for the Red Army.

We crossed the river on this bridge. The bridge was formed of planks lashed in with chains and was very unsteady. The high winds made it even more difficult to keep straight and upright, and some of us almost crawled across bent double and not daring to look directly at the tumbling rapids below. Many of the mules and horses were even more afraid to get onto the bridge and they crowded the bridgehead, screaming and neighing. But our 2nd Bureau's big black horse, the horse that carried the wounded up the "sky ladder" on Laoshanjie, and the horse that carried the wounded across the Wu River pontoon bridge, calmly followed Ah Gen across.

And so, the big black horse is with us on the other side of the river, on the road to victory.

The joy of this victory inspired us. Crossing the Dadu River and stepping off the bridge, we felt that the heavens were wide open to us. Hope was unfolding ahead, new hope that thrilled everyone's heart. What was more, we were expecting to rejoin the 4th Red Front Army soon, and it would be time to stop this seemingly endless trek.

What exactly is the location of the 4th Front Army? Our contact with them was suddenly cut off some time ago. The men of the 3rd Bureau of the Military Commission have been taking turns calling at the appointed time but have never been able to get through. All we know is that they are in the north. All we can do is head north.

We couldn't take the mountain road across Mount Erlang for fear of the enemy's bombers, so we walked through the virgin forest. We hacked our way through thorns and briers because there was no other way through. The primeval forest hid the sky, and only through the thin gaps in the canopy could we catch a glimpse of the snow-capped mountains to the north, as the north wind blew across the lightning-struck tree trunks on the mountain cliffs. We clambered past the kudzu vines, a thick layer of rotting leaves and black mud underfoot, and struggled through thorny thickets, fighting leeches and poisonous snakes and mosquitoes as big as small dragonflies. We were all "mud monkeys" as we marched through the rain, but no one cared about how we looked in this dense, dark forest, and we were more concerned about our luggage. Deputy Chief Zou's backpack was almost lost, but luckily the people behind him found it in time, otherwise it would have been a great loss for our 2nd Bureau! The little black leather-bound notebook of the decoding section was in there.

We crossed Mount Erlang and then broke through the Chuan

Army's Tianquan-Lushan blockade line. Rations were running low, we still had to cross the tall, snowy mountains ahead and the wounded had to stay behind, consigned to the homes of locals. It didn't bear thinking about too much, what it meant to them to stay behind. They were determined to go with the group, willing to die on the road. We all had to be ruthless in persuading them to stay, and we tried loading them down with the silver dollars we had, which they needed more than anything else. Those who were travelling with the army really didn't need that kind of personal belonging. As long as they didn't fall behind, it didn't matter whether they had silver dollars on them or not. But the wounded said, "No, we don't want the money, leave us hand grenades!" One young soldier called out, "I am grateful for your class solidarity, but what I really want from you is a gun!" We could only hope that they were not discovered and killed by the reactionary militia. We could only hope our comrades could recover from their wounds quickly enough to catch up with the main force. We could only hope that we would establish a base camp again soon and be able to go back and pick them up...

The sky is cloudy, but we finally have good news! The 4th Red Front Army is getting signals again! In March and April, the Central Committee and the Military Commission had asked them several times about the situation, and they had replied promptly and confidentially about the enemy deployment on the ground, but then contact was broken for some reason. Now that contact has been restored, they have sent troops to join the Central Red Army.

On 8 June, the Central Committee of the Communist Party of China and the Military Commission of the Chinese Revolutionary Army issued instructions to all the army corps, making it clear for the first time that the strategic aim was to rendezvous with the 4th Red Front Army and that the rendezvous point would be Maogong. We trekked through mountains and suffered great hardships to rendezvous with the 4th Front Army.

We were marching through the gorge towards Mount Jiajin, and although it was summer, the nights were really cold. "Men and horses starved together" and "there was nowhere to shelter at dusk": everyone was in the same boat. All we had were a few Tibetan houses at the foot of the mountain, which could only be used to house our radio station and facilitate its work. Even our commanders, Mao, Zhou and Zhu, had to camp out. Zhu laid himself down under a protruding rock and joked that tonight the commander-in-chief was living in paradise!

As the troops were sorting out the camp, the political commissars were holding a noisy rally, the main message of which was that we are the Red Army of workers and peasants who have won a hundred battles. In the past, we have defeated countless warlords, and now, once again, we have to wage war against Nature. As long as we carry forward the spirit of being willing to make sacrifices, no hardship can stop us from advancing! The mountains will never be too tall for our legs, the snow will never freeze our hearts and we continue to compete with the snowy mountains and duel with the ice and snow!

Jiajinshan is the only route open to us. Chiang Kai-shek thinks he can freeze and starve the Red Army to death without firing a single shot. Few of us from the south have ever seen such a huge, snow-covered mountain, but, once over it, our strategic objective will be achieved. Knowing this, we no longer find it so terrifying. The locals here say that it is a sacred mountain that is difficult even for birds to cross, and that offending the gods who live on it will result in punishment, but there is no other way, we have to go over this mountain.

On arriving at the foot of the snow-covered mountains, we really felt the cold. We were all in thin, unlined clothes at this time of year, and we had given our winter clothes to the "dry people" in Yunnan to show our class solidarity. Luckily, headquarters gave us each a goatskin, which we tied around us to keep us warm. The horses were giving off great clouds of steaming breath, the campfires were blazing, and the troops were boiling up chilli water, even though chillis were in very short supply. With the chilli water inside us, it was time to start climbing.

Birds were flying over the wheat fields, red-billed crows, cawing at us as if giving us a final warning, but we didn't care!

How many people have died on this snow-covered mountain on the eve of our triumphant reunion? The mountain may not be enormously high, but the air is cold and thin, with low air pressure. It squeezes the heart, making breathing difficult. Our faces go blue with the lack of oxygen and we can only move so very slowly. Some of the young soldiers, whose sickly bodies are freezing cold, find themselves out of breath the moment they try to talk. One false step and your foot could catch in a crack in the ice, sending you tumbling down the slope. No loud talking, no laughter (laughter offends the mountain gods and can cause avalanches), no sitting down to rest and no fainting. Some froth at the mouth as soon as they sit down and can't get up again. Some soldiers are so weak and unsteady on their feet that they are blown down into the snowy valley by the wind. Mao Zedong is to be seen walking, leaning a wooden stick, and there too are the senior cadres Xu, Dong and Xie, who are marching with their fellow seniors. Lao Xu is still using his red-tasselled spear as a crutch. He Zizhen is looking very weak, but she is also determined not to ride; rather, she has given up her horse to the seriously wounded and just holds on to its tail to be pulled up the slope. Our bulkiest and most important treasure, the battery charger, is still being carried by Ah Gen and his comrades on the transport team. Halfway up the hill, Chief Zeng suddenly bends over, a little out of breath, with sweat beading his forehead. We hurriedly urge him to get onto his horse and are about to take the unconscious soldier down from the saddle, when Chief Zeng stops us. He straightens up and takes a few slow breaths before stumbling forward again, leaning on his stick. It's not long before we see another female comrade from the command headquarters who can't walk any further. We tell her to take hold of the black horse's tail so she can be pulled along. We are all sockless in our straw sandals, so our feet are covered in snow with every step. Many of us have worn out our sandals and no one has any spares to offer, so we walk barefoot in the snow. Some of us have cracked and bleeding feet, so we wrap them in rags.

It is said that there were some revolutionary romantics who ate cakes of snow dipped in saccharin at the top of the mountain and declared it even better than the famous Shanghai Guanshengyuan ice cream!

Addendum: I recently heard Xiao Jinguang say that this was a story from when they were crossing another mountain later on. Someone shouted that if anyone had any saccharin, they should get it out now in the "spirit of communism", so Guo Huaruo produced his small bottle of the stuff.

The 1st Corps propaganda team left large slogans written on wooden boards: "Comrades, please don't ever stop! Muster your spirits and climb the mountain in one breath! It is only five hours from here to your destination... use all your strength!" A female "political warrior" of the Cadre Recuperation Company who was carrying a stretcher shouted that her eyes were swollen and sore. Someone else said that her eyes were irritated by the glare of the snow and that she was afraid she was going to get snow blindness, so another female soldier rushed to replace her. We stumbled along in the snow and wind, not knowing how long we had been walking, and just when we felt like we were going to collapse within the next few steps, we saw the red flag. The top of the hill was approaching, and there was the red flag planted by the advance guard. When we reached the top, we were ordered: "Sit down and slide down!" Taking our courage in both hands, we did as we were told, sliding down the hill as if on a toboggan, although some of us slipped over into holes under the snow.

At noon on 12 June, a thick fog filled the northern foothills of Jiajinshan, and it was there that the forward troops of the Central Red Army and the 4th Red Front Army met. The Central Red Army forward guard was the 4th Regiment of the 1st Army Corps. Wang Kaixiang and Yang Chengwu saw the men with guns through their binoculars, and they were all wearing the baggy, eight-panel Red Army caps! At first there was a brief stand-off, with the buglers establishing contact with bugle calls, but the two sides had difficulty understanding each other. The 4th Regiment's scouts brought back word that it was the 4th Red Front Army! In the fading mist, both sides recognised each other's red flags, flags with hammers and sickles on them! The two Red Armies swarmed down into the valley which echoed with their cheers.

Xu Xiangqian, commander-in-chief of the 4th Red Front Army, demanded that "the Central Western Expeditionary Force, which has won a hundred battles, be welcomed with 10,000 per cent enthusiasm", and the ragged officers and soldiers of the 4th Regiment were served large plates of yak meat, mutton and potatoes. In the afternoon of 14 June, the leaders of the Central Committee and the Military Commission came down from the mountains to the small town of Dawei. Early the next morning, they left Dawei for Maogong. The 4th Red Front Army and the Central Field Army exchanged congratulatory messages. On 18 June, the Central Red Army arrived in Maogong and the small, snowy city turned into a joyous scene, with everyone shaking hands, hugging and rejoicing. We were welcomed with brotherly enthusiasm, and everyone was delighted. Officers and soldiers from both armies gave each other gifts to celebrate their meeting. The base camp of the 4th Red Front Army was in Mao County, and Zhang Guotao sent a telegram saying that there were problems with food supplies in the area of Maogong. The Central Red Army left Maogong heading north and arrived near Lianghekou. The Red Army officers and soldiers set up a meeting place, and the leaders of the Central Committee and the Military Commission went three *li* out of camp to greet Zhang Guotao on his arrival. Behind them, thousands of Central Red Army troops lined the road, their tattered flags fluttering in the cold wind.

It was raining heavily, and the ranks of soldiers stood in the rain as the chiefs took shelter under the rain canopy. "They're here!" someone shouted in welcome, to be followed by loud and prolonged cheering from the others. People were standing on tiptoe and craning their necks to look at the turning off the main road. First, a few horse heads appeared on the forest road, then, almost immediately, a group of tall horses came galloping along.

"Welcome the leaders of the Fourth Front Army!"

"Learn from the heroic Fourth Front Army!"

"Long live the meeting of the main forces of the Red Army!"

The soldiers beat their gongs and drums as hard as they could, shouting slogans in thunderous voices. They were drenched by the rain and their own tears but jumped and cheered even more vigorously for the joy of this victory. Two majestic people's armies, closely united from now on, marching towards a new victory! The shouting and cheering, the overwhelming enthusiasm of the crowd were such that the whole scene exceeded any description.

The great stallions came galloping in, their hooves splashing in the puddles. These were the chiefs of the 4th Front Army and their

AFTERTHOUGHTS

cavalry guard. In the forefront is a large horse with a white head; that had to be the mount of Zhang Guotao.

With his eight-panel army cap and dark new uniform, Zhang Guotao was smiling as he sat, whip in hand, looking flushed and radiant, while Mao Zedong was wearing an old, patched uniform, and had sunken cheeks and a haggard appearance.

Chairman Zhang Guotao, General Political Commissar Chen Changhao and several more unfamiliar senior generals of the 4th Red Front Army...

This was the moment Chief Zeng had long been waiting for. He was also expecting a familiar figure to appear. His brother Zeng Zhongsheng, leader of the E-Yu-Wan (Hubei-Henan-Anhui) revolutionary base. They had not seen each other for more than six years. The last time they had met was in the spring of 1929 when his brother had just returned from Sun Yat-sen University in Moscow. After a brief meeting at the Central Military Commission of the Communist Party of China in Shanghai, Chief Zeng went north to Yantai to work on subversive measures to incite the enemy to defect or rebel.

When revolutionaries go to the ends of the earth, there are always many partings, and they are always ready to die. We have become used to all kinds of partings, even those of life and death. We had radio contact with the 4th Front Army, although it was intermittent and never steady, so why had he never thought of getting in touch with his brother by radio?

We asked him about this, but Chief Zeng had a look on his face that brooked no challenge. He simply said dispassionately, "We have discipline, comrades. Do you not understand what that means?"

Addendum: Recently, I heard from comrades of the 4th Front Army's 2nd Radio Station that they sometimes had trouble communicating with the Central Red Army because they had lost their codebooks and Chairman Zhang was worried that the enemy had deciphered our secret reports.

We had close and friendly exchanges with our counterparts in the 4th Front Army. We had not expected they could muster more than 80,000 men and horses, while we, the Central Red Army, had come all this way with fewer than a quarter of that total. We were a tired and hungry collection of soldiers, while they were strong and powerful. Our clothes were patched and tattered and many of us were thin and bony, but they were all in good shape. They all had brand-new dark uniforms and even bigger army caps than we did.

Zeng San, a member of the political committee of the Red Army Communication School, was in Hankou without a posting at the time. Zhou Enlai sent Zeng Mian to talk to him about his work and asked him to go to Shanghai to find Wu Yunfu so they could learn radio technology together with Zhang Shenchuan. At the beginning of 1930, Zeng San left Hankou for Shanghai, and Zeng Mian gave him fifteen silver dollars as travel expenses. Zeng San and Cai Wei were both communications cadres trained by Zhou Enlai and had studied in the radio class at Julu Road in Shanghai. Now, Cai Wei was director of the 4th Front Army's 2nd Radio Station. The 2nd Station was the reconnaissance station, and Cai Wei was the best codebreaker in the 4th Front Army. Chief Zeng made an appointment with Wang Zheng, director of the Third Bureau, and accompanied by Zeng San, he took the initiative to visit Cai Wei. After the meeting, when Zeng San and Cai Wei were about to part, Cai Wei ordered the quartermaster to prepare a special meal. The quartermaster brought out bacon and white fungus, and also made a large pot of beef and white rice. They continued their discussions the next day and met again the day after. They seem to have endless topics to discuss.

As he ate his beef and rice, Chief Zeng laughed and asked Cai Wei what the codes had tasted like. It seems that once, when Cai Wei and his men were surrounded by enemy troops, Cai Wei asked the personnel of the 2nd Radio Station to bury the radio equipment and then led everyone in breaking out. He carried the codebook with him. He knew that if he was captured, the consequences were unthinkable, so he pulled the silver dollars and other coins from his pocket and scattered them on the ground. His comrades following behind him did the same. They knew that, as soon as the Kuomintang soldiers saw the silver, they would keep their heads down looking for more money. This would significantly slow their pursuit. As Cao Wei ran, he tore up the codebook and stuffed the pages into his mouth, chewing and swallowing them as he went.

When the man is safe, the codebooks must stay safe, but when the man is lost, the codebooks must become lost too.

Cai Wei attended Fuzhou Gezhi High School in his early years and also the Shanghai Huiling English College, where he was "baptised" in the new culture, embraced the doctrine of Marx and embarked on the revolutionary path. He spoke Fujianese dialect, which sometimes made him difficult to understand, and, as he had studied foreign languages, he was referred to as a "foreign student" by his comrades in the 2nd Radio Station. His English was of great use in his decoding, especially when he broke the enemy's QRC code. In 1932, when Chiang Kai-shek's 300,000-strong army was attempting to encircle and annihilate the E-Yu-Wan (EYW) Soviet area, the 4th Red Front Army was under a tight blockade and hemmed in by many layers of encirclement. The Radio Station was short of equipment and fuel and was often non-operational. Cai Wei then buried himself in the radio room, working day and night to solve one problem after another. The battery charger was missing a compression gasket, so he made a substitute with his own hands and when it needed sanding and polishing, he used ground-up tile ash as a polishing medium. When they ran out of lubricating oil, he rendered down pig and cow fat, refined it twice, filtered it and used that instead. When he saw that the local people used the water flowing from a river channel to drive a wooden turbine to grind their flour, he developed his own wooden water turbine to generate electricity by using the drop of the river water... Chief Zeng had more conversations with Cai Wei, and our 2nd Bureau had more contacts with the 2nd Radio Station. The comrades sometimes played table tennis together, and the 2nd Radio Station also lent us *Fiction Monthly* to read. When Cai Wei heard that our 2nd Bureau battery charger often broke down, he gave us the only one he had as an emergency loan.

As we get to know our comrades in the 4th Front Red Army better, feelings became more complicated. Before the rendezvous, General Commissar Chen Changhao had suggested the slogan "Welcome to 300,000-strong Central Red Army", and that's how the propaganda slogans had all read. But after the rendezvous, when they learnt that the "Great Iron Army" they had been expecting was reduced to so few and that many of them were sick and in poor health, our comrades of the 4th Front Red Army had mixed emotions.

Chen Changhao had gone with Zhang Guotao to the EYW Soviet Zone under the personal escort of Gu Shunzhang. It was on the way back from this mission that Gu was recognised by traitors in the crowd when he was doing his magic act in Hankou. Before Zhang Guotao arrived in the EYW Soviet, Zeng Zhongsheng, Chief Zeng's brother, was secretary of the Special Committee of the Communist Party of China's EYW Soviet and chairman of the Military Committee. The EYW Soviet had been the Communist Party's largest base area. Chief Zeng and Cai Wei had had many dealings with each other as peers and comrades-in-arms, and had formed a close relationship, so there was nothing they couldn't discuss together. When Cai Wei heard Chief Zeng say that he was Zeng Zhongsheng's younger brother, he was more in awe of him, not to say a little terrified. On this occasion, when the two main armies joined forces, there was no sign of the elder brother. Chief Zeng believed he was away on military affairs. Xu Xiangqian, commander-in-chief of the Red 4th Front Army, was not there either. It was said that he was stationed on the front line at Luhua. Chief Zeng had a feeling that his elder brother might be badly injured or seriously ill, but now seeing Cai Wei's frightened expression, his caution and vigilance took on an ominous edge. He knew that his brother was likely to have been sucked into the political maelstrom, which was more deadly than any ailment, however serious.

Over those few days, we heard, from time to time, that Zhang Guotao was staging a "purge" and every cadre in the 4th Front Army was in danger. Could it be that the "purge" had been extended to the chief's older brother? It was said that there were three main types of people who were the target of the purge. One was those from the White Army; regardless of whether they had mutinied, defected or been captured and regardless of whether they had engaged in counter-revolutionary activities, they all had to be investigated. Another was those from landlord and rich peasant families, regardless of performance; they too all had to be investigated. The third comprised intellectuals and young students; "intellectual faction" became a label on its own, and anyone who had studied even for just a few days had to be investigated as well.

In the name of "purifying the revolutionary ranks", decapitation was the most serious punishment, and purging was the lightest. It was said that some female comrades were also purged because of their good looks. Their beauty meant they were suspected of being bourgeois, or the daughters of landlord families who had joined the revolutionary ranks. Comrades from the 2nd Radio Station of the 4th Front Army were spared because the work of radio stations and intelligence was essential to the war effort. Cai Wei was the "nemesis" of the enemy radio station's coding operatives, and also the "Bodhisattva" to whom Chen Changhao made offerings. Chief Zeng now tried to avoid private contact with Cao Wei in order not to bring political troubles down on him.

An oppressive miasma had descended. Two iron armies formed of the best sons and daughters of the proletariat had miraculously and fraternally met, against all odds, in what should have been an overwhelmingly happy victory, but the warmth of the bond was driven off by a chill current. There was a growing and disturbing feeling in the gloom, and political differences began to raise their heads. In the 4th Red Front Army, in the two main Red Armies after their reunion, it was Zhang Guotao who was to have greater power. Zeng Zhongsheng did not get caught up in the political maelstrom because of the widening purge of anti-revolutionaries; rather, he was persecuted for opposing Zhang Guotao's dogmatic leftist stance. As early as August 1933, Zhang Guotao falsely accused Zeng Zhongsheng of being one of "Chen Duxiu's abolitionists" and a "rightist leader" and had him removed from his post and imprisoned. After the Red Army rendezvous, Mao Zedong and Zhou Enlai suggested a meeting with Zeng Zhongsheng, but Zhang Guotao flatly refused.

Chief Zeng learned about his brother's fall from grace from the central leadership. He was thankful that his brother was still alive. How close but far away he felt! Such an oppressive miasma! He was part of our own ranks, he was even a senior leader within those ranks, which were, in turn, led by the Communist Party, but the Central Committee of the Communist Party was unable to rescue him.

The Central Party Committee is facing a brutal struggle, a struggle which concerns the fate and future of the Red Army. In the wake of this great rendezvous, the struggle against opportunism is the most serious task for the Party. The joy of the rendezvous has been short-lived, and soon it is driven away by deep concern. The danger signals have been there since long before the meeting. Before the rendezvous of the two armies, Zhang Guotao and Chen Changhao had telegraphed the Central Revolutionary Military Committee in opposing going north and advocating going south; even if the decision was to go north, they should not develop the northerly movement to the east, but to the west, to Qinghai.

The purpose of going north is to establish the Sichuan-Shaanxi-Gansu Soviet Area, which is closer to the anti-Japanese front line, and would also help the Communist Party play a role in the movement to save the nation from the Japanese. However, Zhang Guotao wants to avoid the strong military pressure from the Kuomintang. His suggestion is that the whole army goes south to the borders of Sichuan and Xikang, or retreats in the direction of Qinghai and Xinjiang. On 22 June, at the expanded meeting of the Central Committee at Lianghekou, most of the participants agree to go north. Seeing that opinion is overwhelmingly against him, Zhang Guotao has no choice but to agree too. The meeting decides that he should be made vice chairman of the Central Revolutionary Military Commission.

Our current enemy is Hu Zongnan. He is commander of the 2nd column of the 3rd Route Army of the Kuomintang's "bandits suppression" campaign. We at the 2nd Bureau will never let down our guard. We have to keep a close eye on Hu Zongnan and Xue Yue of the Kuomintang Central Army, and we also have to watch what is going on with the various factions of the Chuan Army. Hu Zongnan's troops have just arrived in Songpan but have not yet gained a firm foothold.

On 29 June, in accordance with the spirit of the Lianghekou meeting and the enemy situation reported by the 2nd Bureau, the Central Revolutionary Military Commission formulated the Songpan Campaign Plan to take advantage of the first opportunity to annihilate Hu Zongnan's troops and seize control of the road to the north. Although Zhang Guotao agreed to the northward policy at the meeting, he still pressed his case after the meeting and incited some people to suggest he be made chairman of the Military Commission.

I have heard that the Central Revolutionary Military Commission awarded Xu Xiangqian and Chen Changhao the gold Red Star Medal, First Class. I suddenly remembered Chief Qian, the designer of the Red Star Medal. I also thought of Xiao He, and the book *First Love* Chief Qian sent him. And I thought of the last coded message Chief Qian sent. My heart ached at all these thoughts, and I couldn't sleep that night.

In mid-July, as planned, we crossed several more snow-capped mountains, including Mengbishan. The Central Red Army captured Mao'ergai near Songpan and tried to implement the Songpan Campaign Plan, but Zhang Guotao did not cooperate. Forty days later, because of this delay, Chiang Kai-shek had sufficient time to adjust his deployment and Hu Zongnan built a blockade of bunkers in the area west of the Min River and north of Maogong. The opportunity for winning the Battle of Songpan was lost, and the Red Army had no route north except across the great grasslands to the west of Songpan.

Zhang Guotao was a powerhouse who was clearly mobilising troops to extend his influence, and to win him over to lead the army northwards, Zhou Enlai gave up his position as general commissar of the Red Army. In June, in order to be on the same level as the 4th Red Front Army and to facilitate concerted action, the Central Red Army officially reverted to the name 1st Red Front Army and no longer used its field army designation. In mid-July, the various corps of the 1st Red Front Army changed to become "armies": the 1st Red Army Corps became the 1st Army, the 3rd Red Army Corps became the 3rd Army, the 5th Red Army Corps became the 5th Army, and the 9th Red Army Corps became the 32nd Army. The 9th Red Army had not been able to cross the Wu River at first, but not only were they not wiped out, they survived and grew even stronger. Having failed to cross the Wu River, they did manage to cross the Jinsha and join up with the Central Red Army.

The 2nd Bureau's latest report on enemy deployments: Hu Zongnan's main force is completing its assembly in the Songpan area; Xue Yue's corps has moved from Ya'an to the Pingwu area to close up with Hu Zongnan's troops; all divisions of the Chuan Army have occupied Maogong and other places.

A new encirclement was tightening and the enemy's rings of blockhouses were largely complete. In order to get out of this predicament, the Central Party Committee further drew up the "Xia-Tao Campaign Plan" on 3 August, deciding that the main force of the Red Army would turn west to occupy Aba and then head north into southern Gansu. To strengthen the brotherhood and unity of the 1st and 4th Front Armies, and also to avoid the crush of over-large forces on the march which would delay the battle, the plan intermingled the two Front Armies: the Right Route Army, with Xu Xiangqian as general commander, Chen Changhao as political commissar and Ye Jianying as chief of staff, led the 1st Army of the 1st Red Front Army and the 4th and 30th Armies of the Red 4th Front Army from Mao'ergai to Banyou via the Songpan grasslands. The Left Route Army, with the 5th and 32nd Armies of the 1st Red Front Army and the 9th, 31st and 33rd Armies of the 4th Red Front Army, led by Zhu De, commander-in-chief of the Red Army, Zhang Guotao, general political commissar, and Liu Bocheng, chief of staff, set out from Zhuokeji and went to Aba via the Songpan grasslands, then joined the Right Route Army and went north together. The Central Party Committee travelled with the Right Route Army. The 2nd Bureau of the General Command of the Red Army and the 2nd Radio Station of the 4th Red Front Army were grouped together in the Right Route Army and marched with the Forward Army General Command.

Our 2nd Bureau of the Military Commission was posted in the Right Route Army. Before the forces split up and started out, Chief Zeng was overseeing the reconnaissance desk of the Left Route Army, but Chief of Staff Liu Bocheng told him, "You must go with Mao Zedong no matter what, not with Zhang Guotao." After the Maogong rendezvous, Zhang Guotao had been informed by various sources of the important role played by Chief Zeng and our 2nd Bureau, and he had been consumed with envy ever since. He wanted to use his position as chief political commissar of the Red Army to lure Chief Zeng to his side. First, he tried to woo him away, but he was the man who had cruelly persecuted Chief Zeng's brother, and his guilty conscience constrained him. How could he ever get Chief Zeng to come back over to his side? He turned his attention to trying to draw in Cao and Zou from the 2nd Bureau in an attempt to persuade the Bureau, or part of it, to go with him, but all his efforts were in vain. We were also very dissatisfied with the domineering style of Chen Changhao of the 4th Front Army. He was a political commissar of the forward general headquarters of the Red Army, but when he and his guards came to the Central Party Committee's station and galloped arrogantly past us, we were more than a little unhappy. Yes, we were shabbily dressed, few in number and poorly armed but...

The great grasslands of Songpan. A beautiful, natural landscape, but we haven't got very far before we begin to curse it! It is another death march. We are struggling with nature in these oxygen-starved highlands. Our long, winding line of people is an unprecedented miracle in this uninhabited, dead land. The first day we walk, the grass can still be called dry. The second day the grass is growing in water, but it is only ankle deep. The third day we are mired in a mess of water and grass. The grass is still grass, but there is no mud on the ground, only dense waterweed. There are endless self-perpetuating weeds and flowers, and underneath the flowers and grass is muddy, red-brown water. We walk with our trouser legs rolled up high, one foot deep and one foot shallow on the endless muddy grass and roots, with a life-threatening sinkhole beneath our feet at every step. If one man gets stuck, the rescuer will be dragged down too. We try to follow the trail markers left by the advance party that tell us "follow this route". The sky is cloudy and not a single bird can be seen; there are no trees or rocks on the ground.

After a day's trekking, the troops have to camp in puddles, and the soldiers doze off in the water, leaning on wooden sticks or rifle butts. There are still two taels of fried barley powder in the dry ration bag, but no matter how hungry we are, we don't dare to eat them because we don't know how many days walking lie ahead. Many of us ate too much two days before, and since we have exceeded the ration, we have to try a day of fasting. In the freezing wind and rain, the *qingke* barley grains people find on the ground are the undigested ones in bird and animal droppings. Eyes glazed over with unbearable hunger, they gather them up, wash them and eat them. Wild vegetables can fill an empty stomach, but they can't be eaten indiscriminately, as some are deadly poisonous, the mushrooms in particular. Several of our comrades in the 2nd Bureau have eaten poisonous mushrooms. Any wild onions, garlic and grass roots are eaten by the troops at the front of the column, and the grass itself is simply inedible. There is water everywhere, but you can't just scoop it up and drink it; some people have already been poisoned that way. We look forward to the occasional rain and wait to catch it, but there is hardly any dry ground on which to build a fire to boil it. When we camp at night, we are happy if we find just a small patch of grass above the water. The weather is unpredictable, sometimes hot and sunny with clear skies, sometimes there are dark clouds and rain, hail and snow. Without tents or waterproofs, many men die of hunger and cold, and the troops behind the vanguard no longer need signs to guide them, they just follow the line of the corpses of their dead comrades. Our warriors of steel, who have come through so many storms of bullets and shells, cannot break through this grass! At any time as we march, we see people who have fallen behind. Although we do not have the strength to back up our intentions, and although we ourselves are faint with hunger, our feelings of revolutionary fraternity still make us try to help.

One morning, I see a group of people gathered around the ashes of a fire, on which a small pot is steaming. They are sitting quietly with their backs to each other, and everyone is cradling guns in their arms, as if they are asleep. We call to them to get up and go, but there is no answer. We go over to shake one of them, but he collapses at our touch. They had gathered around the fire to get warm before they died. Tearful, we all stop and gently lower them to the ground in order to give them some dignity and to see if there are any comrades who are still alive and cannot be left there. We can't bury them due to the absence of dry earth on the grasslands, so all we can do is pull up some flowering weeds to cover their faces. When we camp at night, it is difficult to see the beauty in the star-filled sky. Luckily, there is always a campfire to gather round to warm ourselves. One cold and miserable night, we hear singing. It isn't loud, but there is still power and emotion in the pathos of the voice. It is Older Sister Cai from the headquarters column who is singing to a dying young soldier who has asked her to sing foreign songs as his last wish. Older Sister Cai Chang is sitting on a piece of tarpaulin. She has not sung for a long time, but she cannot refuse the request. "All right, don't cry. I'll sing." She sings the Marseillaise softly in French, and everyone sits back-to-back to listen. Amid the rain and tears, the song keeps us company as we sit in a torment of hunger until dawn.

We are marching with the 1st Red Army. On the fourth day, the army headquarters give the 2nd Bureau a tent. Previously, Vice Chairman Zhou had specifically instructed the 2nd Bureau staff not to participate in food gathering but to guarantee their food supply. This was not because the 2nd Bureau was being given special privileges, but because their work could not be left unattended at any time. However, the food provided by the troops is very limited, with each person only getting three or four catties of wheat, and the quartermaster cannot give us much either. At Mao'ergai, Commander-in-Chief Zhu personally went out to harvest wheat. He was sharing the common hardships, and the General Headquarters were, indeed, as short of food as everybody else. Vice Chairman Zhou fell ill and, as he was travelling with the 3rd Red Army, Peng Dehuai ordered him to be carried across the grasslands. By this fourth day, we are all completely out of food. Several of our comrades fall sick from hunger. We use the tent to protect the equipment and camp out in the wind and rain overnight. Everyone is suffering from hunger and cold, but we keep our receiver on as usual and do our best to intercept any enemy signals.

The combat troops are not on a battle footing, so we do not have to move in alternating teams, but we are still working in two shifts without stopping for a single minute. We set up the radios in the tent and work under the shelter of a tarpaulin awning. When we run out of good paper, we can't use pencils with the rough and ragged paper left to us as it would tear at the first stroke, so we have to use brushes to copy and decode the messages. When it is cold, the brushes can freeze at any moment, so we have to keep using our hot breath to keep them supple. By the end of the night, everyone has become a black-bearded Zhang Fei. However, when we run out of petrol, we still have to keep the three 15-Watt radios working, with one operator using the hand crank to generate power while another sends and receives messages, for as long as the first operator's strength holds out. When the battery is drained of power, the mechanic drills holes in it and soaks the elements in urine. We have no salt water or salted food, but the urine is just salty enough to keep it running for a while.

On the fifth day, another day of fasting, three comrades can no longer walk unaided, so we let them lean on us to keep them moving forward. The cowhide briefcases from all the different sections have already been eaten, and Ah Gen brings out the remaining half of his belt. The leather is glistening with a salty frost, the crystallisation of countless days of sweat, and has to be scraped down before it can be cooked with wild vegetables, which have a rare savoury flavour. Now, he is cutting the belt into dozens of pieces with a small knife to give to the cooking team. The rainy weather means there is no dry firewood to be found and the precious dry bundles the big black horse had been carrying have all been used up, so Ah Gen chops up some more gun butts. He builds a fiercely hot fire to cook the stew over, and everyone gets a piece of leather to chew on.

Ah Gen's job as a porter is physically demanding and he has always been a big eater, but he has been seen secretly feeding his rations to the horse, and he had already passed out from hunger twice. Since the start of this Western Expedition, his carrying pole has always been fully laden and the machine he carries is always the heavy battery charger. When he crossed the "sky ladder" at Leigongyan in Laoshanjie, there was no room for two people to manhandle the charger, so he climbed it with the charger tied to his back with a rope. Now, when he carries it, his steps are a little unsteady and his face is always covered in sweat. Sometimes the ground is so wet for most of the day that the charger cannot be put down for a moment, so he keeps carrying it on his shoulders no matter how long it takes.

More and more of our comrades fall ill, but all we can do is keep going. We can't leave the sick and wounded behind for the "accommodation team" to take in because they are already swamped by the numbers and are unable to save all those who have fallen behind. Nor can we of the 2nd Bureau afford to slacken our pace. It is another stormy night, and everyone is so cold they are ready to roll themselves into a ball like a hedgehog. A young bugler from the 1st Red Army almost collapses from hunger but, just as he has sunk halfway into the mud, we join together to pull him out. We form a human chain with Ah Gen at the end of it. He realises that he too is being sucked down into the mud, and we see him suddenly throw himself to the ground, clutching the bugler's hand in his and rolling violently to drag the boy out of the mud. Oxygen deprivation, salt deprivation, hunger and dropsy have already sapped Ah Gen's strength, but he still fights to save the bugler as if he were his own little brother. He places the bugler on a straw mound that is at least a little dry and the transport crew unfold a cloth blanket. There are no trees in the grasslands, so they stick their rifles, bayonets down, into the ground, and tie the corners of the blanket to the rifle butts to form a small tent to shelter the lad. During the night, he becomes even more ill, shivering and grinding his teeth, so Ah Gen covers him with his own small blanket. When the bugler wakes up in the morning, he goes to cover Ah Gen with his own blanket and discovers that his body is freezing cold. Hearing the bugler's cries, we run over and see Ah Gen lying with his eyes closed and his face deathly pale. Chief Zeng leans over and feels his hands and feet, then stands up, silently wiping away his tears. The bugler is crying pitifully. We comfort him as best we can, and, still whimpering, he talks about what happened during the night. Gently, we lightly cover Ah Gen with a quilt and open his clenched right hand to find three blood-stained silver dollars. Our Ah Gen, who was the strongest among us and the most able to endure hardship, was exhausted by excessive hunger and fatigue, and it was the severe cold that took away the last trace of his body temperature. He left us in the same way that he toiled, silent to the end. We weep in silence and are thinking of writing his name on his rifle and sticking it into the ground so that it can stay there forever as a memorial. At that moment, we hear a sudden gunshot. We turn to look and see that the tall, black horse has fallen to the ground. Astonishment and dismay hit us like a thunderbolt. Our hearts are in our mouths, and we don't dare look at the horse as it writhes on the ground. We stare blankly at the figure in the distance, at the back of Chief Zeng. He is standing in the grass with his head hanging down, his body still, in the midst of the storm. He is holding a pistol in his right hand, a whisp of smoke rising from its muzzle.

A sorrowful silence envelops us that day. The rest of us all eat the life-saving horse meat with tears in our eyes, but Chief Zeng doesn't take a single bite or even look at it. He just walks on alone, deep in gloom. His guards hurry over to him, but they do not dare to speak either and just follow him in silence. We know that no one will dare try to talk him out of this mood, so we too just follow without a word. We are using our last breaths to keep on marching, and when those breaths are exhausted, men fall to the ground, scarcely able to get up again.

The sky has cleared, but the daylight is as pale and weak as the bony faces of the soldiers. Everyone is as thin as a sack of straw, but their legs are thick and swollen from being soaked in the poisonous waters of the grasslands. We walk on, speaking only in low voices and not willing to look up. The more you look at this endless expanse of water and grass, the more isolated and desperate you feel. Another day and another night pass.

It is dawn again as reveille sounds, followed by the call to fall in and the one to advance. It is not just one bugle, but many bugles blown in unison. We haven't heard the call to advance since entering the grasslands. Every day when we get up, it is a struggle just to move forward, and it is almost impossible for the troops to remain in formation. As the advance sounds, the little bugler we rescued, the little life Ah Gen saved by sacrificing his own, struggles to his feet, strains every sinew to climb onto a slightly higher flat point in the grass, forces himself upright and joins in the call with his own bugle.

It is the seventh day. At dusk, the long and anxiously awaited dry land finally appears! At the edge of the grassland, there is a solid dirt path, and rocks are beginning to appear along our route, rocks that have been absent for such a long time. "Rocks! I see rocks!" The rocks become a symbol of hope. Someone picks up a small one and carries it in his arms as tears of excitement flow down his cheeks. Chief Zeng says loudly, "Forward, comrades, victory is at hand!"

Supplementary note: Comrade Hu Di was poisoned by eating mushrooms while crossing the grasslands with the Left Route Army. After being poisoned, he fell unconscious and cursed Zhang Guotao while delirious. When he woke up, he was dismissed by Zhang as head of the headquarters reconnaissance section, and he had his horse and bodyguards withdrawn. Later, he was taken into custody in the police battalion to accompany the army as part of its "bearing guilt" operation in which convicted officers and officials were kept in post under supervision. By the time the three main Front Armies joined forces in Huining, he was nowhere to be seen.

We finally make it out of these watery grasslands, this most accursed of terrain. The compass leads us to Banyou, where we stop in a house made of dried cow dung. It is not much, but it is enough to keep us safe from the elements. If there is such a thing as going from hell to heaven, that is what we are experiencing now. We are saved, and with a better result than we could have expected. While we are in Banyou, where we fall into a restful sleep, the enemy in Baozuo, seemingly intent on acting like hosts greeting lost travellers, send their reconnaissance teams to lead us to Axi, not far away. Axi is a rural idyll, with wheat and peas ripening, and garlic and crisp daikon radishes. This market town also has a large lamasery, where the various divisions decide to rest and reorganise for a few days. Some companies organise visits to the temple for their cadres and soldiers to open their eyes to new things. The sight of the statues of male and female Buddhas seated "in congress"[1] in the temple causes them both curiosity and embarrassment, because, naturally, they have never seen such things before. Dr Fu, the Central Red Army doctor, teases them, saying, "Are you all like newly-weds? Is this your first time?" This makes the soldiers blush even more.

In late August, the Right Route Army crossed the Great Grasslands and reached Banyou. Part of the Left Route Army also emerged from the grasslands to reach Aba. The only enemy the unit commanders fought during this death march across the grasslands was Nature itself, but we in the 2nd Bureau, while still being part of that battle, day and night, also never forgot the presence of the material enemy. We were still intercepting the enemy's coded reports in the unpredictable and changeable sky. Far away, the Qinghai warlord Ma Bufang's forces were moving southward from northwest China. Closer to home in Gansu, Lu Dachang's regiment of the enemy's new 14th Division was pressing towards the area north of the grasslands.

So, we escaped from the Great Grasslands after all. When we marched out of there, we made it clear that Chiang Kai-shek's attempts to force the Red Army to cut itself off in that no-man's land in northwest Sichuan, in that deadly and unforgiving place, had been thwarted by our brave soldiers. We could leave the taste of grass to the White Army that was chasing us!

All thanks to Axi! Being led here resulted in our discovery of Baozuo and the passage that connected us to Gansu.

At the end of August, the great victory at Baozuo, which destroyed the 49th Division, opened up the Sichuan-Gansu passage.

We arrived in the village of Panzhou with the General Headquarters of the Right Route Army Forward Division.

Addendum: We had long lost touch with the central authorities who were far away from us. The Chinese Communist delegation to the Comintern issued the August 1st Declaration in the name of the Chinese Soviet Government and the Central Committee of the Communist Party of China, without us knowing anything about it until Zhang Hao came to Yan'an from Moscow. If we had been informed in time, we would have been more determined to go north to fight against the Japanese and save our country. Zhang Guotao would certainly have been less cavalier about any international instructions! I later heard that "Sir" had gone to Moscow.

Using his position as chief political commissar of the Red Army and the man in charge of the Military Commission, Zhang Guotao seized the codebooks used by the various armies to exchange information and also the coded telegrams exchanged between the 1st and 3rd Red Armies and Mao Zedong. Our contact with the Party Central Committee was cut off, as was that of the 1st Red Army. Peng Dehuai learnt from Ye Jianying, chief of staff of the Forward Division, that the 1st Red Army was at a Tibetan village called Ejie, but where was Ejie? Peng Dehuai then sent his men with a compass to locate Lin Biao's and Nie Rongzhen's 1st Red Army and give them the newly compiled codebooks.

"The Party Central Committee is the Party Central Committee

plus its radio stations." It was Vice Chairman Zhou Enlai who made this interesting remark. Now it seemed that Zhang Guotao may have had the intention of setting up another "Central Committee" when he seized all the various armies' codebooks. On 29 September, He Long and Ren Bishi received a telegram in plain text from Zhou Enlai:

> "Brother Bishi, we have arrived in Shaanxi, and we have left the code with the Old Fourth. Brother Hao."

He Long and Ren Bishi understood: Hao was Wu Hao, a pseudonym for Zhou Enlai. The Old Fourth was the 4th Red Front Army. But why did Zhou Enlai send the message in plain text? Could this be an enemy trick? Prudently, He and Ren used code to ask Zhou Enlai: "Where are you now? We have been out of touch for a long time. Please state the names of the members of the provincial committee here in your telegram to prove our relationship."

Because Zhou Enlai was not using code, Zhang Guotao was delighted when He and Ren's telegram fell into his hands, and he immediately replied,

> "Your telegram of 29th received. The secretary of your provincial committee is Bishi, and the other members are He Long, Xia Xi, Guan Xiangying, Xiao Ke and Wang Zhen. The 1st and 4th Red Front Armies made rendezvous at Maogong in June, and the Central Committee appointed Guotao as general political commissar."

The telegram was signed "Zhu" and "Zhang". Zhu was commander-in-chief of the Red Army, and Zhang was its chief political commissar. Because He and Ren did not know that the Red Army and the 4th Front Army had split up, when Zhang Guotao's coded telegram replied in this way, they thought they had resumed contact with the Central Committee. The only good thing was that Zhang Guotao's reply alerted the 2nd and 6th Red Army Corps to the direction of the strategic transfer. He and Ren decided to move closer to the 4th Red Front Army, setting out from Liujiaping,

Sangzhi County, Hunan Province and other points, in line with that strategic transfer.

In July of the following year, 1936, the 2nd and 6th Red Army Corps met up with the 4th Red Front Army at Garzê. At this point, He and Ren realised that Zhang Guotao had set up his own "Central Committee" and that Zhou Enlai's telegram, which said "we have left the code with the Old Fourth", meant that the code was in the hands of Zhang Guotao. Ren asked Zhang for the code, but Zhang was reluctant to hand it over even though he could not help but be wary of He Long's explosive temper. Zhu De accused Zhang of deliberately obstructing direct contact between the 2nd and 6th Corps and the Central Party Committee. Realising that he was making himself responsible for undermining the Red Army and threatening its unity, Zhang Guotao reluctantly handed over the code.

After Zhang Hao arrived in northern Shaanxi from Moscow, he gave orders to Zhang Guotao in the name of the representatives of the Comintern. The key to the communication code between the Communist Party and the "distant authorities" was an English edition of *Robinson Crusoe*. After the 1st Red Front Army went north alone, Liu Bocheng, chief of the General Staff who was the keeper of this codebook, had burned it to prevent Zhang Guotao from contacting the Comintern without permission. Zhang Guotao then finally complied with Zhang Hao's orders and went north to join the 1st Red Front Army.

Zhang Hao, whose real name is Lin Yuying, is a native of Huanggang in Hubei Province and a cousin of Lin Biao.

The weather cleared after several days of continuous rain, and a lovely sun rose in the east. In this sparsely populated border area, the Political Department had run out of coloured paper for writing slogans, and we had nowhere to buy paper for copying down our reports, so we bought Tibetan sutra scrolls to use instead. There were scriptures on the paper, so we copied our reports in the gaps, and the writing had to be very small.

I had a strange dream one night, and I wrote it down. There was a sudden buzzing sound like flies, and three black dots came out of the clouds. The air-raid siren sounded, and we all took cover in the banana woods by the river, lying prone with willow wreaths over our heads. The three red-nosed enemy planes looked like strange birds. They hovered in the clouds, now high up now low down, their silver wings glinting brightly. The golden sands of the river strand were picked out with the black and white markings we had laid out, and the enemy planes began to swoop in. This time they weren't dropping bombs, they were dropping letter bags and mail packets, silver dollars, battle plans and codebooks! From this distance, the blue sky and white sun emblems were clearly visible on their wings, and even the pilots could be distinguished. The spiralling air currents from the planes blew swirls on the beach and the fine sand was driven right into our faces, as we still tried to keep our eyes open. Two of the planes finished dropping their parcels and flew back to a higher level, while the other one was still flying level and slow, as if reviewing the troops on the ground from the clouds. Then we saw the face behind the glass of the cockpit. It was Chiang Kai-shek! Who else could it be? The shadowy face looked down, the head suddenly lifted, and we saw how his eyes rolled. Clutching the microphone with one hand and gesticulating with the other, he roared: "Running again! Crossing another river! Get out of here, you useless bastards. Just fuck off out of here if you can't manage a proper revolution! Pull your fingers out and catch me if you can!" We shouted in unison, "Death to Chiang! You useless old fart, you're nothing but a delivery boy!"

Another dream. A nightmare. A memory of 9 September 1935. When I look back on that terrifying night now, it feels like a dream! These days since the Maogong rendezvous were a nightmare for the Central Party Committee and the 1st and 4th Front Armies. And also for Chief Zeng. At the time, he didn't know that his elder brother had been assassinated by Zhang Guotao during the period when the two armies were together. But he knew very well that his brother's life might be in danger because of the way Zhang Guotao was at loggerheads with the central government. What we now know about that emergency departure is that Ye Jianying, chief of staff of the Right Route Army, saw a telegram sent by Zhang Guotao to Chen Changhao and, sensing the seriousness of the situation, rode to the seat of the Central Committee to report to Mao Zedong. Zhang Guotao refused to go north and was trying to force the Right Route Army to go south. The Party Central Committee was accompanying the Right Route Army, while the Red Army was far away on the Southern Gansu-Russian border. In the afternoon of that day, Chen Changhao reported to Mao Zedong and the leaders of the Central Committee that he was prepared to carry out Zhang Guotao's order to recross the grasslands to the south. The situation was critical, and the Central Party Committee decided to move north alone to get out of harm's way as quickly as possible. The night was long and full of dreams. It was time to go!

The 2nd Bureau was very important to Peng Dehuai, and he discussed with Ye Jianying how to "steal" all the maps and the entire 2nd Bureau from the Forward Division command post, so that everyone would be forced to go to the 3rd Red Army headquarters before dawn the following morning. Ye Jianying hurried to the 2nd Bureau, where he told Chief Zeng to prepare for the transfer and asked for strict secrecy and punctuality. They synchronised their watches with Counsellor Ye's.

Chief Zeng made urgent arrangements. He sent men to chivvy back more than twenty comrades who had gone out to fetch grain and, on the pretext of holding a roast lamb dinner, recalled several men who were helping out at the 2nd Radio Station of the 4th Front Army. Chief Zeng also synchronised his watch with Deputy Chief Song Yuhe's and asked Song to bring all the 2nd Bureau's personnel and equipment to Axi in the middle of the night, and to keep the operation absolutely secret. He also gave special instructions to leave behind the battery chargers borrowed from the 4th Front Army.

Under the cover of the night fog, we silently left Panzhou Village and arrived in Axi before dawn. Chief Zeng, Section Chief Cao and Deputy Section Chief Zou were not with us, and we only found out when we reached Ashi that they had preceded us!

Chief of Staff Ye had "stolen" the map from the Forward Division command post. This was the only map of all of Gansu Province that anyone in the whole army had been able to capture. He mounted his horse and chased after us along the road we had taken. He had not even woken his own bodyguards when he left, in order to escape the surveillance set up by Chen Changhao. Nor had he informed any of the many operational staff of the 1st Bureau of the Military Commission.

At dawn, we arrived at the rendezvous with Chief of Staff Ye, where Zeng, Cao and Zou were waiting anxiously for us. Commander Peng Dehuai arrived soon afterwards. He was relieved to see that all of us from the 2nd Bureau had arrived safely. "Good! You're all here! Our victory is guaranteed!" He took Chief Zeng's hand and said excitedly, "Chief Zeng, once more you have done the Party a great service!"

How did Chief Zeng and the others arrive before us? It turned out that he had summoned Cao and Zou to leave quietly after lights out under the pretext of checking the sentry post. Mao had specifically wanted Zeng, Cao and Zou to go first at such a fraught moment.

On 10 September, we hurriedly marched north with the 3rd Red Army. We had to get out of the danger zone as soon as possible. Peng Dehuai led the 10th Regiment to cover our rear, where Mao Zedong also accompanied them. After we had gone some distance and were resting at the roadside on a hill, Li Te, chief of education of the Red Army University, came up after us with a squad of cavalry. The Red Army University cadets were mostly in the 4th Red Army, and Li Te ordered them to stop their march and follow him back immediately. He said, "General Commissar Zhang has ordered you to go south, so why are you still heading north?" He took his horse whip to one of the men who did not want to turn back, shouting that he would take them south so they could eat good white rice. As Li De, the foreign adviser, and Li Te argued in Russian, Mao Zedong came out of a ramshackle house by the roadside, and Li Te asked him, still in an aggressive manner, why he was "deserting". Li Te drew his pistol as he yelled at Mao, and his bodyguard had his finger on the trigger of his weapon. In order to stop Li Te shooting Mao, Li De threw his arms round him from behind and dragged him away. Peng Dehuai was coming from the creek and Mao Zedong pointed over towards him, saying, "Stop it! There's no need to use force! Peng Dehuai is here! It is Peng Dehuai, who has been leading the Third Red Army Corps at our rear, and he is a staunch advocate of going north and a firm opponent of going south. He was furious that Comrade Zhang Guotao wanted to go south!"

Li Te was afraid of Peng Dehuai, so he did not dare do anything rash. Mao Zedong also addressed the Red University cadets from the 4th Front Army, saying, "Comrades, what's all the fuss about? We are all workers and peasants of the Red Army under the leadership of the Communist Party. We are all class brothers. In going north, we are following the correct line of the Comintern and the Central Party Committee. Those who wish to go north can go north, and those who wish to go south can go south. We will go north and open the way for you. I believe that in the coming days, you too will come north, and we will meet again!"

The man I really want to talk about is that tall foreigner, Li De. Although he had long been relieved of supreme command of the Red Army, he agreed with the strategy of going north and firmly believed that this was the correct line. At this critical juncture, he showed no hesitation about stepping up and making a stand. With Li De being nearly two metres tall, Li Te was no match for him. Ha! The comrade counsellor made us look at him with new eyes! He was, after all, an international revolutionary. He had fought bloody battles for the Bavarian Soviet Republic. He had risked his life to enter the Red Soviet Area of China, and he had come with all sincerity to join our glorious cause...

Addendum: On 12 September, the Ejie Conference decided to reduce the size of the army, reorganising the columns of the Military Commission and the main force of the former Red 1st Front Army into the Shaanxi-Gansu Detachment of the Chinese Workers' and Peasants' Red Army, with Peng Dehuai as commander, Mao Zedong as political commissar and Lin Biao as deputy commander. It also set up a five-member team consisting of Mao Zedong, Zhou Enlai, Peng Dehuai, Lin Biao and Wang Jiaxiang to lead the work of the Red Army, and an organisation committee with Li De as director and Ye Jianying and others as deputy directors.

* * *

Heading north. No more intercepting of coded telegrams from the Sichuan network.

We made a hasty exit from Axi. We waded through swamps and thorn bushes, made our way with difficulty along ancient wooden walkways on cliff faces, and swam across rapidly rising rivers. Some fell off the walkways, others were swept away by the rapids. We marched in battle order in case of surprise attacks, and we did not light torches at night. The radio could not be set up for operation on such a treacherous route. As we marched along the Dala Gorge, we were suddenly hit by sneak sniper fire from the other side of the river, which resulted in the death of our oldest operator, Comrade Li Litian. We originally wanted to create a new Soviet area on the Sichuan-Shaanxi-Gansu border, but we had been intending to use the 100,000-strong 1st and 4th Front Armies as the foundation. Now that Zhang Guotao has prevented the Left Route Army from moving north, it was clear that the main force of the 1st Front Army alone, with fewer than 8,000 men, would have difficulty in fighting the powerful enemy forces. Our troops were still moving north, but there was no longer any consideration given to fighting the enemy for the Sichuan-Shaanxi-Gansu area. So where was the next way out? There was no landing point, no end in sight, and for the time being we could only keep going north. On 12 September, in a small village with only a dozen families in Ejie, a meeting of the Central Committee decided that we should head along close to the Soviet Union with a view to opening up international contacts through guerrilla warfare and looking for an opportunity to create a base area. We had suffered so much, and we were at the end of our tether.

If we had been able to intercept Chiang Kai-shek's coded telegrams in a timely manner on the 10th and 11th, the Central Committee and Military Commission would not have had to fret over this. As it was, however, we left in a hurry following the 3rd Red Army on the 10th and made haste to Ejie the next day, so there was no chance of turning the radio on at any stage. On the 10th and 11th, Chiang issued two orders in quick succession, intending to wipe out the Red Army as it headed north on the Sichuan-Gansu border. His first order read,

> "The bandits in Aba have already moved eastward. The bandits in Baozuo, a group of about 10,000, are fleeing northeast

towards Minxian. It seems their intention is to take advantage of our unpreparedness to break us up systematically and join with the bandits in northern Shaanxi to create a new bandit territory in Shaanxi and Gansu."

The Red Army is in Shaanxi! On 17 September, the 4th Regiment of the 2nd Division defeated Lu Dachang's troops and took Lazikou in one fell swoop. Two days later, we crossed Mount Die to Hadapu in southern Gansu. At Hadapu, the leaders of the Central Committee read in the *Ta Kong Pao* published in Tianjin, "The northern part of Shaanxi is a vast area with the potential for comparatively long-term base... The situation in northern Shaanxi now is similar to that of Jiangxi in the twentieth year of the Republic." In another newspaper, there was actually a sketch map of the Northern Shaanxi Soviet Area... Liu Zhidan's Northwest Red Army and the Soviet Area are still there, and the 25th Red Army led by Cheng Zihua and Xu Haidong have also arrived in northern Shaanxi, where they have joined Liu Zhidan's Red Army. The Northern Shaanxi Soviet forms a base with the same area as the Jiangxi Soviet. It is remarkable as the only surviving base.

There is a saying that if there is no light in the east, there is light in the west, and when it is dark in the south, there is still light in the north. We went all that way west, then turned to the north and it seems we should continue in that direction. The revolutionary dawn is with us. Mao, Zhou and Luo have decided: our destination is northern Shaanxi!

Part 2

Sidelights

第二部 側影

"The endless hills, broken and lonely, rolling on and on, resemble the long sentences of James Joyce, but even more tedious, yet their effect is often as eye-catching as Picasso's paintings. As the sun shifts, the steep angular shadows and colours of these hills change strangely, and by dusk the purple summits are joined in a magnificent sea of dark, velvety folds that descend from above like the pleated skirts of the Manchus, all the way down into gullies that seem too deep to see the bottom." This is Edgar Snow's northern Shaanxi.

Edgar Snow, who had reason to dislike Joyce's long, sleep-inducing sentences, was a professor of journalism at Yanjing University in Peking in the 1930s, and in 1936 he became the first Western journalist to enter the Red Zone in China. He was an observer, an experiencer, a searcher and an analyser, and because he wanted to present such deep thinking and analysis, his book *Red Star over China* could hardly be a simple journalistic narrative; he had to express his feelings and thoughts in "long, continuous sentences", because what he found was a "magnificent ocean".

"As eye-catching as Picasso". We can only imagine the rough splendour Picasso's brush would have brought if he had been on the high slopes of northern Shaanxi, or how he would have presented the rolling hills and ravines in cubist form, but Snow's new book did indeed catch the attention of the Western world. In September 1945, Deng Fa went to Paris as a delegate from the Liberated Areas to attend the founding conference of the World Federation of Workers. He was the first director of the State Political Security Bureau and was himself quite a good charcoal artist; he actually used that skill to escape the Nationalist military police when he was involved in revolutionary activities in Guangzhou. In Paris, Picasso asked him to take an oil painting back to Mao Zedong and to present it to him in Yan'an. Deng Fa wrapped the painting carefully and kept it with him at all times. After returning to China on 8 April 1946, he accompanied Wang Ruofei, Bo Gu and Ye Ting on a plane to Yan'an from Chongqing. The plane "crashed" in the Heicha Mountains in Xing County, Shanxi, killing everyone on board. The Picasso painting was also destroyed in the crash.

In *Red Star over China*, Snow sketches an interesting and rather dashing image of Deng Fa in just a few strokes. The American journalist's descriptions of the top leaders, including Mao Zedong, are in continuous, unbroken prose, but the effect is not one of Joycean "tedium". Snow may not have been Joyce's ideal reader, but he clearly had his own narrative logic. As a journalist, he seized this historic opportunity and his rewards far exceeded his expectations.

A revolution is not a dinner party. Revolutionaries rarely talk about family matters. Yet in 1936 in northern Shaanxi, Mao Zedong, Peng Dehuai, Zhou Enlai, Lin Biao and other Red Army leaders explained to him "in words as clear as spring water" the reasons for and aims of the Chinese Revolution, and they spoke frankly about their own family stories. For a dozen consecutive nights, with He Zizhen as a witness, Snow and Mao talked at length in the *yaodong* cave dwelling, which was lit only by an oil lamp. "One evening, after all my other questions had been answered, Mao completed the questionnaire I had compiled under the heading 'personal history'. When he saw the question 'How many times have you been married?', he smiled."

Snow was escorted to northern Shaanxi by the man known as "Pastor Wang". His real name was Dong Jianwu, a graduate of St John's University Seminary in Shanghai, and he was the English-speaking secretary of the "Christian General", Feng Yuxiang. He joined the Chinese Communist Party in 1928 and the Central Special Branch in Shanghai in 1929, but in his public persona he was vicar of St Peter's Church. In the name of the church, he founded the Datong Kindergarten for the Shanghai Party Organisation, to shelter and raise the orphans of the revolution. Mao's three sons were also sent there, but the youngest, Anlong, died through illness soon afterwards. Dong Jianwu and Gu Shunzhang escorted Zhang Guotao and Chen Changhao to the Hubei-Hunan-Anhui Soviet, and it was on their way back that Gu Shunzhang was arrested in Hankou after his identity was revealed through his unauthorised activities. The defection of Gu Shunzhang brought the Central Committee in Shanghai to its knees, and the Provisional Central Committee was moved from Shanghai to the Soviet area in southern Jiangxi. The Comintern advisor, Li De, was also escorted to Ruijin by this Pastor Wang, who was fluent in several foreign languages. After the destruction of the Central Party Committee in Shanghai, Dong Jianwu lost contact with his superiors. In June 1936, he was asked by Song Qingling to go to Xi'an as Pastor Wang to escort Snow and Dr Ma Haide (the American doctor Shafick George Hatem) to the Soviet area in northern Shaanxi.

Dong Jianwu did not know Snow before this. Madame Song wrote two lines of poetry in English on one of her business cards, stamped it with a chop and tore it in half, giving half to Dong Jianwu and sending the other half to Snow. When Dong Jianwu arrived in Xi'an and stayed at the Xijing Guest House, he looked up Snow's and Ma Haide's room number in the visitors' register. When they met, they challenged each other in code and then each showed their half of Madame Song's business card. Once they were correctly matched, the introductions were completed. The Chinese Communist Party had also sent Deng Fa to Xi'an, and after Deng had made contact with Dong Jianwu, he met Snow outside the city. On the third day after meeting, they drove out of the city under the pretext of visiting the ancient monuments, but, after reaching the outskirts, they took a military vehicle straight to the front, where they said their goodbyes. Snow took a bus from the Kuomintang-controlled area to the northern Shaanxi Soviet, while Dong Jianwu returned to Shanghai to resume his duties.

In October of the following year, Snow's *Red Star over China* was published in London, and it proved to be a book that shook the Western world with its description of the Chinese Communist movement. Less than a year later, the "Portrait" edition of Shanghai's *Yijing* magazine published an article of nearly 20,000 words, written by Dong Jianwu under the pseudonym "Yougu", entitled "The Red Army's 25,000-*li* excursion to the west".

Yijing is a fortnightly magazine of literature and history founded by Dong Jianwu's friend Jian Youwen and others. Jian Youwen asked Dong Jianwu for manuscripts, and Dong contributed several articles on research into Li Bai's family background and appreciations of his poetry. It was Pan Hannian who enabled Dong Jianwu to write this "Excursion to the west".

In the preface, Yougu states, "I cannot be exhaustive in this article because of the limitations of space. All I am doing is celebrating this extraordinary feat in order to save a page of the modern history of the Chinese nation. I did not fight in the campaign, nor was I involved in the pursuit, so how can I speak as if I had been there? The only thing I can say is that there were friends of mine on both sides of the confrontation, and each of them told me everything they knew. I have examined the similarities and differences, identified the falsehoods, and then created this article by speaking of what can be spoken of and writing down what can be reported. If the reader wishes to know more about it, he or she will have to consult the books on both sides. What is available in this article is only a summary."

"'Senior Special Envoy': he was only called that as a ruse to get past the official press censorship. At the time of the publication of "Excursion to the West", Snow's *Red Star Over China* was not yet available in Chinese translation, but a translation of *Red Star Over China* did soon follow entitled A Free Record of the Western Expedition. With the two armies fighting at the front and the Kuomintang demonising the Red Army, it was very difficult for the outside world to know the truth, so it could be argued that "Excursion to the West" is the earliest text from behind the lines reporting on the Red Army's Long March."

The colonel turns around and stares blankly at the bottle of "Academy Wine" on his desk, his thoughts still dwelling on a distant past. This is the PLA Academy of Military Sciences in the western suburbs of Beijing, and this doctorate-holding colonel is a very talkative man. He is so excited to explain to his visitors that he cannot stop talking. A peacetime colonel, his body is in good shape and his face and hair are lustrous.

His peroration covers subjects from Snow to Dong Jianwu, and from Pastor Wang to the publishing industry on the Shanghai Bund in the 1930s. He is a leading expert on the history of the Red Army, but his PhD is in sociology, and his very attractive female visitor has a PhD in anthropology, so they were diverted from the subject of the interview from time to time.

"It started off as a military topic, but it got more literary as I went along. In following this trail, I actually made a close study of *Yijing* magazine, and I made an extraordinary discovery! This Jian Youwen was quite something! He was a native of Xinhui in Guangdong and a member of Liang Qichao's clan, but I don't know if he was from Chakeng Village. He lived in Hong Kong in his later years."

The colonel pulled a thick copy of 太平天国革命运动 from his bookcase and took a sip of his tangerine peel tea. "This is the book he published in America in his later years. It's a Chinese translation from the English, but the title is a direct translation of the original published by Yale University called *The Taiping Revolutionary Movement*. His pen name was Da Hua Lieshi [Great Chinese Martyr] and his studio name was Mengjin Shuwu [Boldly Entering the Library]. His motive for founding the magazine in Shanghai was to encourage his readers to help him search for information about the Taiping Heavenly Kingdom, so it was fitting that the magazine should publish this account of Shi Dakai's western expedition and the Red Army's western expedition! He saw the Taiping Army as revolutionaries, and that made the government forces counter-revolutionaries. Just look at the conclusion of this preface by Professor Shi Jingqian of Yale University: 'The rulers of the Tongzhi period were trapped in the context of history. Behind their long-term concerns for the nation, we can hear the sharp and angry cries of the numberless multitude looking for a different way out of their predicament. And those cries were getting louder.' The ideals of the Taiping Heavenly Kingdom had the Christian ideology of the Old Testament. These included egalitarianism and the expression of creativity. Their swords were not only directed at the imperial dynasty, as they had been in countless previous uprisings, but also more directly at the fundamental class divisions and social structures of the time. It is at this level that he expands on the revolutionary significance of the Taiping Heavenly Kingdom. What a man Jian Youwen was! A revolutionary and a scholar at the same time, so he attracted the literati as well, and Zhou Zuoren, Yu Pingbo, Lao She, Liu Yazi, Lin Yutang, Yu Dafu, Xie Bingying and many others were among his contributors. As a matter of fact, Qu Qiubai's last words were also first published in this magazine.

"Of course, many of the revolutionaries also came from literary and artistic family backgrounds, and some had literary talent themselves. Just now I mentioned Feng Xuefeng, who was one of the 'lakeside poets' back then. He was a political instructor during the Long March, and later served as president of the People's Literature Publishing House and secretary of the Party group of the Chinese Writers' Association. Pan Hannian, also a poet, published his fiction debut, *Divorce*, in 1928. Pan Hannian was introduced to Lu Xun by Bao Wenwei. Bao Wenwei was an intelligence agent of the Central Special Branch, who managed to get a confession from Xiang Zhongfa, so that the Central Committee could tell the Comintern that they could confirm that the former general secretary, who had been shot, had indeed defected to the enemy. It should be noted that Bao Wenwei was a young man with the talent of a Cao Zijian and he was also the translator of Rabelais' *Gargantua*.

"But to return to Pan Hannian, who brings us back to our main story. The source of Dong Jianwu's 'Excursion to the West' is certainly not his own personal account. When he escorted Snow, it was not his first trip to northern Shaanxi. He had been there earlier in the year as a special envoy of Song Qingling and arrived with a letter to Mao Zedong. Zhang Xueliang sent a private plane to take him to Fushi, or Yan'an as it is also known, then under the jurisdiction of Zhang Xueliang's Northeast Army. Zhang Xueliang's cavalry company escorted him to Wayaobu, but Mao Zedong, Zhou Enlai and others were leading the Red Army across the Yellow River to the east, so he was received by Bo Gu and Lin Zuhan – Lin Zuhan was Lin Boqu's birth name. Just hold on a moment – I was talking about Joyce just now... let me show you something..."

The colonel took down a copy of *Ulysses* from the bookcase. It had a picture of Joyce on the cover. He also took down a copy of Huang Zhen's *Sketches of the Long March* and turned to the chapter about Lin Boqu, entitled, "The old heroes on the night march". They were shown in the painting full length, in profile, with lean faces and shiny, round-lensed spectacles. Both held walking sticks, but Lao Lin's was, of course, a wooden staff.

"Things were getting more and more literary. But looking back, of course, everybody was a literary youth back then. To tell the truth, I too was rather that way inclined. The Long March is a magnificent human epic, and doesn't *Ulysses* too have an epic prototype? Those long, sleep-inducing sentences...

"But, let's get back to the topic at hand. It is said that when Dong Jianwu returned from his mission, Lin Boqu gave him dozens of copies of the monthly *Struggle*, which might have been a source of material for him for 'Excursion to the West', but the more important material came from Pan Hannian. Pan Hannian was socially adroit and was running around Hong Kong, Nanjing and Shanghai at the time on his latest secret mission. When he heard that the magazine *Yijing* had asked Dong for an article, he felt it was a good opportunity to take him a bundle of material."

The major suddenly stops, glances at the book in the woman doctor's hand, and continues, "In 1936, after the end of the Long March, the Central Committee of the Communist Party of China mobilised everyone who had been through the Long March to write memoirs to be used for international propaganda. Mao Zedong himself organised the initiative, calling on everyone to join in. It was only a few months after the victorious conclusion of the Long March, and with the events of the journey still fresh in their minds, my collection of memoirs is quite truthful and accurate. Many people contributed memoirs. There were long ones and short ones, and, although they might be a bit rough and ready, they were also simple and charming with a youthful energy. There were also people like Ding Ling and Cheng Fangwu who were responsible for the editing, and they tried not to interfere with them too much in order to maintain the original authenticity. Naturally, it was difficult for Dong Jianwu to conduct any research about the Long March in the field, as once the Red Army had passed through, the territory reverted to Kuomintang control. His descriptions of the Long March were also drawn from those memoirs. *Record of the Red Army's Long March*, written in Yan'an, was completed in 1937, but due to the critical stage the war was at, it was not published until 1942. It is a major discovery for military historians. It was first found by Mr Shen Jin of the Yanjing Library at Harvard University in the United States, and Zhu De presented the American journalist Agnes Smedley with a signed copy. What I'm saying is that in this edition, for a variety of complicated reasons, of all those memoirs written back then – some of which were actually written on the battlefield – not all of the ones collected have actually been included."

The doctor looked down again at the old book she was holding. It was not an official publication, just a collection of source material typed out on an old-fashioned typewriter. The pages were a little yellowed and brittle, and the title on the front cover was in a slightly larger font than the contents: *Wu River Variations*.

"Why 'Wu River'?" the woman asked quietly.

"The Long March was a breakout from the enemy's encirclement campaign. In fact, it was multiple breakouts. Its most dramatic period was between the first breakout across the Wu River and the southern crossing of the same river, so of course the author thought that was the part most worth describing. From his point of view, it was his witness testimony. There were many breakouts, but the southern crossing of the Wu River was the crucial battle. That crossing was a strategic operation and the third and fourth crossings of the Chishui River were part of the same campaign. Zhang Wentian also emphasised this concept in the rectification notes he made in 1943. As far as the active combat corps were concerned, it is understandable that morale among the commanders and soldiers was low during the fourth crossing because they did not know the underlying strategy. Where a major campaign was concerned, the Military Commission had to keep everything strictly confidential and maintain the utmost secrecy. Looked at in the terms of a long essay, the third and fourth river crossings were just a foretaste, a foreshadowing of what was to come, for didn't Liu Bocheng go on to secure those pontoon bridges? Those bridges are that 'foreshadowing'. After the third crossing, the radios went silent, the main force of the Red Army suddenly disappeared, but they also made a series of feints which sent out radio signals non-stop. This too was all part of the great foreshadowing, and taken together, they all paved the way for the dramatic climax of the southern crossing of the Wu River. That was the final breakout intended to escape the enemy encirclement once and for all. But if that breakout failed, the Red Army would be in dire straits, facing total annihilation."

The woman nodded in understanding and looked at the colonel

with her remarkable, large eyes. "But who, in fact, is the author of this piece?" she asked.

"I know who you hope it is, but I'm afraid it's not that easy. So many texts from the past are of unknown origin, and so many events go unremembered. After crossing Luding Bridge, the Central Party Committee sent Chen Yun to Moscow to report. Because the Party was only a branch of the Comintern, it had to report to Moscow. The question of the legitimacy of the Zunyi Conference had to be confirmed by the Third International. Pan Hannian had already been dispatched there, but he was unable to arrive in time. Chen Yun left Sichuan disguised as a businessman and first had to get to Shanghai. In fact, I can tell you that it was Comrade Shi Ping who made the report to the Executive Committee of the Communist International on 15 October 1935. It was not until the 1990s that we found out that Shi Ping was actually Chen Yun, and that is why the article was included in the *Selected Writings of Chen Yun*. Lots of things work out like that."

"I had a quick look at your online classes just now and I discovered a few details—"

"Don't use the word 'discover' too lightly! It is fine to make bold assumptions, but you have to be very careful to seek proof. You can't rely on conjecture alone, or just rely on your feelings... you say 'details' too, but don't forget this is a typescript from the seventies! Double Pigeon brand mechanical typewriter, several thousand Chinese characters crammed into a single character plate... some obscure characters were simply not there, so a different, incorrect one had to be used instead, or the character was handwritten. As you can see, that happened quite a lot."

"It was really hard work for the typists!"

"Truly! So hard on the eyes! They used to say that finding the right characters was like catching fleas. So, this typescript is clearly not the original manuscript, and there are definitely some minor errors. Are there any other corrections? I doubt it. Some of the foreign terms may have been altered in accordance with the conventions of the 1970s, so different characters were used to transliterate words such as 'Bolshevik' or 'Stalin', as well as perhaps some modes of expression, punctuation and so on, but on the whole, this is a very rare document, authentic, unpretentious and not without its own vivid style. It stands up to examination and scrutiny and could only have been compiled by someone who lived through the whole experience. There is no way anyone could have fabricated it."

The colonel took a thick pile of photocopied sheets from the bookcase, which she accepted eagerly. She thanked him repeatedly, as if she had been given a great treasure. She still handled the typewritten document carefully and lovingly, her manner both graceful and dignified.

"So, a nameless martyr! There's not even a name on the cover," the woman said with more than a hint of sadness in her expression.

"We should look on the bright side. Maybe he was going to write it out by hand, maybe even with a brush, but in the end, it never happened."

"Are you saying that he typed this himself?"

"Not necessarily, but if he did type it himself, that would at least suggest the author was still alive in the 1970s–"

"What I don't understand is how a document like this ended up on a street stall."

"It was a chaotic time – lots of houses were raided and had their possessions confiscated... I am touched by your interest, so I am willing to help you, but whether I can do so is another matter. To tell the truth, I'm not very optimistic. It's very difficult! Let me give you another example: Regimental Commander Wang Kaixiang and Political Commissar Yang Chengwu of the Fourth Regiment of the First Red Front Army. The Heroic Fourth Regiment! In the historical sequence of the First Red Army Corps, its predecessor was the Ye Ting Independent Regiment during the Northern Expedition. Breaking out across the Wu River, capturing Luding Bridge, making rendezvous with the 4th Front Army, seizing Lazikou Pass, always blazing the trail and leading the way! But as for his name..." The colonel took down a heavy military dictionary from the bookshelf, leafed through it to a particular page and read out, "Wang Kaixiang, 1901-1935, also known as Huang Kaixiang..."

Barely containing her curiosity, the woman waited for him to continue.

"Wang or Huang? The troops were predominantly southerners, so perhaps it was just that they couldn't hear the difference between the two and used them indiscriminately. In the case of the lightning crossing of Luding Bridge, it was the newspaper reporter who galloped on horseback and brought a note to the corps commander, telling him he must make haste to take the bridge the next day. This order, which came from Lin Biao, was addressed to 'Wang, Yang'. Twenty-two brave soldiers risked their lives in this most thrilling attack on the bridge, but who were they? There is no way of checking now, nothing can be found in the battle records of the First Red Front Army except only for the names of eight men. It is not even known what eventually happened to Liao Dazhu, the company commander who led the flying assault on the bridge. He may have died on the Long March or he may have been killed in the Sino-Japanese War... 'how cold were the iron cables of Dadu Bridge',[1] and what of the storming of that bridge, the sound of the bugles, those thin, starving young soldiers, braving the flying bullets, stepping out onto those wobbly iron cables and wooden planks....." The colonel suddenly seemed to be choked with emotion, but then he raised his voice with a feigned solemnity and continued, "Heaven and Earth felt the shock and the gods wept!"

Neither of them broke the silence for a while. The woman got up to refill the colonel's teacup, and the colonel himself looked out the window without speaking. The hills in the distance were ablaze with large leaves the colour of fire or blood. A breeze was blowing, and the red leaves were as gorgeous in the sunlight as clouds at sunset. The doctor sat quietly back on the sofa. The colonel was right, the leaves there were more beautiful than those at the Fragrant Hills. There were too many tourists at the Fragrant Hills, and the leaves were polluted by the dust and the people. The military compound was closer to the city than the Fragrant Hills, so, of course, the colonel and his team didn't have to go to the Fragrant Hills to see the leaves, and it was also more private in the compound because it was difficult for outsiders to get in. This was an important military site and the place where Marshal Ye lived in his later years.

The colonel regained his composure slightly and began to speak again, his voice no longer so high-pitched. His tone was contemplative. "A day and night of non-stop running for two hundred and forty *li*. That is the length of three marathons. It was the longest rapid march, entirely on foot, in military history... and it was along clifftops and mountain passes, fighting all the way. This was beyond the limits of human physical ability. Roman legions won campaigns by being good runners, but they were nowhere near as fast."

The woman was looking breathlessly at an entry in the encyclopaedia and mused, "Wang Kaixiang, Huang Kaixiang, just a portrait, not even a picture–1"

"At least we still have that portrait. Too often, all that remains of battlefield comrades are just their shadows in our memory."

The woman stood up excitedly and looked directly at the colonel. The colonel didn't know how to react for a moment and felt rather embarrassed.

"You asked me why I am so stubborn, didn't you? I am so stubborn in my pursuit because it was my mother's dying wish. She never met her biological father, but she heard my grandmother tell me more than once that I had my grandfather's eyes... maybe it has been passed on to me, more than to my mother..."

"I understand," said the colonel, nodding seriously. "Chen Shuxiang was commander of the Thirty-Fourth Division, and the enemy ordered that his head should be hung from the Xiaowumen city gate tower in Changsha, while his mother still lived on Wawu Street opposite the tower... I will do my best to help you, Dr He, following all the clues that I can. What is clear at this point is that the group about which *Wu River Variations* is written was undoubtedly the Second Bureau of the Central Revolutionary Committee and the Military Commission. These people worked on the covert frontline. Their names cannot be published, their achievements cannot be made public and even the most decorated war heroes among them have had to remain in obscurity. It is even more difficult to identify ordinary members. The good thing is that the people written about in this book, these important characters, are all identifiable through the pseudonyms the author uses. Zeng Mian is Zeng Xisheng, who also used the name 'Mian' when he was working undercover, infiltrating the Kuomintang in Chongqing. He was Yu Mian, and his wife's name was Yu Shu. Qian Chao is Qian Zhuangfei. Qian Chao was his pen name, and back then he starred in *A Hero Hidden in Mount Yan* using the stage name Qian Xixi. This was the first black-and-white Chinese martial arts film, and he designed this poster himself. It is one of the earliest surviving Chinese film posters. His daughter Li Lili was a major star in the 1930s. Cao Daye may be Cao Xiangren, a native of Daye in Hubei. He did not want to be buried in the Babaoshan Revolutionary Cemetery, so his grave is among the green hills of his hometown. The original for Zou Sheng may be Zou Bizhao. The descendants of all these people are still alive."

There is a certain moment, a certain melody, that seems to come floating in on the wind, as if from a dream. This music that comes from some deep, dark place actually has images associated with it. It is a flowering tree trembling in the wind, it is a wave that rolls in during the dark hours of the night. You hear that sound in the leaves and the waves, it is a loved one who has passed on far away, telling you...

In the late afternoon, at this mountain inn, as the music of the ocarina drifts in from outside the window, the woman listens for a moment and can't hold back her tears. The music of *Hometown Scenery*, a lonely and melodious sound, is accompanied by the waving pines on the mountains and the white clouds shimmering in the wind. She looks at the clouds with tear-filled eyes. There is bright sunshine, the singing of birds and the scent of flowers, and when she sees the waving of amaranth flowers next to the fence, the tears flow even more freely. She is sitting alone in the small dining room of the inn, facing the window.

When the innkeeper appears at the door, he sees her sobbing at the table. Her small, bare arm is bruised, and her shoulders are shaking slightly. He does not want to disturb her and stands silently in the doorway.

His lady guest was almost mugged on the mountain road the night before, but she had fought back to protect the newly acquired information she had in her bag. When she returned to the inn, the innkeeper's wife treated her injured arm. At the time she thought the city woman was crying over her injury, but that was not the case at all. There was nothing delicate, nor fragile about her.

Such a difficult search, the more so because it relies on a particular kind of determination. Nor is it a smooth process. She is currently in Shaoyang, Hunan Province, where Zou Bizhao had been the first commander of Shaoyang Military District. He was the last of the Red Army's "three decipherers" to die. He died in 1999 at the age of eighty-four. After such a long life, he might have left more memories behind than the others. This is why the woman decided to make it the first stop on her quest.

Zou Bizhao had taken a photograph of Mao Zedong at the end of the arduous trek that came to be known as the Long March. Before leaving Lazikou, he shared a horse with Cao Xiangren. On the last day of the Long March, when they reached Wuqi Township, Zou Bizhao could not walk any more, so Mao Zedong made him ride on his own stretcher. In December 1936, the Military Commission of the Central Revolutionary Army decided to centralise the technical and intelligence departments of the 2nd and 4th Front Armies in Bao'an, the seat of the Military Commission, and merged them with the 2nd Bureau of the Military Commission. "Without the 2nd Bureau, the Long March is hard to imagine. With the 2nd Bureau, it was as if we were walking at night with lanterns." In his view, the 2nd Bureau of the Military Commission was not only a "lantern" for the Long March, not only a "scientific clairvoyant and omniscient entity", but also the "Lu Ban Rock of the Revolution".[2]

According to the memoirs left by Zou Bizhao, the top-level secrecy of the 2nd Bureau was maintained throughout the Red Army's Long March. After reaching Hadapu in Gansu, when newspapers and magazines were at last readily available, the Central Party Committee saw a way out of northern Shaanxi, and the 2nd Bureau staff were able to glean more information about the enemy.

"Every issue of the Kuomintang military affairs periodical had an article detailing the awarding of regimental flags, which announced the military unit numbers of regiments batch by batch. In the same magazine, you could also find the names of some of the commanding officers. As we passed through Tongwei on the Xilan Highway, there was mail being carried on buses, but when I tried looking for these magazines, Liu Shaoqi stopped me doing so."

Zou Bizhao was on the look-out for these magazines to find clues to help his deciphering work. Liu Shaoqi was director of the Political Department of the 3rd Red Army Corps and an alternate member of the Central Political Bureau, but even he didn't know why Zou wanted the magazines. This just goes to show what a secretive existence the 2nd Bureau of the Military Committee led. During the later stages of the Long March, paraffin and diesel fuel were in short supply, and Liu Shaoqi, in his role in the General Political Department, could not understand the 2nd Bureau's excessive use of fuel. He once asked, "The central leaders don't even have oil to light their lamps, so why do *you* need so much?"

Of course, the fuel was needed for the battery chargers to keep the radios running. Chief Zeng was in a rush, and he replied brusquely, "What's the problem? I eat it! I drink it!" Zhou Enlai then politely explained to Liu Shaoqi that the central leaders would have to light their lamps without oil, but the 2nd Bureau had to have oil to carry out its work.

In fact, even some corps commanders might not have been aware of the deciphering capability of the 2nd Bureau and the role its decoded messages played in the command decisions of the Central Committee and the Military Commission. The 1st and 3rd Red Army Corps were the two main forces of the Central Red Army, and Yang Shangkun, political commissar of the 3rd Red Army Corps, later recalled, "It was a military emergency, and when an order was given to go, you had to go, even if it was pouring with rain. Likewise, when an order was given to retreat, one had to retreat, and no one felt they had to ask why. The purpose of the operation at that time was not only unknown to the cadres at the division level, but even I, as a political member of the corps, did not fully know it either. Anyway, we listened to orders every day and went when told to go. In general, we only knew that the purpose was to be rid of the enemy."

The Red Army had finally shaken off the enemy, and the northward march was to join in the resistance to the Japanese. Japan was the new enemy. After the Lugouqiao Incident, the Chinese Workers' and Peasants' Red Army was reorganised into the 8th Route Army of the National Revolutionary Army, and the work of the 2nd Bureau of the Military Commission was changed from reconnaissance of the Nationalist Army to reconnaissance of the invading Japanese army. With the change in the target, all 2nd Bureau personnel had to learn Japanese. Zou Bizhao and others were formed into a "special class", with Cao Xiangren as overall head and Zou Bizhao as group leader, to make an intensive study of Japanese. However, the way it was carried out was something of a surprise. The Japanese language instructor was Tu Tingrong, who had returned from studying in Japan to join the anti-Japanese resistance. In addition to general and specialised classes, the 2nd Bureau also held a spy training course to teach espionage duties. Later, when the textbook for the spy class was sent to the front line, it was intercepted by the Nationalist secret service. When the head of the secret service, Dai Li, saw it, he was so impressed that he issued it in an altered form as a compulsory textbook for the Nationalist secret service. After graduating from the special class, the students formed Section 4 of the 2nd Bureau of the Military Commission and went to the front line of the anti-Japanese resistance in Shanxi, Chahar and Hebei. In order to master the Japanese telegram format and encoding principles, in July 1938, Chief Zeng Xisheng and Zou Bizhao made a special trip to the 8th Route Army Office in Wuhan to collect information gleaned from the Japanese Foreign Ministry. It was said that Chiang Kai-shek's intelligence agencies had deciphered the Japanese diplomatic service's coded telegrams, and after careful arrangements by Li Kenong, Zeng Xisheng and his men secretly met with Kuomintang codebreakers such as Yang Xuan in the French Concession, in order to obtain relevant technical information. The 2nd Bureau also obtained relevant information by working with Japanese prisoners.

In July 1939, the 2nd Bureau finally made a breakthrough in its cryptographic attack on the Japanese, a milestone in the implementation of their technical reconnaissance and the first victory in their assault on the Japanese imperialist cryptographic fortress. In 1944, however, Zou Bizhao asked to be transferred out of the 2nd Bureau. He had a superb memory but was tormented by neurasthenia. The monotonous and boring work, which did not allow for fatigue of the nerves, now brought him insomnia, headaches and hallucinations. Suffering unbearably and unable to wrestle with the codes any longer, he advanced into the Central Plains with the 359th Brigade of the 8th Route Army (formerly the 6th Red Army Corps) and became deputy chief of staff of the 8th Route Army's Southbound Detachment.

"I suffered from terrible insomnia, all kinds of noises in my head, headaches, even to the point of developing neuroses. I really didn't want to keep working in the Second Bureau, and was constantly asking about a transfer... In 1939, I went to study at the Marxist-Leninist Institute under the auspices of Chairman Mao, and it was he who wrote the letter too... One day, I went round to relax at Comrade Ye Zilong's house and when Chairman Mao saw me there, he called me over for a chat. I told him that my brain was not in a good state and asked if I could go to the front. Chairman Mao talked about the connection between my individual state of affairs and the overall situation and asked me to give priority to the overall situation and not leave the Second Bureau... Ye Jianying, the chief of staff, told me that Comrade Cao Xiangren was leaving the bureau and asked me to take charge. He said that he could ask Wang Yongjun and another comrade to be the deputy directors. I had already made up my mind to leave and I did not agree... I worked as deputy chief of staff in the Southbound Detachment Branch and had a very enjoyable time because of my good physical strength and ability to walk fast. The head of the Military Commission did his very best to look after me, but I was already suffering from severe insomnia and headaches. I had done my best for the work of the Second Bureau, but I had changed from loving the deciphering to being afraid of the books and documents. I feel very deeply that 'brain workers' have a very hard time."

In considering the documents available at Shaoyang, and the recollections of Zou Bizhao's children, the doctor paid careful attention to every detail that matched her hypothesis, but the two-month search did not lead to the discovery she had expected. The insomnia caused by the deciphering work during the war years was not easily shifted, and when Zeng Xisheng was in charge of Anhui in the 1950s, Zou Bizhao went to stay for a few days and he was still tormented by it. He went downstairs at night so often that the children in the compound made up a little song they used to sing: "That Zou Bizhao, he's an odd one, / Always awake in the middle of the night."

She returned to the typed manuscript of the book she had obtained from the colonel, the two most important details of which were the man called "Xiao He" of the 2nd Bureau of the Military

Commission and the "sketch" that mentioned the amaranth flowers.

The woman's maternal grandfather was called He and her mother had insisted that she take her mother's name, which was unusual back then. Coming from a literary family, her mother was a woman of strong opinions. The man called He had sacrificed his life on the banks of the Wu River and sent his last coded message to command headquarters there. Were the mentions of amaranth flowers in *Wu River Variations* merely examples of a fleeting lyricism?

"We didn't report back to our parents or tell anything to our wives and children. Truth be told, many of us had already lost our parents who had died of hunger in the famines or of illness, or been killed in the reprisals by reactionary factions. Nor did we have wives and children. Perhaps there might have been a lover, now disappeared from our ken in a distant hometown. Perhaps there was still the lingering memory of a certain type of flower, like those amaranth flowers in autumn…"

There are millions of flowers and trees in the world, but in Dr He's heart, only the amaranth holds special memories for her. Her mother once told her that it was one of her grandmother's favourite flowers because it had a story to tell about her grandfather. She said that there was a patch of amaranth along the wall of her grandmother's garden that flowered dark red in autumn. She regrets not writing down the story during her mother's lifetime before she died suddenly that autumn. Now through her bitter regrets, she still remembers her mother's last wish. She has her grandfather's eyes, and she wants to find memories connected to him.

As a Doctor of Anthropology, she had thought that her mother was a so-called "posthumous child" simply because she had never met her biological father. But if it turned out that her biological father was still alive when she was born, then that was not actually the case. It was a simple matter of an inadvertent, but longstanding, misinterpretation. She could not forgive herself for her carelessness over this, and after her mother's death, she was quite certain she had some kind of mission to fulfil. Her mother had given birth to her at the age of forty-five, and now she too has reached that age. Her university employment contract has expired, and there is no chance of it being renewed. Now, as a freelancer, she feels this mysterious calling. This search may be what gives meaning to the rest of her life.

Zou Bizhao's little black leather-bound notebook, which he called "The Offering of My Heart's Blood". When the Red Army arrived in Shaanxi, he had not filled the entire book to the last page. His expectations of victory had been realised before that happened, although, in the later stages, he had written in slightly smaller characters. He kept a record of every decipherment: from October 1934, when the Central Red Army left the Soviet Area, to October 1935, when the Long March ended, the 2nd Bureau of the Military Commission deciphered 177 of Chiang's codes on battlefronts in Guangdong, Hunan, Guangxi, Guizhou, Yunnan, Sichuan and Shaanxi.

The codebreakers of the 2nd Bureau of the Military Commission were, in fact, the three men Zeng, Cao and Zou. From the autumn of 1932, when they broke the first enemy's codes, to the autumn of 1936, when the three main forces of the Red Army met, they had personally deciphered as many as 860 different types of Kuomintang military code. In Zou Bizhao's memoirs, written in 1988 and entitled *The Glass Cup*, the opening line is, "Mao Zedong said, 'When we fought Chiang Kai-shek, we gambled on the glass cup. We got it right and won.' That glass cup was the work done breaking the enemy's codes."

With the 2nd Bureau of the Military Commission, the Red Army was "gambling on the glass cup", and, in return, the 2nd Bureau deciphered all the important secret communications of Chiang Kai-shek and the warlords. As for the enemy side, they learned nothing at all from the secret communications of the Red Army. It is true that, as the *Art of War* says, "The enemy reveals itself, but I stay hidden" and "If I am hidden and cannot be spied on in the depths of my concealment, then I can take control of the enemy's orders." The Red Army code was based on a code called "Hao's Secret" created by Zhou Enlai in his early days, which was later upgraded in several variations. This is a "re-encoding method" double-operation cipher system. The base adds random numbers, one at a time, and the arithmetical rule is that addition is not rounded up and subtraction is not rounded down. Because the numbers are randomly generated (like today's random authentication codes), even if there are repetitions of Chinese characters in the original copy, the added random numbers mean that the message has "different codes for the same character and different characters for the same code". Although Hao's Secret was created based on the Soviet cipher system, the Chinese code was actually more difficult to decipher than one using the foreign alphabet. Such an advanced encryption method did not give the enemy any opportunity to analyse it, thereby ensuring the security of telegraphic communications. It was the most secure encryption system of that era. Chiang ordered Huang Jibi, a cryptography expert in the chairman's Attendants Office, to decipher the Red Army's coded communications, but Huang laboured in vain.

"Huang Jibi's Report" of 24 August 1933 read,

> "After two months of studying the telegrams of the Red bandits, we still have no idea where to start. It is clear from what we have seen that the bandits have an excellent and painstaking understanding of how to compile and encode their telegrams and how to compile the ciphertext. Thorough examination of all the reports we obtained showed that the content is encoded from beginning to end. It seems that they use a quantity of numbers to substitute for the names used in the message, and the telegrams are encrypted using a re-encoding method to create tables with thousands of pages of variations that can be used to change the size of the codebook being employed. The tables contain the numbers from 0000 to 9999 and those 10,000 numbers can be used freely at any time as the encoder wishes. Both the sender and the recipient have these tables to consult, so there are any number of codebooks, and each one can be used at any time. Moreover, there is no way to analyse when these changes are made... After repeated discussions with all personnel, everyone believes it is impossible to resolve this matter."

So, in 1933 they had "no way to analyse" the Red Army ciphers, and this remained the case in the following years. The 2nd Bureau of the Military Commission continued to develop its decoding abilities, and to ensure that its own codes could not be broken, it used its own deciphering experience to work with the 3rd Bureau to make them more difficult to crack. The secrecy surrounding the Red Army's codes was then far greater than that of the Nationalist Army, so it had the upper hand over the enemy in both attack and defence. The Kuomintang Army, despite the establishment of a large radio reconnaissance bureau, despite the purchase of the most advanced deciphering equipment at the time and despite the employment of foreign cryptologists, many of their personnel were "virgin soldiers" who could not stand hardship. They had joined the army for profit and promotion and worked only to the letter of the military handbook, sticking to the so-called rules about how much they got to eat and how far they could be ordered to march. They wouldn't take another step on reaching the prescribed distance. Outside their official working hours, however urgent a telegram might be, they wouldn't let it interfere with their eating, sleeping and relaxing time. The Red Army, on the other hand, was fighting for the liberation of the toiling masses of the world, with an iron will and a glorious dedication to unselfish struggle. Moreover, its coding techniques were more sophisticated, and the enemy could not break them. The Red Army's victory of the weak over the strong in this intelligence war, which lasted for several years, is a unique occurrence in the history of human warfare, even though our intelligence team started from scratch. Many years later, Otto Braun, a German who went under the pseudonym Li De, described in his "China Diary" how he first met the personnel of the 2nd Bureau of the Military Commission. Li De arrived in Jiangxi in September 1933, and in November he went with Bo Gu from Ruijin to the Red Army General Headquarters in Jianning, Fujian:

> "On the third night, we arrived in Jianning. Zhu De and Zhou Enlai met us at the forward headquarters. They led us through the complex. The headquarters consisted of a dozen houses and several hundred people, including guards, and a whole company of young intelligence officers called "little devils" who were on duty day and night, eavesdropping on and deciphering Kuomintang radio messages."

The Offering of My Heart's Blood is a record of the results of the decipherment work of the 2nd Bureau of the Central Military Commission, and *The Glass Cup* is subtitled "Radio Reconnaissance of the Central Red Army and the Red 1st Front Army". Zou Bizhao's account of the decipherment work is the main focus, and there are few personal accounts, so naturally, it was difficult for Dr He to make the discoveries she hoped for.

As early as 1933, Zou Bizhao was awarded the Red Star Medal, the highest honour of the Chinese Workers' and Peasants' Red Army, but when he was promoted in 1955, it was only to the rank of colonel. Recipients of the Red Star Medal, Third Class in 1933, including Deng Hua, Yang Yong and Yang Dezhi, were generals by 1955, but Zou Bizhao was still only a colonel. Even Xiao Yuehua, who had divorced Li De during the Yan'an period, returned to work in the army in the 1960s and was made an honorary colonel. When she thought of that erudite colonel at the Academy of Military Sciences, Dr He found herself very confused. The truths that she had actually discovered were not at all what she had expected.

Back during the War of Liberation, Zou Bizhao was head of the Special Service Corps of the 359th Brigade, commander of the 1st Military Division of the Northwest Military Region of Hubei, commander of the Jingzhong Command of the Jianghan Military Region and commander of the central command of Tianjingqian (Tianmen, Jingshan and Qianjiang). The four military divisions of the Northwest Hubei Military Region fought separately, and all of them were broken up. In 1946, he led his troops to camp in a village in the Dabie Mountains when they were suddenly attacked by the enemy. Most of the soldiers died in their sleep, and Zou Bizhao was wounded in his left hand. After the smoke cleared, he could no longer find the rest of his troops. He spent more than a month in the mountains, eating wild fruits and drinking from mountain springs; his clothes were torn and his feet were frozen. He was finally rescued by an old villager called Huang. After hiding in a cave for more than a week to avoid the enemy's frantic search, he had to bury his pistol in the cave and disguise himself as a commoner. After returning to his hometown several months later, he escaped several arrest attempts by the Shaoyang Security Regiment. As soon as he recovered his strength, he went back to the army again. After many hardships, he finally found the Shanxi-Hebei-Shandong-Henan Field Army. Its commander, Liu Bocheng said, "I know this man."

In those turbulent years, it was difficult for the authorities to send anyone to investigate what Zou Bizhao had reported. He could only provide his own version of events, unsupported by any other evidence. The fact that no one could prove this part of his life story caused him a great deal of distress and anguish later on, and he had to endure much loneliness because of it. It wasn't until 1972 that Zou Bizhao, with the help of his old comrade Yue Jun, went back to Hubei and found the old man named Huang who had rescued him. He also went back to the cave where he had been hiding and found the rusty pistol! This proved the veracity of what he had said back then and that he had not, in fact, been arrested.

He was awarded the Independence and Freedom Medal, Second Class, the Liberation Medal, Second Class, and the August 1st Medal, Second Class. He retired in 1983 with deputy ministerial status.

"So, that is what war is like," she muses in the glow of the sunset. In those tragic sieges, in those night raids by the enemy, how many people were left alive and how many died? Some you thought had sacrificed their lives, actually struggled through terrible difficulties to return to their units.

There are even different versions of how the martyr Qian Zhuangfei met his end. Some say he fell off a cliff after dropping his glasses while avoiding an air raid. Some say he was killed by looters when he asked for directions, while others say he died at the hands of a local militia group. Another example is the veteran revolutionary He Shuheng, who stayed on in the Soviet Area and was a delegate to the Communist Party of China's First Congress in Hunan with Mao Zedong. Legend has it that he jumped off a cliff to his death while breaking out of the encirclement, but the truth is even more tragic: when he found that he couldn't run any farther, rather than drag his comrades down with him, he shouted to Deng Zihui who was leading the group, to shoot him. Instead, Deng ordered some of his men to support him as he ran, but when they reached a cliff edge, he suddenly broke free and jumped off. He survived the fall and then fought with the local reactionary militia unit that was searching the mountainside. In the end, it was these reactionaries who shot him. Zou Bizhao returned to his unit alive, but before that, he was certainly listed as a casualty. During the Long March, the officers and men were willing to shed their last drop of blood for the Red Soviet Area, and as long as they were alive, they still cherished the hope of returning there alive.

There on the banks of the Wu River in April 1935, how did Xiao He of the 9th Red Army Corps shed his last drop of blood as he sent those coded messages back to headquarters? If he had survived, would he have had any hope of getting out alive? Dr He is shaken by this sudden thought.

If he had survived, he might have been able to cross the Jinsha River with the 9th Army Corps, and would have been able to reach northern Shaanxi with the main Red Army...

The little amaranth garden at my maternal grandmother's house seems to me now to have been a memorial to love. It is a garden that no longer exists, remembered first by my mother and now, most fondly, by my daughter. My mother said that before he joined the Revolution, my grandfather was a freshman college student who was recruited by the Communist underground, but soon afterwards he was betrayed by traitors and fled. Grandma's family was also implicated, so they fled to Tianjin to escape disaster. My mother was born in the Tianjin Concession, and my grandmother also grew an amaranth plant in a pot on her balcony.

"The last time they saw each other... was it in that little garden?"

She had asked her mother that and had expected an answer in the affirmative. Instead, her mother's expression had slowly changed and grown rather cold. She shook her head painfully and said, almost to herself, "No... Chongqing."

The foggy mountain town. After more than a decade of separation, they had made contact with each other. A large part of the country had fallen, and people were fleeing to Chongqing, the "provisional capital". He found her through the underground, but she had no idea about his current status. She had fled to Chongqing so husband and wife could be reunited, and to have someone to turn to. They agreed to meet at a "hanging gallery" hotel built out on stilts over the river.

That night, she looks out of the window and sees a strange yet familiar figure. Dressed in a suit and carrying a black leather briefcase, he stands at a distance, directly under the streetlight, and raises his eyes towards the window. The woman waves joyfully at him, but he looks around warily, not moving a step. Suddenly, a group of plainclothes men burst out of the alleyway, brandishing pistols, and rush into the hotel. The woman upstairs does not see what is going on below; she is still waving anxiously at the man. At that moment, he waves desperately back at her, gesturing for her to take cover. He lifts his briefcase in desperation and shakes it, waving even more violently at the woman. Her figure leaves the window and the man walks quickly away...

"I hate him!" Even in that distant memory, her mother's hatred was still vivid. She was nine years old at the time. Her mother had gestured to her from the window but she was fast asleep. She was exhausted from the long journey.

This was her only chance to meet with her biological father, and it had been missed. Many years later, all she remembered was the all-pervasive night fog and the sound of the riverboat's whistle.

The world of that meeting was an eternity away. Did Grandpa survive the Long March? Did he reach northern Shaanxi? She was sure Grandpa had gone to the South Jiangxi Soviet, which is why she asked that expert from the Academy of Military Sciences for help. If he had later arrived in Shaanxi, then what was he doing in Chongqing? What was his identity in Chongqing? Why the suit and briefcase?

Suppose he was the Xiao He who sent messages back to headquarters on the banks of the Wu River, and suppose he had been captured before he had shed his last drop of blood...

If that Xiao He was not her grandfather, then why, as the author of *Wu River Variations*, did he write about the amaranth flowers in his notes on the Long March?

She is deeply immersed in this vexing mystery. Zou Bizhao, one of the "three decipherers", left no clues in his writings, and his descendants had had trouble providing any more information. All that remained of his history was in those words. Indeed, he seldom talked about it with his children during his lifetime. This had nothing to do with the discipline of secrecy; in his later years, as mankind was moving into the computer age, these methods of codebreaking used during the Long March had long since become obsolete, and this secret history had long since been declassified. In fact, as early as 1936, not long after the end of the Long March, Zhou Enlai declassified it in his own inimitable way. In December of that year, Zhang Xueliang and Yang Hucheng were trying to force Chiang to join the resistance against Japan by giving him a "military warning". Zhou Enlai went to Xi'an to deal with the incident on behalf of the Chinese Communist Party. Zhou was the director of the Political Department of the Huangpu Military Academy. He admired his student, Li Mo'an, who had been in the first cohort of cadets, for his combined military and literary talents, so he transferred him directly to the Political Department as his assistant. Later, as lieutenant general of the 10th Division of the Kuomintang Army, Li Mo'an was stationed in Xi'an and was asked by He Yingqin to attack Zhang and Yang's "rebel army". Zhou Enlai, who no longer wore a long beard as he had during the Long March, went to Li's division alone to pay a visit to his student. Li Mo'an greeted "Director Zhou" as a disciple. During the meeting, Zhou Enlai praised Li's poetry and recited two lines from one of his poems: "Climbing the Immortals' Bridge [*Dengxian* in Chinese] to cross to the other side, how many tears dry on the cheeks of the beauties they leave behind?" Li Mo'an was dumbstruck and looked at Zhou Enlai in disbelief. Zhou Enlai burst out laughing. Three years ago, the Kuomintang army was defeated at Dengxian Bridge, and Li Mo'an, wearied and disillusioned by the war, had sent these lines as a private message to his wife in Shanghai.

Zou Bizhao was transferred out of the 2nd Bureau of the Military Commission in 1944, and what happened after that can only be investigated along different lines. "The Offering of My Heart's Blood" is a record of one victory after another, and represents the most cherished memories of his long life. At the beginning of *The Glass Cup*, he fondly recalls a scene from many years ago:

> "In January 1933, I was resting during a night march to destroy the 90th Division of Wu Qiwei, known as the 'Iron Army', and then turn towards Nanfeng. Although it was winter, it was not

cold, only cloudy with a light wind, which felt very soothing. Comrade Cao Xiangren was talking about telling revolutionary stories in the future to the next generation: 'You will tell one story and I will tell another. There are so many of them to be told.'"

They were still in the joyful innocence of youth back then, not yet twenty years old. Then, after the triumph of the revolution, they too entered middle age. They were busy with revolutionary work as the New China was still in the process of being built, and later, as politics changed, they met with all sorts of different situations. They rarely told their stories to the younger generation and took countless secrets to the grave.

Fragments of innumerable memories in the depths of time. What is "credible history"? The original archives from the flames of war may be flawed, and there may be subjective elements in the accounts of individuals and their descendants. It is for this reason that the memories of "third parties" may be the most reliable. They put them into writing, and they are responsible for their authenticity.

As far as our friend, the Doctor of Anthropology, while she is certainly looking for authentic and credible history, she is also reluctant to give up on the wider search, praying she will find the clues she seeks in the memories of other individuals...

"At the end of 1938, Cao Xiangren became director of the 2nd Bureau of the Military Commission. How old was he? Twenty-four! The central political and military apparatus was in Yan'an, and our 2nd Bureau was in Diezigou Village in Ansai District. We had to be kept secret and the people in Yan'an didn't know we were there. Situated several dozen miles northwest of Yan'an, we were also sheltered from the enemy bombers. Cao Xiangren rode to Yan'an for a meeting. The 2nd Bureau set up Section 4 which focused on the deciphering of Japanese codes. On 1 July 1939, the bureau informed Yan'an of the first batch of Japanese intelligence. The Central Party Committee and the Central Military Commission immediately gave them a special commendation."

"To Comrade Cao Xiangren and to pass on to the comrades of Section 4:

We are very pleased to hear that, with Bolshevik perseverance, concentrated effort and hard work, you have recently begun to achieve results in the study of enemy codes. We wish you well in your efforts to overcome all the inevitable difficulties of victory and to fight for the accomplishment of the most difficult and most glorious task given to you by the Central Party Committee and the Military Commission! Now we are specially sending Comrade Teng Daiyun to you to express our fellow feeling on behalf of the Central Committee and the Military Commission, and to present to each comrade of Section 4 a reward of one pair of cloth shoes, one pair of lined socks, one tube of toothpaste and one large notebook for their hard work. The Central Committee and the Central Military Commission of the Communist Party of China on 7 July 1939."

In his book *On the General Staff in the War of Resistance Against the Japanese*, Yang Di, an operational staff officer back then, gives a detailed account of the "Great Intelligence Leak in Yan'an" in July 1943:

"One day, when I was on combat duty, Director Wu [Xiuquan] came to me and said, 'Call Director Cao Xiangren of the 2nd Bureau at once and tell him that Chief of Staff Ye has ordered him to hurry with all speed to the Central Party Committee's Secretary's office in Yangjialing... he is to put down the phone and come post-haste, the sooner the better. I'm going to Yangjialing now for a meeting.'

It was early the next morning when Director Wu returned... [Overnight] he called a meeting to convey to us the determination of the Party Central Secretariat and Chairman Mao... [Wu Xiuquan then told us] that Chairman Mao said it is Party discipline to keep Party secrets, and today, after a discussion in the Secretariat of the Central Party Committee, it was resolved that we want to leak a big secret. Director Wu said to Director Cao of the 2nd Bureau that they had heard that all information they had received on the movements of the Kuomintang Army, the telegrams from Chiang Kai-shek to Hu Zongnan and the telegrams from Hu Zongnan to the various units, had all been simultaneously intercepted and deciphered by him [Cao Xiangren] and his 2nd Bureau. Chairman Mao also said to Comrade Li Kenong, [deputy] head of the Central Social Department, that our

Party comrades who had infiltrated the key core departments of the Kuomintang Army had done an excellent job, as they had promptly transcribed the orders received by Hu Zongnan and Yan Xishan from Chiang Kai-shek and the orders issued by Hu and Yan to attack us, and secretly transferred them to us. The information provided by your two experts, Li Kenong and Cao Xiangren, has enabled the Central Party Committee and the Central Military Commission to have an excellent grasp of the enemy's situation. This is the biggest and most important secret our Party and our army possess.

Now, to crush Chiang Kai-shek's attack on the border area and on Yan'an, we have to transfer troops from northern China to Yan'an, and it is too late to do so. We, the Central Secretariat, have studied this and have only one practical plan... to publish the telegrams and written orders sent by Chiang Kai-shek and Hu Zongnan to all Kuomintang groups and armies to attack the border area and Yan'an. We are using this major leak to save the border area and Yan'an from danger. We are making this dangerous move at a very perilous time, as we are using the leak as the price for stopping Chiang Kai-shek's attack. Do you think it is a good deal or not?"

Hu Zongnan and Yan Xishan assembled an army of 400,000, and the Kuomintang outnumbered the Communists forty to one. Li Kenong and Cao Xiangren said they were determined to obey and execute the orders of the Central Party Committee and Chairman Mao. Chairman Mao asked the 1st Bureau quickly to compile the relevant information uncovered by the 2nd Bureau and send telegrams to Zhou Enlai in Chongqing and Peng Dehuai at the front, telling them to announce it publicly in the name of the 8th Route Army Office and the 8th Route Army headquarters in Chongqing. At the same time, they were to call Chiang Kai-shek and Hu Zongnan, in the name of Zhu De, commander-in-chief of the 8th Route Army, to raise serious protests about and warnings against the Kuomintang's anti-Communist acts which undermined the unity of the resistance against Japan.

Chiang Kai-shek wanted to take advantage of the disbanding of the Comintern to destroy the Chinese Communist Party in one fell swoop, but this big leak from the Communist Party of China exposed his plot. The previously defenceless Yan'an was turned into a safe place. Ye Jianying, then chief of staff of the Central Military Commission, was the mastermind of this "empty city strategy" and later commented, "The third anti-Communist surge launched by Chiang Kai-shek and the Kuomintang was extremely fierce, but they were reduced to chaos without bloodshed, and we won by using our wits. Chairman Mao wisely and decisively used the secret information from the Second Bureau to expose the fact that the stubborn faction within the Kuomintang had moved heavy troops to attack the border areas. The Second Bureau did an excellent job in fully understanding the enemy's deployments in a timely and accurate fashion. The Second Bureau's technical intelligence was used by Chairman Mao to maximum effect."

The cost of this big leak was that the Kuomintang Army swiftly changed to a new code, but the 2nd Bureau rose to the challenge and soon succeeded in breaking it. By this time, the 2nd Bureau had a team of several hundreds. Before that, in 1941, it also detected Hitler's Barbarossa plan to attack the Soviet Union from a coded Kuomintang message. In July 1945, Director General Cao Xiangren led a team to the Shanxi-Chahar-Hebei Military Region to carry out reconnaissance of the forward divisions of the main Japanese force. The 2nd Bureau of the Shanxi-Chahar-Hebei Military Region was known as the "Meteorological Bureau" to outsiders. In the early summer of 1947, Cao Xiangren took another team to the northeast to establish the Second Bureau of the Northeast Democratic Alliance Army headquarters. Cao Xiangren was also director general and later deputy chief of staff of the Northeast Field Army.

"As a senior commander in our army, Lin Biao had his own unique personality. He was by nature a quiet man and somewhat introverted, quite the opposite of Old Commander Peng. Lin Biao used to take only four or five staff officers with him in the field, but on the night of 30 September 1948, when he went south from Harbin to Jinzhou, he took with him three or four hundred men from the Second Bureau. Three or four hundred men! Two railway trains with the Second Bureau of the Northeast Field Army led by Cao Xiangren at the front and the commanders of the field army at the rear. Lin Biao's principle in fighting a war was not to fight if the situation was unknown. He said that to fight a war is 'to fight with secret information' and that 'intelligence is victory'. 'The operational plan is decided, the troops are deployed but the enemy situation has changed. Instead of waiting for me to give my orders, we should wait for the Second Bureau to give theirs'."

On the night of 30 September 1948, that train, the one that went south in the misty night, carried dozens of radios all working at the same time and 300 to 400 men from the 2nd Bureau. This is only an approximate figure, and today we cannot be sure of the exact names of the men in this group. Although some of them are still alive, they are all in their nineties, and several have reached their century. And in their memories, in the dreamy past seen through the clouds of time, those youthful figures are far away and indistinct. Names appear in the fragments of their memories, but there is no young man called He.

She listens carefully to each of the old men's reminiscences, from which she draws out any information related to that name. As a Doctor of Anthropology, she also uses the professional methodology of fieldwork. She doesn't know her grandfather's given names. If he was using a pseudonym back then, it will be even more difficult to corroborate.

Walking through the brightly lit and vibrant city streets, Dr He is physically and mentally exhausted, but she is not depressed. On this snowless winter day, her thoughts are far away on the snowy plains of the northeast, a wilderness bordering Siberia, with its pale green sea of forests, vast stands of birch trees, howling wolves and horse-drawn sleighs.

It was a romance that belonged to another era. These were once real, living people.

They had lived real but invisible lives in the gaps in the historical records. Walking through the streets of Beijing in this cold winter, for no apparent reason, the theme song of a Soviet film, *War and Love*, rings in her ears. She can't shrug that tune off. She doesn't want her grandfather to have had another romance. The biting wind sobers her up; she doesn't have to worry about that. If Grandpa wasn't on that southbound train in 1948, there couldn't be another love affair.

Assuming that her grandfather was not on that southbound train with the Northeast Field Army, she will have to go back in time and look for his tracks in that land of yellow earth in northern Shaanxi. Another possibility also exists in that typewritten volume from the seventies, *Wu River Variations*. She can hardly rule out the possibility that her grandfather was its author, and she wants to confirm this. She will just have to search through it systematically. It mentions amaranth, and Cao Xiangren's work records include "revolutionary grass", a farmers' crop he had made notes about during his time as secretary of the Zhejiang Provincial Committee Secretariat.

In August 1975, Cao Xiangren died in Beijing at the age of sixty-one. He was one of the first ambassadors of the New China to foreign countries, and along with the Long March painter Huang Zhen, they were both "ambassadors general". After returning to China, he served successively as vice minister of the First Mechanical Industry Department of the State Council, secretary of the secretariat of the Heilongjiang Provincial Party Committee of the Communist Party of China and secretary of the secretariat of the Zhejiang Provincial Party Committee of the Communist Party of China. In 1966, while in Zhejiang, he experienced a number of political shocks, including the issue of rural household production contracting. In 1961, when his old chief and comrade Zeng Xisheng was working on "contracted farmland" in Anhui, he went to visit him and learn about the process. He wanted to implement it in Zhejiang, but he faced opposition and was later criticised for it. In early 1967, Premier Zhou sent a special plane to collect him and Jiang Hua and bring them to Beijing to protect them, along with a number of other old cadres. There were, in fact, many provincial and ministerial cadres involved, and he was actually owed this protection due to his role as the former director of the 2nd Bureau of the Military Commission, although it was only a limited and temporary form of protection. Amid the two-fold pain of mental and physical illness, in the evening of his life, it was this distant memory that gave him rare comfort. Looking back on his life, although he later served as an ambassador abroad and a senior provincial and ministerial official, what he was most proud of was "the name I made for myself in the Second Bureau of the Military Commission". It was those years of the Long March that he missed the most, those youthful days amid the flames of war, those dark nights lit by the flares of countless battles with...

In the middle of the night, I long for the brightness of day. In the depths of winter I long for the spring breezes. If you want the Red Army to come over the ridge, it will turn the mountain as red as Indian azaleas...[3]

The morning light is clear and the first thing she hears is this music drifting in through the window, a melody from long ago. It is a beautiful tune, pure and natural, full of deep emotion. It is coming from the women who get up early in the morning and dance in the square. The song is so beautiful, she doesn't think of it as noise. As she listens to the music in a daze, she feels her heart stir.

If you want the Red Army to come over the ridge, it will turn the mountain as red as Indian azaleas...

A woman's song. They had such great tunes in the seventies and such excellent lyrics. It is hard to find such innocent songs these days. The sun shines through the trees and spills onto the tabletop by the window, bringing a shimmering light. She lies on the hotel bed and listens to the song coming in through the window.

She is still terrified by last night's dream. At midnight the dream returned when the power went out in the hotel. The receptionist said it was just a breaker switch. She lay down again in the darkness, with the light from the tall building opposite shining in through the window. What lingered in the darkness was a vision of that power cut many years ago: the foggy night when Grandma looked out of the window and saw that figure; a group of plainclothes men rushing into the hotel brandishing pistols; the man downstairs waving desperately at them upstairs...

Her mother is asleep. She was only nine years old. Grandma pulls her out of the room. They dodge the plainclothes men rushing upstairs. Her mother turns the electric switch off downstairs. The guests are running downstairs in a panic. They escape from the hotel building in the confusion...

Grandma's father was an electrical engineer, and she has been interested in electricity since she was a child. The issue is that, at that fateful moment, the man should not have gone too far. Even if he was fleeing for his life, he should have looked back again. He had left his wife and daughter in the hotel room, and they had become his cover. If he had looked back then and seen that the building was in darkness, he would have realised his situation was not so dangerous, as he wouldn't, after all, have been trapped in the hotel room by plainclothes men. But he did not turn back to look for his wife and daughter. He disappeared in the darkness of the night. All that was left for his daughter was the memory of the riverboat's whistle.

Even if he was on an urgent mission, he had still come to meet his wife and daughter. Perhaps he was feeling exposed and was afraid of endangering that briefcase, which must contain top secret documents of exceptional importance, but he was certainly not putting his personal life before his duty.

This is as far as the woman's deductions can take her. It is too difficult for her to go any further with them. In these circumstances, she has to conclude that the briefcase was more important than three lives. The fact that he was willing to abandon his wife and daughter when they were in danger could only mean that he was on a mission, that he had to protect that briefcase, and to do so he would even put his wife and daughter at risk... Chongqing, that strange, foggy city, that hot and humid mountain town, that enigmatic galleried hotel...

That was the last trace of him. Now, she has no choice but to go back on her tracks. There is no trace of him in the sixties and seventies, no record of him in the Liao-Shen Campaign. The last words of the booklet, *Wu River Variations* by an unknown author, are "Destination, northern Shaanxi"... Northern Shaanxi. Chongqing. Her inquiries are revealing a nebulous path.

The first director of the 2nd Bureau of the Central Military Commission, Zeng Xisheng, went to northern Shaanxi after the victorious conclusion of the Long March and remained as director of the bureau. He was transferred to the Social Department of the Central Party Committee at the end of 1938 and then followed Zhou Enlai to Chongqing.

She has to suspend her search for Cao Xiangren. All the interviewees mentioned the Red Star medal that he received in 1933 and how she would like to have seen it with her own eyes, but this wish too goes unfulfilled. The truth is that the medal has long since sunk to the bottom of the sea.

In 1947, when Bureau Director Cao Xiangren was posted to work in the northeast, he set out from Weihai, Shandong Province, on a small steamer, but soon after going to sea, he encountered a patrol ship of the Nationalist Army.

According to Peng Fujiu, who was deputy director of the 2nd Bureau of the Shanxi-Chahar-Hebei Military Region, "Early the next morning, Cao Xiangren brought me a small black leather-bound notebook, telling me it was the decipherment record of the Central Red Army: 'Zou Bizhao gave me this when he left the Second Bureau. It is very precious. Now I will take a boat from Weihai in Shandong to North Korea and then transfer to Harbin. It is a dangerous journey, so it is up to you to keep this book safe. It is the book I call *The Offering of my Heart's Blood*.'

Director Cao's premonitions proved correct. They did encounter a dangerous situation on the way, which forced them to jettison everything that might reveal their identity, and even the Red Star medal that Director Cao had won in the Central Soviet area was dropped into the sea.

A medal sinks to the bottom of the sea. It doesn't float on the choppy surface but sinks into the eternal silence of the ocean depths, at one with the rocks and seaweed. There is starlight on the water, the dense secret whispers of the wind, and there are also those young lives sunk into the mire of the grassland. They all disappear in an instant. And there are those who plunged into the ice chasms of the snowy mountains, who never had a chance to leave behind their last words. Zeng Xisheng's Red Star medal, too, sank into the water. That was during one of the great perils of the Long March of Ten Thousand Miles: the Wu River.

She stops for a long time in the history gallery of the Memorial Hall of the Central Revolutionary Base in Ruijin. On both sides of the gallery are huge, imposing oil paintings of dozens of "Fathers of the People's Republic who emerged from Ruijin", including Zeng Xisheng. They are majestic, epic pictures, and the characters portrayed in them are all alive with personality. There is Mao Zedong walking at the front of the column, dressed in a coat and holding a cigarette, gazing into the distance with a smile on his face, while Zhu De rides a tall white horse, a robust and powerful figure. In an ingenious and creative piece of design, the gallery is located in the last hall of this giant memorial, where the visitors exit the building, as if it were the end of some kind of historical tunnel. It serves to highlight the theme of the whole memorial: this is where the People's Republic came from. In December 1931, Zeng Xisheng moved from Shanghai to the General Headquarters of the Red Army in Ningdu. Here, he met Chairman Mao. When Mao heard the name of Zeng Xisheng, he shook his hand and said jokingly with a big smile, "What talents the proletariat has! We already have a Xixian in our ranks, and now we have a Xisheng. The Communist Party has a saint and a sage, but how pitiful the Kuomintang is!"

Deng Xixian was the name given to Deng Xiaoping by his school master. Zeng Xisheng's work in the 2nd Bureau of the Military Commission is of course extremely mysterious, and the only reason there is more information about him publicly available is because he later held political office at the local level. The 8th National Congress of the Communist Party of China was the first national party congress after the founding of the New China, and there were only ninety-seven members on the Eighth Central Committee, of which Zeng Xisheng was one. Zeng Xisheng's life achievements are also extensively described in the relevant memoirs edited and published by authoritative institutions such as the Communist Party History Press and the Central Literature Press. Dr He hopes to find something out among Zeng Xisheng's descendants, and to this end she studies the relevant literature as hard as she did when she was studying for her PhD. This is the necessary preliminary information-gathering phase.

"When he went to work in the local area, it was, of course, well before the implementation of the new ranking system introduced in 1955, which could not be retrospectively applied. During the War of Liberation, he was deputy chief of staff of both the Shanxi-Hebei-Shandong-Henan Field Army and the Central Plains People's Liberation Army. In 1933, he was awarded the Red Star Medal, Second Class along with Liu Bocheng and Nie Rongzhen, both of whom had the rank of marshal! His brother Zeng Zhongsheng, a graduate of the Fourth Huangpu cohort, was one of the thirty-six military strategists of the Republic, as determined by the Central Military Commission. He had been the main leader of the Hubei-Henan-Anhui Red Army until Zhang Guotao arrived in the Hubei-Henan-Anhui Soviet. Unfortunately, he was secretly assassinated by Zhang Guotao at the age of thirty-five. His wife, Huang Jie, a sixth cohort Huangpu graduate, was a contemporary of Zhao Yiman. She later married Xu Qianqian, who was a member of the first Huangpu cohort and another of the thirty-six strategists. They both lived to a grand old age. Just think, in those days when the 1st and 4th Front Armies met in August 1935, the brothers were so close and yet so far apart, unable to meet. In the emergency exodus on 9 September, Mao Zedong let Zeng, Cao and Zou go first, and Zeng Xisheng still did not yet know that his brother had been killed."

Zeng Xisheng left Yan'an for Chongqing in early 1939. Dr He is once again combing through the historical materials of the Yan'an era. As a woman intellectual, she has always had a particular interest in the subject of "revolution and love", and life in Yan'an had a special romantic air. She searched for her grandfather in the documents related to Zeng Xisheng and made no small number of interesting and unexpected discoveries in the process. When talking about her marriage, Zhuo Lin recalled, "Deng Xiaoping and Deng Fa both came back from the front and lived in a cave house. He was then a political commissar of the 129th Division, working in the Taihang Mountains, and was still unmarried. Deng Fa wanted him to find a suitable match in Yan'an, so he brought him to his study class. Once, when I went to Zeng Xisheng's house, Zeng said there was someone who wanted to marry me and asked if I was happy about the idea. I said no, because I was still young at the time and wanted to work for a few more years. In fact, Zeng Xisheng talked to me twice, and I was not happy about it on either occasion."

In this, she is, of course, being a little evasive. She wrote what she really thought in her memoirs: "At that time, the old cadres of the Long March were all worker and peasant cadres, so we were afraid of marrying them, afraid that they were uneducated and inarticulate." But Deng Xiaoping was not put off. He got someone to take a message asking if they could meet to talk. Zhuo Lin agreed. They went to Zeng Xisheng's house together.

Deng Xiaoping said, "I am an old man already and fighting at the front is very hard. I want to marry you, but Zeng Xisheng and you talked it over and you don't agree. I am not very good with words, but I do hope you will give this job your consideration. I am a few years older than you and I recognise this is a shortcoming on my part, but I hope to make up for it in other ways."

On the day of the wedding, Zhuo Lin said to Deng Xiaoping, "In the future, you have to pay attention to what I say. When you have heard me out, if you have an opinion, speak up."

Deng Xiaoping replied, "Well, the way things stand with me is that, if you want to say something, say it. If I have an opinion on it, I'll tell you, and if I don't, that's that…"

Deng Xiaoping, the veteran cadre of the Long March, was actually only thirty-five at the time, which was the same age as Zeng Xisheng. He was also an educated man and had been to France, so he could certainly be considered an intellectual. Dr He is full of hope that she will find more similar material in the historical records, because there is one particular person she is searching for.

At the age of thirty-five, Zeng Xisheng, who had been transferred out of the 2nd Bureau of the Military Commission, moved to Chongqing to work. After the Red Army arrived in northern Shaanxi, he had requested a transfer, but Mao Zedong and Zhou Enlai did not approve it. Mao Zedong once said wryly, "In my early years, I wrote an essay that contained this sentence, 'The only modern figure I am convinced by is Zeng Wenzheng '. I have also heard that Chiang Kai-shek admires Zeng Guofan, so I am obliged to disagree with him, which only leaves me Zeng Xisheng to put my belief in!"

The shift from the Revolutionary War in China to the People's War of Resistance Against the Japanese brought relative stability to life in Yan'an compared with the treacherous conditions during the Long March, but all kinds of contrasting factions emerged within the ranks. Zeng Xisheng's desire to be transferred had a number of causes. The main one was that there were some people who belittled his achievements and exaggerated his shortcomings and the favouritism they considered he received. The victorious conclusion of the Long March led to Mao, Zhou, Zhu and Peng, the heads of the Military Commission, singling out Zeng Xisheng and the 2nd Bureau for special treatment. After arriving in northern

Shaanxi, Mao and Zhou instructed the supply department always to favour the 2nd Bureau, even if supplies were short. They signed the Order on the Regulation of Office Expenses and Allowances, giving Zeng Xisheng a preferential first-class monthly allowance of twelve yuan, which was two yuan more than the standard divisional monthly allowance. The monthly allowance of Luo Fu and others on the Central Committee was only five yuan. During the Spring Festival of 1936, Lu Xun asked someone to bring him a few Jinhua hams, and Mao Zedong made sure to share one of them with Zeng Xisheng.

The great military sage of the ancients, Sunzi, once said, " In your whole army, none should be closer to you than your spies; none should be more richly rewarded; and no secret should be more closely guarded than your spy network." The demonstration of such respect and affection was just as it should be and not unusual, but some individual comrades who were spurred on to cause trouble both by their belief in absolute egalitarianism and by envy and jealousy, often criticised Zeng, saying, "What's so great about Zeng Xisheng? He doesn't lead the troops into battle but makes a big fuss about setting up a new base and gets treated like a king and has honours heaped on him!" This sour, mean-spirited gossip wounded him deeply.

For reasons of secrecy, the role of Zeng Xisheng and the 2nd Bureau was known only to the leaders of the Central Committee and the Military Commission. Their achievements could not be publicised, nor could they explain the reasons for any grievances they provoked. As this situation persisted for a long time, it was inevitable that a certain sense of loneliness would develop. He had to keep on top of all the changes in the enemy's codes and had little time to interact much with his comrades in other departments. This led some people to believe he was out of touch and too aloof. In fact, this behaviour was just a manifestation of his no-nonsense character, although he did have something of a temper. When he was concentrating on codebreaking, no one was allowed to disturb him. Once on the Long March, when Commander-in-Chief Zhu was in a rush for some information and Chief Zeng was working as fast as he could to decipher it, he just pushed Zhu out the door without batting an eyelid. When he broke the code and went outside, there was the commander-in-chief squatting on his haunches, waiting. The fact is that the commander-in-chief was a gentle and warm-hearted man, and he certainly understood the nature of Zeng Xisheng's work, so he was not bothered in the slightest. Some people, however, took this incident as evidence of Zengs' lack of respect for leadership and his high-handedness. In fact, his character began to change right from the time the 2nd Bureau of the Military Commission was established. The pressure was enormous, the work was dry and boring, it was a lonely existence and required a high level of brain power. He could not allow himself or his team to take a step back in the face of difficulties, nor could he permit any mistakes in their work. He became more irritable and would flare up at anyone who disturbed him. When he asked for a transfer, he was greatly angered by those people who took the opportunity to stir up old grievances. During the Long March, when the authorities decided to assign a political commissar to the 2nd Bureau, he publicly expressed his disapproval. He approached Wang Jiaxiang, director of the General Political Department, to state that the 2nd Bureau had a strong and sound Party organisation, carried out highly effective ideological and political work, and that he and other cadres had a solid political stance. Since the 2nd Bureau consisted of only a few dozen people, there was no need for a political commissar. Besides, didn't the 1st Bureau have a political commissar? But there were people who seized on this and criticised him in terms of the class struggle and the two-line struggle, accusing him of finding the post of political commissar unacceptable. He had been a revolutionary for many years, was still only in his thirties and was bursting with vim and vigour. In a fit of anger, he said he was leaving the 2nd Bureau to raise his own army, start a guerrilla campaign and actually get something done.

In fact, Zeng Xisheng was not acting in a fit of pique, as he had long believed that "famous heroes are not particularly remarkable, it is the unsung heroes who are the most valuable". He was acting because he could no longer stand the gossip, because he considered that Cao Xiangren, Zou Bizhao and others were already able to take on the heavy responsibility that he currently carried, that his departure would not be detrimental to the work of the 2nd Bureau, and that he should be leading troops into battle to toughen himself up and gain experience. Although Zeng Xisheng now wore round-rimmed glasses, he was originally trained as both a scholar and a soldier. When he was young, he had studied at the Huang Yang Academy run by his grandfather, and he could throw a millstone weighing more than eighty catties up from the ground and catch it in his hands, repeating the exercise seven or eight times without any change in his expression.

Zeng Xisheng did indeed raise a guerrilla band and make something happen.

On 4 January 1941, Ye Ting and Xiang Ying led more than 9,000 men of the New 4th Army south from their headquarters in Yunling, Jing County, Anhui Province, and three days later, they were surrounded and attacked in Maolin by seven divisions of the Kuomintang's "Stubborn Army" consisting of more than 80,000 men. The New 4th Army fought a bloody battle over seven days and nights, but finally, outnumbered and out of ammunition and food, they died a heroic death, with the exception of 2,000 men who managed to break out. The army's commander, Ye Ting, went to the enemy's divisional headquarters to negotiate, but he was arrested and detained. Deputy Army Commander Xiang Ying, Chief of Staff Zhou Zikun and Director of the Political Department Yuan Guoping, were all killed. In an act of self-exculpatory retaliation, Chiang Kai-shek declared the New 4th Army action a "mutiny", revoked its unit number and "relieved" its commander, Ye Ting, from his post. The Ye Ting Independent Regiment had been part of the 4th Army of the National Revolutionary Army during the Northern Expedition, a heroic "iron army", but now Ye Ting, commander of the New 4th Army, was to be "court-martialled". Chiang Kai-shek also ordered Tang Enbo and Li Pinxian's more than 200,000 troops to attack the Jiangbei (north of the Yangtze) Command of the New 4th Army. At the beginning of the Northern Expedition in 1926, Zeng Xisheng served as a battalion political instructor in Li Pinxian's 3rd Division, and now, in the second Nationalist-Communist collaboration, the Kuomintang Army was attacking the Communist-led army. Zeng Xisheng was in charge of organising the rescue teams sent across the river, and, as a result, more than 700 people were rescued. On 20 January, the Central Military Commission issued an order to rebuild the New 4th Army, appointing Chen Yi as acting commander, Liu Shaoqi as political commissar and establishing its headquarters in Yancheng, north of the Yangtze. On 18 February, the Central Military Commission appointed the military and political heads of the seven divisions of the New 4th Army. Zhang Dingcheng was commander of the 7th Division, and Zeng Xisheng was the political commissar. At this time, Zhang Dingcheng was studying at the Yan'an Central Party School and had not yet arrived at his post. The heavy responsibility of forming a new 7th Division in these blood-stained circumstances fell on Zeng Xisheng's shoulders.

When one is entrusted with the management of a crisis, there are many difficulties that must be overcome. On 15 April, the Central Committee of the Communist Party of China issued a letter of instruction to Zeng Xisheng and the other cadres in Jiangnan: "Our Party and our army must make certain to establish a position in southern Anhui, Wuwei, Lu and Tong, and not readily give it up. This glorious task is given to all the comrades of Wannan and Wuwei, and we expect they will accept it with Bolshevik courage and determination and abandon all doubt, hesitation and fear of difficulties." On 1 May, the founding meeting of the 7th Division was held in Wuwei, Anhui Province, and more than 1,900 men were enrolled into it.

Wuwei was a place that offered a great deal of promise. The New 7th Division, born out of the blood of the Southern Anhui Incident, had grown to nearly 30,000 men by 1945, the eve of victory in the war. Their weapons were all Japanese. Zeng Xisheng had a codebreaker's brain and a good head for economics, so, under his leadership, the New 7th Division was transformed from the "poor 7th Division" to the "wealthy 7th Division". There was a saying that "the wealthy 7th Division is the provider and protector for the whole army". The New 7th Division continued to provide a large amount of funds to the headquarters of the New 4th Army and the 8th Route Army. From 1944 to 1945 alone, it provided the headquarters of the New 4th Army with Nationalist *fabi* currency worth about 200,000 taels of gold. By the time its military unit registration was revoked in the spring of 1947, there were more than 500,000 taels of gold in the accounts of the 7th Division.

This was a glorious new chapter in the life of Zeng Xisheng.

However, for Dr He, in her current research work, these discoveries are taking her further and further from Chongqing. Her thoughts are still in that city.

Zeng Xisheng left Chongqing with Ye Ting and his wife in early July 1940, and his identity moved out of the cover of secrecy into the public eye. He was only in Chongqing for a year and a half. Dr He is surprised to discover that it was also in the early summer of 1940 that her grandmother took her mother to Chongqing to join her grandfather!

The figure of the man standing under the streetlamp; the woman's pose, beckoning from the hotel window; the sleeping girl in the room; the sound of the steam whistle by the river...

The public documents available today show that Zeng Xisheng was transferred to southern Anhui because his identity in Chongqing had been exposed, and Zhou Enlai and Ye Jianying decided to transfer him secretly to the headquarters of the New 4th Army. At that time, Ye Ting, commander of the New 4th Army, was in Chongqing and about to leave to return to the army headquarters. This would have facilitated his transfer.

Zeng Xisheng's secret trip to Chongqing took place in February 1939, and the location was the Zhou Mansion, No. 50 Zengjiayan, the Southern Bureau of the Central Committee of the Communist Party of China and the Chongqing Office of the 8th Route Army. The Central Committee's Bureau had been formally established in January, with Zhou Enlai as its secretary. Its remit was to lead the Party's work south of the Yangtze River and to head up the united front work with the Kuomintang at the rear. The situation in the "provisional capital" was as unpredictable and confusing as the mist in the mountain city. Zeng Xisheng was able to gather information on the enemy from the public press, and he was also a master in deciphering secret information on the covert front, so Zhou Enlai proposed to the Central Committee that he be transferred to the Military Group of the Southern Bureau. The Communist Party of China had two covert fronts: one was "underground" and the other was in the ether. It was underground during the Central Military Commission's time in Shanghai, and the radio code-breaking during the Soviet period and the Long March was in the ether. Zeng fought on both of these covert fronts. On arriving in Chongqing, although he remained anonymous, he could not help but encounter the secret agents of the National Military Council on the ground. In June of that year, Ye Jianying also arrived in Chongqing in order to assist Zhou Enlai in presiding over the Southern Bureau and to serve as head of the Military Department and deputy secretary of the United Front Work Committee. Dark clouds loomed over the mountain city, and an anti-Communist storm was due to come crashing in at any moment.

One day, two young men dressed as students came to No. 50 Zengjiayan. One of them was Zhang Weilin and the other was Feng Chuanqing, staff members of the Kuomintang Military Council's Telecommunications Office. They hated the Kuomintang rule and asked to go to Yan'an. Zeng Xisheng investigated their backgrounds and motives, determined that they were not secret agents and wanted to use them. The General Telecommunications Station of the Military Intelligence was a very advanced outfit, set up with the aid of the United States, through which Dai Li commanded and controlled the Kuomintang agents scattered all over the country, providing intelligence to Chiang Kai-shek and issuing secret orders. One night in September, Zhang Weilin and Feng Chuanqing were quietly inducted into the Party in Lei Yingfu's room downstairs in the Zhou Mansion. Under the bright red Party flag, Ye Jianying and Zeng Xisheng administered the oath of membership to them.

The White Terror was getting worse day by day. It was too dangerous for them to come to the Zhou Mansion to deliver information, so the comrades in the Department of Military Affairs needed a reliable way of contacting them. In November, Li Lin, a female student of the Chinese People's Anti-Japanese Military and Political College came to Chongqing from Yan'an. Li Lin, formerly known as Yu Jiaying, was sent to the Southern Bureau by the organisation to make use of her father-daughter relationship with Yu Anmin, a major general in the Chuan Army, to carry out liaison work with the Chuan Army. Ye Jianying, Zeng Xisheng and the others repeatedly offered the opinion that it would be more useful to send her to establish a secret contact point with Zhang and Feng. It was therefore decided that she would change her name to Zhang Luping and pretend to be Zhang Weilin's sister, who had come up from Shanghai. Zeng Xisheng had them find two rooms in

Niujiaotuo for Zhang Weilin to move to, to be away from the Military Intelligence establishment. Zeng Xisheng then gave Zhang Luping three tasks: first, to lead Zhang Weilin, Feng Chuanqing and five or six other members of the Party in the Telecommunications Department of the Military Intelligence Bureau to set up a special branch of the Chinese Communist Party; second, to transfer the information provided by Zhang and Feng to the Zhou Mansion through a transit station; and third, to continue to recruit Party members in the Telecommunications Department of the Military Intelligence Bureau if possible. During this period, Zhang Luping's daily activities, her costume, little details that needed particular attention, contact signals in case of emergency and so on, were all arranged by Zeng Xisheng himself.

From then on, important Kuomintang intelligence was constantly transmitted from the Military Intelligence operation to the Communist Party of China's Southern Bureau, including even top-secret information such as the staffing of the secret service organs and the arrangements for their work. The coded call signs of the General Telecommunication Station, the wavelengths used and the information transmitted through the communications network were also obtained by Zhang Weilin and his men. Despite the fact that the Military Council was equipped with two teams of men at the radio station and kept changing the codes, we were still able to decipher their secret messages. On one occasion, Dai Li sent a three-man undercover team with a small radio station to infiltrate the Shaanxi-Gansu-Ningxia border area through Hu Zongnan's defence zone to carry out secret intelligence operations. Zhang Weilin and his team sent this information to the Southern Bureau, and Zeng Xisheng immediately telegraphed to Yan'an. As a result, the infiltration team was captured as soon as they showed up, and Dai was furious when he learned about it.

The establishment of a secret branch of the Communist Party's military radio station led to a series of leaks of important Kuomintang information, which alerted Chiang Kai-shek to the situation. He was furious about it and cursed Dai for his incompetence, ordering him to investigate more closely. It was at this point that an accident occurred. Zhang Weilin inadvertently burned out a vacuum tube at work and this caught the attention of keen-eyed military intelligence agents. Zhang was arrested and imprisoned by the Inspection Department. Zhang Weilin's lack of experience led him to act impetuously when he was locked up. He escaped from the guardhouse and went straight to the Zhou Mansion to ask for instructions. Zeng Xisheng and his comrades in the military group analysed the situation and decided that burning out the vacuum tube would be treated as a work demerit and would result in a fine at most; whereas escaping would expose the whole organisation and affect the overall situation. They told Zhang Weilin to buy a replacement vacuum tube and go back as quickly as possible.

However, while Zhang Weilin was away, the Inspection Department sent men to search his residence in Niujiaotuo and found the configuration sheets and radio codes of the various radio stations of the Military Council, as well as the names and materials of several other operators. Zhang Weilin was arrested immediately upon his return. That night, several Party members, including Yang Guang, Zhao Ligeng, Wang Xizhen and Chen Guozhu, from the Military Council's main telecommunication station, were also arrested. Feng Chuanqing, who was on duty at the time, escaped over the wall and went to No. 50 Zengjiayan the next morning to report the circumstances of the "great radio arrest". Ye Jianying personally arranged to send Feng Chuanqing across the Jialing River to work in Yan'an. Unfortunately, after crossing the river, he too fell into the hands of the enemy.

At this time, Zhang Luping was visiting her family in Chengdu, unaware of what had happened in Chongqing, when a telegram was sent to her in the name of Zhang Weilin, asking her to return to Chongqing. On receipt of the message, she rushed back to Chongqing, but as soon as she got off the train, she was arrested by agents who were lying in wait for her at the station.

Zeng Xisheng's situation also became very dangerous, as information was now repeatedly being leaked, especially after the incident with Zhang Luping and the seven others. The military intelligence agents intensified their close surveillance of the Zhou Mansion and they had already sniffed out that the Chinese Communist Party must have an important "mystery figure" in Chongqing.

At the beginning of the second Nationalist-Communist collaboration, Chiang Kai-shek sent a delegation to Yan'an. The delegation made it a point to visit the 2nd Bureau and to meet the "mystery Chinese Communist" who had helped uncover important information about them on several occasions. By then they had already been informed of Zeng Xisheng's name, perhaps because of the confession of Chen Zhongshan, the staff officer in the translation section who was captured in Yunnan in 1935 (it was later confirmed that Chen was killed by the Dian Army, but he had not had any information forced out of him). The investigation team were disappointed and amazed by the results of their mission: all the 2nd Bureau's communication equipment was so rudimentary, and most of it was captured from the battlefield. What was even more unbelievable was that the man who had caused them so much trouble and whom they had been unable to deal with, even with the help of foreign experts, was so unimpressive and just like any of the other "8th Routers". The delegation could not help but feel a little ashamed and in awe.

Now they suspected that Zeng Xisheng, a Chinese Communist intelligence expert, might be in Chongqing. In order to confirm this suspicion, they sent spies posing as friends and relatives of Zeng Xisheng to the Zhou Mansion to find out the truth. The spies sometimes stayed in the parlour downstairs all day, saying they had to wait for Zeng Xisheng and that they had something to tell him. The situation was so tense that Zhou Enlai and Ye Jianying decided to send Zeng Xisheng to the Hongyan Village Office of the 8th Route Army for a while to hide out. In order to avoid being seen by the secret agents, Zeng Xisheng disguised himself as Zhou Enlai's bodyguard, then hid in boot of Zhou's car. In this way, he was able to make good his escape from the Zhou Mansion.

At the 8th Route Army Office in Hongyan, Zeng Xisheng could not go out by day and had to wait quietly for the organisation to make arrangements. Fortunately, he met Qian Jiang there, an old subordinate and comrade from the 2nd Bureau. Qian Jiang had come on a mission with a team from the bureau, so the two of them ate and slept together, talked about the past, looked forward to the future and often stayed up all night talking. When Qian Jiang left

Chongqing, Zeng Xisheng wrote a fond farewell message in his notebook:

> "We have been together for seven or eight years, through several encirclements and annihilations, and the Long March of more than 20,000 li, and I never thought we would have to part. I wish you all the best, and I hope that you will work hard and study hard to build your great achievements and develop your great future in your new environment and in the great new era.
>
> This is a parting at a distance today, so please accept my fond regards, my good friend.
>
> 20 January 1940 Xisheng"

Zeng Xisheng had always been a selfless worker and could not bring himself to be idle for a moment. Hiding out in the Hongyan office, he found it very difficult to do nothing all day. He was anxious for the organisation to arrange his work as soon as possible so that he could be useful and help make a difference. Since his identity in Chongqing had been exposed, Zhou Enlai and Ye Jianying decided to transfer him secretly to southern Anhui.

* * *

The black and white of these public documents, these yellowed pages and dull handwriting, speak of a different reality on this breezy night. The figures hidden in the scrolls of history, who emerge from these words in the image of their youthful years, are accompanied by the distant sound of a wind that is strong enough to chase away the peaceful drowsiness of this good night. It is the faint sound of waving pine trees in which a human voice can clearly be heard. It is like a soprano in a symphony, singing lyrically without words, except that this occasional female voice is coming out of the distant, hazy background. It is a sound that can't be denied; you can't just close the window and you can't just go peacefully back to sleep. The sound is both a chant and a summons.

In the night, in the pale, hazy background and from among the flowering trees outside the window, you can clearly hear another kind of music being played in the overwhelming silence. The players in the dark background are not tuxedoed musicians on a stage, they are playing against the profound backdrop of waves and pines. Theirs are not the shiny golden instruments of the theatre, but a truer sound, a trumpet that carries a secret message through the fog and the mountains, a bugle call ordering the daredevils to charge. It is also the truer sound of drums, of roaring voices and of sirens. This sound broke through the night mists of the mountain town, painting memories and dreams with the colour of blood. The blood of the waves and the pines. The figure scrambling over the wall is also the colour of blood. There is the sound of a gunshot that is real and does not need to be simulated; it too is a note in the symphony. The hazy canvas of the dark night is also punctuated by this note, along with these branches that dance in the wind like dry arms waving. They are all embellishments to this image, and the figures that float across the canvas, despite their silence, are the voices in this symphony. These figures, resurrected in countless fragments, appear in the depths of time, in the depths of memory, like reliefs on the base of a monument. A towering monument, surrounded by pines and cypresses, and spreading clusters of bright coloured flowers. At dusk, when the setting sun is the colour of blood, the amaranth flowers look particularly bright. Their names are not recorded on the base of the monument, which is also part of the background of this picture. In the depths of that background is the city skyline ranged against the night sky that promises rain, the sky that was once ignited by the flames of war. The strains of that symphony still rise amid the swelling sounds, and above the noise and through the twilight, the red star is still shining. It is the red star on the spire of the monument, illuminated by a powerful laser light, and rising out of the music...

She wakes from her dream in the middle of the night, in the midst of the storm. She recalls the dream in the dim light of dawn, and outside the window the noise of rain hitting the leaves is like the sound of that old typewriter. Back then, Zeng Xisheng had set Zhang Luping three tasks, the third of which was, if possible, to continue recruiting Party members in the Military Council's

Telecommunications Office. Seven people including Zhang Luping met heroic martyrs' deaths. Were there others who slipped through the net at the Military Council's headquarters? Unfortunately, they too were among those arrested, as they were on the list of names discovered in the search of the Niujiaotuo residence, but they did not betray anyone else.

After being arrested, Zhang Luping and the other seven "heroes of the tiger's lair" held fast in the face of severe torture and coercion from the enemy and were prepared to die. They were rivetted into leg irons and imprisoned first in the Bai Mansion and then, in March 1941, they were transferred to the Xifeng concentration camp. Under the leadership of the secret Party branch in the camp, Zhang Luping fought hard to resist the special agents of the Military Council. She took the risk of sending their group escape plan out of the prison and expressed her love for life and her confidence in the victory of the revolution in a poem: "The pomegranate blossoms in the mountain town in July are still bright red upon the branches. / They look like the blood of warriors, like the vermilion lips of a young girl…"

However, in 1943, when Yan'an was working on a "rescue campaign" and Zhang Luping (Li Lin) was fighting the enemy in the Xifeng concentration camp, Kang Sheng, head of the Central Social Department, fabricated accusations against her in a meeting, saying, "Li Lin has defected! She is a traitor and a spy for the Military Council!" On 14 July 1945, the enemy secretly shot the seven heroes on their way into Chongqing under the pretence of transferring them for release. After their heroic sacrifice, they suffered a long period of unjust disgrace, labelled as counter-revolutionary members of the "Military Intelligence Telecommunications Staff". In 1968, before Zeng Xisheng fell seriously ill and was on his deathbed, he continued to vouch for Zhang Luping and the other seven martyrs, hoping that one day they would be rehabilitated. After the third plenary session of the 11th Central Committee of the Communist Party of China, when the relevant departments reviewed the case, comrades Ye Jianying and Lei Yingfu came forward to confirm that the seven comrades were indeed underground workers for the Party. Thus, the stain that had besmirched the names of the seven comrades was finally removed, and they were restored to the light of revolutionary martyrdom.

* * *

Back in 1968, the historical problems of many people were being unearthed, and investigators were being sent all over the place. At that time, my father stayed first in the official government Jingxi Hotel and then in the PLA General Hospital. His stomach problems were getting worse, all stemming from his time in the Central Soviet Area. At that time, he was under great pressure, and during the four "encirclements", times were particularly hard for him. Sometimes he couldn't even eat the pumpkin soup, but survived on a daily diet of bamboo shoots, no salt, just bamboo shoots cooked in water. In the end he got sick to his stomach just at the sight of bamboo shoots, and he eventually developed a serious stomach ulcer. My mother was from Zhejiang and she loved fresh bamboo shoots, but after the liberation, when there were many more things to eat, my father was still afraid of eating them and never touched them again. It was not only bamboo shoots; he wouldn't eat horse meat either, and he prohibited us from eating both dishes too. He was a local cadre and was admitted to the PLA General Hospital with the special approval of the prime minister. At that time, conditions for the army were much better than for local government. Once he started living in guest houses and hospitals, his life was much less carefree, and he was often obliged to accept a variety of investigative postings which annoyed him. But the years had smoothed his previously violent temper, and, looked at objectively, these transfers also helped him in his last intention of caring for his old comrades.

One day, personnel from the 4th Machinery Department came to look into Minister Wang Zheng's historical issues. He definitely served as radio station chief of the 18th Division of the Kuomintang Army and was captured during the encirclement of the Red Army in early 1931. At that point, he joined the Red Army and immediately set up a radio team for them, going on to become director of the 3rd Bureau of the Military Commission of the Chinese Revolutionary Army, and was awarded the rank of Lieutenant General by the

People's Republic in 1955. When my father described Wang's exploits, the external investigators were moved to tears and Wang avoided disgrace. Wang was the father of radio communications in the New China, and the 5G and 6G mobile phone technology we have today are derived from his early wireless communication technology. Today, everyone uses the QQ call code, but Wang Zheng's first radio contacts used just Q. There was also Dai Zhongrong, who worked undercover in Hu Zongnan's office as deputy director of Governor Hu's confidential office and head of the telecommunications section. He later became a pioneer and patriarch of the new Chinese chip industry in the 1970s, when our photolithography machines were still able to keep up with the rest of the world's high-tech advances.

But, to return to those changes of posting. On one occasion, they were sent to investigate the history of Li Lin (Zhang Luping) and the others. It was only then that my father learned that seven of his comrades, including Li Lin, were still suffering under an undeserved stigma. Feeling very sad, he gave a detailed account of their history to the investigators and strongly suggested they be rehabilitated and posthumously recognised as revolutionary martyrs. He said that the premier and Marshal Ye were well aware of this and hoped that the relevant authorities would implement his suggestion as soon as possible. As he was dying, he still held Zhang Qinghua's hand tightly and said, "What's going on with Li Lin? I cannot die in peace, if her problem is not resolved."

"Apart from these seven martyrs, will we find any others who were recruited by Zhang Luping in the Military Council's radio station?"

"How can we know this? They are all gone... My father rarely talked to us about such topics during his lifetime, not just to us children, but also to my mother, a comrade in the struggle for many decades."

* * *

Some third-party recollections. When Zeng Xisheng was critically ill, Song Yuhe went to visit him again. After Qian Zhuangfei's disappearance, he was the one who took over as deputy director of the 2nd Bureau of the Military Commission. He said to Zeng's wife, Yu Shu, "This Lao Zeng of yours was really quite something!" When Yu Shu asked him why he was so impressed, he replied that Lao Zeng had achieved miracles and went on to talk about the secret telegram he sent, pretending to be Chiang Kai-shek, before crossing the Wujiang River in 1935. Guo Huaruo, who was an officer graduate of the fourth intake at Huangpu, along with Zeng Xisheng, had twice refused to be Chiang Kai-shek's secretary, but instead became a senior counsellor in the Red Army's operational command. The newspaper *Reference News* published on the occasion of the First National Congress of the Chinese Soviet Republic was named by him. He was present at the "Night of the Wu River". One day, not long after Zeng Xisheng's death, he said to Yu Shu, "Lao Zeng did a great deed, something truly, truly great, but it is a secret and I can't tell you about it." "Was it the fake telegram?" Yu Shu asked. "Did Lao Zeng tell you about it?" Guo asked. "No," Yu Shu replied. Zeng San, who was political commissar of the Red Army Communication School, mentions it in his memoirs. Zeng Xisheng himself kept it top secret to the end.

To Zeng Xisheng's descendants, this extreme secrecy is not at all surprising. Under conditions of such tight security, which amount to a state of total seclusion, it is inevitable that a person begins to feel cut off from the rest of the world. The Red Star Medal was the highest honour of the Red Army, but Zeng never talked about it afterwards. This might not have been a deliberate omission but rather the natural product of his personality and his attitude to honour and glory. From his point of view, this physical representation of the highest honour was a mere worldly trinket, and there would be no need to devote time to searching for it if it was lost. In fact, he did indeed lose his medal when he dropped it into the water during the crossing of the Wu River.

"This matter was also mentioned by Bureau Chief Song. He said that Lao Zeng was such an extraordinary man that he thought nothing of it when his Red Star Medal fell into the Wu River while he was crossing it. This was the only way my mother learned that my father had won the medal, so she asked what kind of award it was. It was the right question to ask, as Chief Song was the man in charge of the awarding of the medal at the time… There are many things about the men and women of that generation which may be difficult for people to understand today, in particular their high ideals and noble character."

Some more third-party recollections: "In 1960, the Central Committee of the Communist Party of China decided to set up six central bureaus to act as the dispatching bodies for the Central Committee in the regions. The central leadership originally wanted Zeng Xisheng to take up the post of first secretary of the East China Bureau, but he took the decision for himself to step back from the appointment. He said that Ke Qingshi was senior to him, had a higher theoretical level, and after all, 'Ke was a man who had met Lenin'. These were the terms in which he made his position clear to the chairman. After that, the '7000 Cadres Conference' excused him from the posting in Anhui and he remained second secretary of the East China Bureau."

Some secrets are meant to be taken to the grave. Those who were tortured in prison, for example, were determined to die, set their jaws and never reveal their identities. Only at the last moment of their heroic deaths did they shout the slogan, "Long live the Communist Party". One day at dusk in Yeping, Ruijin, Dr He was looking at the artillery-shell-shaped Red Army Martyrs' Memorial Tower and meditating upon it. It was designed in 1933 by Qian Zhuangfei, deputy director of the 2nd Bureau of the Military Commission. The dark brown tower is studded with countless small stones, each of which represents the spirit of a martyr. The arrest of Gu Shunzhang in Hankou and the information intercepted by Qian Zhuangfei saved the Shanghai Central Party Committee from extinction. Xu Enzeng, head of the Kuomintang Central Committee, who was the individual involved on that side, deliberately concealed the true story of this incident, and Chiang Kai-shek was unaware of the truth until his death: "I will never talk about this, even in death."

The kind of patience and fortitude required to keep secrets and endure violence in silence has to do with Party spirit as well as personality. "When the job is done, you go away and hide your work and your name." She also thought of Mo Xiong, a native of Yingde, Guangdong. In his youth, Mo Xiong joined the secret underground resistance movement founded by Sun Yat-sen and known as Tongmenhui.[4] He was known as "Brother Mo" within the Kuomintang and the army, as well as the "Five-Colour General", a reference to him having friends all over the country and in all organisations and societies. He was not part of Chiang Kai-shek's direct chain of command, but Chiang ordered him to attend a secret high-level military meeting at Guling in Lushan, where Mo got hold of the "Iron Barrel Plan" for the fifth encirclement and annihilation campaign against the Red Army. Mo Xiong risked destroying his family by handing over the plan to his Communist liaison officer Xiang Yunian. He was then sent by Chiang to join the encirclement of the Red Army at the meeting point of Yunnan, Guizhou and Sichuan, where he secretly provided cover for the Red Army to evacuate the area. During the War of Resistance Against the Japanese, he was active in protecting and rescuing Communists in Guangzhou. After the founding of the New China, Mao Zedong specifically instructed Ye Jianying, who was in charge of Guangdong, to invite Mo Xiong, who was living in Hong Kong, to return to Guangzhou to work. During the land reform in the early 1950s, the local peasants and land reform cadres were unaware of Mo Xiong's history and demanded that he be shot on the spot after mass criticism. This was approved by the relevant leaders of the South China Bureau, and even at this critical moment, Mo Xiong was silent and did not mention his important contribution to the revolution. Fortunately, someone reported the truth to the first secretary, Tao Zhu, just in time and Mo Xiong escaped execution.

Mo Xiong handed over the Iron Barrel Plan to Xiang Yunian. At the time, Mo Xiong was commissioner of the 4th Administrative Office of the Kuomintang in northern Jiangxi and also head of security, while Xiang Yunian was secretary at the security headquarters. After receiving the information, Xiang Yunian discussed the matter with Liu Yafu and Lu Zhiying, members of the Party underground, and decided to activate the secret radio station overnight to report the key points of the Iron Barrel Plan to the Central Soviet. They also decided that Xiang Yunian himself would be responsible for delivering the information as he spoke Hakka and could easily get past the enemy checkpoints. The three of them spent the night writing down the entire Iron Barrel Plan in four copies of the "Student Dictionary", including the deployment of troops, firepower, attack routes and command structures, and also traced the battle map onto transparent paper. The task took them until dawn.

To avoid the Kuomintang troops stationed in the village, Xiang Yunian had to walk through the mountains and sleep in the open, feeding himself with a small amount of dry food and wild fruits and drinking from the mountain springs. After many days of trekking, he was bearded and skinny. On arrival at Xingguo, he found that the Kuomintang Army had tightened its siege, with blockhouses in almost every village and guard posts at every hilltop road junction. Whenever young and able-bodied men approached, they were taken away as "Red bandit spies". Xiang Yunian had to retreat to the mountains to wait for an opportunity. Time, however, waits for no one. Growing anxious, he soon came up with a plan. He bent down, picked up a stone from the ground and knocked out his four front teeth. The next day his cheeks were badly swollen, his face looked hideous and frightening, his hair was as tangled as a clump of mugwort, and his clothes had long since been tattered and torn by thorns. The whole effect was of a disgusting old beggar with a messed-up face. He hid his four secret books in a filthy bag with rancid scraps of food on top and went down the mountain barefoot. When the Kuomintang sentries along the way saw him, they covered their noses and chased him away. However, the further south he travelled, the tighter the scrutiny became, and the hidden dictionaries could be discovered at any time. He had to find another, better plan. Fortunately, as a Communist liaison officer, he had established many secret contacts along the way, so with the help of underground members, overnight, he wrote all the information onto thin silk paper in invisible ink, hid it in the padded layers of the cloth shoes he wore on his feet and continued his journey. In this way, he passed through successive Kuomintang Army checkpoints and reached Ruijin on 7 October.

He found the Provisional Central Committee in Shazhouba and handed the information to Zhou Enlai, one of the Team of Three. When Zhou Enlai and Li Kenong received the top-secret information from Xiang Yunian, they could hardly recognise the ragged tramp in front of them as their old subordinate, and were moved beyond words. After the Team of Three circulated the Iron

Barrel Plan, the shock set in as they digested the fact that the Central Red Army was in extreme danger and would soon fall under the encirclement of the Kuomintang Army if no decisive measures were taken. The deciphered information from the 2nd Bureau of the Military Commission also showed that, even before all this, Chiang Kai-shek had advanced his large-scale attack by about a month. The plans from two different sources corroborated each other, and the troops on the front line were in a constant state of emergency. The enemy, implementing a new strategy of blockade by blockhouse, was fighting without haste, advancing step by step, while the Red Army was in a desperate, step-by-step retreat. The situation was already critical, and it was necessary to withdraw from the Central Soviet before the "iron barrel" was closed. On the very same day, the Central Revolutionary Military Commission issued an order to leave the area on 10 October.

Thus, the Long March began ahead of schedule.

* * *

"In Shanghai they were all working undercover under Zhou Enlai's leadership. The demands of their secret work required Xiang Yunian to change his name to Liang Mingde. After years of fighting in the north and south, galloping from east to west, he had lost all contact with his family. He heard nothing about the whereabouts of his wife and children. His son, Liang Dechong, has been studying hard since parting from his father in Shanghai at the age of sixteen. When the war broke out in 1937, he changed his name to Xiang Nan and joined the revolutionary movement to save the country from the Japanese. In 1949, at the beginning of the founding of the New China, Xiang Yunian (who was still using the name Liang Mingde) was overjoyed to hear that his son had grown up and joined the revolution, working as a cadre in the Anhui Provincial Youth League. Xiang wrote to Zeng Xisheng, who was then first secretary of the Anhui Provincial Committee, asking him to find his son, who had been lost to him for more than ten years. Zeng Xisheng took on the search for an old comrade's sake. Once, when he was in a provincial meeting, he specifically stayed behind to talk with Xiang Nan, secretary of the provincial Youth League

Committee, asking him on behalf of an old fellow soldier, to search for a young man surnamed Liang among the cadres of the Youth League."

In the early 1980s, Xiang Nan was first secretary of the Fujian Provincial Committee of the Communist Party of China. This is a true story and a strange twist of fate. According to Xiang Nan's recollection:

In 1951, the Anhui Provincial Working Committee of the New Democratic Youth League was formed by merging the Northern and Southern Anhui Working Committees. Xiang Nan was its secretary and at the same time also secretary of the Party Committee of Anhui University. One day, he went to a meeting of the Provincial Committee and Zeng Xisheng, secretary of the committee, gave him the task of helping him to find the lost son of an old comrade. He said that his old comrade, Liang, was working in the northeast and had heard from someone that his son was working for the Youth League in Anhui. He had written to Zeng Xisheng to ask for help in finding him. Sometime later, Zeng Xisheng and Xiang Nan saw each other at another meeting and Zeng asked if he had met with any success. Xiang Nan said he couldn't find the lad as there were as many as 100,000 people in the Youth League in northern Anhui, and a lot of them had the surname Liang.
Zeng Xisheng told Xiang Nan frustratedly that perhaps if he met his old comrade's child, he might still be able to recognise him because, years ago, they had all lived on Rue Vouillemont in the French Quarter of Shanghai. Xiang Nan said, "I also lived on that same street in Shanghai." Zeng Xisheng was surprised and asked, "What number did you live at?" Xiang Nan gave the number of the house. Zeng Xisheng went on to ask him who had brought him to Shanghai from western Fujian as a child. Xiang Nan said that it was a silk merchant and his young assistant. It dawned on Zeng Xisheng that it was he who had personally arranged for the "silk merchant" and the "young assistant" to transport a batch of radio parts urgently needed by the Central Red Army, from Shanghai to Ruijin. It was he who gave them the instructions to bring Xiang Yunian's wife and children to Shanghai after completing their mission. After Xiang Yunian's wife and children had got themselves settled on Rue

Vouillemont, he often visited, pretending to be a merchant called Hu, to talk "business" with Xiang Yunian. Xiang Yunian's clever young son was a delight, always calling him "Uncle Beardy" [Hu means "beard"] and offering him a chair and a cigarette whenever they met. Of course, Zeng always took a handful of sweets to give the boy every time he went. Remembering this, Zeng Xisheng laughed out loud with relief and asked Xiang Nan if he remembered an uncle with a big beard. Xiang Nan replied, "Of course I do. He took me to the movies!" Zeng then asked him, "Do you think I look anything like that Uncle Beardy?"

Dumbfounded, Xiang Nan took a closer look. Zeng Xisheng pointed at his nose and said, "Look carefully! Who do I look like?" Xiang Nan stared at him, then stood up and exclaimed, "Uncle Beardy!" The young man and the old man embraced and wept.

It turned out that, when Zeng Xisheng was working undercover in Shanghai, he often used to grow his beard so that, in case of emergency, he could shave it off and disappear. At that time, Zhou Enlai's cover identity was that of an antiques dealer, and he too wore a long beard as a disguise to conceal his identity, so his alias as Hu Gong, which can also be understood as "Lord Beard", was also very appropriate.

Xiang Nan had been looking for himself! Dr He is fascinated by this story and equally engrossed in the fantasy of finding her own miracle. She had been shocked by her lightbulb moment at the Red Army Long March Memorial Hall in Wujiang, Guizhou. In the multimedia exhibition hall, the route of the Long March was displayed in lights on a map. When those dozens of little lights flashed on for a moment, she realised that the route of the Long March, from Jiangxi to Shaanxi, clearly formed the character 毛 (Mao). In those poems Mao Zedong wrote in cursive script, there is indeed the character 毛, whose shape and strokes resemble the route of the march.

Xiang father and son were fortunate indeed that they had obtained each other's information through Zeng Xisheng. How many people's identities have remained unknown to their wives and children until their death and have had to suffer all sorts of misunderstandings about their service? Aliases, the confusion of war, the changing times, but those aspects of physical appearance the memory retains can still inform recognition. She prayed she would have the same kind of luck, even though she had no idea what her grandfather had looked like. She did know she had her grandfather's eyes, and she also knew his original name, but none of that provided conclusive proof of identity. She had hoped that her grandfather's surname would not have changed, but Xiang Yunian had changed his name to Liang Mingde, altering even the surname. There were so many pseudonyms in those days, some of which did not even sound like pseudonyms. For example, Chen Yun's Party pseudonym was just "Mister", while Zhou Enlai and Qu Qiubai probably had a hundred or more different aliases.

Wu said that he deliberately stayed silent for a long time, so quiet that the five or six people in the courtroom could hear each other's breathing. He even stood up and paced back and forth in the room, occasionally scrutinising Qu Qiubai's expression, only to see him sitting like a meditating monk, his eyes half closed and his face pale and thin. After a long silence, he suddenly turned around and slapped the table with great force, saying loudly, "You are Qu Qiubai, not Lin Qixiang! I heard you speak in Wuhan in the sixteenth year of the Republic." When Wu threw this abrupt accusation at Qu Qiubai, Qu's expression changed slightly, but he still said unhurriedly, "You are mistaken, I am not Qu Qiubai!" Wu then made his last move and shouted, "Bring him in!" The man who came in was a traitor from the Red Army who had been captured and defected to the enemy. He had been waiting outside to deliver his statement, and as he pointed at Qu Qiubai, he said to Wu obsequiously, "I stake my head on it, he is Qu Qiubai. If my word isn't enough, don't just rely on that, there is a photo of him to check against." Qu Qiubai just smiled at the traitor's on-the-spot identification and said, "In that case, there is no need for this good man to stake his head on it, and I can stop trying to pull the wool over your eyes. I am Qiu Qiubai, and you can treat as fiction all the stuff you have heard from people in Shanghai about what I did as Lin Qixiang over the last ten days or so!"

She believes in luck. If Xiang Nan could find Xiang Nan, she herself can find her grandfather, even if he had more than one alias. It is by no means too extravagant to hope he is still alive, and anyway, it should certainly be possible to find some kind of information about him. Even if in the end it all turns out to be in vain, she has to continue this challenging search, or she will never have any peace. She has to do it not only for her peace of mind but also for the strength to go on living. "My personal opinion doesn't matter as there is a photograph of him that can be used for verification."

That photograph. She cannot bear to look at the image of Qu Qiubai before his martyr's death. A lieutenant colonel in the Kuomintang Army, Song Xilian, regaled him with food and wine but all to no avail. He could get nothing out of this man who had once been the one of the highest-level leaders of the Chinese Communist Party, about the secrets of the Party organisation or any intelligence on the Red Army. Qu Qiubai steadfastly refused to give in to Song Xilian. Which ideology could save China, Communism or the Three Principles of the People? Qu Qiubai was one of the men who drafted the Great Manifesto of the Kuomintang, and Song Xilian had himself been secretly inducted into the Communist Party through his introduction by Chen Geng. Qu said that Chiang Kai-shek, as he now was, had forfeited the right to talk about the Three Principles of the People because he was a fascist. He refused to discuss ideology any further with Song Xilian. Song received a coded telegram from Chiang, which read, "Execute on the spot and present the photographs for inspection." Qu Qiubai walked to the execution ground with his head held high, singing the *Internationale*. This anthem, which stands for the Great Revival of the People, was originally translated by him from the French, but by then it was also accessible to the Chinese people. He sang it in Chinese and also in Russian. He posed for a photograph in front of the Octagonal Pavilion in Zhongshan Park, then drank several glasses of whisky before walking out of the park with a cigarette in his hand towards the execution ground at the foot of Luohan Ridge. Kneeling on a patch of grass, he smiled at the executioner, nodded and said, "This spot will do. Shoot!"

A whistle blows and shots ring out. This black-and-white photograph preserves the last of the revolutionaries: a man in a white shirt and black trousers. His demeanour is poised as he stands with his arms folded. His gaze is stoic and there is a smile on his lips...

The uncertain light of the setting sun. A golden fountain of falling leaves. Those figures that have not been preserved have left no photographs to check against.

The colonel had said that there could be a batch of photos from the Long March, and Geng Biao, the head of the 4th Regiment of the 1st Red Army Corps, certainly took many photographs, some of battlefield scenes, some of prisoners or trophies, and even more that captured the daily life of his comrades. Unfortunately, his diary of the Long March and these photographs were handed over to the American journalist Snow for foreign propaganda purposes after he arrived in Shanbei, and their whereabouts are unknown.

What a collection of candid photographs that would have been!

Perhaps moved by her sincerity and hard work, the gods of luck are still favouring her. An unexpected clue appears among the voluminous historical data. When Zeng Xisheng and Zou Bizhao went to Wuhan to gather Japanese intelligence in 1938, they made contact with Yang Si, a Kuomintang expert in deciphering. At that time, Yang Si was working in the Department of Electronics and Communications of the Nationalist government's Ministry of Communications, breaking Japanese codes. The director of the department was Wen Yuqing. After Wuhan fell, the Telecommunications Department moved to Chongqing. Dai Li asked Wen Yuqing for an expert, and Yang Si was persuaded by Li Kenong to infiltrate the Military Intelligence Bureau. Yang Si had secretly joined the Communist Party of China in Chongqing in the summer of 1940. Because of his outstanding achievements, Yang Si was later promoted by Dai Li to the rank of major general as director of the Special Skills Research Office.

Chongqing again! The summer of 1940 again! And someone connected to Zeng Xisheng! Following up on this clue, Dr He finds a copy of *The Memoirs of Chi Buzhou*.

Chi Buzhou, a native of Minqing, Fujian, went to Japan in his youth, studied at Tokyo University and Waseda University, and married a Japanese woman, Eiko Shirahama. After the outbreak of the War of Resistance Against the Japanese, Chi Buzhou returned to China to fight against Japan. In 1937, he sought refuge with the

Nanjing Nationalist government and joined the Central Bureau of Investigation and Statistics of the Kuomintang. It is said that in 1943, Chi Buzhou cracked the secret Japanese LA code, and US military cryptography experts also deciphered messages containing information on the itinerary of the Japanese Admiral Isoroku Yamamoto. As a result, his plane was shot down and he was killed. In January 1952, Chi Buzhou was sentenced to twelve years in prison because he was identified as a member of the Kuomintang's Central Bureau of Investigation and Statistics. After serving his sentence, Chi Buzhou returned to Shanghai in May 1963. In March 1983, Chi Buzhou happened to meet Li Zhifeng and Huo Shizi in Shanghai. Li Zhifeng was able to prove that, although Chi Buzhou was in the Central Bureau of Investigation and Statistics, he was not part of the espionage apparatus. Huo Shizi also proved that everything Chi Buzhou did was in the anti-Japanese cause and benefitted the country and the people. He was not only innocent but had, in fact, performed meritorious service. The Shanghai Higher People's Court declared Chi Buzhou innocent. In 2003, Chi Buzhou died in Kobe, Japan, and his ashes were brought back to China. Minqing County in Fujian Province erected a monument to him in Taishan Park.

The Military Commission's Research Group on Coded Messages was headed by Mao Qingxiang of the Research Office of the Military Commission, with Huo Shizi and Li Zhifeng as chief and deputy chief respectively. The former was a student studying in Japan and had assisted Wen Yuqing, chief secretary for telecommunications at the Ministry of Communications, in researching and translating diplomatic Japanese codes. He was said to have achieved something remarkable, but when I worked with him from June to the end of November 1938, I never heard him talk about it. Li Zhifeng was an expert in Chinese ciphers and had been head of the Second Classified Unit of the Military Intelligence Bureau, which he had been ordered to infiltrate by Vice Chairman Zhou Enlai. In order to break the deadlock, the Military Commission's Cipher Telegraph Research Group, led by Li Zhifeng, proposed to Huo Shizi that he send his men to the various headquarters in the different war zones to collect complete and partial Japanese telegraph codebooks and coded Japanese telegrams captured after fighting with the Japanese Imperial Army. This was with a view to helping the army's research on deciphering Japanese coded messages. Li's suggestion was agreed by Mao Qingxiang, who commissioned Li Zhifeng as a major general counsellor of the Military Council and Li Yu as a colonel counsellor of the Military Council so they could openly carry Chiang Kai-shek's orders and make haste to the various war zone headquarters to collect the material. Relying on his special relationship with the Chinese Communist Party, Li Zhifeng set out in the hope of being able to provide the relevant information. Once they arrived in Xi'an, Li Zhifeng left Li Yu behind and went on alone to Yan'an to ask for help. With the consent of the Communist Party, he handed over three Japanese double-coded telegrams captured by the 8th Route Army to the Kuomintang Military Commission back in Chongqing and openly requested a reward. Li then resumed his post in Chongqing. Later, when the three secret telegrams were sent to the Kuomintang Military Council, Huo Shizi publicly signed a request to Chiang Kai-shek to award him a medal for shooting down a Japanese Air Force bomber.

Subsequently, I got to learn more about how the Communist Party supplied the army with Japanese codebooks, and the story pleased me greatly. I hoped the Military Commission's Coded Telecommunications Research Group could make a breakthrough, but that good news never came. I don't know much about what the army did with the Japanese codebooks after they were supplied by the Chinese Communist Party. I have reproduced below, for the benefit of readers, the full text of the second half of page nine to the first half of page ten of *Some Matters Relating to the Kuomintang's Coded Telecommunications Research Group and the Military Technology Office* (hereinafter referred to as *Some Matters*) written by Li Zhifeng and Huo Shizi.

In the winter of 1939, the Chongqing coded telegram detection and decipherment community said with one voice, "The three highly important Japanese Imperial Army double-coded telegrams supplied to the Kuomintang by the Chinese Communist Party are a concrete manifestation of the second phase of cooperation between the Communist Party and the Kuomintang in the common cause of the struggle against Japan. They are the first such priceless treasures that the Communist Party has handed over to the Kuomintang."

Li Zhifeng took this as a great honour. Consequently, Wei Damin of the Military Intelligence made an earnest formal request to have copies transcribed. Wen Yuqing of the Institute of Coded Telegram Inspection and Decipherment used a devious trick and spent a lot of money to bribe Zhao Youquan to transcribe a copy. This all led to a fierce competition among the three different groups comprising the Military Control Commission's Coded Telecommunications Research Group, the Military Intelligence's Coded Telecommunications Group and the Coded Telecommunications Investigation and Translation Research Institute, to decipher the Japanese Army's double-code telegrams. The three types of Japanese Army double-coded telegrams were: i) a four-digit cipher with "5678" as the key, plus or minus four random numbers from a 101-page codebook; ii) a four-digit cipher plus or minus four random numbers from the Japanese language "come-and-go" codebook; iii) a three-digit cipher with "111" as the key, plus or minus three random numbers from a thirteen-page codebook. After secret analysis and research by each of the three parties, it was confirmed that the telegrams used the current Japanese Army double-code system but that was all. As for how many random numbers were added or subtracted to each coded telegram, which page the addition or subtraction began and ended, and the actual number of sets of random numbers added or subtracted to the key at the beginning and end of the telegram, that information we have never been able to find out. Thus, it was next to impossible to unravel this jumble of added and subtracted numbers and to find a practical formula for peeling away the "skin" of superfluous numbers. We were at a loss and simply didn't know what to do. Although the Military Office's Coded Telecommunications Group hired Osborne and Yardley, former US Naval Intelligence Service code-breaking experts, to lead a study on ways to solve the problem of stripping away the double-coding framework, it was all to no avail.

Li Zhifeng, who was originally secretary of the Attendant's Office of the Xi'an Appeasement Bureau, set up a coded telegram research office for Yang Hucheng soon after taking up his post. He quickly

deciphered top-secret telegrams which disclosed that Ma Qingwan's team in southern Gansu had defected from Yang to join Chiang, and Chiang's orders to kill Qu Qiubai, Fang Zhimin, Ji Hongchang and others. Zhou Enlai personally arranged for him to infiltrate the Kuomintang Central Bureau of Investigation and Statistics. The *Jiangnan Times* of December 2005 said of the affair, "During the Xi'an Incident, the Attendant's Office of the Appeasement Bureau was ordered by Yang Hucheng to send the contents of deciphered coded telegrams to Zhou Enlai, head of the Communist Party of China's Central Committee delegation, for his information, thereby attracting Zhou's attention. When he learnt that the telegrams had been deciphered by the cipher room headed by Li Zhifeng, Zhou instructed Nan Hanchen to bring Li to a secret meeting at the Communist Party delegation's residence. When Nan Hanchen introduced Li Zhifeng to Zhou Enlai, Zhou rose to greet him and warmly shook his hand and expressed his encouragement.
Zhou Enlai said, "You joined our Party's United Front in Wuhan in 1926, and now the revolution needs you more than ever. The fact that you have done such a good job in deciphering shows how much you love the country and want to save the people. I hope that you will join us in this revolution." Choked with emotion, Li Zhifeng replied, "I will obey Vice Chairman Zhou's instructions. I will fear no hardship or dangers, and for the rest of my life I will work hard to complete my mission." Zhou Enlai then ordered Li Kenong and Zeng Xisheng, who were waiting in the vestibule, to come in and receive their instructions: "This is Comrade Li Zhifeng, Director Yang's confidential secretary. He has expressed his willingness to participate in the revolution. I am now putting him under your orders for his future work."

In March 1983, Chi Buzhou met Li Zhifeng and Huo Shizi in Shanghai. In Dr He's imagination, such a chance encounter was both lucky and predestined. And she finally has her own piece of luck. These fragments of memory from the depths of time, these figures that appear and disappear in the mist, all point to that mountain town in Sichuan, that foggy, wartime capital. And in Chi Buzhou's memories of later years, those figures in the mist might indeed take on real substance.

The expulsion of Wei Daming from the Army Technology Office was dramatic, and the sabre rattling and tit-for-tat dealings were even more combative. I was in a minor position at the time and did not hear about it. I only learned a little about it afterwards. The following excerpts are based on *Some Matters*.

When Wei first arrived, he acted in an overbearing manner, gradually trying to bring the secret service style of Military Intelligence to the Military Technology Office. First of all, he ordered all the personnel in the room to provide three one-inch half-length portrait photographs...

Some Matters was co-authored by Li Zhifeng and Huo Shizi. Li was not publicly identified until the liberation of Shanghai in 1949. In 1957, he accompanied his old boss Zeng Xisheng to Hefei as a counsellor in the Counsellors' Office of the Anhui Provincial People's Committee and as a member of the Provincial Committee of the Chinese People's Political Consultative Conference. He was elected to the National Committee of the Chinese People's Political Consultative Conference in 1983.

The Technical Research Office of the Military Commission of the national government, established in April 1940, was a huge institution, with as many as 300 to 400 staff. The director, Dr Wen Yuqing, was a technocrat, while, of the two deputy directors, Mao Qingxiang was Chiang Kai-shek's brother-in-law, and Wei Daming was a member of Military Intelligence. In the early days of the Military Technology Office, Mao Qingxiang was the first to take control, but it was wrested from him by Wen Yuqing, then later fell into Wei Daming's hands. The book *Some Matters* records the incident in which Wei Daming ordered the entire office to supply the photographs, and Li Zhifeng was one of the people involved. As a counsellor in the Counsellors' Office of the Anhui Provincial People's Committee and a member of the Provincial Committee of the Chinese People's Political Consultative Conference, Li Zhifeng would have left more relevant memories. The 1950s was also the time when Zeng Xisheng was in charge of Anhui.

Whereas the Long March was a "night march" through darkness and surrounded by danger, the New China was a cause for fanfare and celebration. The old world had been destroyed and the new world was unfolding in all its grandeur and splendour. However, the 1950s were sixty years ago, a whole cycle of the lunar calendar. It is ancient history for today's youth. The residents of Anhui look back on the control of the Huai River as a major project that brought benefits to both the country and the people. It involved the construction of the five huge reservoirs including the one at Fuziling, and the construction of the Pi-Shi-Hang Rivers Irrigation System, which linked up the Huai River system. This was a major campaign that spanned many years, and Zeng Xisheng, who was first secretary of the Anhui Provincial Party Committee, was the commander-in-chief of that campaign. As early as 1944 to 1945, Zeng Xisheng led the 7th Division of the New 4th Army in building the Huang-Si-Tan Rivers Embankment Project in the Wanjiang base area, which was the largest water conservancy project built anywhere in the country during the War of Resistance Against the Japanese. The management of the Huai River in the New China is another demonstration of his great talent. He had the passion and tenacity to dare to imagine and to dare to break through barriers. He sometimes rode a horse to inspect the bustling construction sites and would take his family to join in the work. Inspired by the revolutionary drive of the masses, he strove to be the best in the country in everything he did and wanted to build the new world as soon as possible. In 1959, when the Great Hall of the People was completed in Beijing, the design of the huge screen in the Anhui Hall was also masterminded by Zeng Xisheng, who gladly inscribed the *tiehua* pictorial metalwork screen with the characters 迎客松 (Welcoming Pine). In 1978, a memorial service for Zeng Xisheng was held in Beijing ten years after his death. It was attended by Deng Xiaoping and other leading members of the central government, and Hu Yaobang delivered a eulogy. Li Xiannian wrote a commemorative article which described Zeng Xisheng as "the founder of our Party's intelligence-deciphering work" and "the pioneer of China's rural economic system reform".

In 1961, during the Great Famine, Zeng Xisheng piloted the implementation of "contracted farmland" in Anhui Province to address the food shortages. The people called this initiative "life-saving fields". He was also first secretary of the provincial committees of two large provinces, Anhui and Shandong; such a dual responsibility was exceptional. "Contracted farmland" enabled the people of Anhui not only to have enough to eat, but also to have surplus food to support neighbouring provinces such as Henan. Zeng Xisheng was very ambitious, but he could not have anticipated the sudden change in the prevailing wind of the times. At the beginning of 1962, the Seven Thousand Cadres Conference was held in Beijing, and contracted farmland was criticised as a serious error in direction and as "turning back the clock". The Central Committee sent people to "expose and criticise" the initiative. The atmosphere at the meeting was so hostile that Zeng Xisheng was not even given a seat, so he pulled up a chair and sat at the edge of the meeting. Some people there advocated his expulsion from the Party, and others his execution. At this point Mao Zedong said, "Without Zeng Xisheng, the Long March would have been unthinkable. Don't mention the idea of executing him again!"

Back in 1933, Zeng Xisheng was awarded the Red Star Medal, which some people said was a "gold medal for exemption from execution", and the Provisional Regulations on Discipline of the Workers' and Peasants' Red Army did have such a stipulation. The Central Committee removed Zeng Xisheng from his post as first secretary of the Anhui Provincial Committee and transferred him out of Anhui. Although he had been removed from his post, some grassroots Party organisations and cadres in Anhui took the great political risk of petitioning the central government for the continuation of contracted farmland. On 2 July, the Secretariat of the Central Committee met to discuss the issue of contracted farmland. Deng Xiaoping, general secretary of the Central Committee, said, "In areas where the peasants are in difficulty, various methods can be adopted. Our comrades in Anhui Province say, 'It doesn't matter if a cat is black or yellow; as long as it can catch mice, it is a good cat.' There is certainly some truth in this statement. Contracted farmland is a new phenomenon and can be tried again." However, at the Beidaihe Conference in August and the Tenth Plenary Session of the Eighth Central Committee in September, Zeng Xisheng was criticised for "representing the interests of the wealthy and petty bourgeois farmers" and the contracted farmland scheme was criticised for restoring a "capitalist-style monopoly". The criticism escalated and a large number of cadres in Anhui were implicated. Zeng Xisheng repeatedly told the central government, "Contracted farmland was my proposal, and I implemented it according to my own opinions. I was personally responsible for everything and no other comrades should be implicated."

Zeng Xisheng was transferred out of Anhui in 1962, and Li Zhifeng went to Hefei in 1957. Older Hefei residents still remember the time when Zeng Xisheng accompanied Mao Zedong to meet 200,000 people there in September 1958. He accompanied Mao Zedong in an open car as he was driven down Changjiang Road, which was lined with rejoicing crowds of citizens, singing and dancing. Such a spectacle had never been seen before in any other provincial capital city. The twenty-five-metre-wide Changjiang Road was also something to be seen in few other cities in China at the time.

Even today, Changjiang Road is still the number one street in Anhui. It is hard to imagine how different it once was, as you walk along this bustling street, day and evening. People are in a hurry to move on, and those old folk who have now slowed down are hidden in the deep alleys behind the tall buildings. They sit in the sun on bamboo chairs in front of their doors and watch the world go by.

The main street is lined with lively shopping malls and the kind of places where social media influencers gather. The wind of the times blows full in your face and historical records are mostly hidden in old buildings away from the main street. They are not given an inch of space on either side of the street, but they do have their place. At one point, she stands on the street and stares in awe at the giant screen on the facade of a multi-storey shopping mall: a herd of elephants marching north from Xishuangbanna.

Even though a stranger to the place, Dr He walks among the whitewashed Huizhou-style buildings, not missing any clues related to Zeng Xisheng and Li Zhifeng. She searches out all the living people who had contact with Li Zhifeng and does not miss a single text or document concerning him.

In the early summer of 1940, the Shanghai Insurance Association

SIDELIGHTS

received a shipping order from Hong Kong. On the surface, it appeared to be a standard telegraphic sea freight order with a ship registration number belonging to the British company Swire, the sailing time, and a list of goods such as penicillin, Dowling paper, bristles and amaranth. The destination was Jardine Wharf and the consignor was He Dizhi. The full name of the Shanghai Insurance Association was the Shanghai Insurance Amateur Association. It was a united front anti-Japanese organisation led by the Shanghai Underground Branch of the Communist Party of China. Its base was on Avenue Edward VII. In fact, the Insurance Association had no cargo business with Hong Kong, and it was only due to the lack of experience of the staff that this telegram went unnoticed. After careful checking, this coded message revealed the name of a Kuomintang spy who had sneaked into Yan'an. The great danger was that this person had actually infiltrated our top-secret 2nd Bureau of the Central Military Commission. Fortunately, the Shaanxi-Gansu-Ningxia border area guards in Yan'an acted promptly and eliminated more than fifty spies from the Hanzhong special training class of the Kuomintang Military Intelligence in one fell swoop. Among them were some female spies who were married to Party and government officials at the bureau level. The background of the consignor, He Dizhi, was unknown, but Li Zhifeng speculated that this person might be a member of the Kuomintang Military Technology Office. Wen Yuqing, the director of that office, was being manoeuvred out of his post and left on the pretext of going to Hong Kong for medical treatment. This mysterious He Dizhi person may have had some connection with Wen.

This is an excerpt from the *Collected Literary and Historical Materials Series* of the 1990s; just an anecdote. But for Dr He, this is a rare piece of proof. Her grandfather's original name was not He Dizhi, but his surname was indeed He. Chongqing, the early summer of 1940, a man in a suit and leather shoes, a black leather briefcase, the Military Technology Office, amaranth...

Amaranth. In 1940, the Japanese Army was still unable to enforce a complete blockade of Chinese shipping. The transport of medicines and Dowling paper from Hong Kong to Shanghai was understandable, but why amaranth? Amaranth is nothing more than a type of herbaceous flowering plant. Of course, this is not an ordinary dispatch, but a message transmitted in code. And she feels an intuition stirring: this is more like a suicide note! Another name for amaranth is "Love-lies-bleeding".

The author of this story was a local writer who had been a subordinate of Li Zhifeng when he was in Anhui, and now they are both very old men. Only a few dozen issues of the *Collected Literary and Historical Materials Series* were published, but fortunately the old editor is still alive, and equally fortunately he is soon found.

He says he has seen a picture of this man!

This old gentleman is a bit of a pedant. He calls himself a "miscellaneous scholar", the kind who knows a lot about everything. Although he is bedridden, his mind is still clear, and he speaks in a very organised manner: "The world is just a big dream, and life is a few degrees cooler in autumn. You say you and the colonel are fellow countrymen, from the same province. In the end, how much does that matter? Times change. 'For thirty years east of the river prospers, then for thirty years west of the river is favoured.' Xue Yue and Wu Qiwei were sworn enemies of the Red Army and were trying to drive the Red Army to extinction, but later they were both famous anti-Japanese generals, and Wu Qiwei was to be seen on the viewing platform of the Founding Ceremony. History is history. But history is sometimes difficult to explain clearly, especially when you come to so-called 'questions of personal history', which require 'survival skills'.

"At that time, there was a mathematics genius named Yang Si. He infiltrated the Kuomintang military command to provide information for Yan'an, and Dai Li promoted him to major general. This rank was to prove a big problem later on! Because both his Party sponsor and his single intelligence contact had passed away, it was very difficult to prove his story. How could such a creature of the shadows protect himself? But just see how smart he was! When things began to happen, he took the initiative to go to the Public Security Bureau and ask to be locked up. He reasoned that he knew too many people and held too many secrets. This was the safest and most certain way to keep those secrets... Hah! If someone comes to see me, I turn into a chatterbox! Let's talk about this photo. It is said that there used to be a Mr Mei here, a middle school maths teacher, but he was not a local. No one knew where he came from, but it was said that there was a problem in his past and maybe he was implicated in the Pan Hannian case. He had no wife and no children and lived alone for the rest of his life. The story is that he had to abandon his wife and daughter at a critical moment when he was working for the revolution, and she covered for him. After that, he was never able to see them again, not only because of the chaos, but also because of his own guilt and because of the troubles he encountered during the rest of his life. It seems that he was too ashamed to see them again. He dared not even consider it because he couldn't bear the thought that they might be killed because of him. There could be no redemption from the consequences of a single thought. In his later years, he left this manuscript with a few photographs, one of which was of him in Hong Kong. It was a photo of a businessman's tea party. It was a casual snap, not a record of a formal occasion. I don't remember the name of the businessman's company, but the owner was Bo Gu's younger brother. You must know that Bo Gu was once the top leader of the Chinese Communist Party. His real name was Qin Bangxian, and his younger brother was Qin Bangli. When he was in Shanghai that year, Chen Yun gave him two gold bars and asked him to use them as capital to build a secret communications station under the cover of opening a shop. After Xiang Zhongfa's defection, it was through him that Zhou Enlai and others reached the Central Soviet Area. He was also the escort for Chen Yun when he went to Moscow for a meeting during the Long March. So his company can therefore be described as a 'Party property', and it was an important contact point in Hong Kong. As for this photo, how do I remember so much about it? It is because I have a cousin who also has the two-character given name 'Dizhi'. And because the names of all the people in it are written on this photograph of Teacher Mei, and one of those names is He Dizhi."

"Does this photo ring a bell with you? The face, for example, the eyes–I"

"How could it? I've only glanced at it... it's a group photo, just a snapshot really. He only appears in profile."

"Yes, only a side view, but it's probably the only picture of him that remains."

"I understand that. When the person is gone, a photo can be useful. But after all these years, who knows if they're still around. The good thing is that the material is in a state-run library, so I don't think they'd just throw it away. County-level cities are generally managed quite formally and systematically. Fortunately, it is not too far from here either, and the high-speed rail is very convenient."

"I would go to the ends of the earth."

"I take my hat off to you! Back then, it was mostly men who defected, very few women! A question of faithfulness!"

"You are using an elder's prerogative to make fun of me."

"Not at all, I wish you good luck!"

It is the warm scent of spring. The scenery that sweeps by outside the car windows shows the ink-smudge of distant mountains, farmers working in the fields, children flying kites, puppies gambolling, swifts swooping and turning, and new leaves trembling in the breeze.

Everyone has their own hometown or village, and the deaths of those who have no home to return to or have passed on far away, demand your compassion. Strangers who die are part of your family too. They have a home village of their own as well; it is to be found in the landscape of this great world. You search for them down through the depths of the years, and you must retain their images to make them a memory that will never be obliterated.

In February, the grass is long and the birds are on the wing. The sun is warm and bright, replete with wonderful expectations. Even the raucous sounds of the city, you hear as beautiful music.

You have come here, to this strange little town. For the first time in your life, you have the feeling of being close to home. It is not your hometown, but there is a real feeling of closeness, a real summons reaching out to you. At this time, at this moment, in this body, you find some kind of genuine consolation in your life. You come here, to this old library, and your heart flares with an even greater joy. The age and simplicity of its exterior, the vines on its wall, all combine to make this small building feel genuinely grounded. This is not your hometown, but you can hear someone speaking to you. You look around in disbelief, and then you look up at the camera, the electronic eye of the 5G era, which has 360 degrees of coverage. You can't see him, but you hear his voice. "As long as you remember me, I'm alive." Suddenly you remember where you read that phrase. Your heart flutters with awe. Who is this speaking to you from the depths of the ages, who is looking at you fondly, and whose gaze you can feel so vividly?

You slowly turn around and look at the little red brick building. As the sun sets, there is a warmth to its brick walls. You expect to find some kind of secret here, some kind of confirmation about your life. A dusty manuscript, a yellowed photograph, and the person in that photograph waiting for you. You came here this Friday afternoon, but you were too late. It is a fine weekend, too, and a fine weekend starts on Friday afternoon. The little building is closing. You shouldn't let your own passion make you angry. That passion is all your own, and you shouldn't be protesting so loudly.

You are careful to maintain the good mood you have been in all the way here, and you can only wait patiently for the next working day. Suit yourself to your circumstances; the hotelkeeper understands the situation better than you. Of course, he wishes that there were more weekends for people to enjoy, so his living would improve. You hesitate to speak, not daring to address him. You dare not say that you have already discussed the matter with the curator, who was conducting a poetry recitation for a group of women on the nearby riverbank. Your arrival piqued her interest.

You come with joy in your heart, and they have a joy of their own. The times are peaceful and quiet where the silken willow branches flutter in the wind. The women are all wrapped in bright silk scarves, they wear exercise leggings and sunglasses. Facing the river, they joyfully recite a poem. A poem about happiness. They want to communicate with everyone they hold dear, and tell everyone about their happiness.

"How sweet, how sweet our dreams": the music accompanying the recitation has such a beautiful melody! On this particular morning, the music makes you weep too.

* * *

Sitting with the map on the bed, you look for a place to go for the weekend. One name draws you in: Wu River.

It's just a name. This is another Wu River, it is not that Wu River. Those warriors who feared no sacrifice back then, successfully crossed the Wu River to the north and then crossed it to the south. Their enemies threatened them, saying that the Wu River was a killing ground, but the Red Army once again survived through sheer desperation. The photocopy of *Wu River Variations* is in your suitcase. You came here for another manuscript, and for that photograph pasted into it, even though the man is only seen in profile. Time flies. How many manuscripts have disappeared into its depths? During this sleepless night, you think of Zeng Xisheng and deep in your heart you comprehend the memory his descendants keep dearest of all their limited memories: the unforgettable scene of that summer day in 1968 when the hearse is slowly driven out of the People's Liberation Army General Hospital. The first to run to the side of the road to see him off was a group of children who were complete strangers to him. They raised their hands to salute the hearse... More manuscripts disappeared forever: Zeng Xisheng's three notebooks. In the last six months of his life, he returned to his old work in his hospital bed and resumed his research into ciphers, which he had abandoned for nearly thirty years. He asked his daughter to buy computer materials for him at a bookstore and invited a teacher from Tsinghua University to give him computer lessons, until his doctors strictly forbade him to read or write. After his death, his wife, Yu Shu, gave Premier Zhou the three notebooks that contained his work on codes from the last days of his life, and Premier Zhou gave them to the Third Department of the General Staff of the Chinese People's Liberation Army, but now, they too have disappeared.

It is impossible to imagine how Zeng Xisheng's wife felt when she made her final request to the premier. She said she has no demands of the central government, but she did want to follow her husband's last wish and take the children back to her hometown to farm. That was Zeng Xisheng's hometown in Hunan. On New Year's Eve in 1960, he had taken advantage of his illness to go back for a visit. It was the first time he had returned in thirty-six years. After making his New Year's greetings around the village on the first day of the New Year, he walked around the place with a heavy heart and left that very morning.

To the end of his life, he kept completely silent about the top-secret southern crossing of the Wu River, and he never even revealed it to his wife with whom he shared everything that life threw at them. The Red Star Medal, that highest of honours, also sank into the waters of the Wu River, never to be seen again. Although the "Three Heroes of Deciphering" of the Red Army's Long March – Zeng Xisheng, Cao Xiangren and Zou Bizhao – all became provincial and ministerial officials later, and also made considerable contributions to the construction of the New China, deep in their hearts, their memories of their time on the Long March were the most cherished.

Made of material "even more special than those special materials" – a particularly simple material. Long-term immersion in cryptographic technology also gave them a special character. Their temperaments tended to be inward-looking, a special kind of simplicity and loneliness. When they returned to the real world, this simplicity was not enough to deal with complicated human affairs. In times of peace, many things became more complicated. Back in 1946, despite his impressive record of forming the 7th Division of the New 4th Army and his development of the anti-Japanese base in the Wanjiang River area, Zeng Xisheng wrote in a letter to Wang Yongjun, deputy director of the 2nd Bureau of the Military Commission, "Thirty-nine years of separation: although I could never bear to be parted from this cause, for a variety of reasons, I have become separated from all of you... I have not achieved anything in eight years, yet I have been very busy all that time, so I have not been able to write to you. I do not deserve the praise heaped upon me and feel ashamed at it. Peace will now soon be achieved. I have nothing more to offer, and my physical strength is no longer anything like what it used to be. I have lived a mediocre life and feel now that my time has passed."

But this monograph still survives. It is written in an elegant, eye-catching cursive script, with restrained brushstrokes, both supple and rigid, which are at once imposing and yet at the same time calm and upright, truly of ancient quality. It is hard to imagine that this is the handwriting of a man in the midst of a war. It is rare for such a manuscript to survive. And here in this hotel, in your travelling suitcase, there is a copy of it. What kind of manuscript is now about to appear in the little library of this little town? It may be the relic of a martyr, a relic he has left behind for the world, and perhaps you are his relic too!

Wujiang Township, the number one town on the 800-mile Wan River. In those days, it was also the anti-Japanese base for the region. A township with a history of thousands of years, the Wujiang of the Western Chu where the Overlord (Bawang) of the Western Chu, Xiang Yu, is commemorated. The Bawang Ancestral Hall. The Bawang Pavilion. Bawang crispy pastry. In this legendary place where Xiang Yu killed himself, there is also a legend about Zeng Xisheng. Legend has it that this native of Hunan would occasionally perform Beijing opera here, singing a few lines of *Farewell My Concubine* by the riverside.

He was born a hero and died a devil. Even now, one still thinks of Xiang Yu, who refused to cross the river. A legend in the clouds of history. A legend about a legend. He said that the people of Hunan were also the people of Chu because back in the Spring and Autumn and Warring States periods, Hunan was also part of Chu territory.

You have come here, to this legendary river crossing. The crossing is deserted, and you see only a flat-bottomed boat on the shore. You look silently at the wild reeds, at the misty landscape on the other side. At this moment, it is as if you hear a voice: "Swim across! You must swim across alone!" It is a ritual that you must perform; a mysterious summons from the surging river; a secret word from the evening breeze whispering through the reeds: "Swim across and you will see that person as you wish to see him. You will see him complete."

This is how you pass the weekend, in this place called Liyang in ancient times, in this modern-day Wujiang Township. On Sunday night, your phone rings as promised. A call from your boyfriend.

"If things go as I hope tomorrow, I'll give you a present."

"What kind of present? Not a Bawang crispy pastry?"

"No, not food, something anthropological–l"

"Huh! You and your PhD in anthropology. I think I know what you mean... "

"Do you want it?"

"If I've guessed right... but what about your age?"

"Medical science can help!"

"Just think about it! What a great woman your grandma was! A real-life Wonder Woman! If she hadn't switched off the power that night, if they had fallen into the hands of those plainclothes men–l"

"Then you and I wouldn't be talking like this, and I would never have come here. What am I doing here? Is it just to see a river called the Wu?"

"Some experts say that this section of the Yangtze flows north-south. The poet Yian Jushi said, 'I will not cross the river to the east', but he was actually referring to the Yangtze. So the question is, where is the Wu River?"

"Some people in the local area say the same thing. They have the gift of the gab! They have lifted themselves out of poverty and become propserous, and what they have to say is always interesting. They are neither humble nor overbearing. I went to a stall to buy fruit, and I asked if there was any pesticide on it. The stall-holder said, 'No, you'll have to add your own!'"

"No kidding! You have to be careful! If fruit sellers are that quick with words, how much better is a librarian going to be? You'll have to sharpen your own wits!"

"It has been slumbering away there for decades. I hardly think it's going to disappear over the weekend! Tomorrow is Monday, you just have to restrain yourself. Is there something in your genes? Think of those saints of men back then, and the miracles they performed even when their minds and bodies were pushed to the very limit! If they were around to help today, there is nothing that could not be achieved!"

"Ha, yes, I get it. I'll do my very best. I believe in miracles, in some kind of telepathic influence... I heard the voice quite clearly: 'Swim across this river and all will be well with you.'"

"Telepathy and belief are all well and good, but it is courage and action that are needed! It couldn't be more right! Think about it, though. If you don't handle it properly, it will mean... that photograph, even though it's just a side view... It would mean there is no one left with any memory of the image. He would be gone forever. It's quite simple. If whoever is there isn't happy with you, they will just say it's not there. It's that simple!"

"I will never let that happen."

"Then you'd better learn how to smile!"

Late into the night, you relax your taut nerves. On this moonlit spring night, in this hotel in a strange place, you silently freshen yourself up in the mirror, because you are going to meet your relative. You practise smiling over and over again in anticipation of tomorrow.

The sky is beginning to grow light but there are still stars twinkling on the water. Once again you go down to the riverbank.

Swim across the river!

>   There is a silence in the depths of time
>   Which is the starlight on the water
>   And the secret whispers in the wind.

NOTES

TONGDAO

1. According to the traditional nominal age system, a person is counted as being one year old at birth
2. Taking these place names literally, they mean "level/equal" and "way through" respectively

MOVING WEST

1. Zhuge Liang is one of the most famous political and military strategists in Chinese history. He was active during the Three Kingdoms Period (220-280 CE)
2. Wang Jialie was chairman of the Guizhou government from November 1931 to May 1935. He continuously resisted Chiang Kai-shek's attempt to unify China under his central government
3. The old-style Hanyang rifle, which was replaced in the main National Revolutionary Army in 1925 by the Hanyang 88, still had an old-fashioned barrel shroud, a length of tubing that overlayed the main barrel to protect both the barrel from damage and the user from contact with hot metal.

BUREAU CHIEF

1. Matching couplets are auspicious or wise sayings in black ink on red paper, posted up on door surrounds at festivals and celebrations with the two main sentiments flanking the door vertically either side, and a linking element horizontally over the lintel
2. Bo Gu's real name was Qin Bangxian, but when he was studying in Russia he called himself Bogunov. On his return to China, he shortened this to Bo Gu
3. a form of mobile barricade, dating back to ancient times, comprising canopies made of tree trunks and wooden stakes
4. known in the West as *cheval de frise*, this is another simple form of barrier composed of a linked row of crosses of sharpened stakes. In China, it dates back to the earliest Bronze Age dynasties

SECTION CHIEF

1. This a reference to a quotation from the chapter on warfare in the ancient Legalist text *The Book of Lord Shang*

NOTES

TUCHENG

1. Li Bozhao, 1911-1985 was married to the former president of the PRC, Yang Shangkun. Later in life she became a famous dramatist, but in her youth she joined the Communist Party in 1931 and took part in the Long March
2. This phrase is a pun on Chiang Kai-shek's name as pronounced in Mandarin: Jiang Jiashi. This is supposed to sound like *Jiang gai si*, which means "Jiang deserves to die"

FOUR CROSSINGS

1. A quotation from *The Lament of Gaixia*, supposedly written by Xiang Yu, one of the contenders for the throne after the fall of the Qin dyansty, when he was routed by his rival, Liu Bang, at the Battle of Gaixia in 202 BCE
2. "Three Tigers Roaring in the Mountain Forest" is a nickname based on the constituent elements of the characters of Lin Biao's name: 林 = woods and 彪 is formed of the characters 虎 = tiger and 三 = three
3. A picul is a traditional unit of weight, literally "as much as a man can carry on a shoulder pole", usually taken as 60-64kg

AFTERTHOUGHTS

1. Male and female deities seated in the act of sexual union are common in Tantric Tibetan Buddhist art, but unknown in mainstream Chinese Buddhism

2. SIDELIGHTS

1. A quote from Mao Zedong's poem *The Long March*
2. A famous scenic spot in Gansu province, this rock is where the legendary master mason Lu Ban is said to have sat as he planned the magical construction of a bridge over the Jishi Canyon.
3. From a song written by Lu Zhuguo, composed by Fu Gengchen and sung by Deng Yuhua. In May 2009, it was selected as one of the five "Patriotic Songs Recommended by the Propaganda Department of the Central Committee of the Communist Party of China"
4. Tongmenghui was a secret society and underground resistance movement founded by Sun Yat-sen, Song Jiaoren and others in Japan in 1905, with the goal of overthrowing the Qing dynasty. It was a forerunner of the Kuomintang.

ABOUT THE AUTHOR

Pang Bei, born 1966 in Tsingtao, is chairman of the Writers' Association of Guangzhou. A graduate of the Foreign Languages Institute of the People's Liberation Army, he also served as a staff officer.

His other novels include *Midnight Banquet* and *The Unicorn*. He has also written for the stage, including dramas *Life After Life* and *Sound of the Sword*, and for film, including a screenplay credit for *Lord of Shanghai*. Shortlisted for the Mao Dun Literature Prize, *Midnight Banquet* won the top-ten Asia Weekly Annual Chinese Novel Award. *Wu River Variations* won the 2022 Best Books of China Prize and 2022 Best Novel of the People's Literature magazine. His drama *Life After Life* won the Best Playwright Award of the Chinese Drama Festival and was performed at the Avignon Festival in France.

ABOUT THE TRANSLATOR

James Trapp has an honours degree in Chinese from the School of Oriental and African Studies, University of London, with special papers in pre-Han archaeology and early Buddhist sculpture. After graduating, he spent ten years as an art dealer working for companies based in London, New York and Hong Kong.

Subsequently, with the rise in interest in Mandarin in UK schools, he refocused on making Mandarin accessible to young learners. He has produced a comprehensive Programme of Study for Primary Mandarin, with a focus on the constructive use of Chinese art and culture in Mandarin teaching. He has developed this in classrooms and after-school clubs across a wide range of primary and secondary schools, as well as through his work at the British Museum.

James first visited China in 1982 and has since travelled extensively throughout the country. He has published China-related books on characters, proverbs, astrology, science and technology. His translation works include new versions of Sunzi's *The Art of War* and Laozi's *Daodejing*, and, for Sinoist Books, Wang Hongjia's *Final Witness*, Ma Pinglai's *The Elm Tree*, Su Tong's *Shadow of the Hunter* and Zhou Daxin's *Longevity Park*. When not translating, James is to be found walking his dog, Pebbles, and perfecting his versions of classic Sichuan dishes.

About **Sino**ist Books

We hope you enjoyed this story about the codebreaking efforts of the 2nd Bureau.

SINOIST BOOKS brings the best of Chinese fiction to English-speaking readers. We aim to create a greater understanding of Chinese culture and society, and provide an outlet for the ideas and creativity of the country's most talented authors.

To let us know what you thought of this book, or to learn more about the diverse range of exciting Chinese fiction in translation we publish, find us online. If you're as passionate about Chinese literature as we are, then we'd love to hear your thoughts!